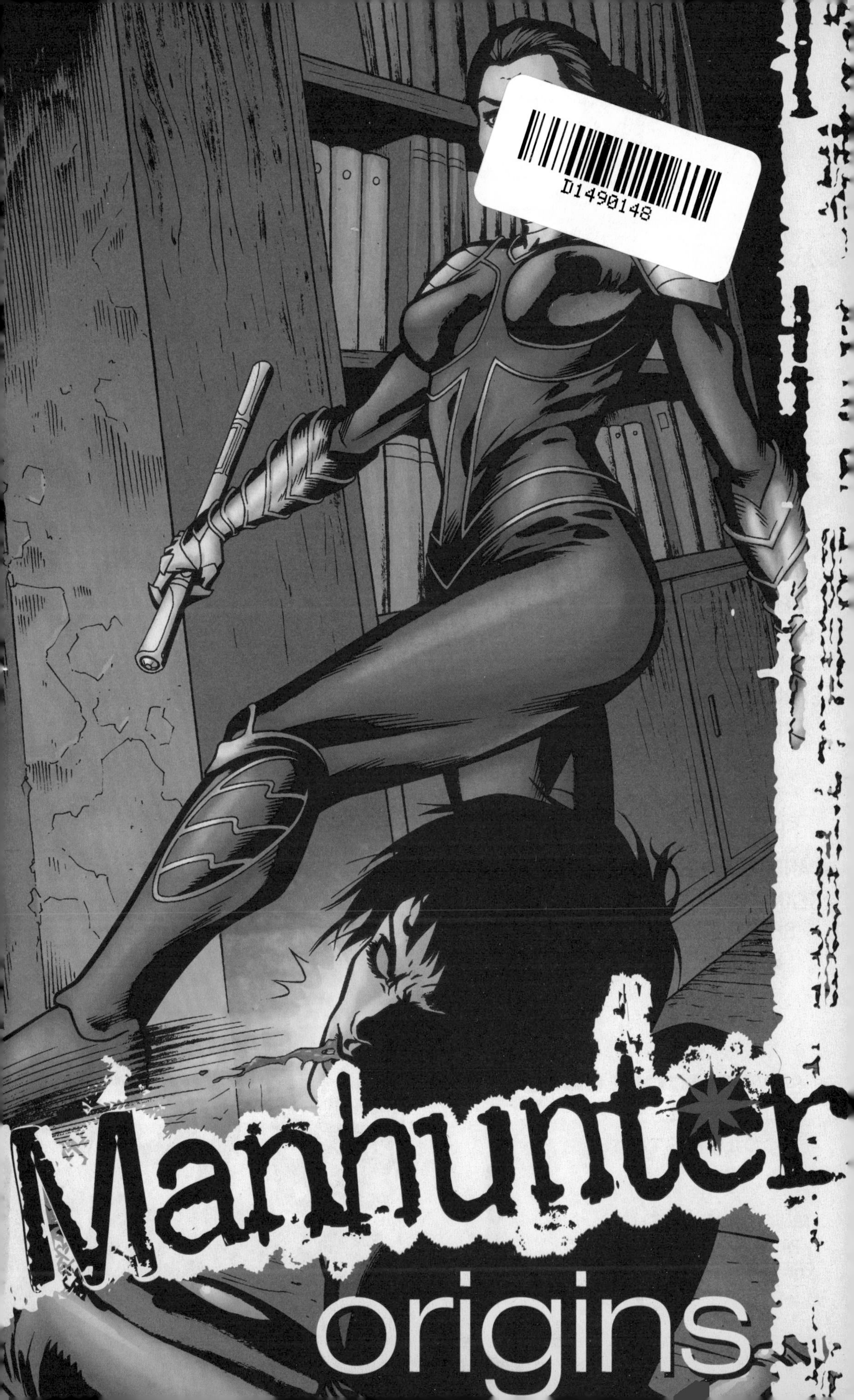

Manhunter origins

origins

MARC **ANDREYKO**
WRITER

JAVIER **PINA**
DIEGO **OLMOS**
STEPHEN **SADOWSKI**
SEAN **PHILLIPS**
SHAWN **MARTINBROUGH**
RAGS **MORALES**
PENCILLERS

FERNANDO **BLANCO**
ANDREW **PEPOY**
SEAN **PHILLIPS**
SHAWN **MARTINBROUGH**
BOB **PETRECCA**
INKERS

STEVE **BUCCELLATO**
JASON **WRIGHT**
COLORISTS

TRAVIS **LANHAM**
PAT **BROSSEAU**
PHIL **BALSMAN**
LETTERERS

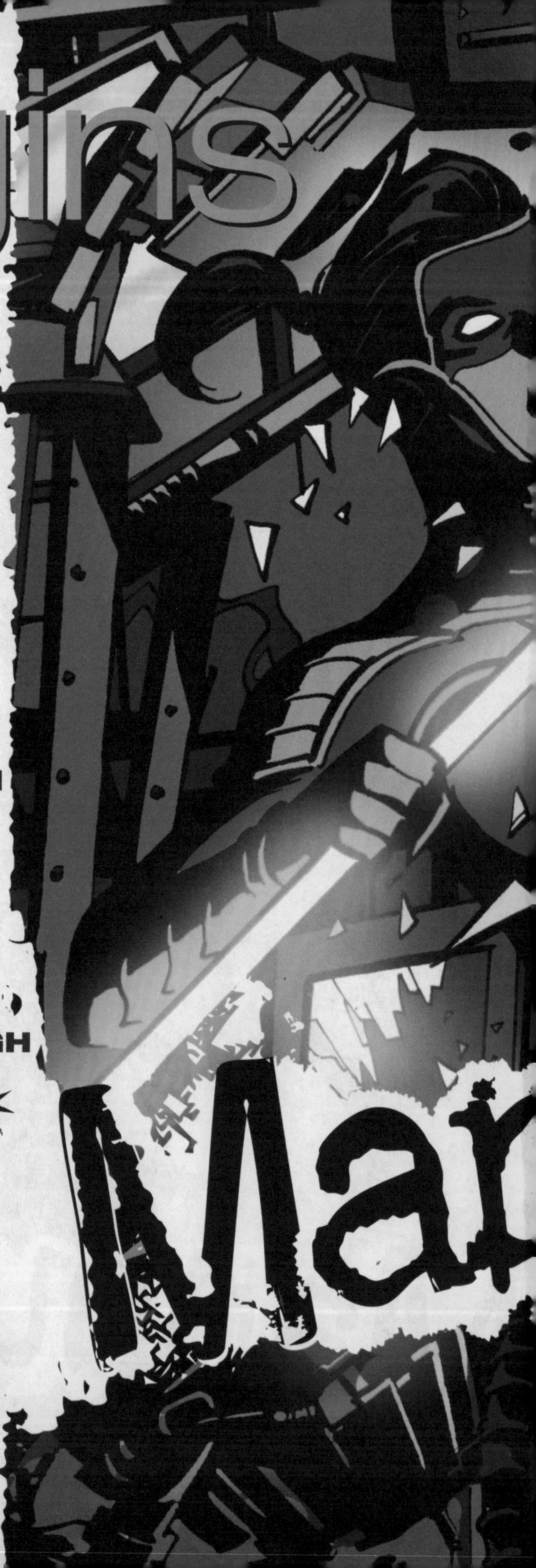
Mar

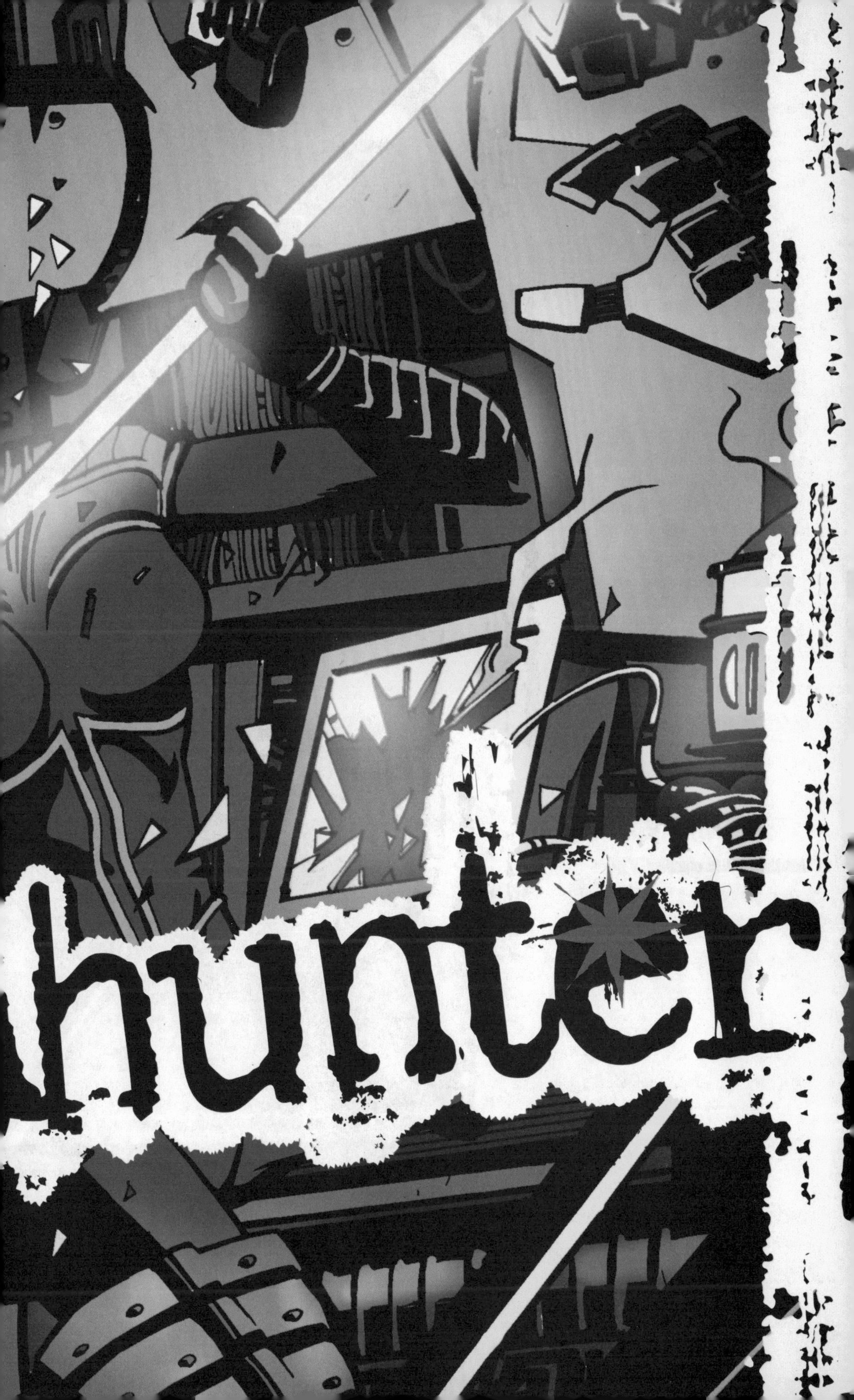
hunter

Cover by Stephane Roux

MANHUNTER: ORIGINS

Published by DC Comics. Cover and compilation
copyright © 2007 DC Comics. All Rights Reserved.

Originally published in single magazine form in MANHUNTER
#15-23. Copyright © 2005, 2006 DC Comics. All Rights
Reserved. All characters, their distinctive likenesses and
related elements featured in this publication are trademarks
of DC Comics. The stories, characters and incidents
featured in this publication are entirely fictional. DC Comics
does not read or accept unsolicited submissions of ideas,
stories or artwork.

DC Comics, 1700 Broadway, New York, NY 10019

A Warner Bros. Entertainment Company

Printed in Canada. First Printing.

ISBN: 1-4012-1340-5

ISBN 13: 978-1-4012-1340-4

CAST OF CHARACTERS

MANHUNTER

Kate Spencer is a federal prosecutor by day, and crime-fighting vigilante by night. Roaming the streets of Los Angeles, Kate hunts down the super-villains who have escaped justice with the help of high-tech weaponry that she acquired from an evidence locker. The origins of these weapons was unknown…until now. Kate has a son, Ramsey, from her former marriage to novelist Peter Robinson. Kate and Peter's relationship deteriorated mostly due to Kate's extreme dedication to her job. But after a complicated series of events, the family seems to be reunited for now. Kate's estranged father might have something to say about that, though…

DYLAN BATTLES

A former henchman for various villains (Black Manta, Two-Face, Killer Frost, etc), Dylan Battles testified against his former employers in a court case for which Kate was prosecutor. Dylan then relocated with his wife and baby as part of a Witness Protection Program, but Kate tracked him down and offered him a position as her technician, assisting her in her exploits as Manhunter. At first he refused, but Kate reminded him that she could easily reveal his location to any number of super-villains that he used to work for. When Dylan's wife walked out with their baby after a fight, Dylan finally called Kate and agreed to work with her. A master technician, Dylan has made numerous improvements to Kate's uniform and weaponry.

CAMERON CHASE

Cameron is a longtime friend of Kate's who was recruited by the Department of Extranormal Operations (D.E.O.) — a government agency that oversees metahumans and uncovers all their secrets. But Cameron has a few of her own: she is the daughter of a little-known hero known as the Acro-Bat, who was killed by the villainous Dr. Trap when she was only seven. The incident left her scarred, and left her with a mistrust of metahumans. Ironically, she discovered that she had powers of her own — the ability to dampen the powers of other superbeings.

MARK SHAW

One of the previous people to bear the name Manhunter, Mark Shaw has been both a hero and a villain — sometimes both at once, due to some complicated government programming that messed with his psyche. Now on the side of the angels, Shaw has a new destiny awaiting him…

OBSIDIAN

Todd Rice is the son of Alan Scott, the original Green Lantern, and Rose Forrest, the original Thorn. As Obsidian, Todd can become a living shadow with the ability to pass through solid objects, fly and create objects out of shadows. He is currently in a relationship with Damon Matthews, who is Kate's legal assistant.

OUR STORY SO FAR

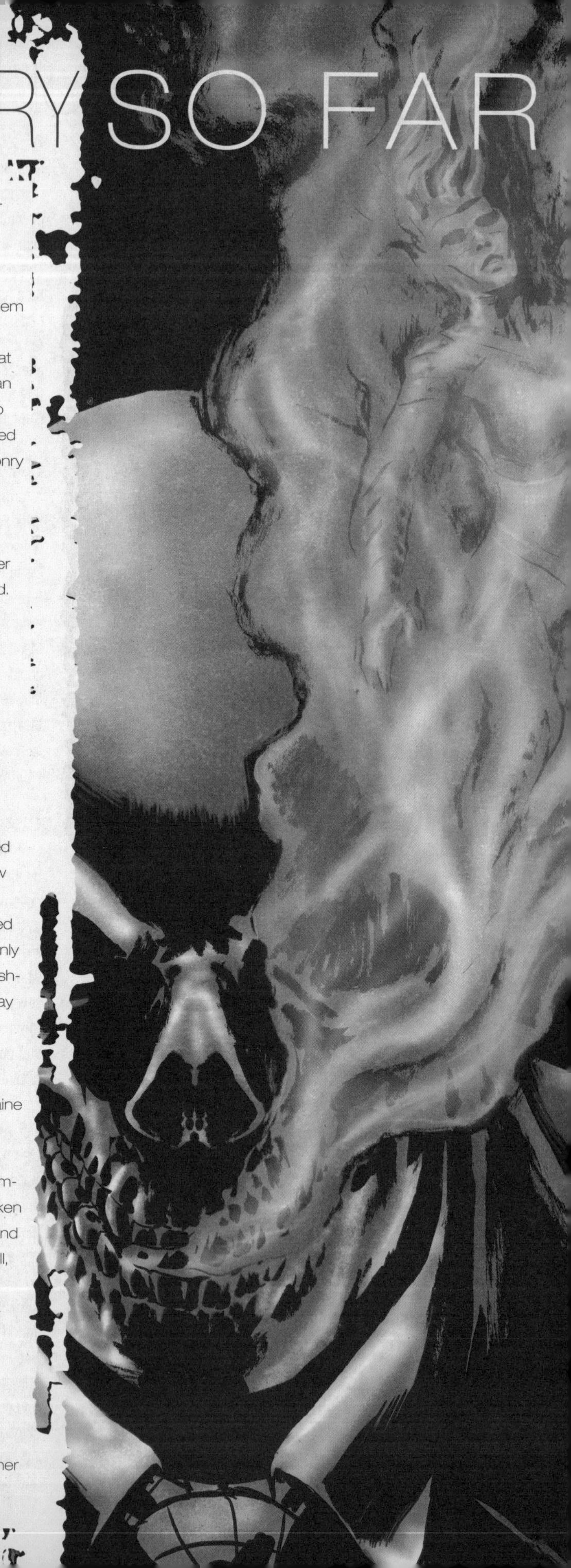

Kate Spencer was a federal prosecutor in Los Angeles who watched as yet another super-criminal — Copperhead — escaped justice. But this time, it would be the final straw.

Tired of putting villains behind bars, only to see them escape prison soon after (or avoid a sentence completely with a good lawyer), Kate decided that something needed to be done. When the reptilian Copperhead escaped while being transported to prison, going on another killing spree, Kate donned a costume and obtained some high-tech weaponry that she appropriated from a high-security evidence locker to become… the Manhunter. Hunting down and ultimately executing Copperhead before he had the chance to murder more innocents, her actions did not go unnoticed. The villain community didn't take well to the knowledge of a costumed "hero" who was willing to actually kill criminals.

Carl Sands, the deranged menace known as Shadow Thief, saw the news of his friend Copperhead's death, and made it his mission to get revenge against Manhunter. When Kate later learned that Sands was also responsible for the recent death of the hero Firestorm, she turned the tables and decided to hunt down the Shadow Thief. But before she had the chance to kill the villain, the heroes of the Justice League intervened and took Sands into custody. Kate realized the only way to get the Shadow Thief now was the old-fashioned way: a trial. Though it became no typical day in court: criminals such as Phobia, Merlyn and Cheshire tried to kill Sands before he could talk about the super-villain community on the stand, but ultimately Manhunter — with the help of Lorraine Reilly (formerly Firehawk) — thwarted the villains.

Meanwhile, the villainous Dumas had been systematically murdering every person who had ever taken the "Manhunter" name, including Chase Lawler and Kirk DePaul. Mark Shaw was on this hit list as well, until it was revealed that Shaw was being controlled by complicated government programming and was actually committing the murders himself. With Kate's help, Shaw was able to fight against his programming, putting an end to the Manhunter hunt.

Back at home, a person claiming to be Kate's father approached her son Ramsey in a park, and later visited Kate's ex, Peter, at a book signing — only to mysteriously disappear…

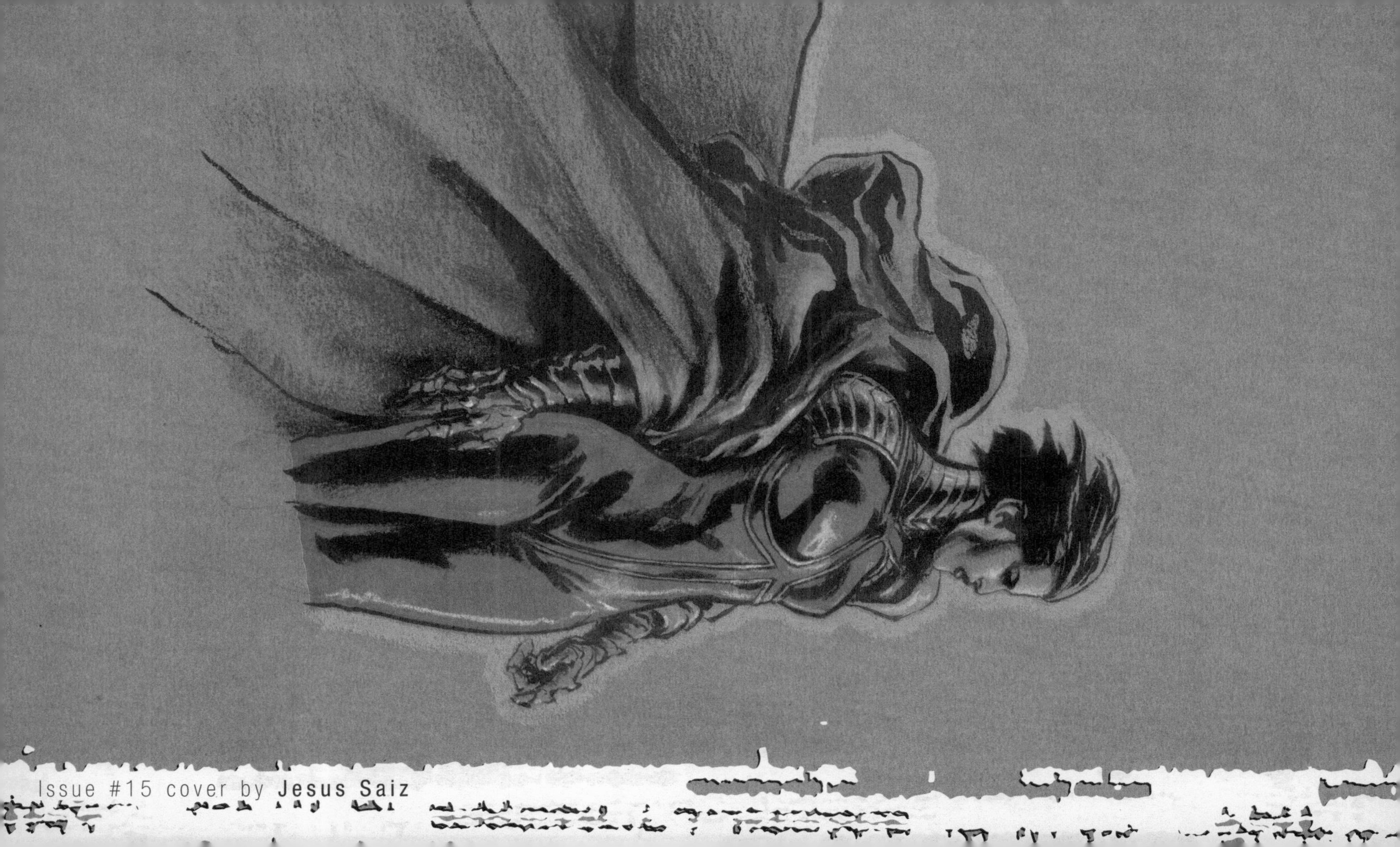

Issue #15 cover by **Jesus Saiz**

Interior art by Javier Pina & Fernando Blanco, Stephen Sadowski & Andrew Pepoy, Sean Phillips, Rags Morales & Bob Petrecca, Shawn Martinbrough

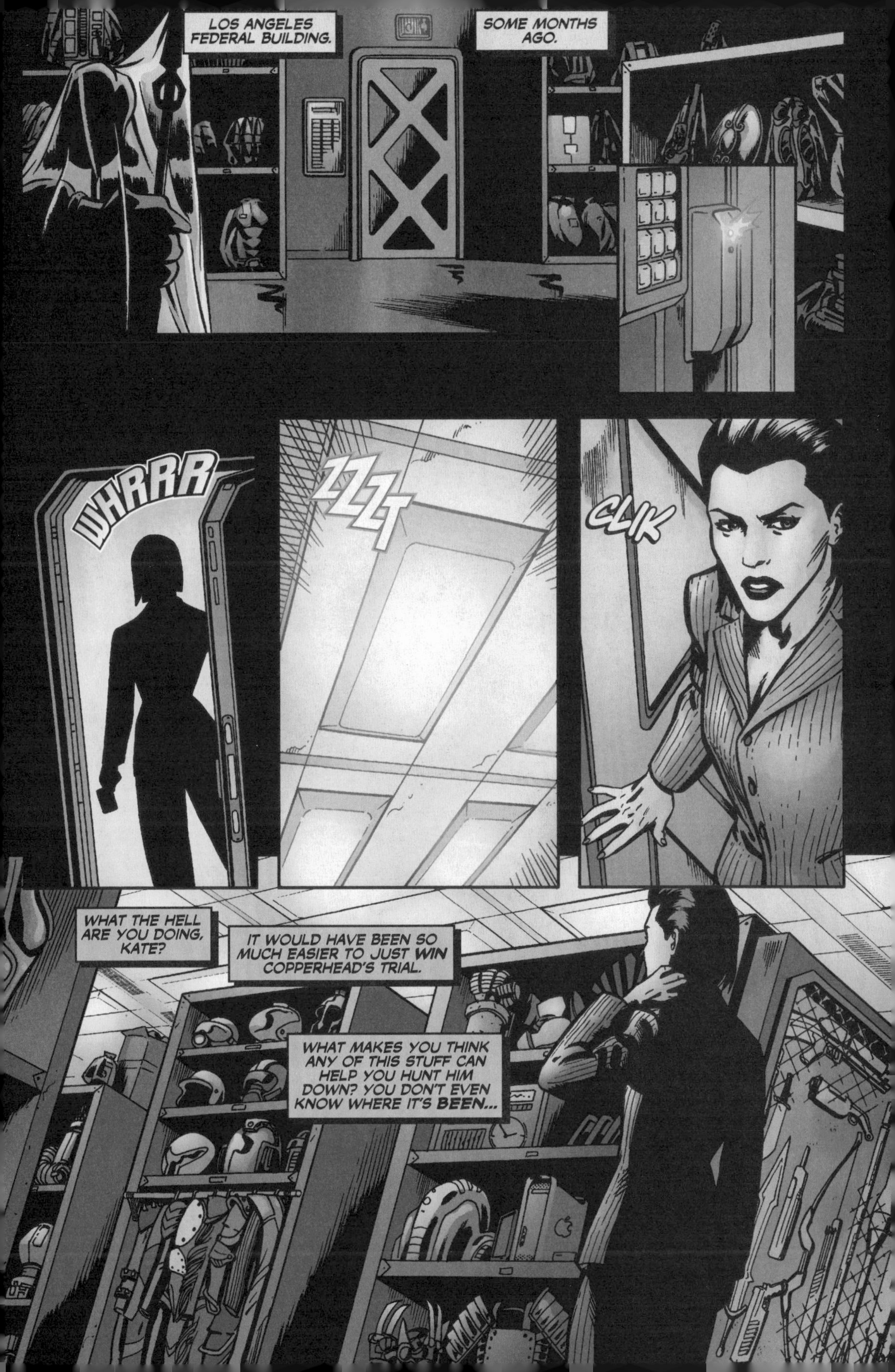
LOS ANGELES FEDERAL BUILDING.
SOME MONTHS AGO.
WHRRR
ZZZT
CLIK
WHAT THE HELL ARE YOU DOING, KATE?
IT WOULD HAVE BEEN SO MUCH EASIER TO JUST WIN COPPERHEAD'S TRIAL.
WHAT MAKES YOU THINK ANY OF THIS STUFF CAN HELP YOU HUNT HIM DOWN? YOU DON'T EVEN KNOW WHERE IT'S BEEN...

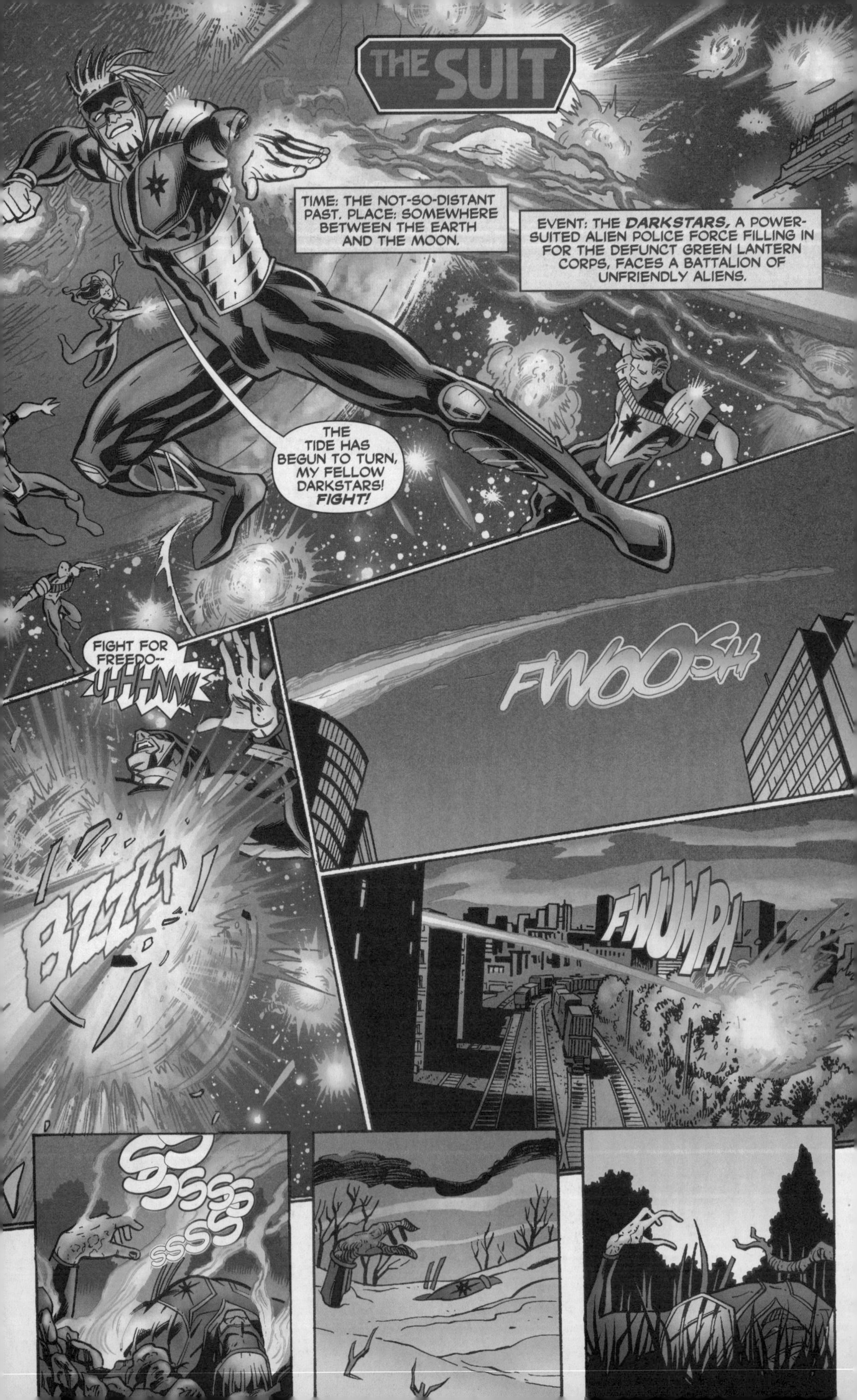
THE SUIT
TIME: THE NOT-SO-DISTANT PAST. PLACE: SOMEWHERE BETWEEN THE EARTH AND THE MOON.
EVENT: THE DARKSTARS, A POWER-SUITED ALIEN POLICE FORCE FILLING IN FOR THE DEFUNCT GREEN LANTERN CORPS, FACES A BATTALION OF UNFRIENDLY ALIENS.
THE TIDE HAS BEGUN TO TURN, MY FELLOW DARKSTARS! FIGHT!
FIGHT FOR FREEDO--UHHHNN!!
FWOOSH
BZZZT
FWUMPH
SSSSSSSSS

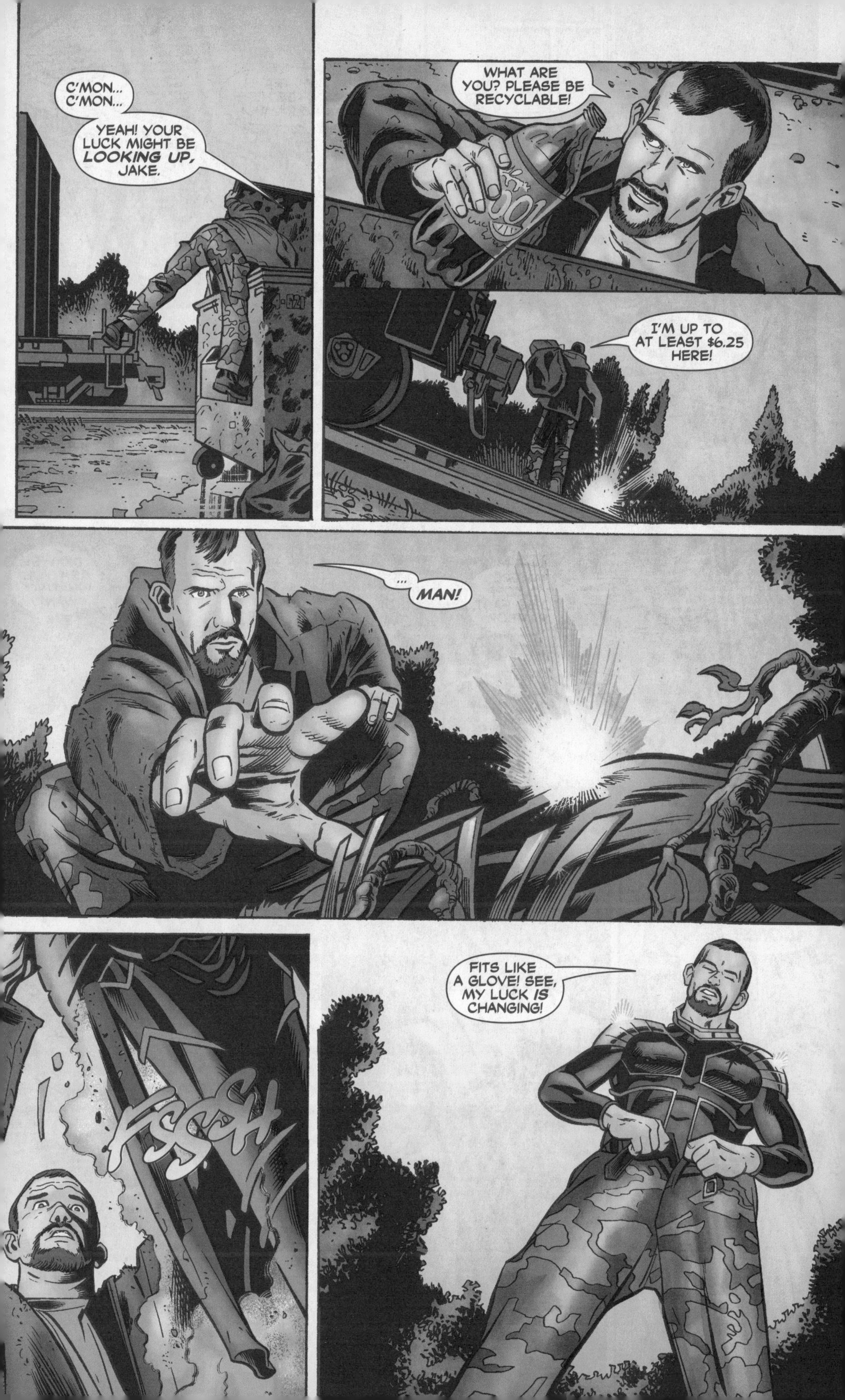
C'MON... C'MON...
YEAH! YOUR LUCK MIGHT BE LOOKING UP, JAKE.
WHAT ARE YOU? PLEASE BE RECYCLABLE!
I'M UP TO AT LEAST $6.25 HERE!
... MAN!
FSSH
FITS LIKE A GLOVE! SEE, MY LUCK IS CHANGING!

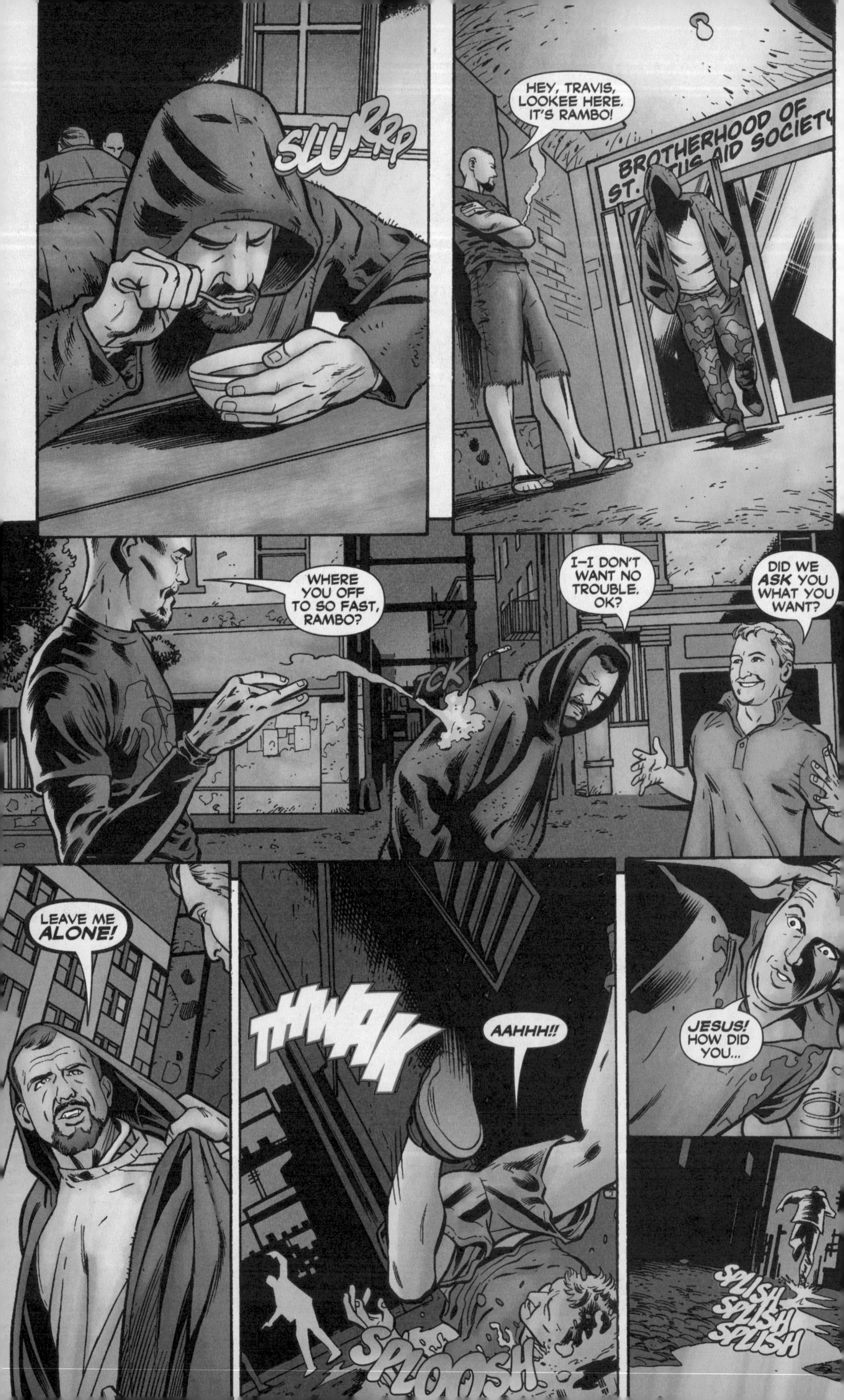
SLURRP
HEY, TRAVIS, LOOKEE HERE. IT'S RAMBO!
BROTHERHOOD OF ST. [...]US AID SOCIETY
WHERE YOU OFF TO SO FAST, RAMBO?
TCK
I-I DON'T WANT NO TROUBLE. OK?
DID WE ASK YOU WHAT YOU WANT?
LEAVE ME ALONE!
THWAK
AAHHH!!
SPLOOSH
JESUS! HOW DID YOU...
SPLISH SPLISH SPLISH

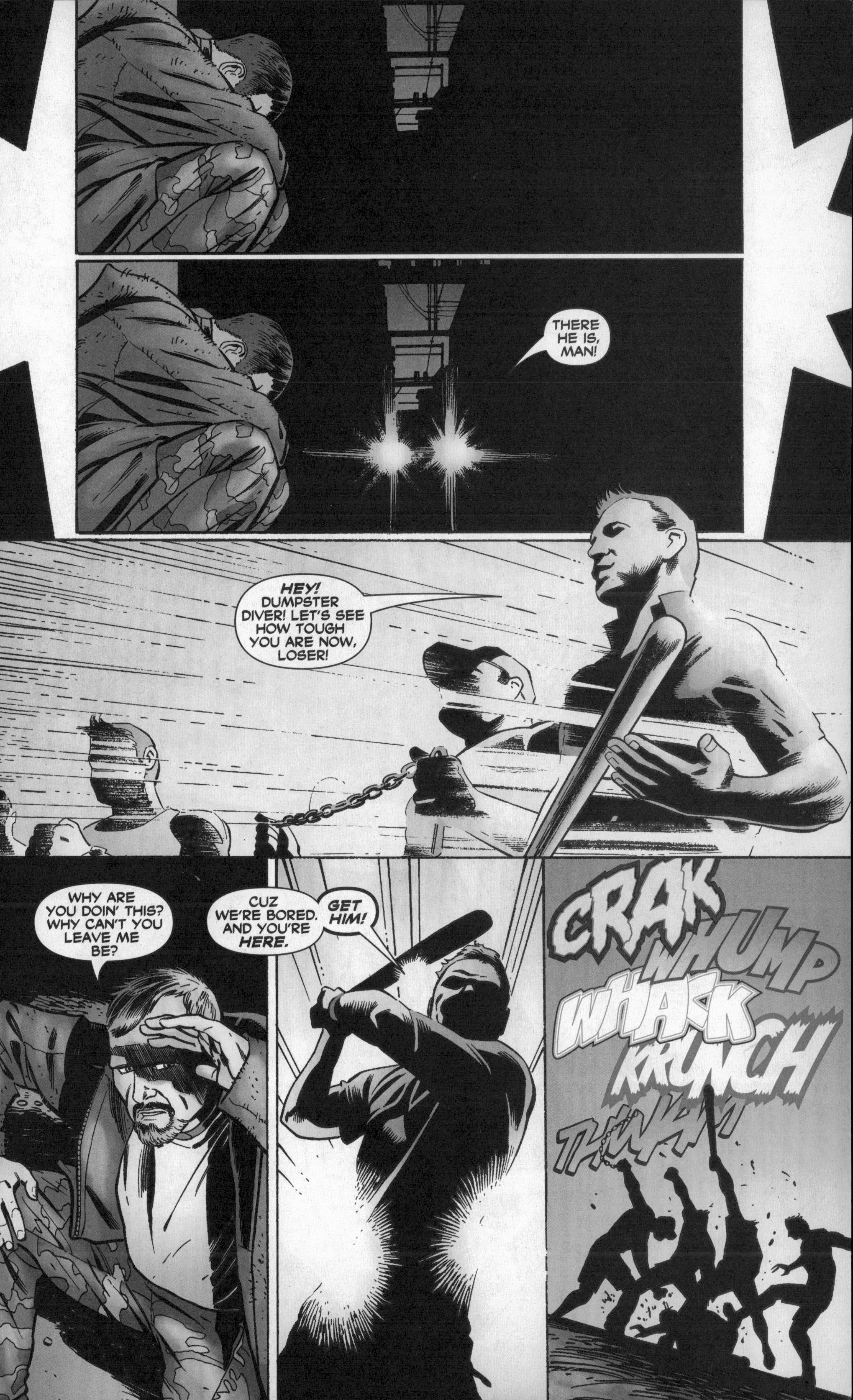
THERE HE IS, MAN!
HEY! DUMPSTER DIVER! LET'S SEE HOW TOUGH YOU ARE NOW, LOSER!
WHY ARE YOU DOIN' THIS? WHY CAN'T YOU LEAVE ME BE?
CUZ WE'RE BORED. AND YOU'RE HERE.
GET HIM!
CRAK
WHUMP
WHACK
KRUNCH

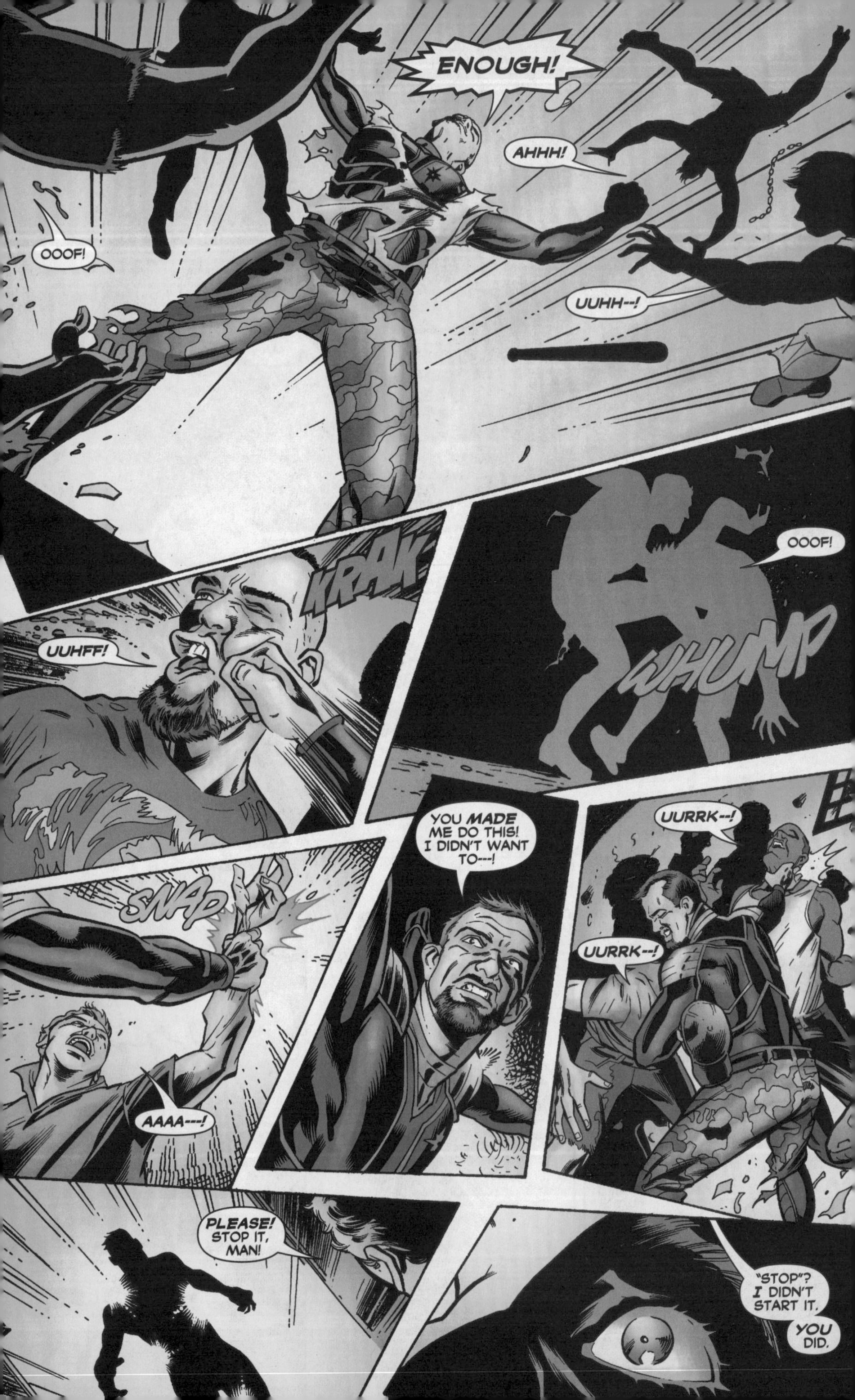
ENOUGH!
AHHH!
OOOF!
UUHH--!
KRAK
UUHFF!
OOOF!
WHUMP
SNAP
AAAA---!
YOU MADE ME DO THIS! I DIDN'T WANT TO---!
UURRK--!
UURRK--!
PLEASE! STOP IT, MAN!
"STOP"? I DIDN'T START IT.
YOU DID.

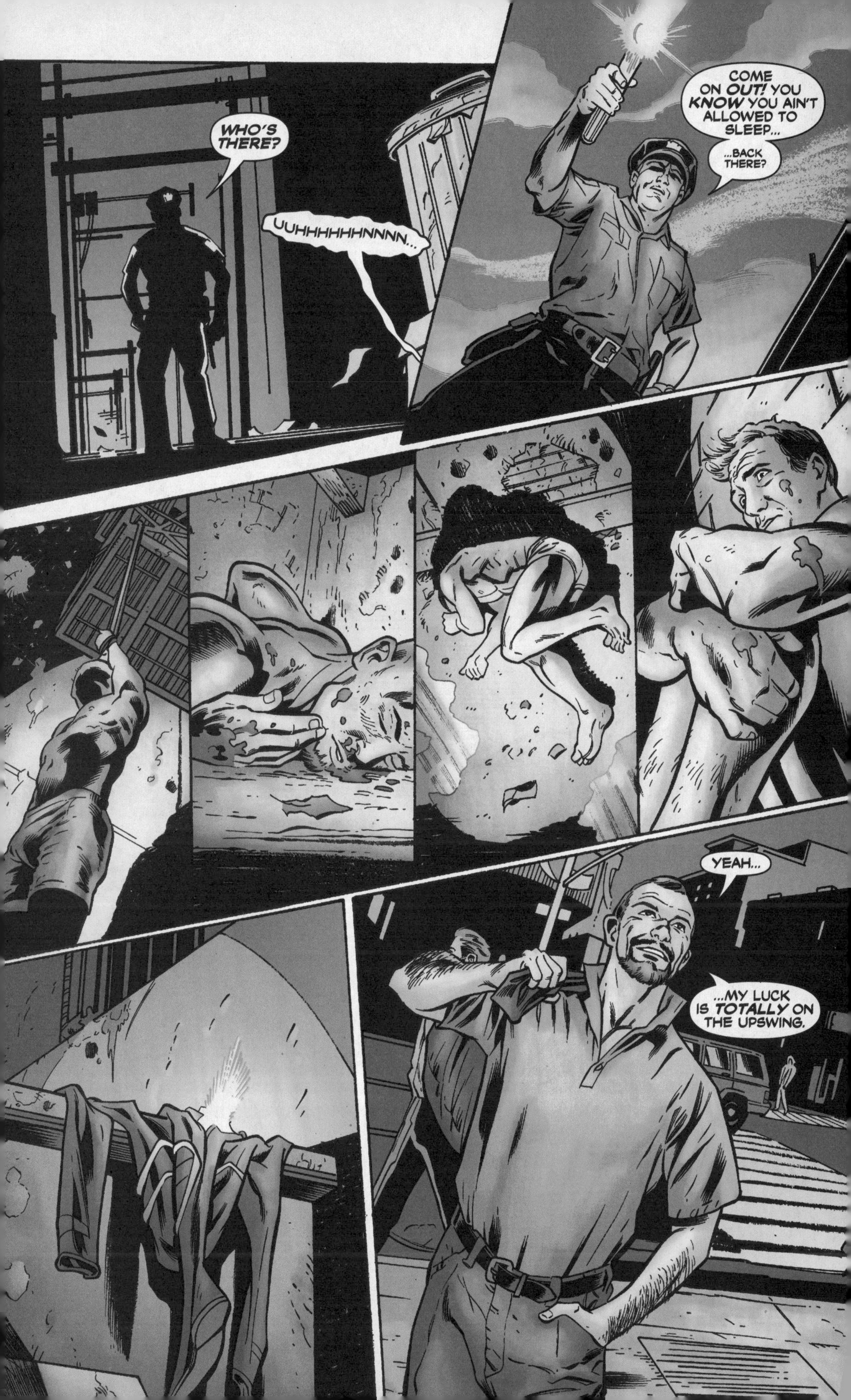
WHO'S THERE?
UUHHHHHHNNNN...
COME ON OUT! YOU KNOW YOU AIN'T ALLOWED TO SLEEP...
...BACK THERE?
YEAH...
...MY LUCK IS TOTALLY ON THE UPSWING.

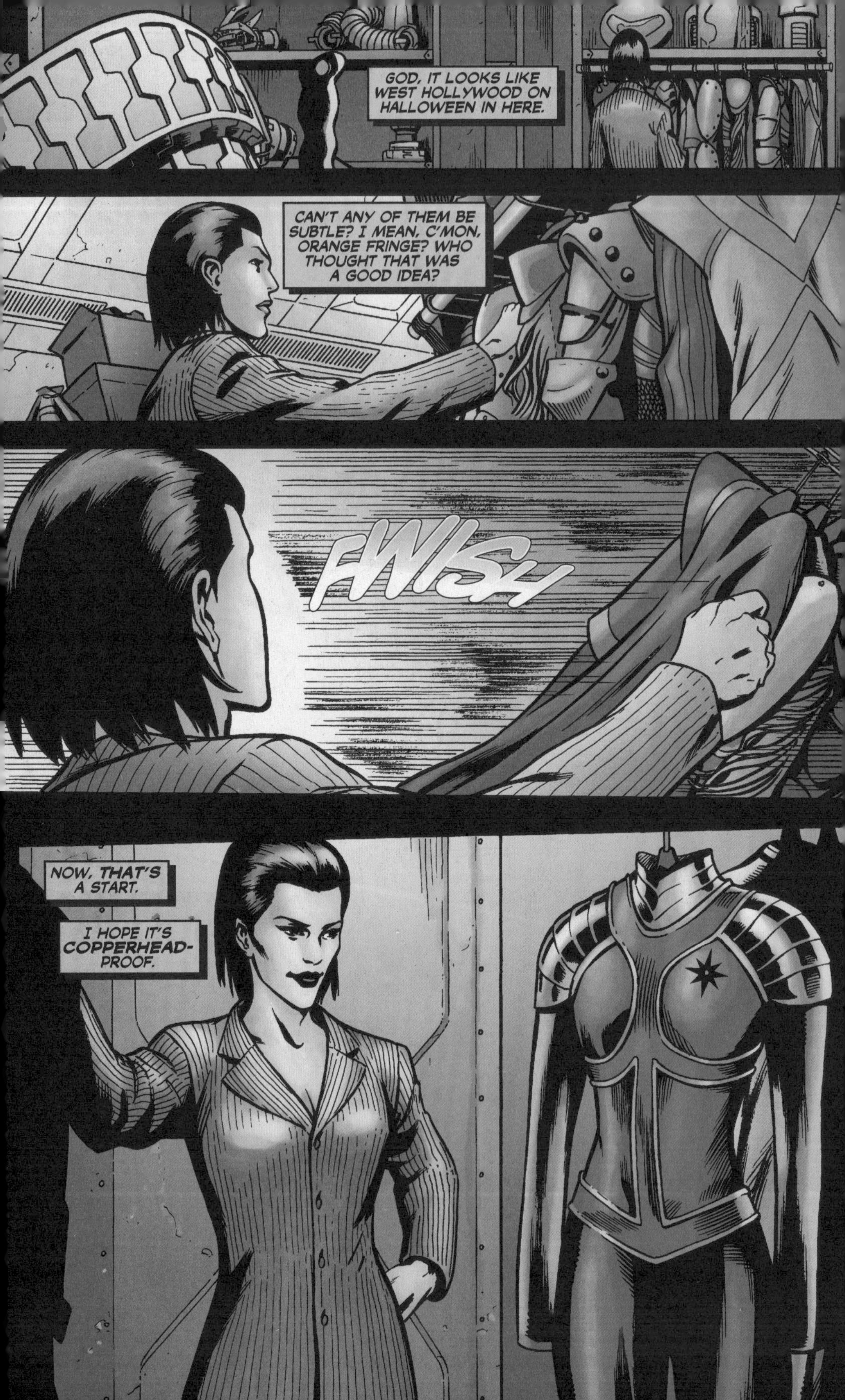

GOD, IT LOOKS LIKE WEST HOLLYWOOD ON HALLOWEEN IN HERE.
CAN'T ANY OF THEM BE SUBTLE? I MEAN, C'MON, ORANGE FRINGE? WHO THOUGHT THAT WAS A GOOD IDEA?
FWISH
NOW, THAT'S A START.
I HOPE IT'S COPPERHEAD-PROOF.

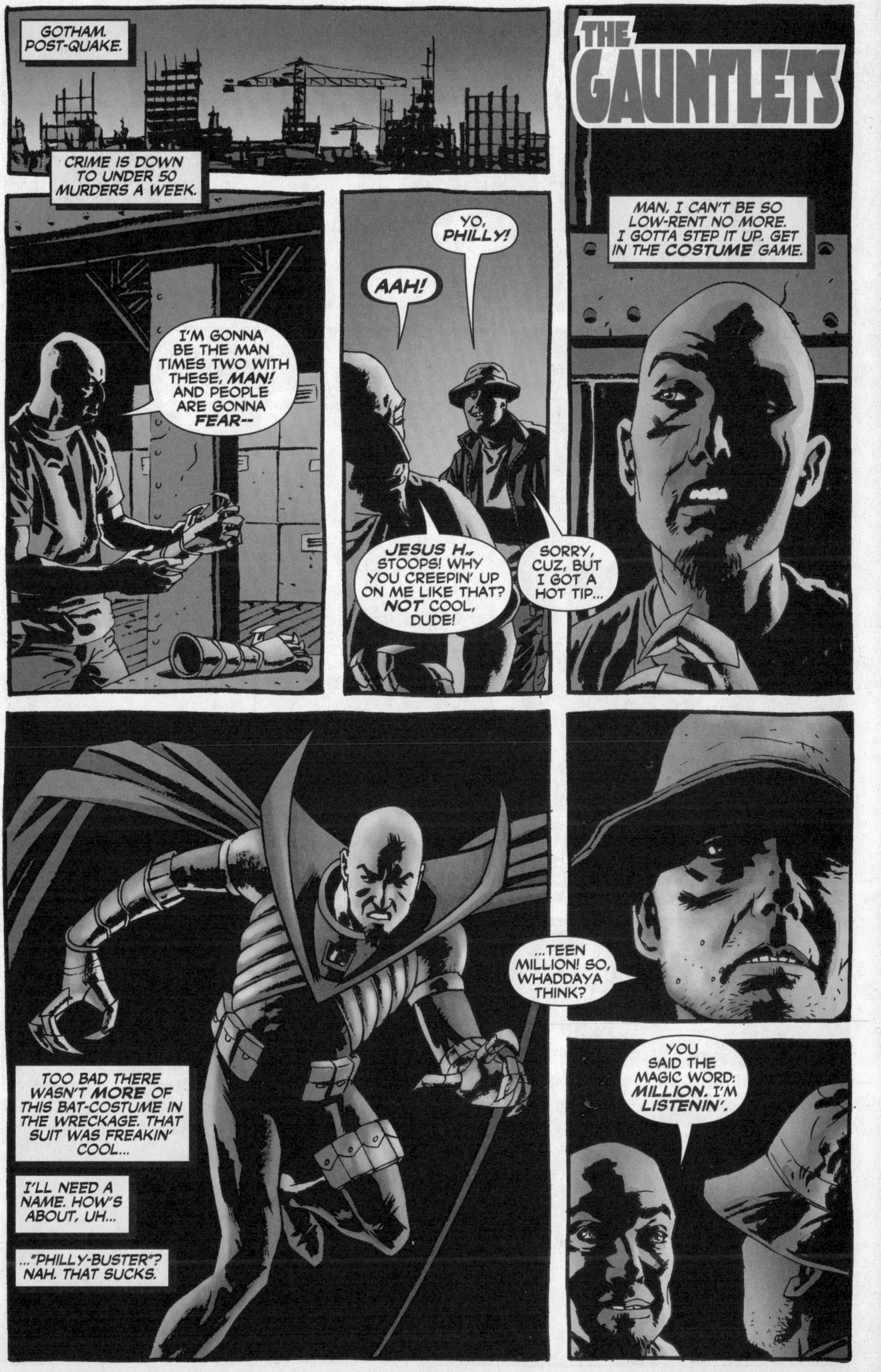
GOTHAM. POST-QUAKE.
CRIME IS DOWN TO UNDER 50 MURDERS A WEEK.
THE GAUNTLETS
I'M GONNA BE THE MAN TIMES TWO WITH THESE, MAN! AND PEOPLE ARE GONNA FEAR--
YO, PHILLY!
AAH!
JESUS H., STOOPS! WHY YOU CREEPIN' UP ON ME LIKE THAT? NOT COOL, DUDE!
SORRY, CUZ, BUT I GOT A HOT TIP...
MAN, I CAN'T BE SO LOW-RENT NO MORE. I GOTTA STEP IT UP. GET IN THE COSTUME GAME.
TOO BAD THERE WASN'T MORE OF THIS BAT-COSTUME IN THE WRECKAGE. THAT SUIT WAS FREAKIN' COOL...
I'LL NEED A NAME. HOW'S ABOUT, UH...
..."PHILLY-BUSTER"? NAH. THAT SUCKS.
...TEEN MILLION! SO, WHADDAYA THINK?
YOU SAID THE MAGIC WORD: MILLION. I'M LISTENIN'.

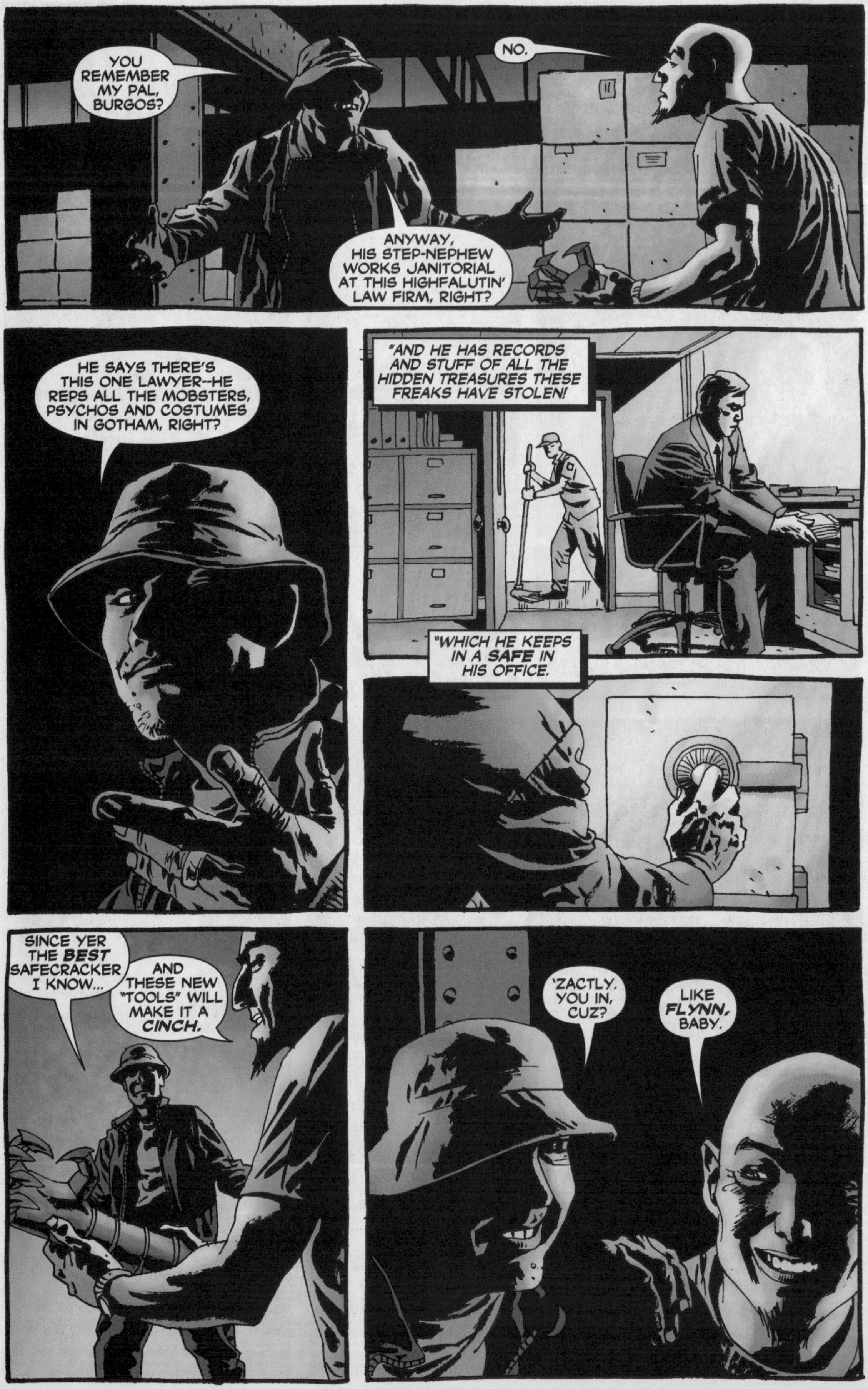

YOU REMEMBER MY PAL, BURGOS?
NO.
ANYWAY, HIS STEP-NEPHEW WORKS JANITORIAL AT THIS HIGHFALUTIN' LAW FIRM, RIGHT?
HE SAYS THERE'S THIS ONE LAWYER--HE REPS ALL THE MOBSTERS, PSYCHOS AND COSTUMES IN GOTHAM, RIGHT?
"AND HE HAS RECORDS AND STUFF OF ALL THE HIDDEN TREASURES THESE FREAKS HAVE STOLEN!
"WHICH HE KEEPS IN A SAFE IN HIS OFFICE.
SINCE YER THE BEST SAFECRACKER I KNOW...
AND THESE NEW "TOOLS" WILL MAKE IT A CINCH.
'ZACTLY. YOU IN, CUZ?
LIKE FLYNN, BABY.

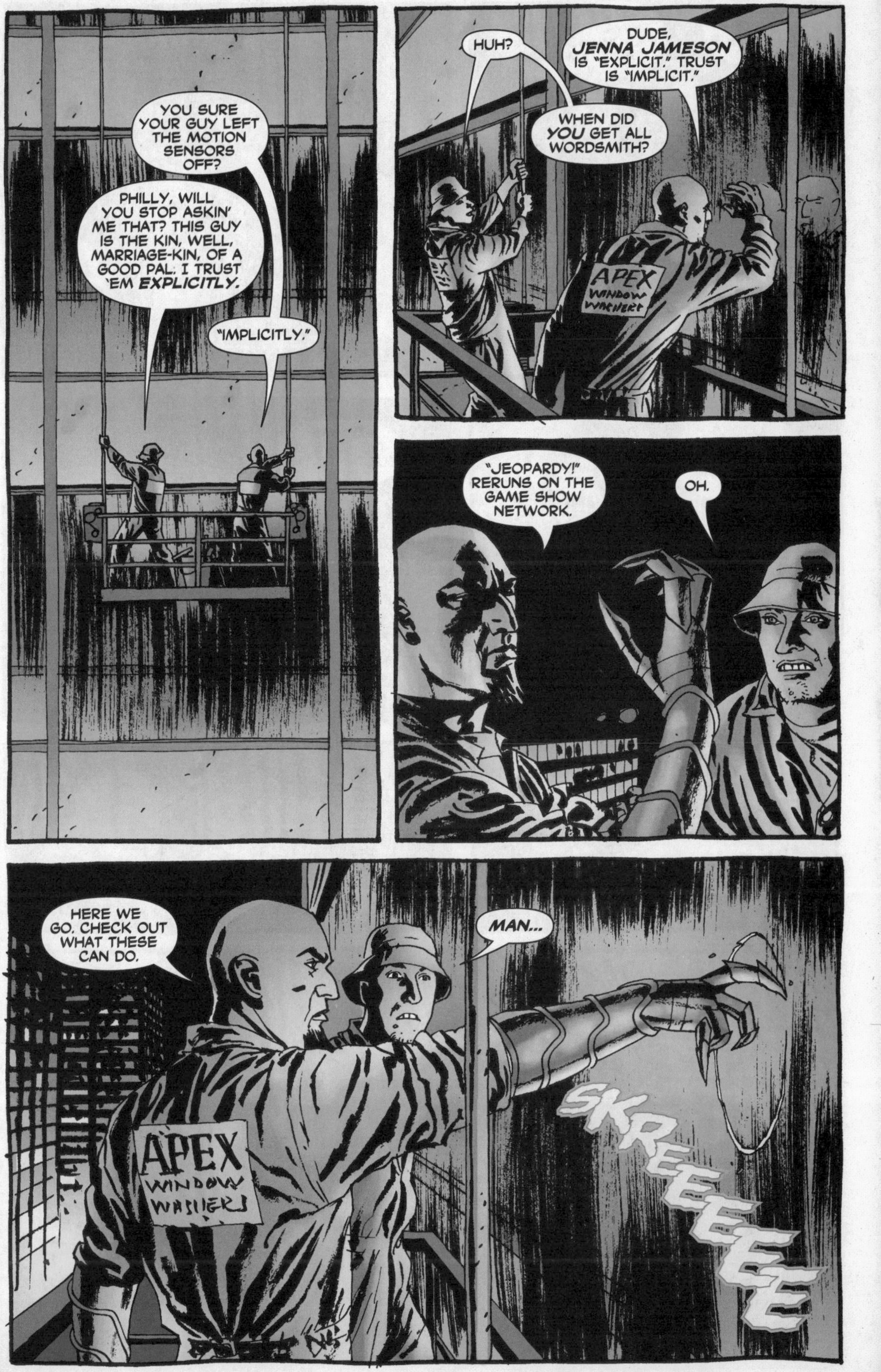
YOU SURE YOUR GUY LEFT THE MOTION SENSORS OFF?
PHILLY, WILL YOU STOP ASKIN' ME THAT? THIS GUY IS THE KIN, WELL, MARRIAGE-KIN, OF A GOOD PAL. I TRUST 'EM EXPLICITLY.
"IMPLICITLY."
HUH?
DUDE, JENNA JAMESON IS "EXPLICIT." TRUST IS "IMPLICIT."
WHEN DID YOU GET ALL WORDSMITH?
APEX WINDOW WASHERS
"JEOPARDY!" RERUNS ON THE GAME SHOW NETWORK.
OH.
HERE WE GO. CHECK OUT WHAT THESE CAN DO.
MAN...
APEX WINDOW WASHERS
SKREEEEEEE

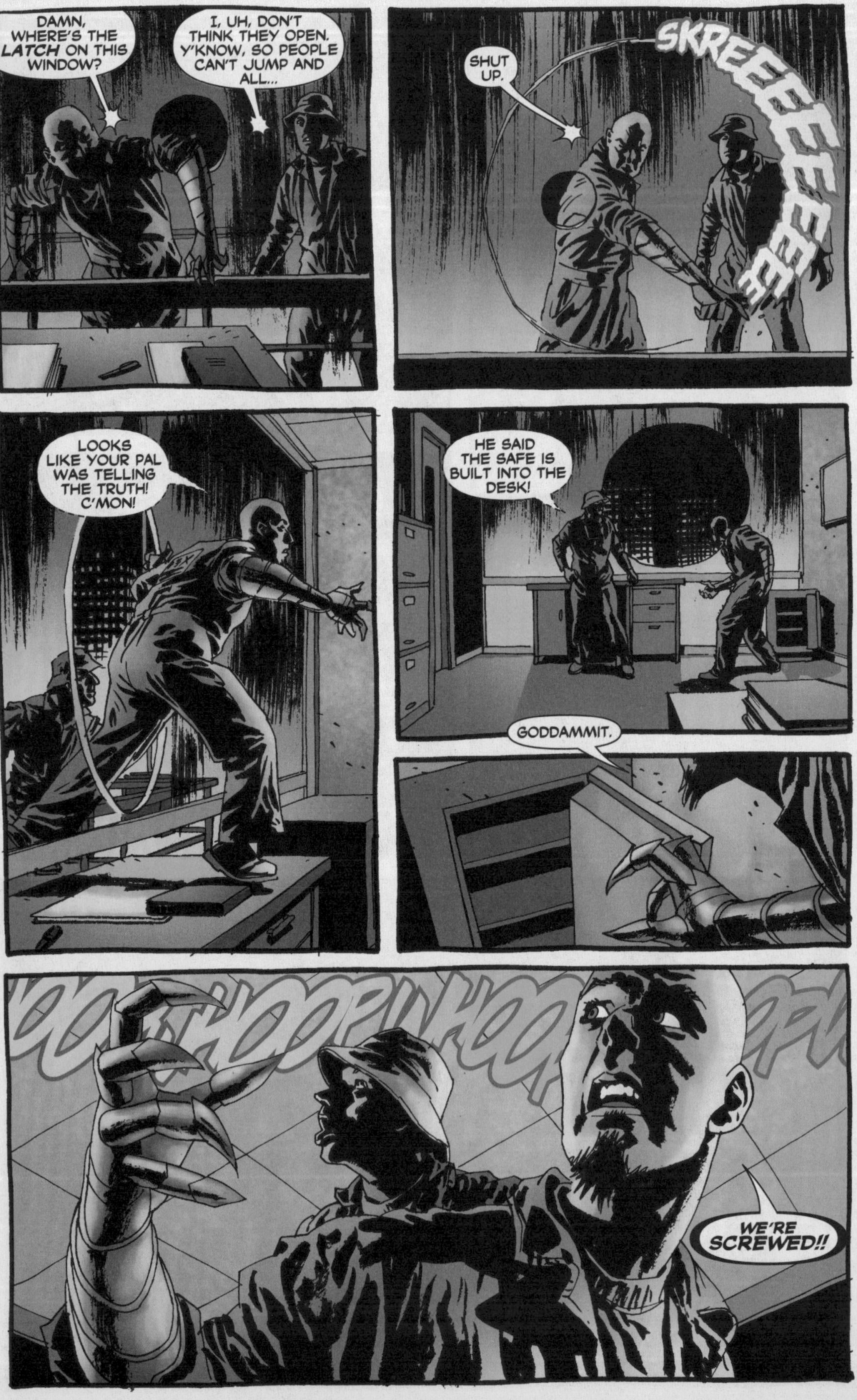
DAMN, WHERE'S THE LATCH ON THIS WINDOW?
I, UH, DON'T THINK THEY OPEN. Y'KNOW, SO PEOPLE CAN'T JUMP AND ALL...
SHUT UP.
SKREEEEEEEEE
LOOKS LIKE YOUR PAL WAS TELLING THE TRUTH! C'MON!
HE SAID THE SAFE IS BUILT INTO THE DESK!
GODDAMMIT.
THOOP!
WE'RE SCREWED!!

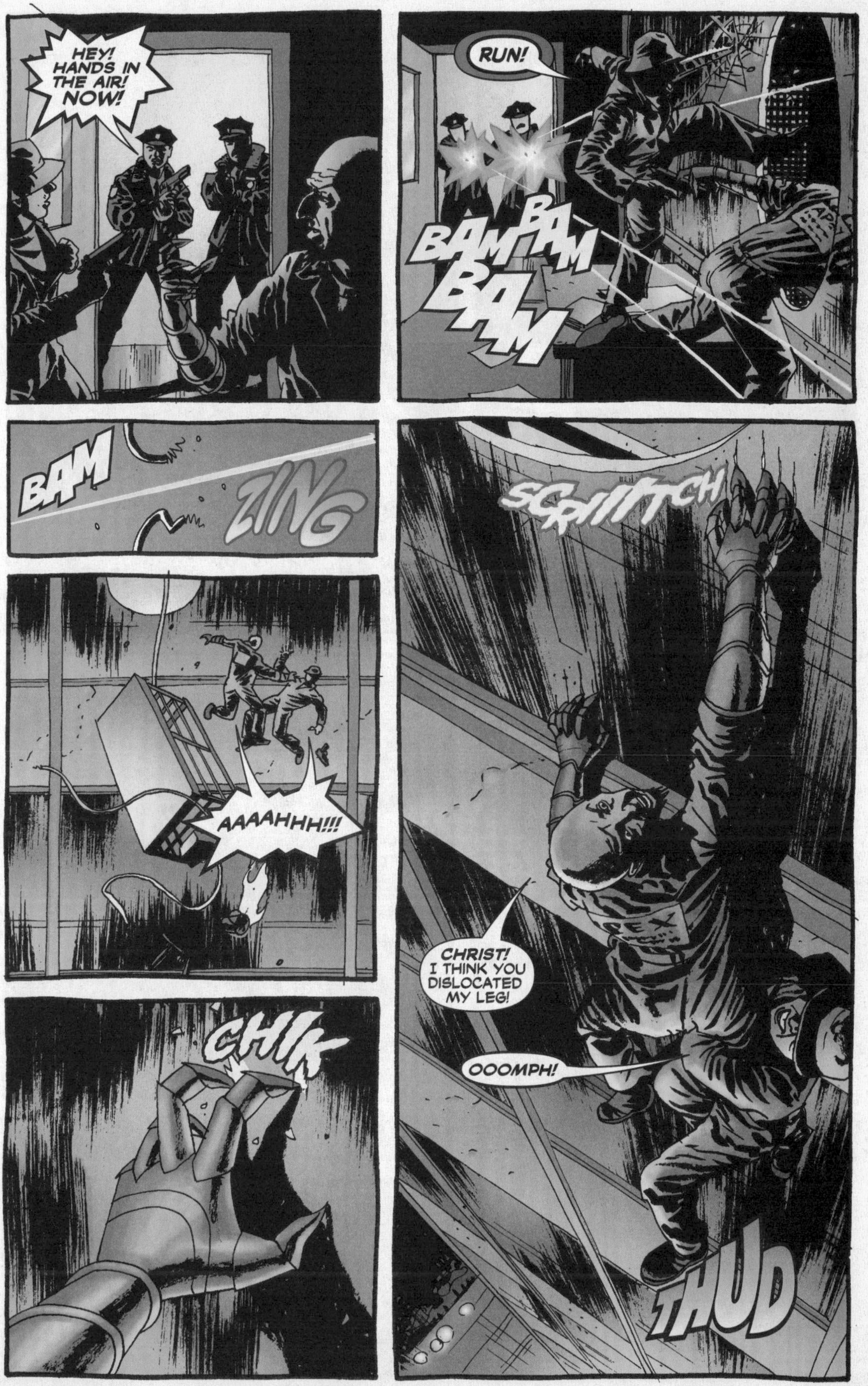

HEY! HANDS IN THE AIR! NOW!
RUN!
BAM BAM BAM BAM
BAM
ZING
SCRIIITCH
AAAAHHH!!!
CHRIST! I THINK YOU DISLOCATED MY LEG!
OOOMPH!
CHIK
THUD

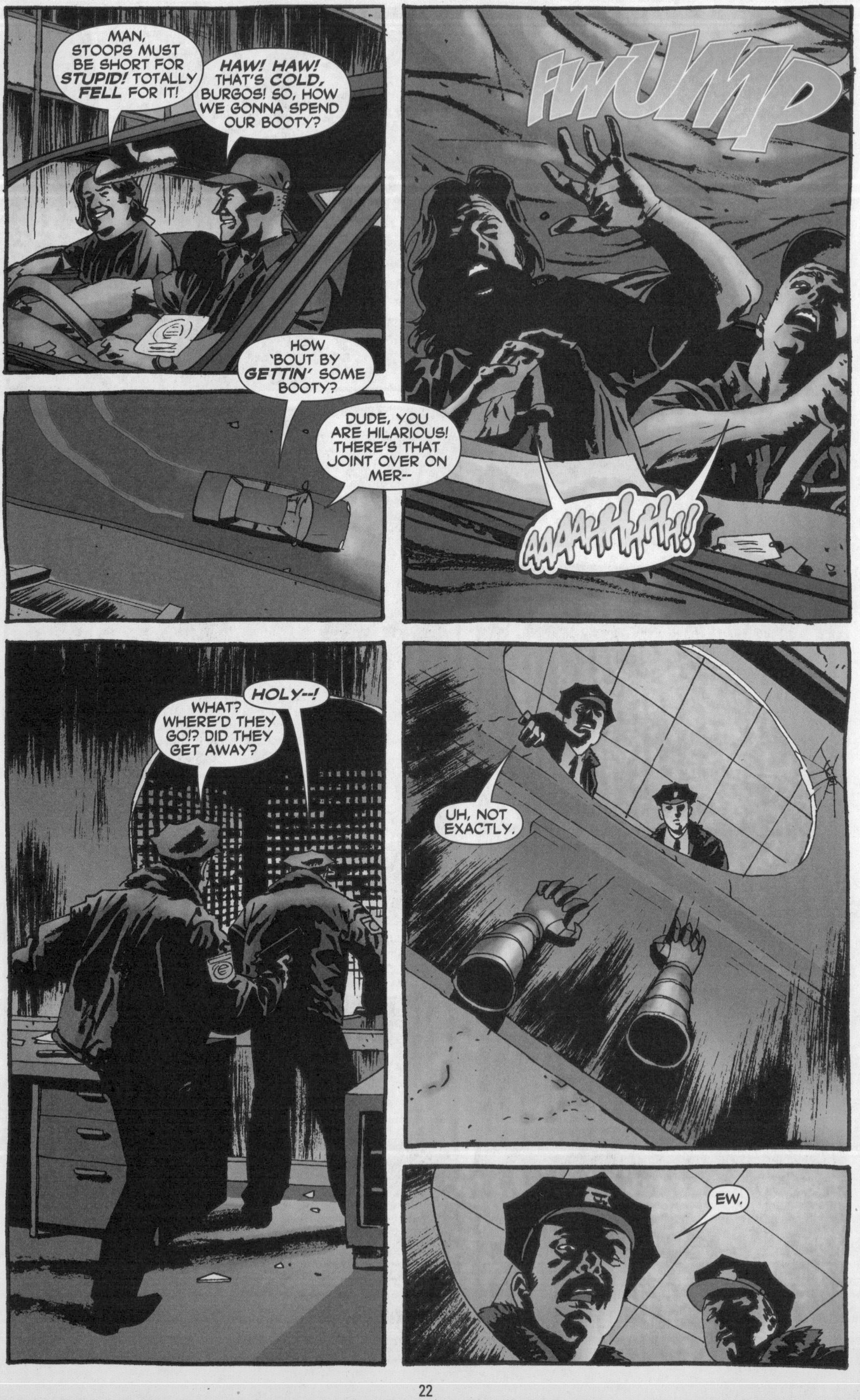
MAN, STOOPS MUST BE SHORT FOR STUPID! TOTALLY FELL FOR IT!
HAW! HAW! THAT'S COLD, BURGOS! SO, HOW WE GONNA SPEND OUR BOOTY?
HOW 'BOUT BY GETTIN' SOME BOOTY?
DUDE, YOU ARE HILARIOUS! THERE'S THAT JOINT OVER ON MER--
FWUMP
AAAAHHHHH!
WHAT? WHERE'D THEY GO!? DID THEY GET AWAY?
HOLY--!
UH, NOT EXACTLY.
EW.

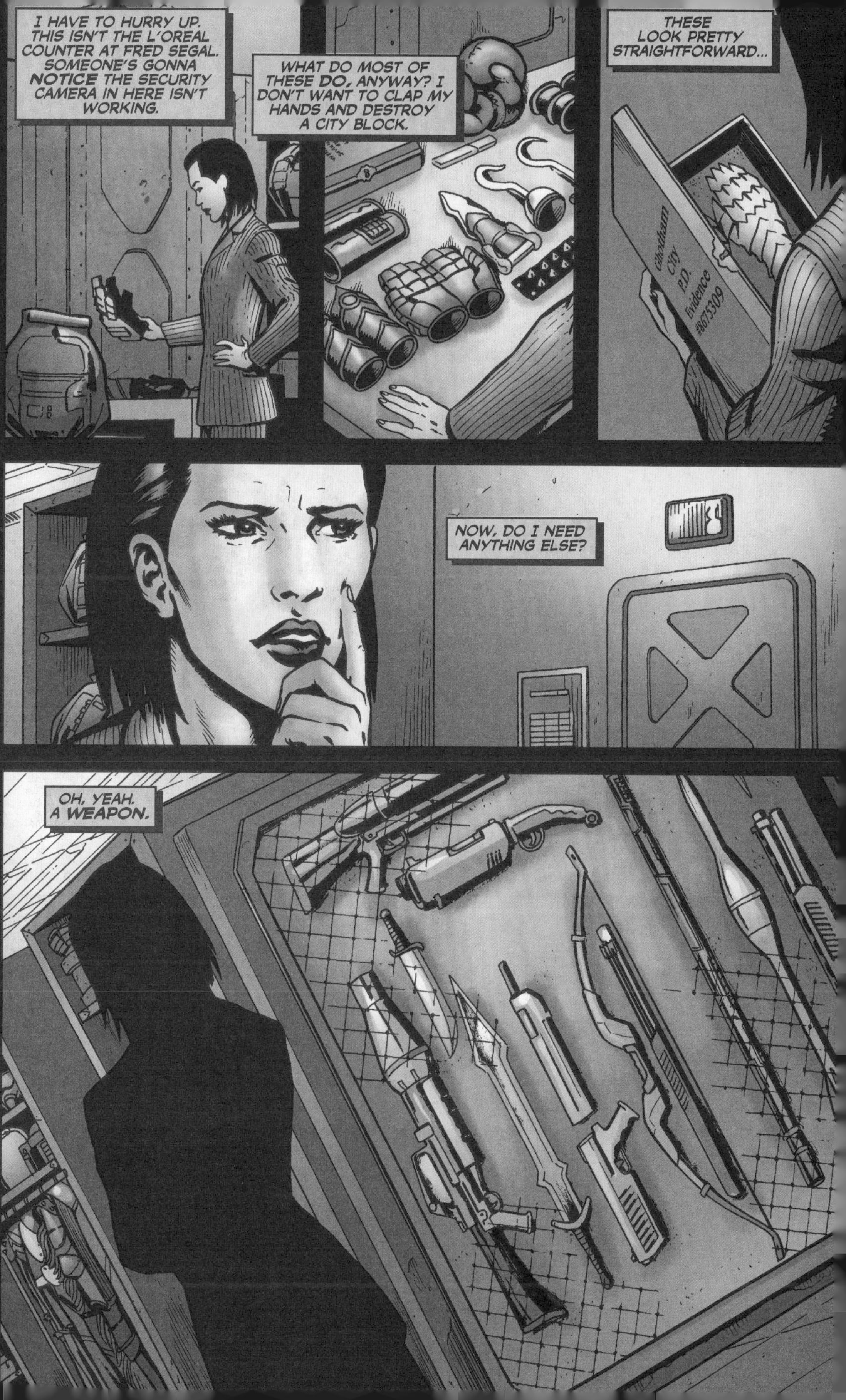
I HAVE TO HURRY UP. THIS ISN'T THE L'OREAL COUNTER AT FRED SEGAL. SOMEONE'S GONNA NOTICE THE SECURITY CAMERA IN HERE ISN'T WORKING.
WHAT DO MOST OF THESE DO, ANYWAY? I DON'T WANT TO CLAP MY HANDS AND DESTROY A CITY BLOCK.
THESE LOOK PRETTY STRAIGHTFORWARD...
Ghotham City P.D. Evidence #8675309
NOW, DO I NEED ANYTHING ELSE?
OH, YEAH. A WEAPON.

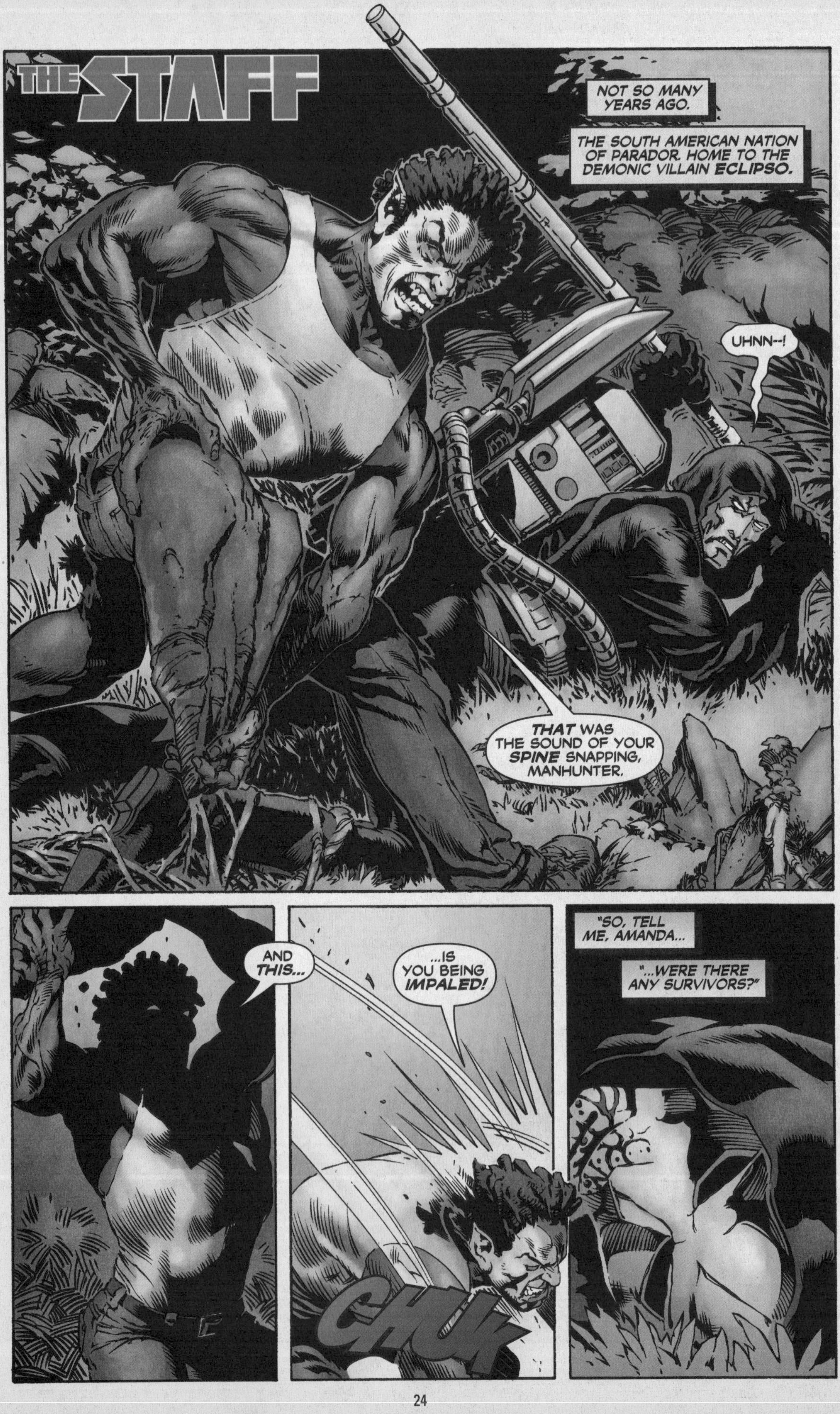
THE STAFF
NOT SO MANY YEARS AGO.
THE SOUTH AMERICAN NATION OF PARADOR. HOME TO THE DEMONIC VILLAIN ECLIPSO.
UHNN--!
THAT WAS THE SOUND OF YOUR SPINE SNAPPING, MANHUNTER.
AND THIS...
...IS YOU BEING IMPALED!
CHUK
"SO, TELL ME, AMANDA...
"...WERE THERE ANY SURVIVORS?"

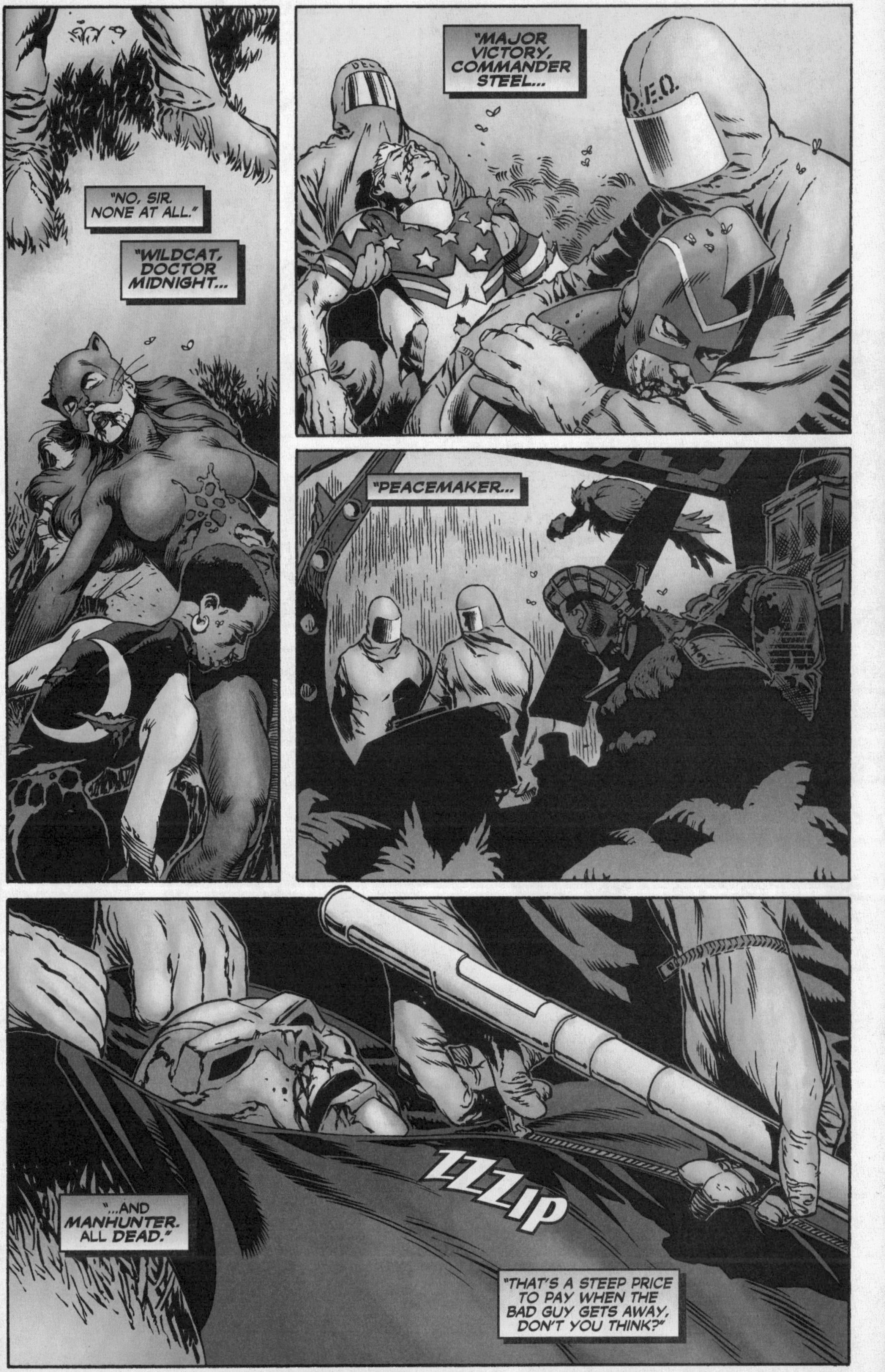
"NO, SIR. NONE AT ALL."
"WILDCAT, DOCTOR MIDNIGHT...
"MAJOR VICTORY, COMMANDER STEEL...
D.E.O.
"PEACEMAKER...
"...AND MANHUNTER. ALL DEAD."
ZZZIP
"THAT'S A STEEP PRICE TO PAY WHEN THE BAD GUY GETS AWAY, DON'T YOU THINK?"

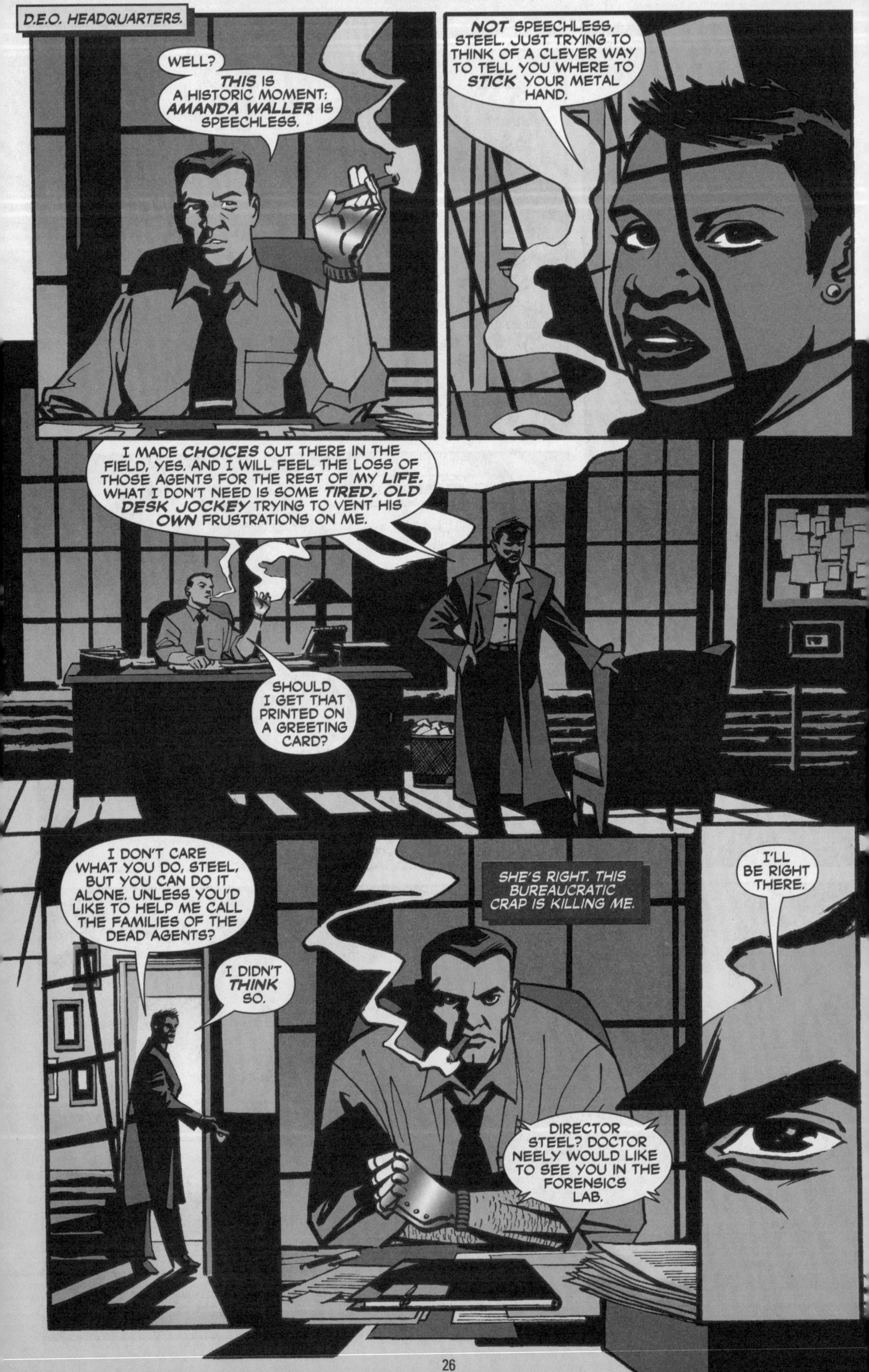
D.E.O. HEADQUARTERS.
WELL?
THIS IS A HISTORIC MOMENT: AMANDA WALLER IS SPEECHLESS.
NOT SPEECHLESS, STEEL. JUST TRYING TO THINK OF A CLEVER WAY TO TELL YOU WHERE TO STICK YOUR METAL HAND.
I MADE CHOICES OUT THERE IN THE FIELD, YES. AND I WILL FEEL THE LOSS OF THOSE AGENTS FOR THE REST OF MY LIFE. WHAT I DON'T NEED IS SOME TIRED, OLD DESK JOCKEY TRYING TO VENT HIS OWN FRUSTRATIONS ON ME.
SHOULD I GET THAT PRINTED ON A GREETING CARD?
I DON'T CARE WHAT YOU DO, STEEL, BUT YOU CAN DO IT ALONE. UNLESS YOU'D LIKE TO HELP ME CALL THE FAMILIES OF THE DEAD AGENTS?
I DIDN'T THINK SO.
SHE'S RIGHT. THIS BUREAUCRATIC CRAP IS KILLING ME.
DIRECTOR STEEL? DOCTOR NEELY WOULD LIKE TO SEE YOU IN THE FORENSICS LAB.
I'LL BE RIGHT THERE.

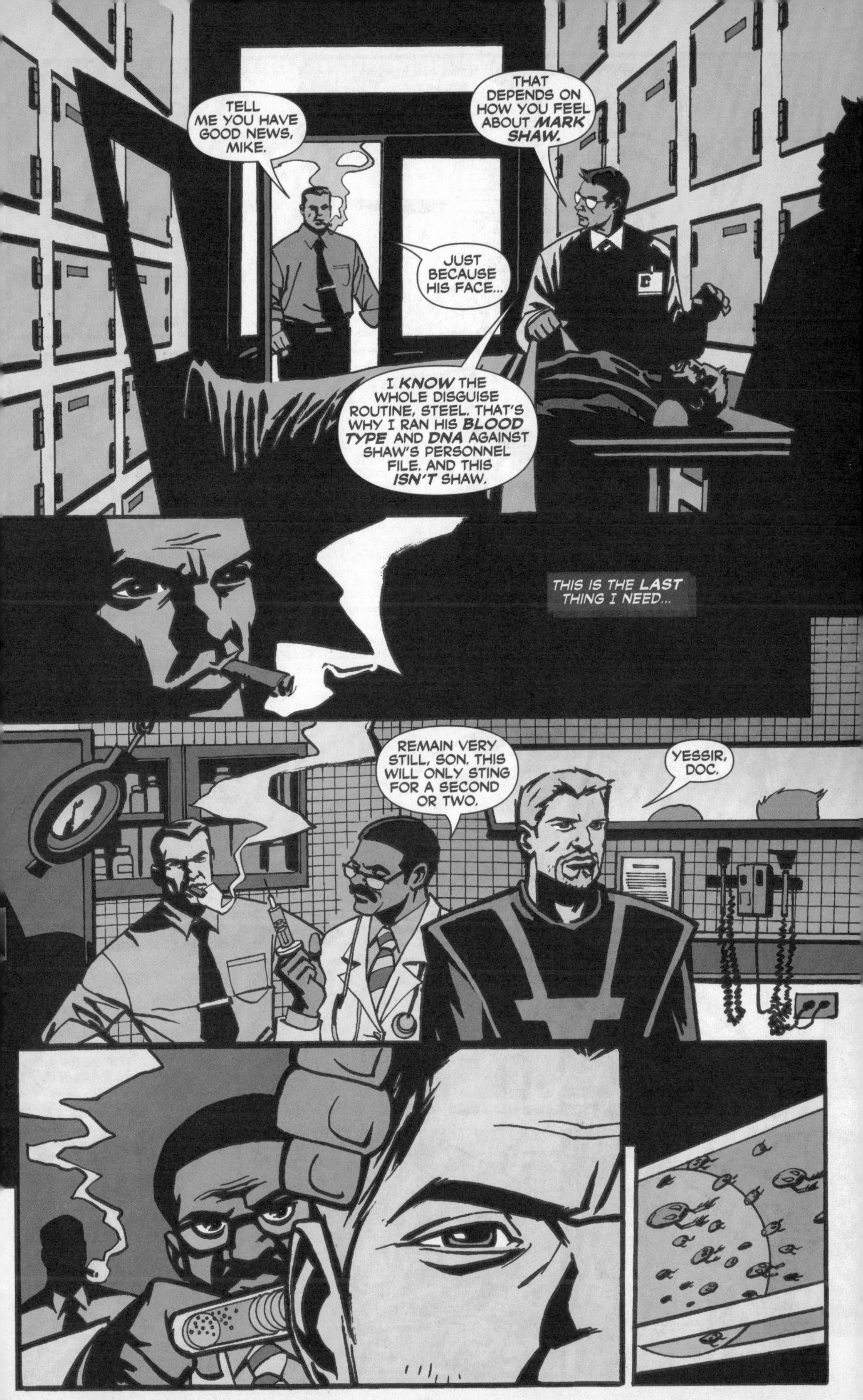
TELL ME YOU HAVE GOOD NEWS, MIKE.
THAT DEPENDS ON HOW YOU FEEL ABOUT MARK SHAW.
JUST BECAUSE HIS FACE...
I KNOW THE WHOLE DISGUISE ROUTINE, STEEL. THAT'S WHY I RAN HIS BLOOD TYPE AND DNA AGAINST SHAW'S PERSONNEL FILE. AND THIS ISN'T SHAW.
THIS IS THE LAST THING I NEED...
REMAIN VERY STILL, SON. THIS WILL ONLY STING FOR A SECOND OR TWO.
YESSIR, DOC.

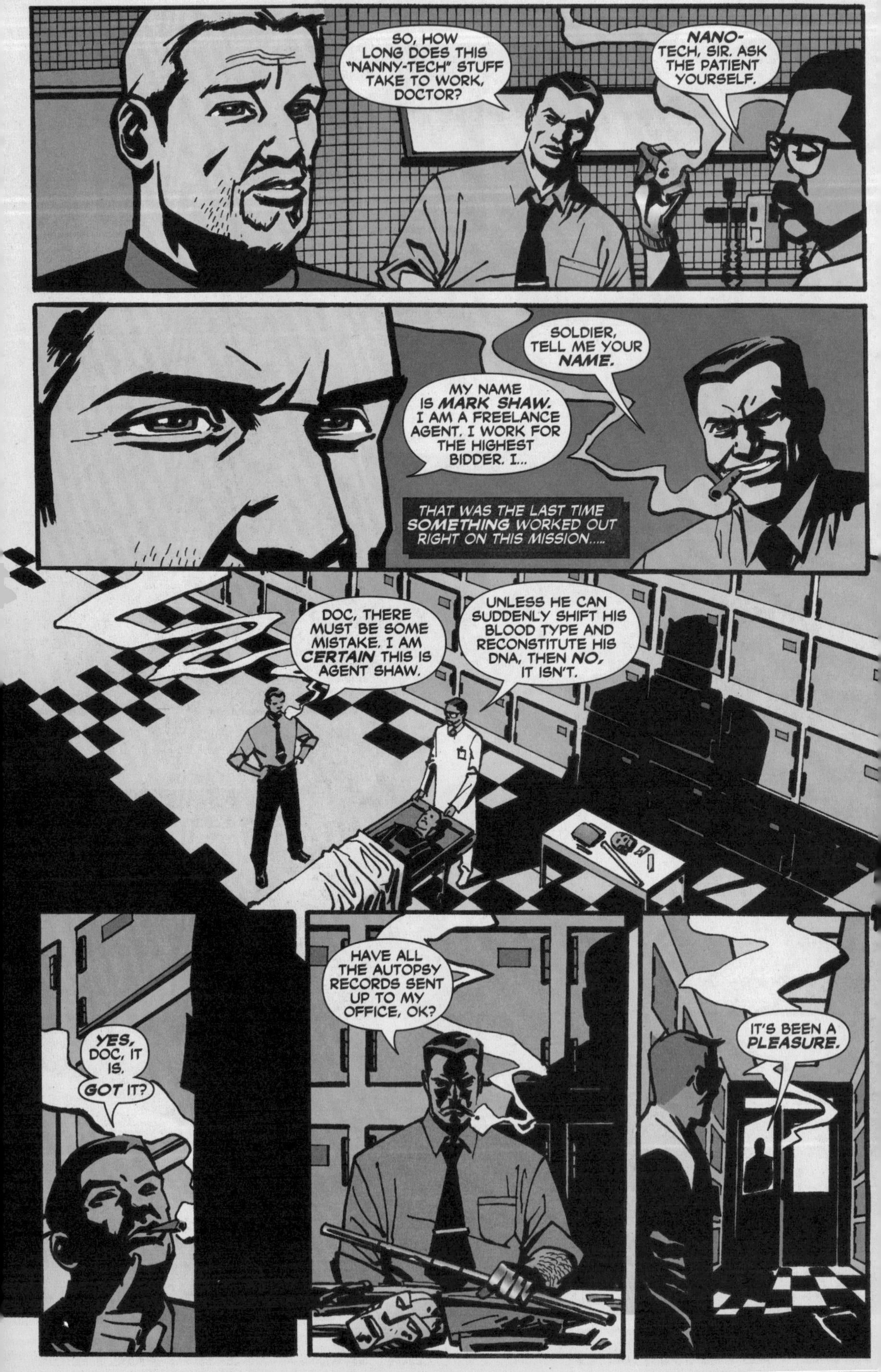
SO, HOW LONG DOES THIS "NANNY-TECH" STUFF TAKE TO WORK, DOCTOR?
NANO-TECH, SIR. ASK THE PATIENT YOURSELF.
SOLDIER, TELL ME YOUR NAME.
MY NAME IS MARK SHAW. I AM A FREELANCE AGENT. I WORK FOR THE HIGHEST BIDDER. I...
THAT WAS THE LAST TIME SOMETHING WORKED OUT RIGHT ON THIS MISSION.....
DOC, THERE MUST BE SOME MISTAKE. I AM CERTAIN THIS IS AGENT SHAW.
UNLESS HE CAN SUDDENLY SHIFT HIS BLOOD TYPE AND RECONSTITUTE HIS DNA, THEN NO, IT ISN'T.
YES, DOC, IT IS.
GOT IT?
HAVE ALL THE AUTOPSY RECORDS SENT UP TO MY OFFICE, OK?
IT'S BEEN A PLEASURE.

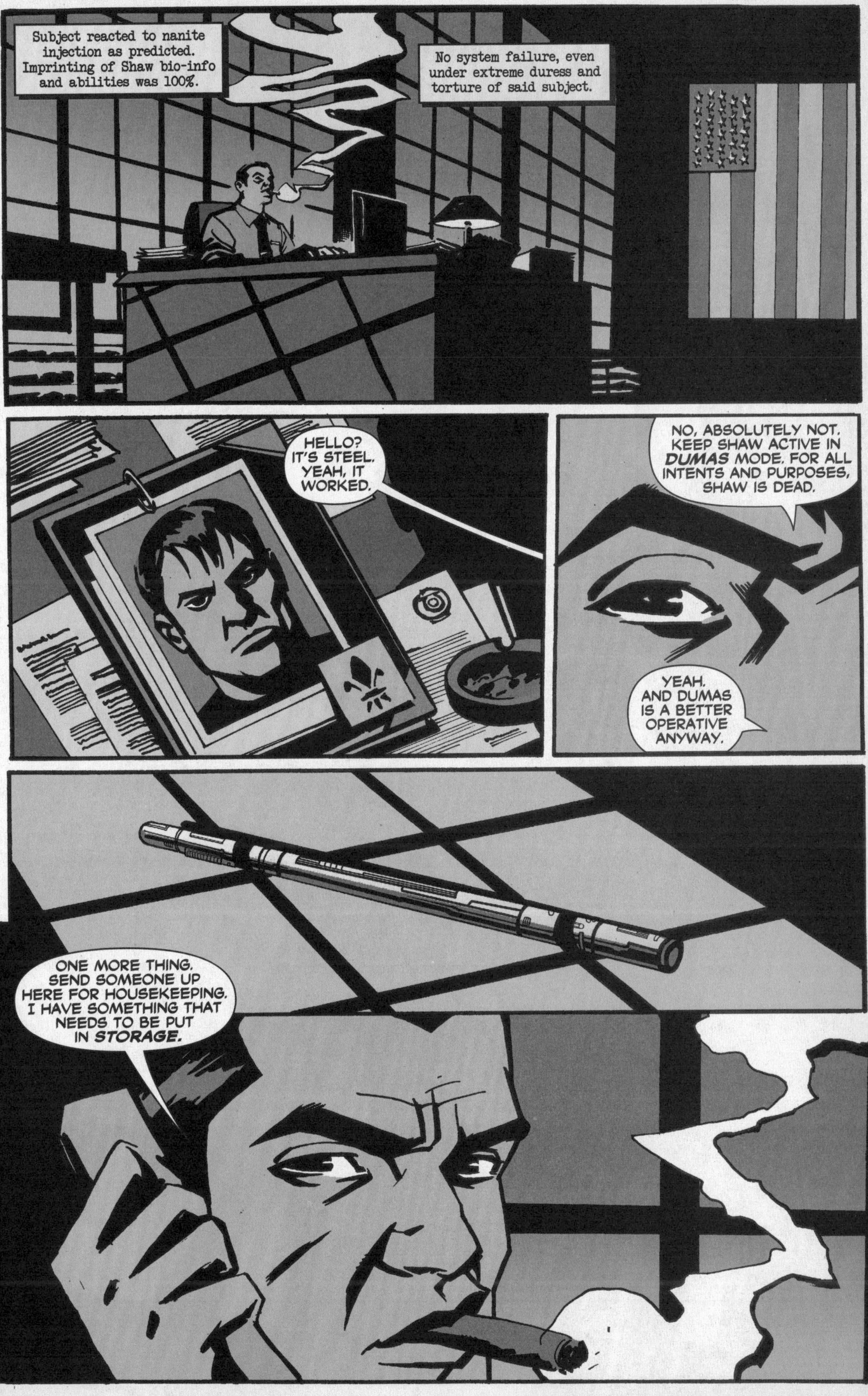
Subject reacted to nanite injection as predicted. Imprinting of Shaw bio-info and abilities was 100%.
No system failure, even under extreme duress and torture of said subject.
HELLO? IT'S STEEL. YEAH, IT WORKED.
NO, ABSOLUTELY NOT. KEEP SHAW ACTIVE IN DUMAS MODE. FOR ALL INTENTS AND PURPOSES, SHAW IS DEAD.
YEAH. AND DUMAS IS A BETTER OPERATIVE ANYWAY.
ONE MORE THING. SEND SOMEONE UP HERE FOR HOUSEKEEPING. I HAVE SOMETHING THAT NEEDS TO BE PUT IN STORAGE.

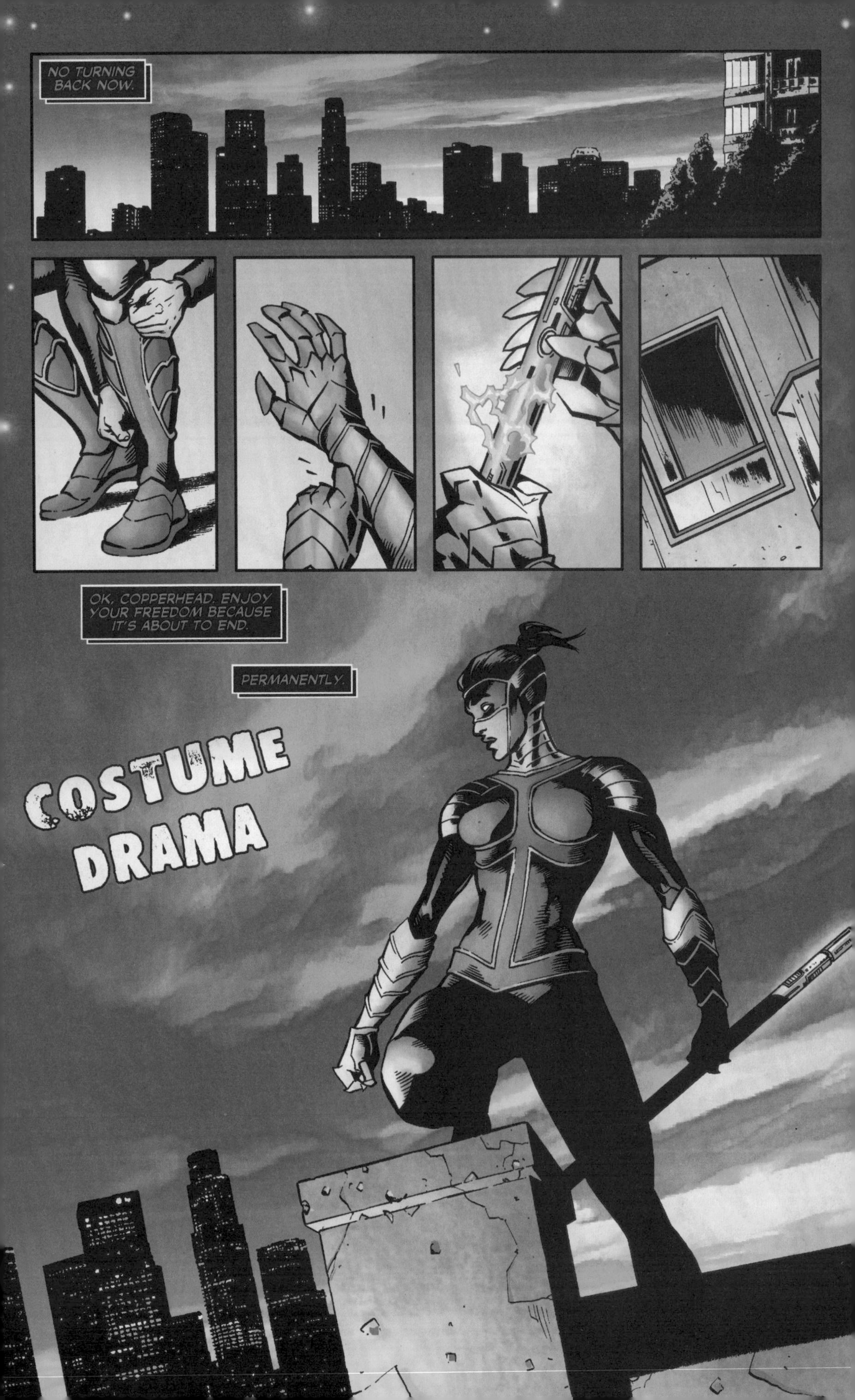
NO TURNING BACK NOW.
OK, COPPERHEAD. ENJOY YOUR FREEDOM BECAUSE IT'S ABOUT TO END.
PERMANENTLY.
COSTUME DRAMA

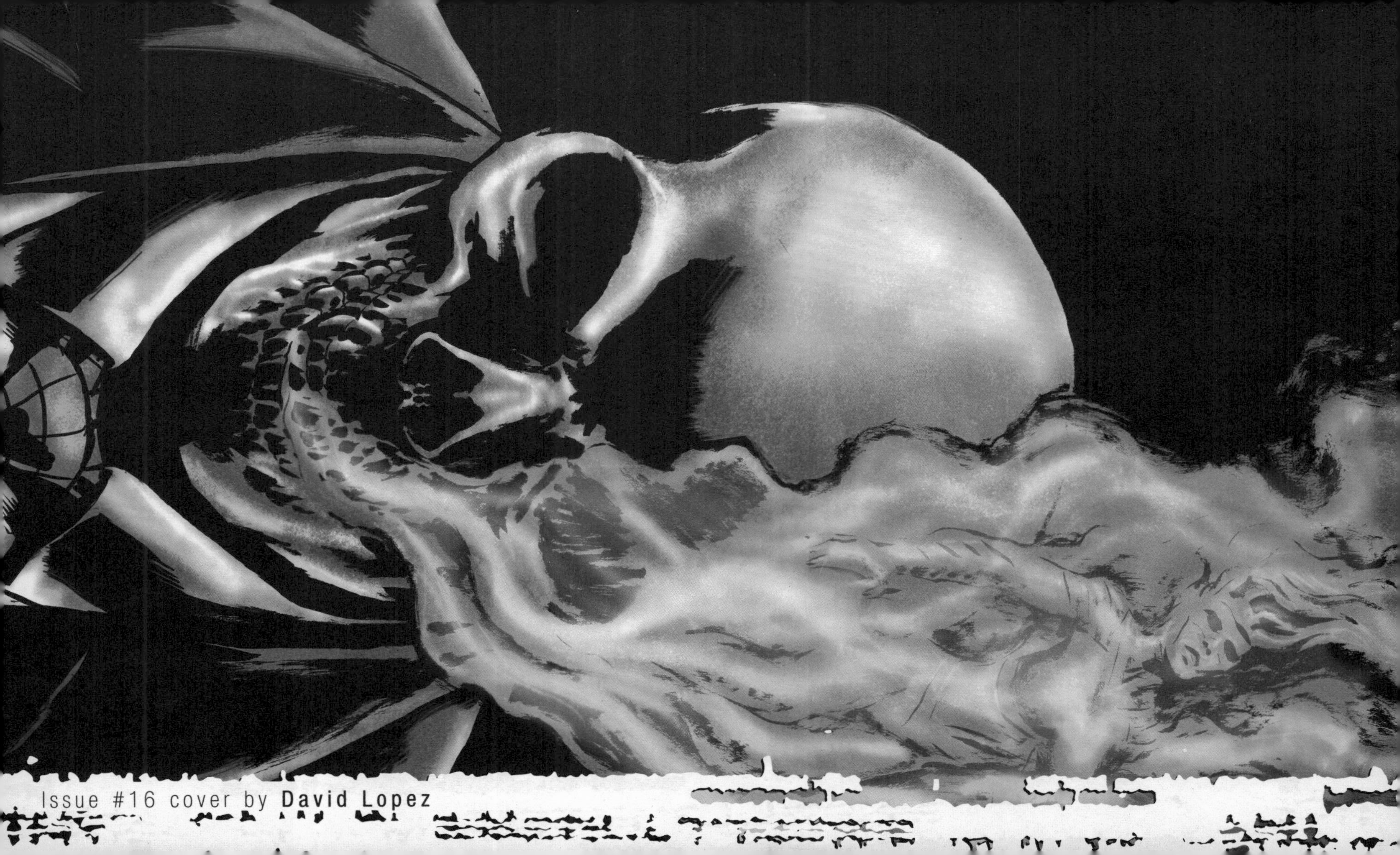

Issue #16 cover by David Lopez

Interior art by Javier Pina & Fernando Blanco

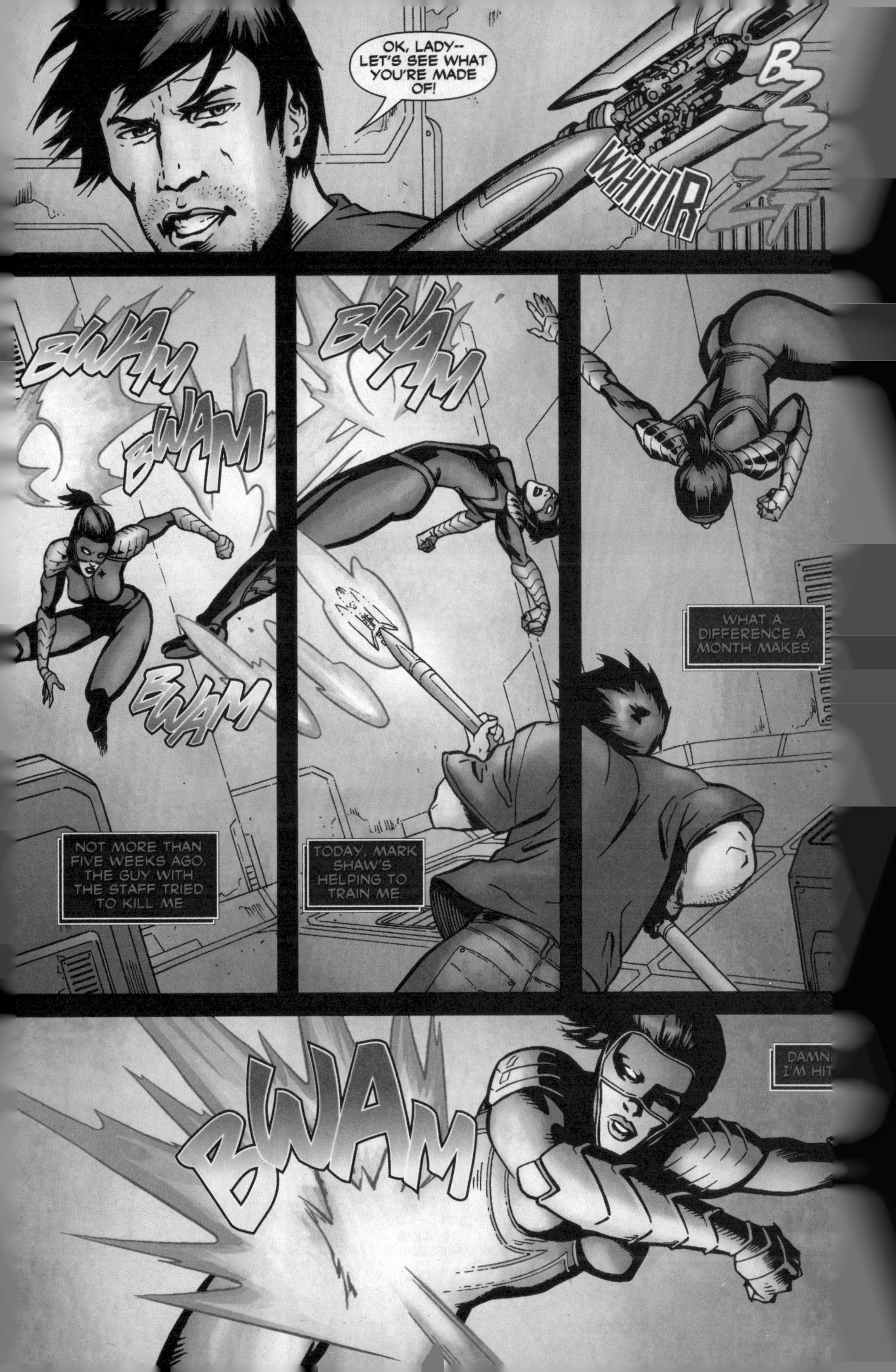
OK, LADY-- LET'S SEE WHAT YOU'RE MADE OF!
WHIIIR
BZZZT
BWAM
BWAM
BWAM
NOT MORE THAN FIVE WEEKS AGO, THE GUY WITH THE STAFF TRIED TO KILL ME.
BWAM
TODAY, MARK SHAW'S HELPING TO TRAIN ME.
WHAT A DIFFERENCE A MONTH MAKES.
BWAM

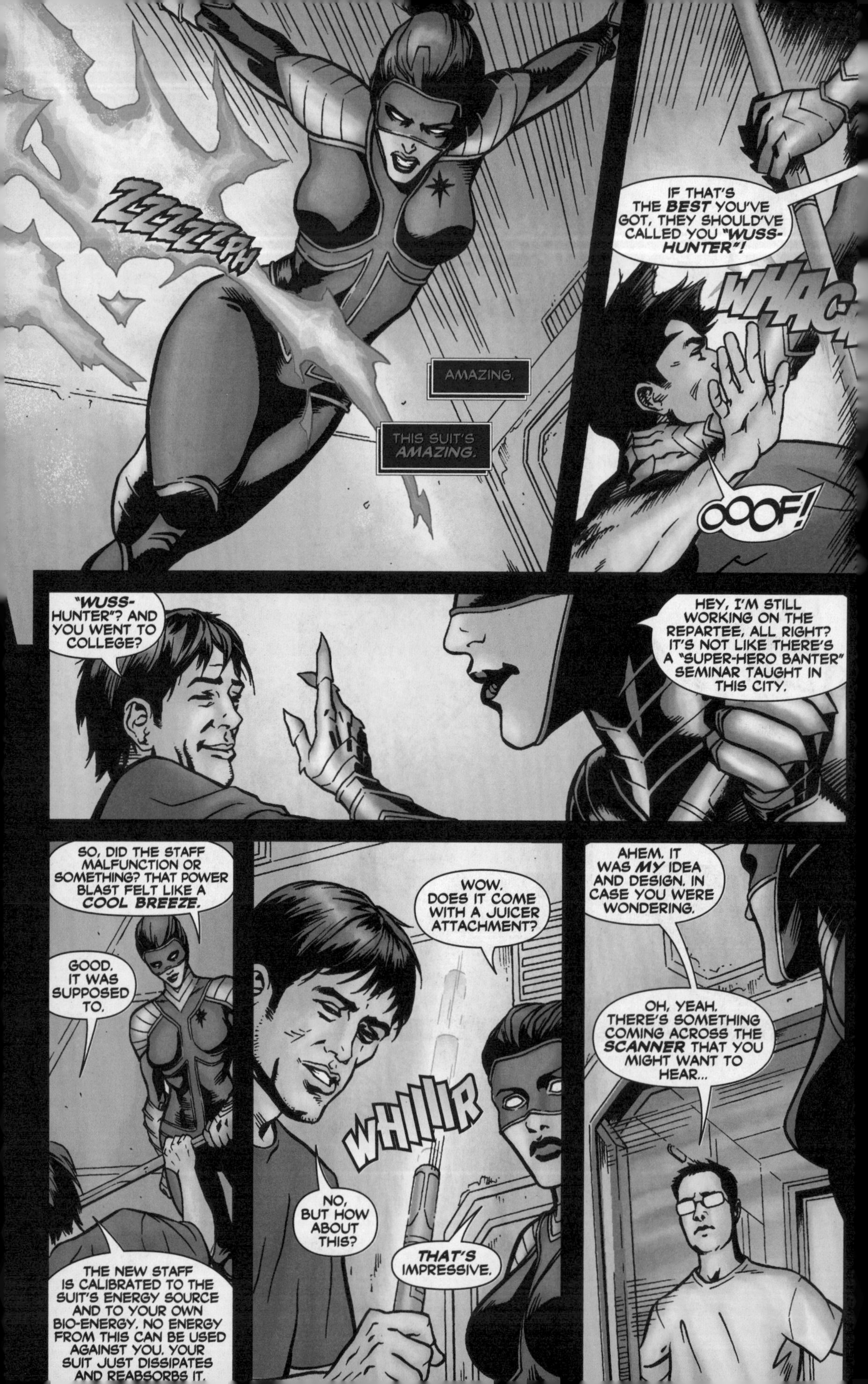
ZZZZZZZPH
AMAZING.
THIS SUIT'S *AMAZING.*
IF THAT'S THE *BEST* YOU'VE GOT, THEY SHOULD'VE CALLED YOU *"WUSS-HUNTER"*!
WHAC
OOOF!
*"WUSS-*HUNTER"? AND YOU WENT TO COLLEGE?
HEY, I'M STILL WORKING ON THE REPARTEE, ALL RIGHT? IT'S NOT LIKE THERE'S A "SUPER-HERO BANTER" SEMINAR TAUGHT IN THIS CITY.
SO, DID THE STAFF MALFUNCTION OR SOMETHING? THAT POWER BLAST FELT LIKE A *COOL BREEZE.*
GOOD. IT WAS SUPPOSED TO.
THE NEW STAFF IS CALIBRATED TO THE SUIT'S ENERGY SOURCE AND TO YOUR OWN BIO-ENERGY. NO ENERGY FROM THIS CAN BE USED AGAINST YOU. YOUR SUIT JUST DISSIPATES AND REABSORBS IT.
WOW. DOES IT COME WITH A JUICER ATTACHMENT?
WHIIIIR
NO, BUT HOW ABOUT THIS?
THAT'S IMPRESSIVE.
AHEM. IT WAS *MY* IDEA AND DESIGN, IN CASE YOU WERE WONDERING.
OH, YEAH. THERE'S SOMETHING COMING ACROSS THE *SCANNER* THAT YOU MIGHT WANT TO HEAR...

FAMILY PLOTS

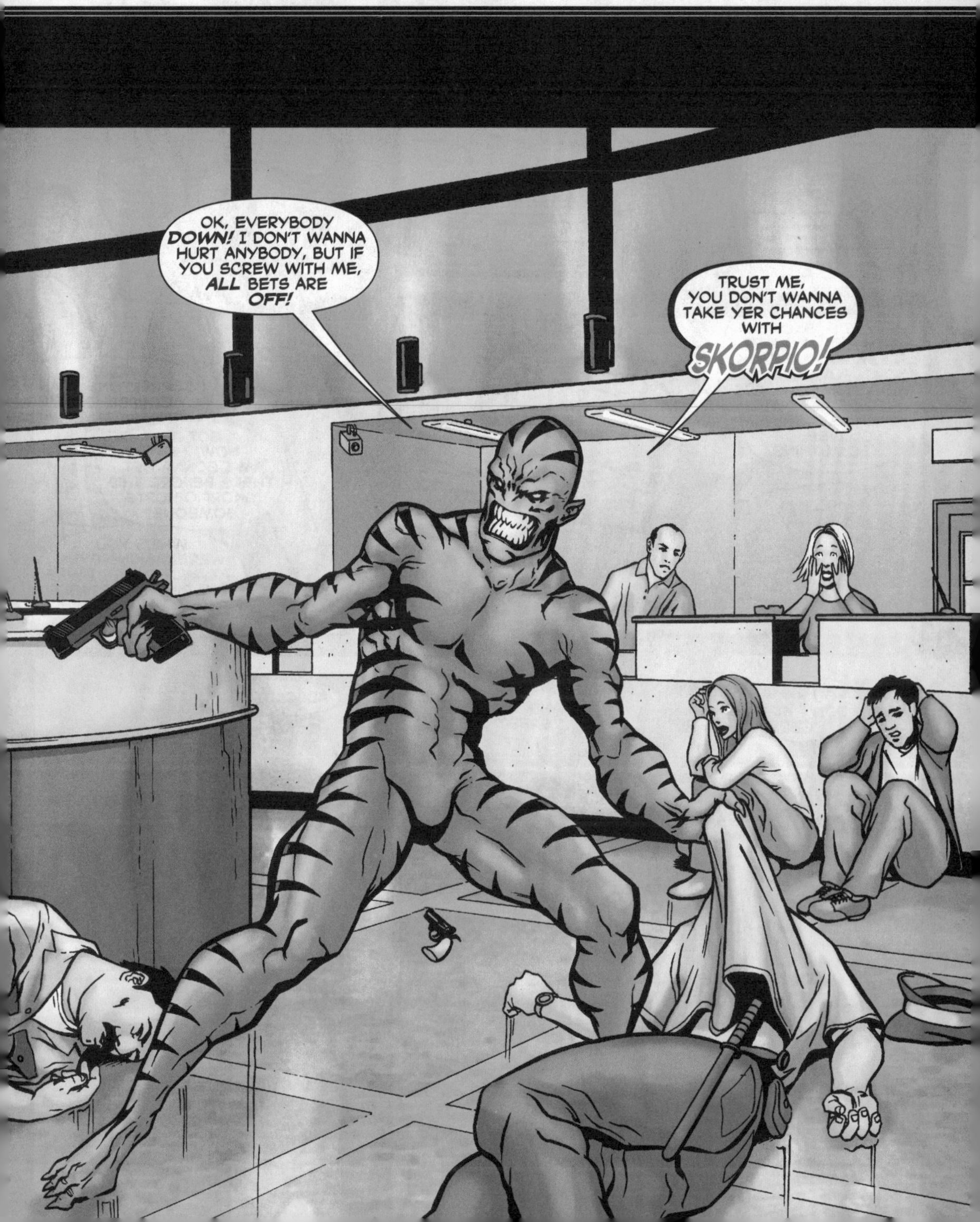
OK, EVERYBODY DOWN! I DON'T WANNA HURT ANYBODY, BUT IF YOU SCREW WITH ME, ALL BETS ARE OFF!
TRUST ME, YOU DON'T WANNA TAKE YER CHANCES WITH SKORPIO!

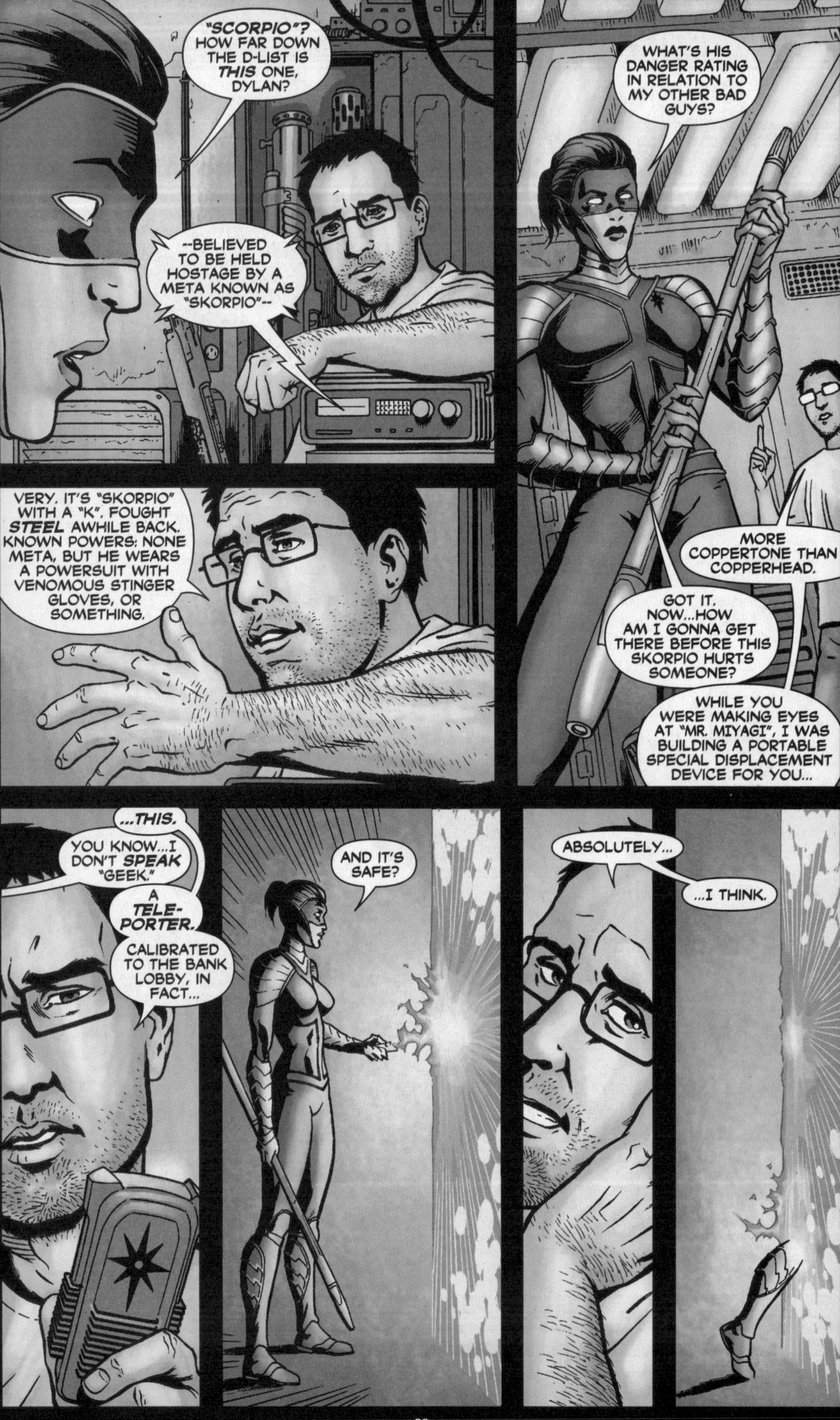
"SCORPIO"? HOW FAR DOWN THE D-LIST IS THIS ONE, DYLAN?
--BELIEVED TO BE HELD HOSTAGE BY A META KNOWN AS "SKORPIO"--
WHAT'S HIS DANGER RATING IN RELATION TO MY OTHER BAD GUYS?
VERY. IT'S "SKORPIO" WITH A "K". FOUGHT STEEL AWHILE BACK. KNOWN POWERS: NONE META, BUT HE WEARS A POWERSUIT WITH VENOMOUS STINGER GLOVES, OR SOMETHING.
MORE COPPERTONE THAN COPPERHEAD.
GOT IT. NOW...HOW AM I GONNA GET THERE BEFORE THIS SKORPIO HURTS SOMEONE?
WHILE YOU WERE MAKING EYES AT "MR. MIYAGI", I WAS BUILDING A PORTABLE SPECIAL DISPLACEMENT DEVICE FOR YOU...
...THIS.
YOU KNOW...I DON'T SPEAK "GEEK."
A TELE-PORTER.
CALIBRATED TO THE BANK LOBBY, IN FACT...
AND IT'S SAFE?
ABSOLUTELY...
...I THINK.

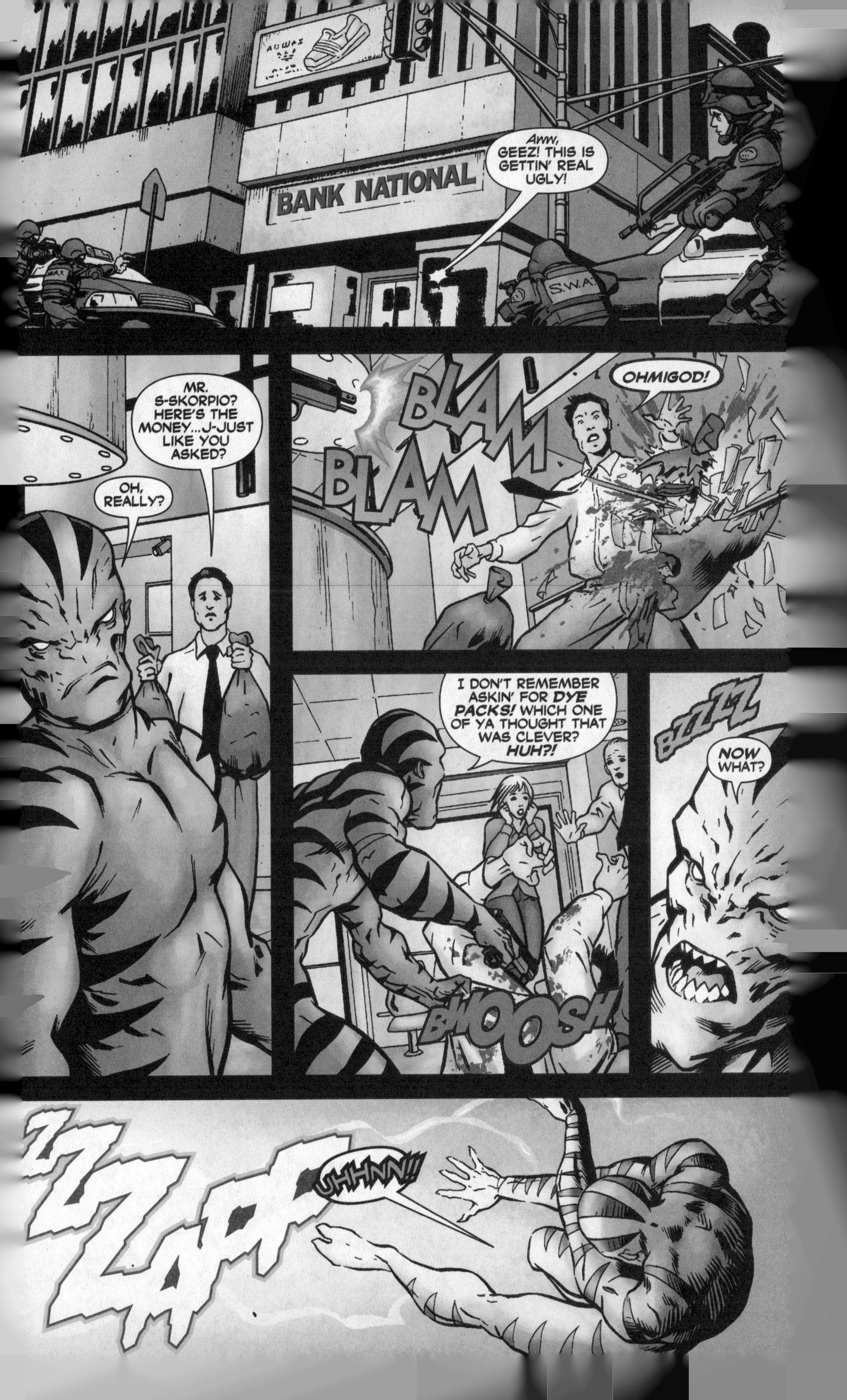
BANK NATIONAL
AWW, GEEZ! THIS IS GETTIN' REAL UGLY!
MR. S-SKORPIO? HERE'S THE MONEY...J-JUST LIKE YOU ASKED?
OH, REALLY?
BLAM
BLAM
OHMIGOD!
I DON'T REMEMBER ASKIN' FOR DYE PACKS! WHICH ONE OF YA THOUGHT THAT WAS CLEVER? HUH?!
BWOOSH
BZZZZ
NOW WHAT?
ZZZAP
UHHNN!!

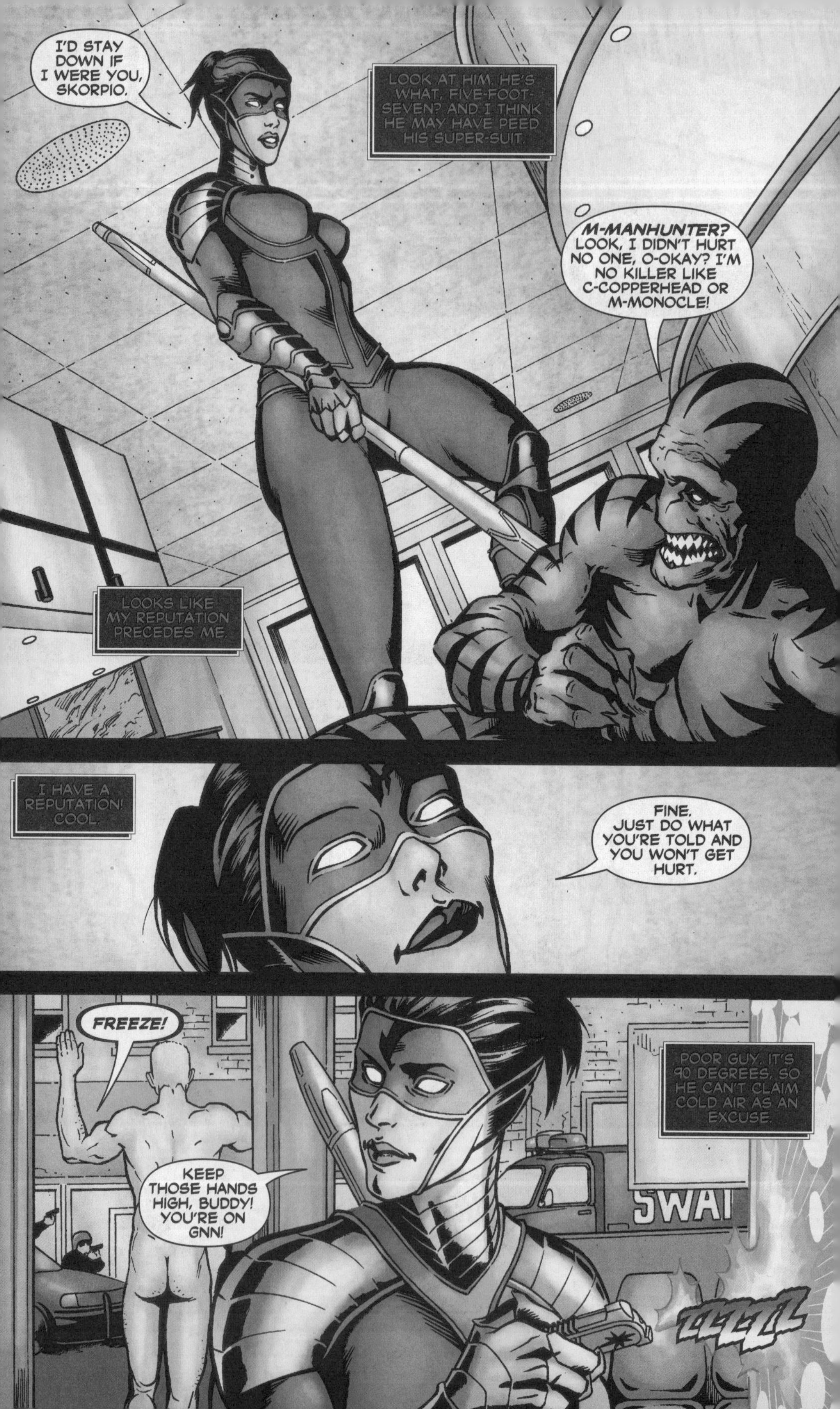
I'D STAY DOWN IF I WERE YOU, SKORPIO.
LOOK AT HIM. HE'S WHAT, FIVE-FOOT-SEVEN? AND I THINK HE MAY HAVE PEED HIS SUPER-SUIT.
M-MANHUNTER? LOOK, I DIDN'T HURT NO ONE, O-OKAY? I'M NO KILLER LIKE C-COPPERHEAD OR M-MONOCLE!
LOOKS LIKE MY REPUTATION PRECEDES ME.
I HAVE A REPUTATION! COOL.
FINE. JUST DO WHAT YOU'RE TOLD AND YOU WON'T GET HURT.
FREEZE!
KEEP THOSE HANDS HIGH, BUDDY! YOU'RE ON GNN!
POOR GUY. IT'S 90 DEGREES, SO HE CAN'T CLAIM COLD AIR AS AN EXCUSE.
SWAT
ZZZZT

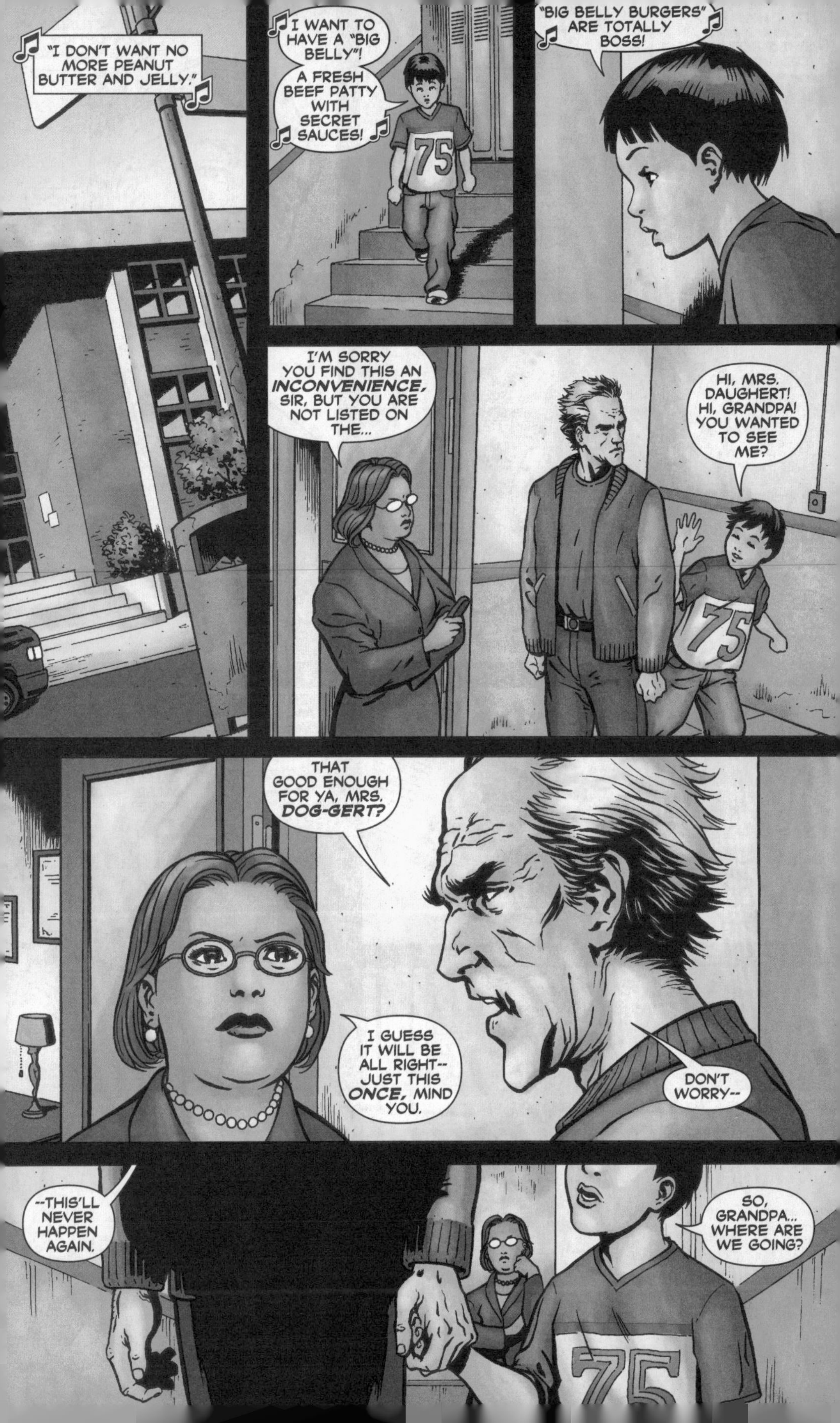

"I DON'T WANT NO MORE PEANUT BUTTER AND JELLY."
I WANT TO HAVE A "BIG BELLY"!
A FRESH BEEF PATTY WITH SECRET SAUCES!
"BIG BELLY BURGERS" ARE TOTALLY BOSS!
I'M SORRY YOU FIND THIS AN INCONVENIENCE, SIR, BUT YOU ARE NOT LISTED ON THE...
HI, MRS. DAUGHERT! HI, GRANDPA! YOU WANTED TO SEE ME?
THAT GOOD ENOUGH FOR YA, MRS. DOG-GERT?
I GUESS IT WILL BE ALL RIGHT-- JUST THIS ONCE, MIND YOU.
DON'T WORRY--
--THIS'LL NEVER HAPPEN AGAIN.
SO, GRANDPA... WHERE ARE WE GOING?

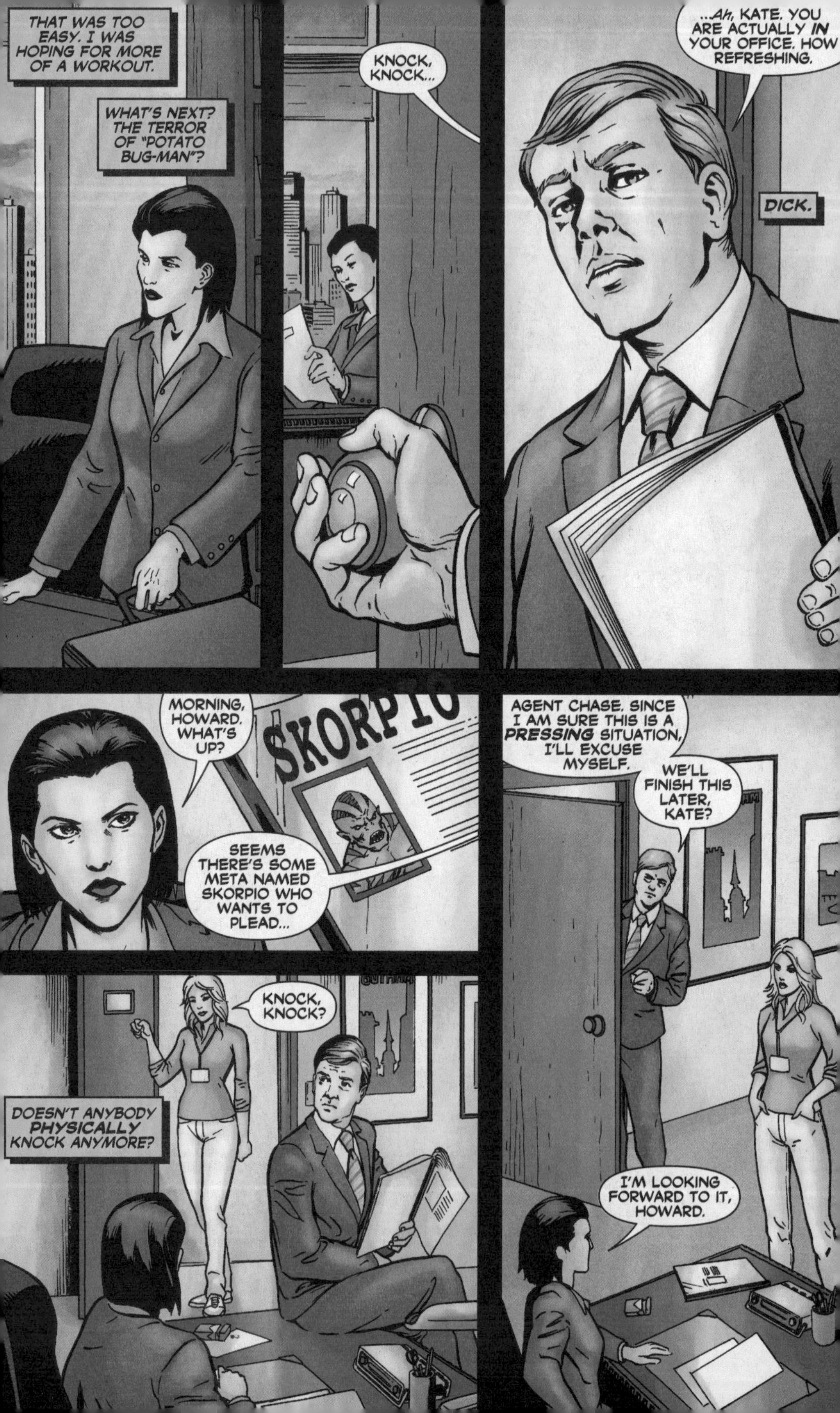
THAT WAS TOO EASY. I WAS HOPING FOR MORE OF A WORKOUT.
WHAT'S NEXT? THE TERROR OF "POTATO BUG-MAN"?
KNOCK, KNOCK...
...Ah, KATE. YOU ARE ACTUALLY IN YOUR OFFICE. HOW REFRESHING.
DICK.
MORNING, HOWARD. WHAT'S UP?
SKORPIO
SEEMS THERE'S SOME META NAMED SKORPIO WHO WANTS TO PLEAD...
KNOCK, KNOCK?
DOESN'T ANYBODY PHYSICALLY KNOCK ANYMORE?
AGENT CHASE. SINCE I AM SURE THIS IS A PRESSING SITUATION, I'LL EXCUSE MYSELF.
WE'LL FINISH THIS LATER, KATE?
I'M LOOKING FORWARD TO IT, HOWARD.

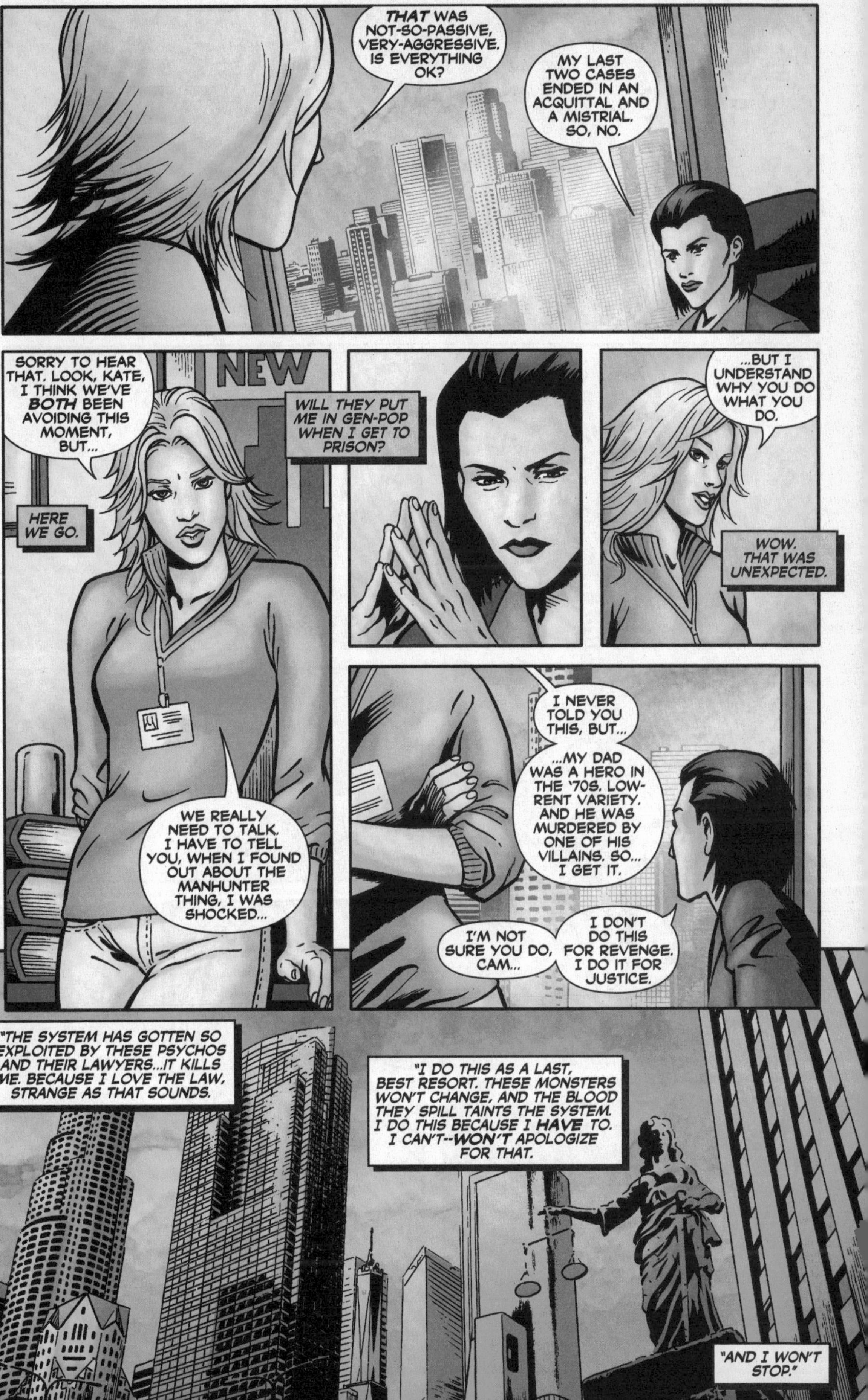
THAT WAS NOT-SO-PASSIVE, VERY-AGGRESSIVE. IS EVERYTHING OK?
MY LAST TWO CASES ENDED IN AN ACQUITTAL AND A MISTRIAL. SO, NO.
SORRY TO HEAR THAT. LOOK, KATE, I THINK WE'VE BOTH BEEN AVOIDING THIS MOMENT, BUT...
NEW
WILL THEY PUT ME IN GEN-POP WHEN I GET TO PRISON?
HERE WE GO.
WE REALLY NEED TO TALK. I HAVE TO TELL YOU, WHEN I FOUND OUT ABOUT THE MANHUNTER THING, I WAS SHOCKED...
...BUT I UNDERSTAND WHY YOU DO WHAT YOU DO.
WOW. THAT WAS UNEXPECTED.
I NEVER TOLD YOU THIS, BUT...
...MY DAD WAS A HERO IN THE '70S. LOW-RENT VARIETY. AND HE WAS MURDERED BY ONE OF HIS VILLAINS. SO... I GET IT.
I'M NOT SURE YOU DO, CAM...
I DON'T DO THIS FOR REVENGE. I DO IT FOR JUSTICE.
"THE SYSTEM HAS GOTTEN SO EXPLOITED BY THESE PSYCHOS AND THEIR LAWYERS...IT KILLS ME. BECAUSE I LOVE THE LAW, STRANGE AS THAT SOUNDS.
"I DO THIS AS A LAST, BEST RESORT. THESE MONSTERS WON'T CHANGE, AND THE BLOOD THEY SPILL TAINTS THE SYSTEM. I DO THIS BECAUSE I HAVE TO. I CAN'T--WON'T APOLOGIZE FOR THAT.
"AND I WON'T STOP."

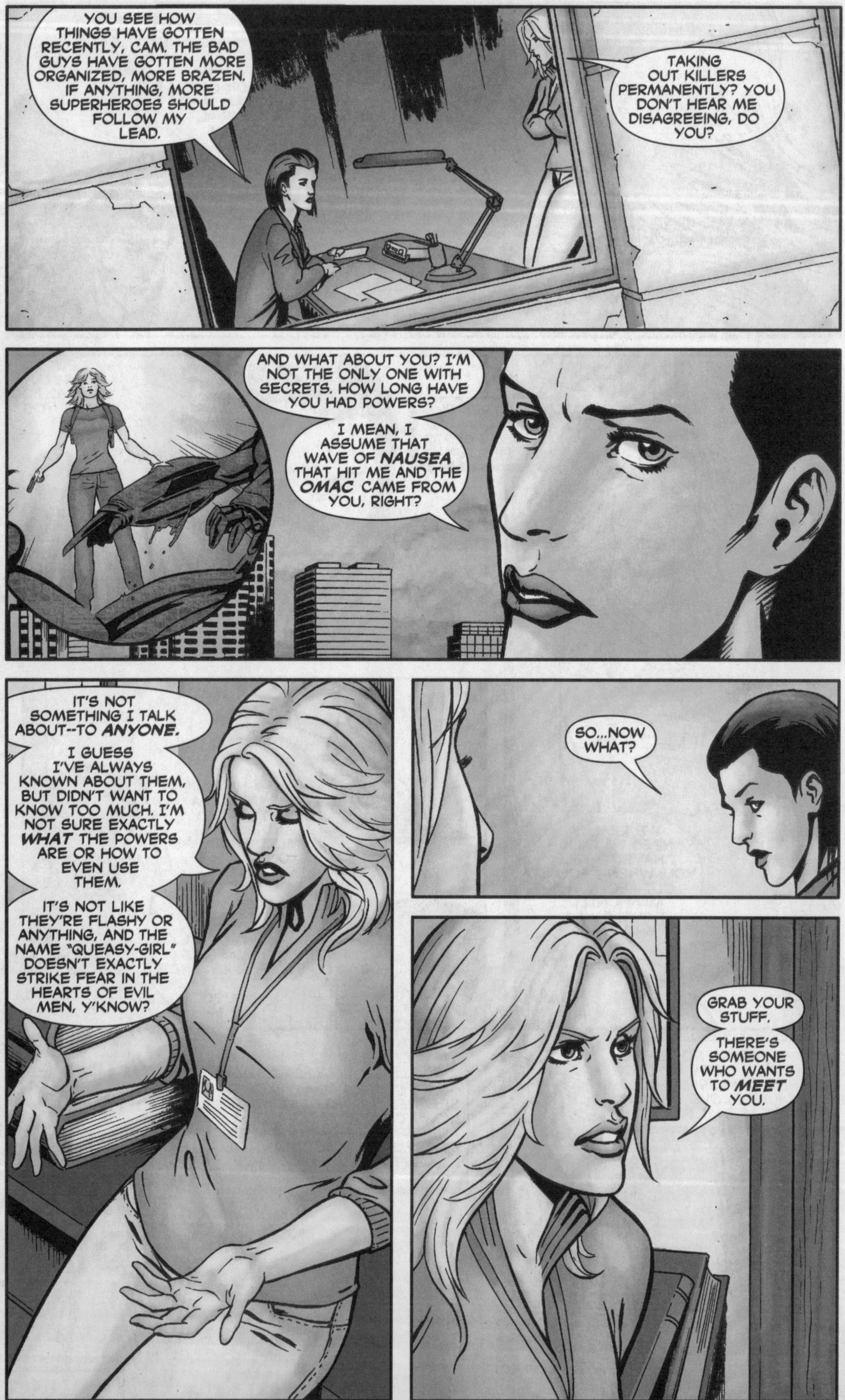

YOU SEE HOW THINGS HAVE GOTTEN RECENTLY, CAM. THE BAD GUYS HAVE GOTTEN MORE ORGANIZED, MORE BRAZEN. IF ANYTHING, MORE SUPERHEROES SHOULD FOLLOW MY LEAD.
TAKING OUT KILLERS PERMANENTLY? YOU DON'T HEAR ME DISAGREEING, DO YOU?
AND WHAT ABOUT YOU? I'M NOT THE ONLY ONE WITH SECRETS. HOW LONG HAVE YOU HAD POWERS?
I MEAN, I ASSUME THAT WAVE OF NAUSEA THAT HIT ME AND THE OMAC CAME FROM YOU, RIGHT?
IT'S NOT SOMETHING I TALK ABOUT--TO ANYONE.
I GUESS I'VE ALWAYS KNOWN ABOUT THEM, BUT DIDN'T WANT TO KNOW TOO MUCH. I'M NOT SURE EXACTLY WHAT THE POWERS ARE OR HOW TO EVEN USE THEM.
IT'S NOT LIKE THEY'RE FLASHY OR ANYTHING, AND THE NAME "QUEASY-GIRL" DOESN'T EXACTLY STRIKE FEAR IN THE HEARTS OF EVIL MEN, Y'KNOW?
SO...NOW WHAT?
GRAB YOUR STUFF.
THERE'S SOMEONE WHO WANTS TO MEET YOU.

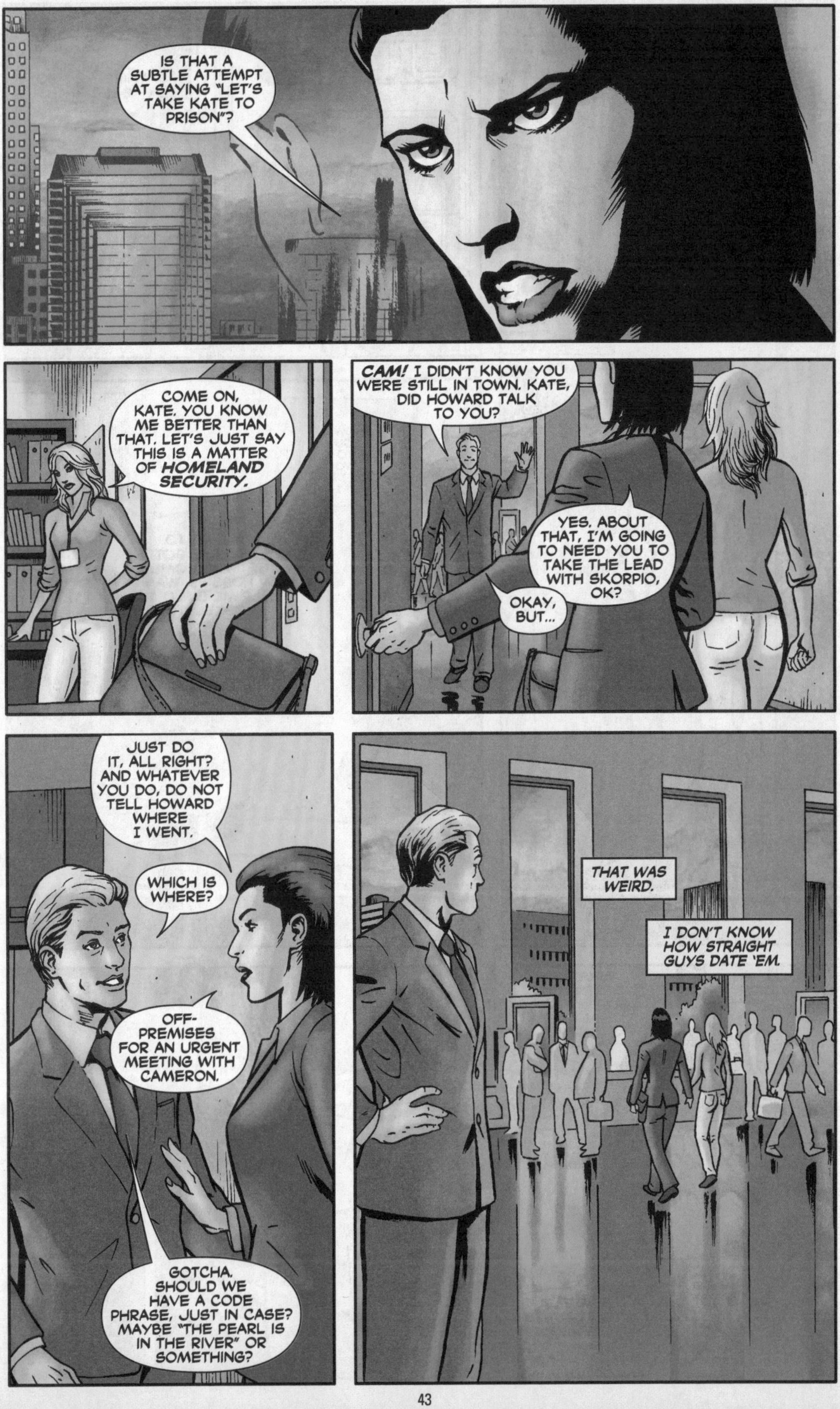
IS THAT A SUBTLE ATTEMPT AT SAYING "LET'S TAKE KATE TO PRISON"?
COME ON, KATE. YOU KNOW ME BETTER THAN THAT. LET'S JUST SAY THIS IS A MATTER OF HOMELAND SECURITY.
CAM! I DIDN'T KNOW YOU WERE STILL IN TOWN. KATE, DID HOWARD TALK TO YOU?
YES. ABOUT THAT, I'M GOING TO NEED YOU TO TAKE THE LEAD WITH SKORPIO, OK?
OKAY, BUT...
JUST DO IT, ALL RIGHT? AND WHATEVER YOU DO, DO NOT TELL HOWARD WHERE I WENT.
WHICH IS WHERE?
OFF-PREMISES FOR AN URGENT MEETING WITH CAMERON.
GOTCHA. SHOULD WE HAVE A CODE PHRASE, JUST IN CASE? MAYBE "THE PEARL IS IN THE RIVER" OR SOMETHING?
THAT WAS WEIRD.
I DON'T KNOW HOW STRAIGHT GUYS DATE 'EM.

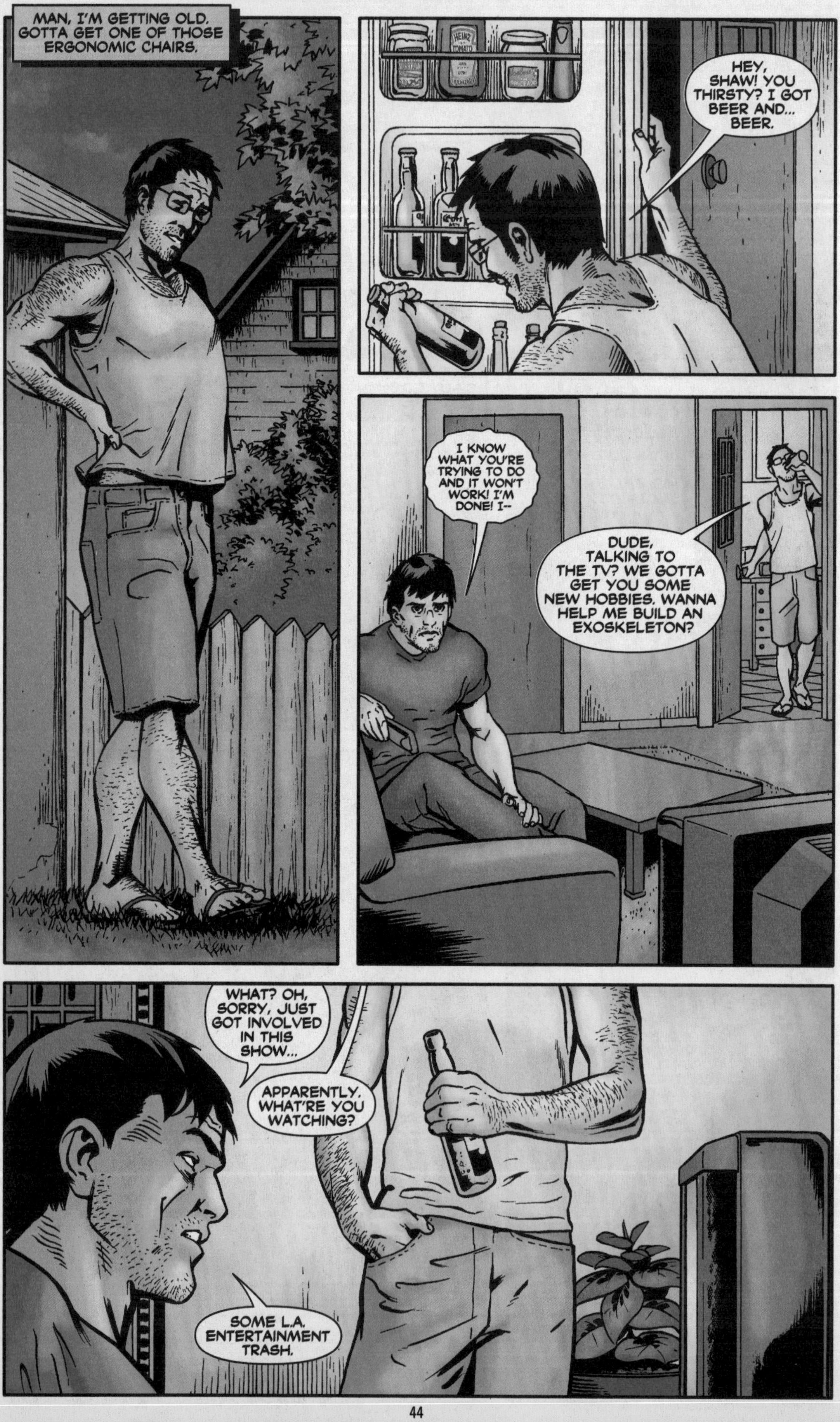
MAN, I'M GETTING OLD. GOTTA GET ONE OF THOSE ERGONOMIC CHAIRS.
HEY, SHAW! YOU THIRSTY? I GOT BEER AND... BEER.
I KNOW WHAT YOU'RE TRYING TO DO AND IT WON'T WORK! I'M DONE! I--
DUDE, TALKING TO THE TV? WE GOTTA GET YOU SOME NEW HOBBIES. WANNA HELP ME BUILD AN EXOSKELETON?
WHAT? OH, SORRY, JUST GOT INVOLVED IN THIS SHOW...
APPARENTLY. WHAT'RE YOU WATCHING?
SOME L.A. ENTERTAINMENT TRASH.

BE MORE SPECIFIC. ARE WE TALKING "THE INSIDE; "E.G.," "EXCESS...

TED SHOEMAKER · LIVE

..."HOLLYWOOD"?

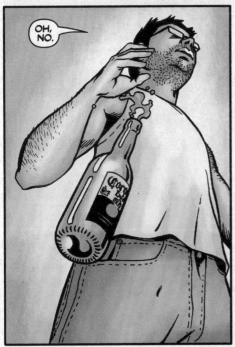

OH, NO.

WHAP

HEY, YOU OK? I THOUGHT YOU'D DIE TO SAVE A COLD BEER.

UM, YEAH. I'M FINE. MUSTA SLIPPED FROM THE CONDENSATION. I, *UH*, I GOTTA GO FINISH SOMETHING UP IN THE WORKSHOP.

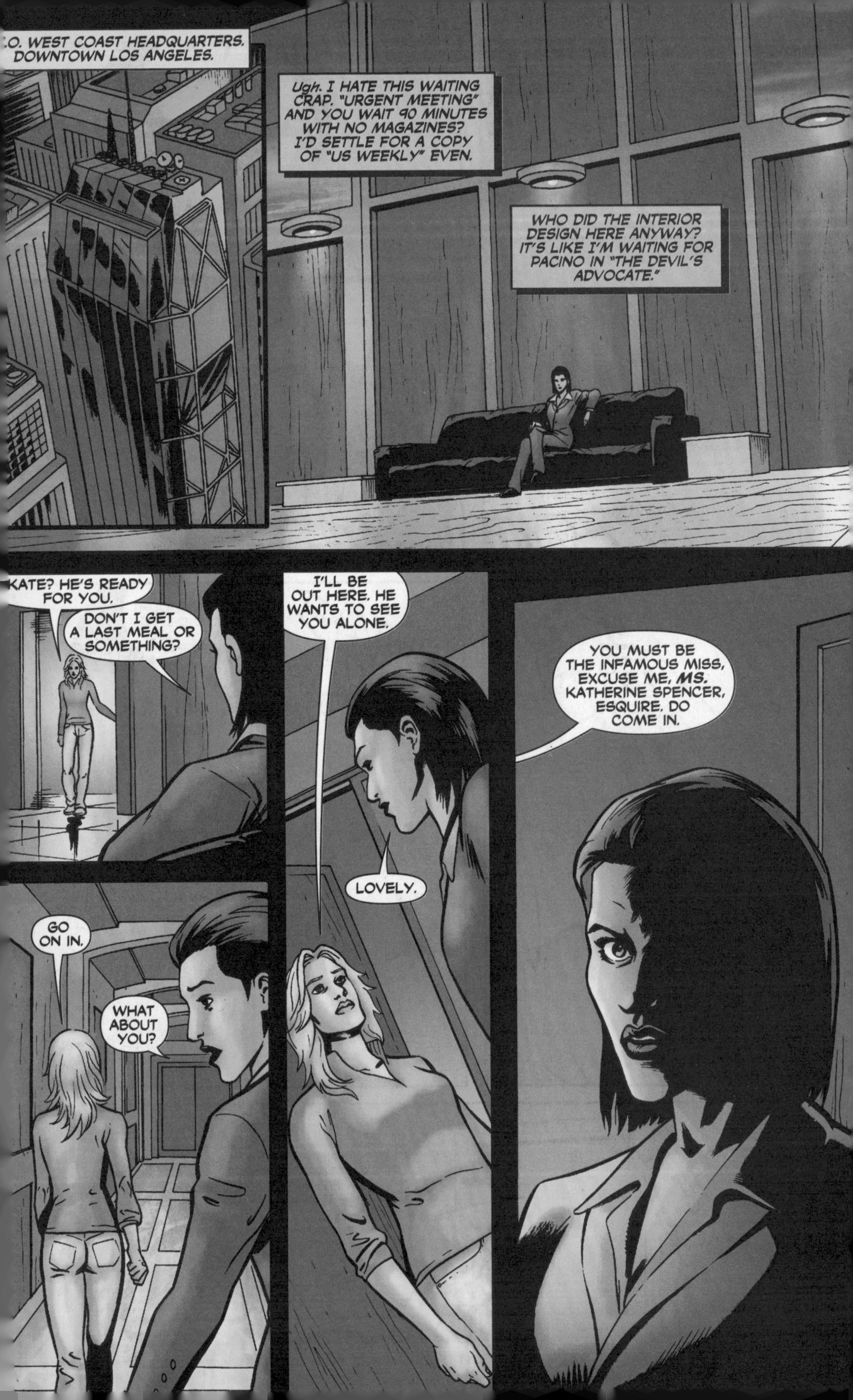

.O. WEST COAST HEADQUARTERS. DOWNTOWN LOS ANGELES.
Ugh. I HATE THIS WAITING CRAP. "URGENT MEETING" AND YOU WAIT 90 MINUTES WITH NO MAGAZINES? I'D SETTLE FOR A COPY OF "US WEEKLY" EVEN.
WHO DID THE INTERIOR DESIGN HERE ANYWAY? IT'S LIKE I'M WAITING FOR PACINO IN "THE DEVIL'S ADVOCATE."
KATE? HE'S READY FOR YOU.
DON'T I GET A LAST MEAL OR SOMETHING?
GO ON IN.
WHAT ABOUT YOU?
I'LL BE OUT HERE. HE WANTS TO SEE YOU ALONE.
LOVELY.
YOU MUST BE THE INFAMOUS MISS, EXCUSE ME, MS. KATHERINE SPENCER, ESQUIRE. DO COME IN.

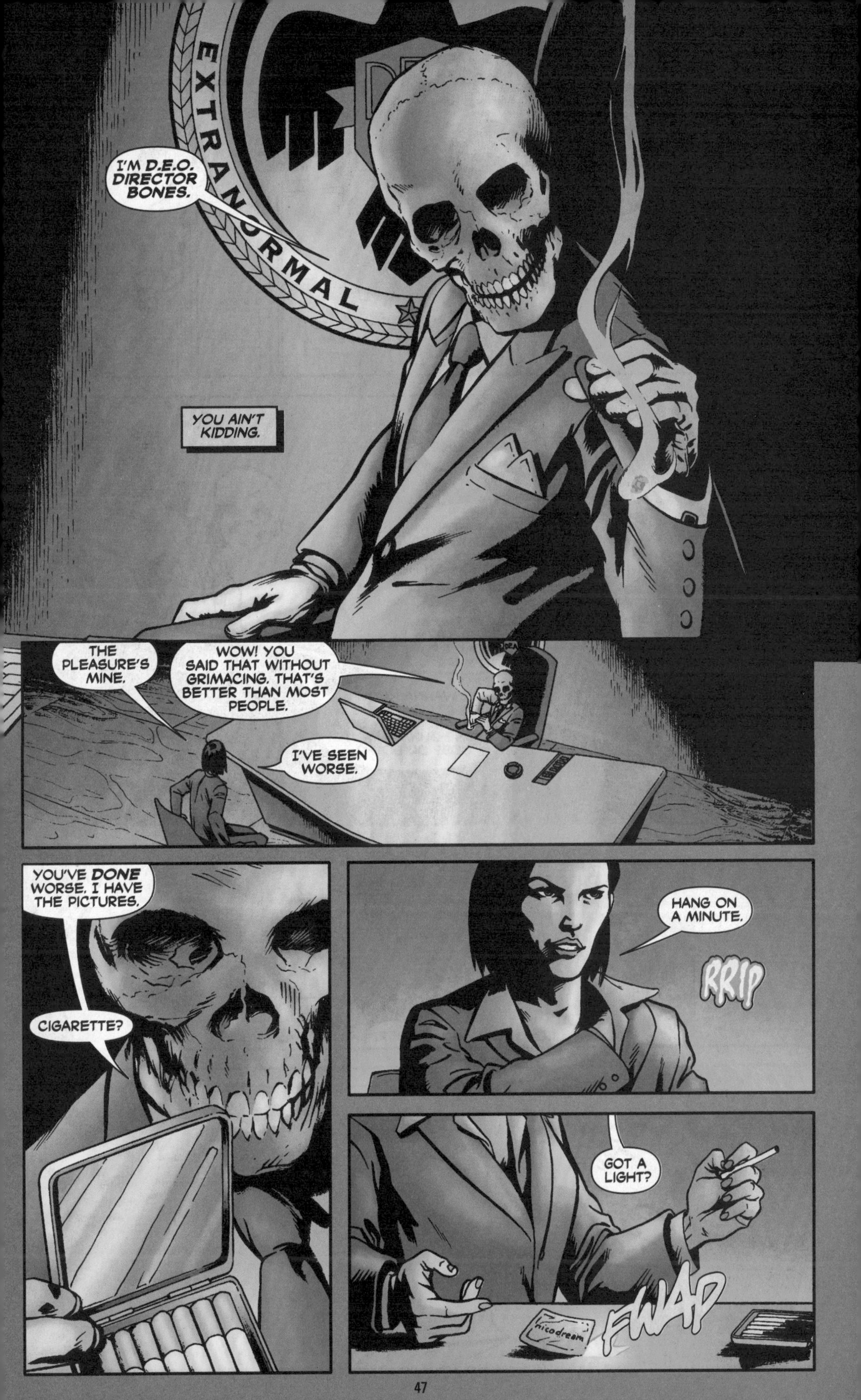
I'M D.E.O. DIRECTOR BONES.
YOU AIN'T KIDDING.
THE PLEASURE'S MINE.
WOW! YOU SAID THAT WITHOUT GRIMACING. THAT'S BETTER THAN MOST PEOPLE.
I'VE SEEN WORSE.
YOU'VE DONE WORSE. I HAVE THE PICTURES.
CIGARETTE?
HANG ON A MINUTE.
RRIP
GOT A LIGHT?
nicodream
FWAP

NICE, HUH? I GET 'EM SPECIALLY MADE.

YOU HAVE **NO** IDEA.

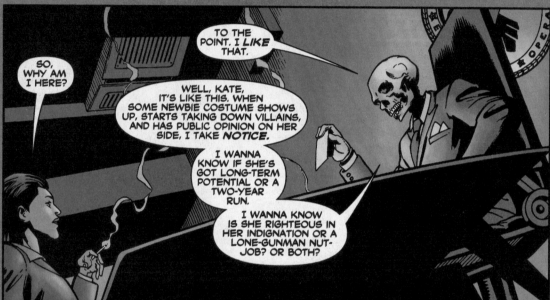

SO, WHY AM I HERE?

TO THE POINT. I **LIKE** THAT.

WELL, KATE, IT'S LIKE THIS. WHEN SOME NEWBIE COSTUME SHOWS UP, STARTS TAKING DOWN VILLAINS, AND HAS PUBLIC OPINION ON HER SIDE, I TAKE **NOTICE.**

I WANNA KNOW IF SHE'S GOT LONG-TERM POTENTIAL OR A TWO-YEAR RUN.

I WANNA KNOW IS SHE RIGHTEOUS IN HER INDIGNATION OR A LONE-GUNMAN NUT-JOB? OR BOTH?

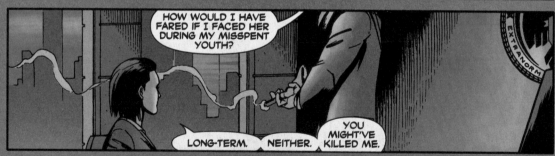

HOW WOULD I HAVE FARED IF I FACED HER DURING MY MISSPENT YOUTH?

LONG-TERM.   NEITHER.   YOU MIGHT'VE KILLED ME.

LIKE YOU DID WITH "SKYMAN," REMEMBER?

ANY **OTHER** QUESTIONS?

JUST ONE...

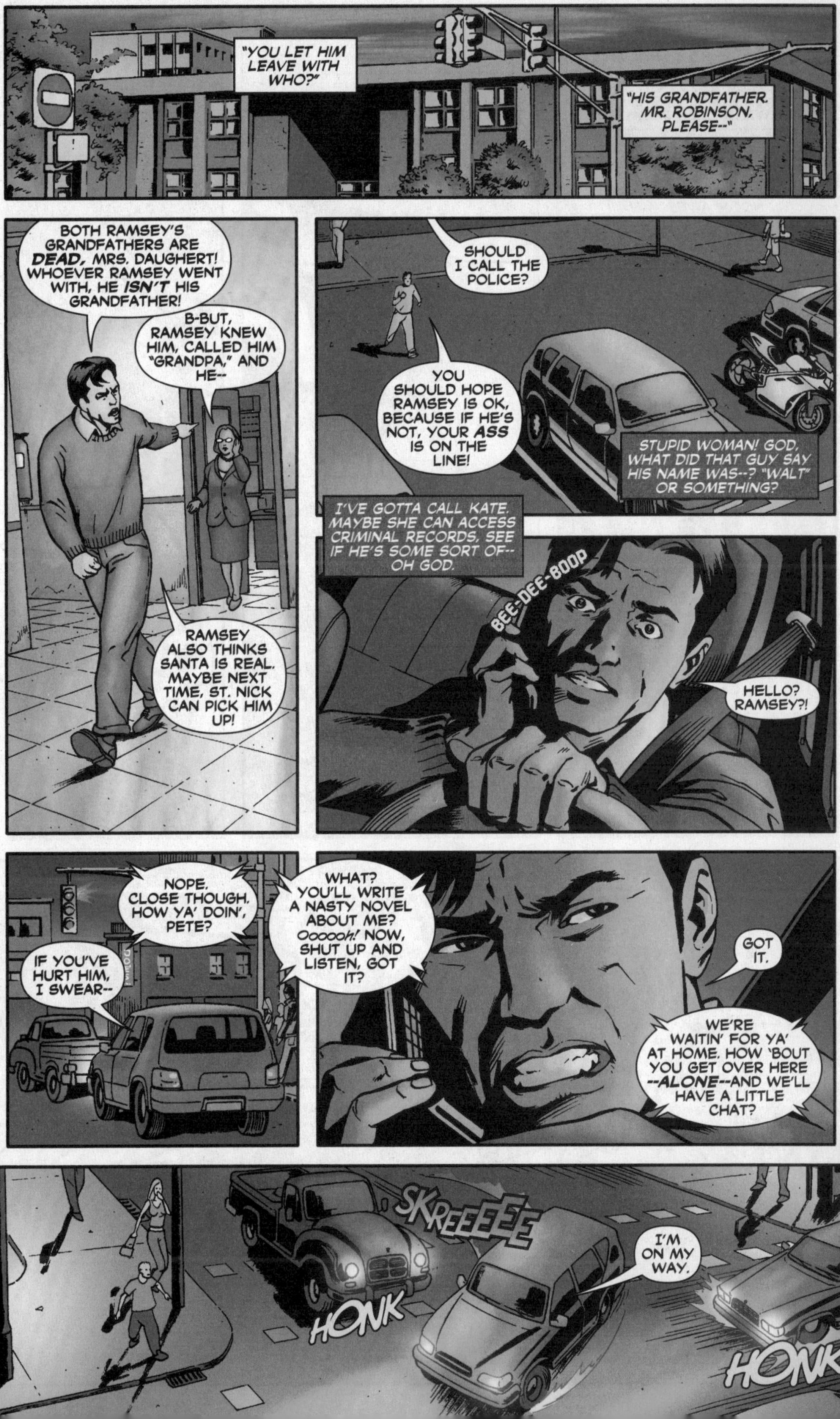
"YOU LET HIM LEAVE WITH WHO?"
"HIS GRANDFATHER. MR. ROBINSON, PLEASE--"
BOTH RAMSEY'S GRANDFATHERS ARE DEAD, MRS. DAUGHERT! WHOEVER RAMSEY WENT WITH, HE ISN'T HIS GRANDFATHER!
B-BUT, RAMSEY KNEW HIM, CALLED HIM "GRANDPA," AND HE--
RAMSEY ALSO THINKS SANTA IS REAL. MAYBE NEXT TIME, ST. NICK CAN PICK HIM UP!
SHOULD I CALL THE POLICE?
YOU SHOULD HOPE RAMSEY IS OK, BECAUSE IF HE'S NOT, YOUR ASS IS ON THE LINE!
STUPID WOMAN! GOD, WHAT DID THAT GUY SAY HIS NAME WAS--? "WALT" OR SOMETHING?
I'VE GOTTA CALL KATE. MAYBE SHE CAN ACCESS CRIMINAL RECORDS, SEE IF HE'S SOME SORT OF-- OH GOD.
BEE-DEE-BOOP
HELLO? RAMSEY?!
NOPE. CLOSE THOUGH. HOW YA' DOIN', PETE?
IF YOU'VE HURT HIM, I SWEAR--
WHAT? YOU'LL WRITE A NASTY NOVEL ABOUT ME? Oooooh! NOW, SHUT UP AND LISTEN, GOT IT?
GOT IT.
WE'RE WAITIN' FOR YA' AT HOME. HOW 'BOUT YOU GET OVER HERE --ALONE--AND WE'LL HAVE A LITTLE CHAT?
SKREEEEEE
I'M ON MY WAY.
HONK
HONK

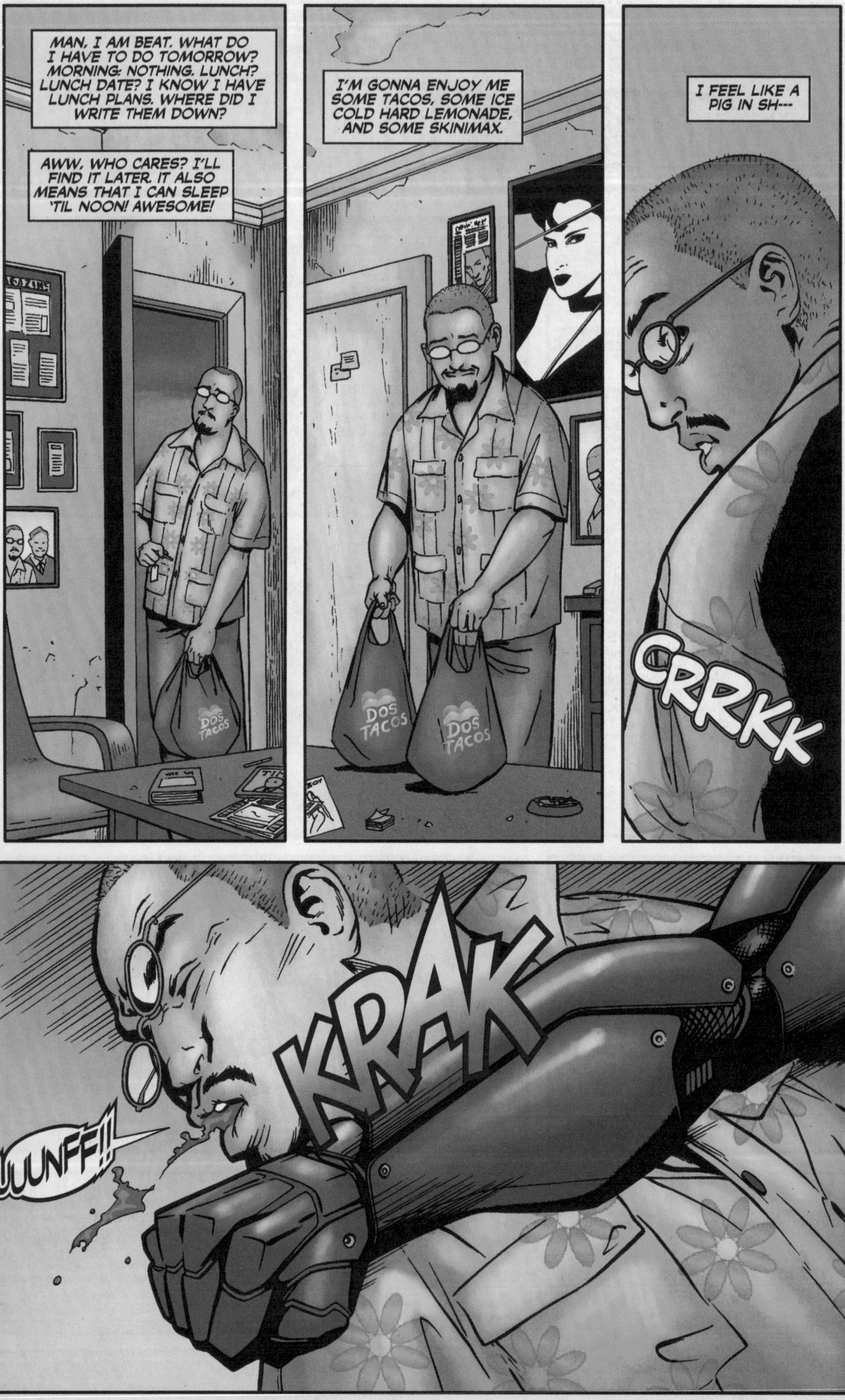
MAN, I AM BEAT. WHAT DO I HAVE TO DO TOMORROW? MORNING: NOTHING. LUNCH? LUNCH DATE? I KNOW I HAVE LUNCH PLANS. WHERE DID I WRITE THEM DOWN?
AWW, WHO CARES? I'LL FIND IT LATER. IT ALSO MEANS THAT I CAN SLEEP 'TIL NOON! AWESOME!
DOS TACOS
I'M GONNA ENJOY ME SOME TACOS, SOME ICE COLD HARD LEMONADE, AND SOME SKINIMAX.
DOS TACOS
DOS TACOS
I FEEL LIKE A PIG IN SH---
CRRKK
KRAK
UUUNFF!!

...HOW'D YOU LIKE TO **WORK** FOR ME?

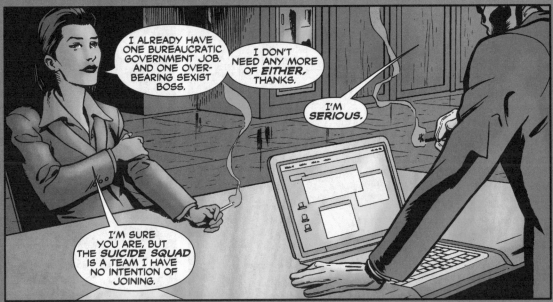

I ALREADY HAVE ONE BUREAUCRATIC GOVERNMENT JOB, AND ONE OVER-BEARING SEXIST BOSS.

I DON'T NEED ANY MORE OF *EITHER*, THANKS.

I'M **SERIOUS.**

I'M SURE YOU ARE, BUT THE *SUICIDE SQUAD* IS A TEAM I HAVE NO INTENTION OF JOINING.

AMANDA DOESN'T DESERVE YOU. BESIDES, I'M NOT TALKING SUICIDE SQUAD *OR* THE D.E.O.

I WANT YOU TO WORK FOR *ME.*

I'M LISTENING.

GOOD. NOW WHAT I AM TELLING YOU HAD BETTER NOT LEAVE THIS ROOM, GOT IT?...

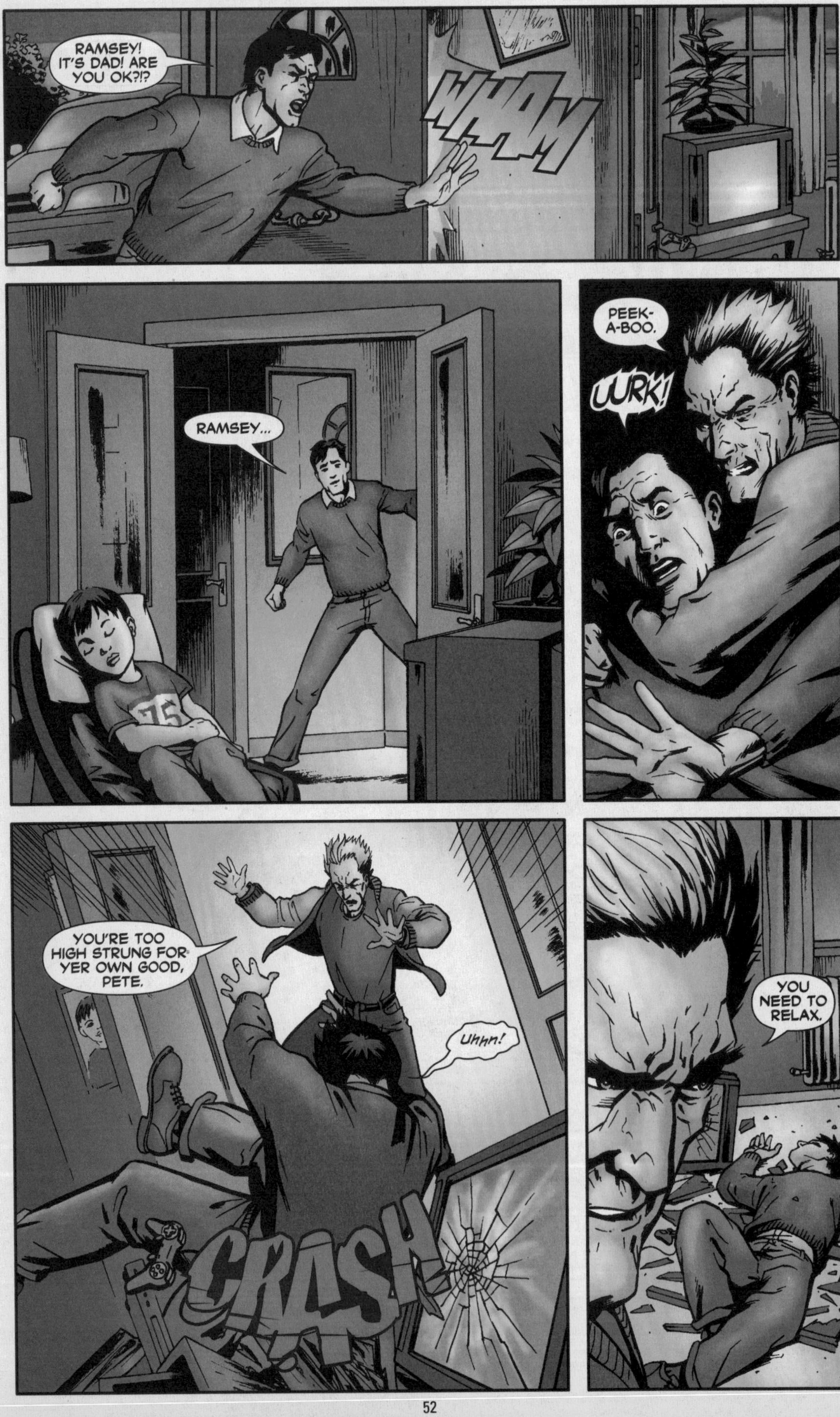
RAMSEY! IT'S DAD! ARE YOU OK?!?
WHAM
RAMSEY...
PEEK-A-BOO.
UURK!
YOU'RE TOO HIGH STRUNG FOR YER OWN GOOD, PETE.
Uhhn!
CRASH
YOU NEED TO RELAX.

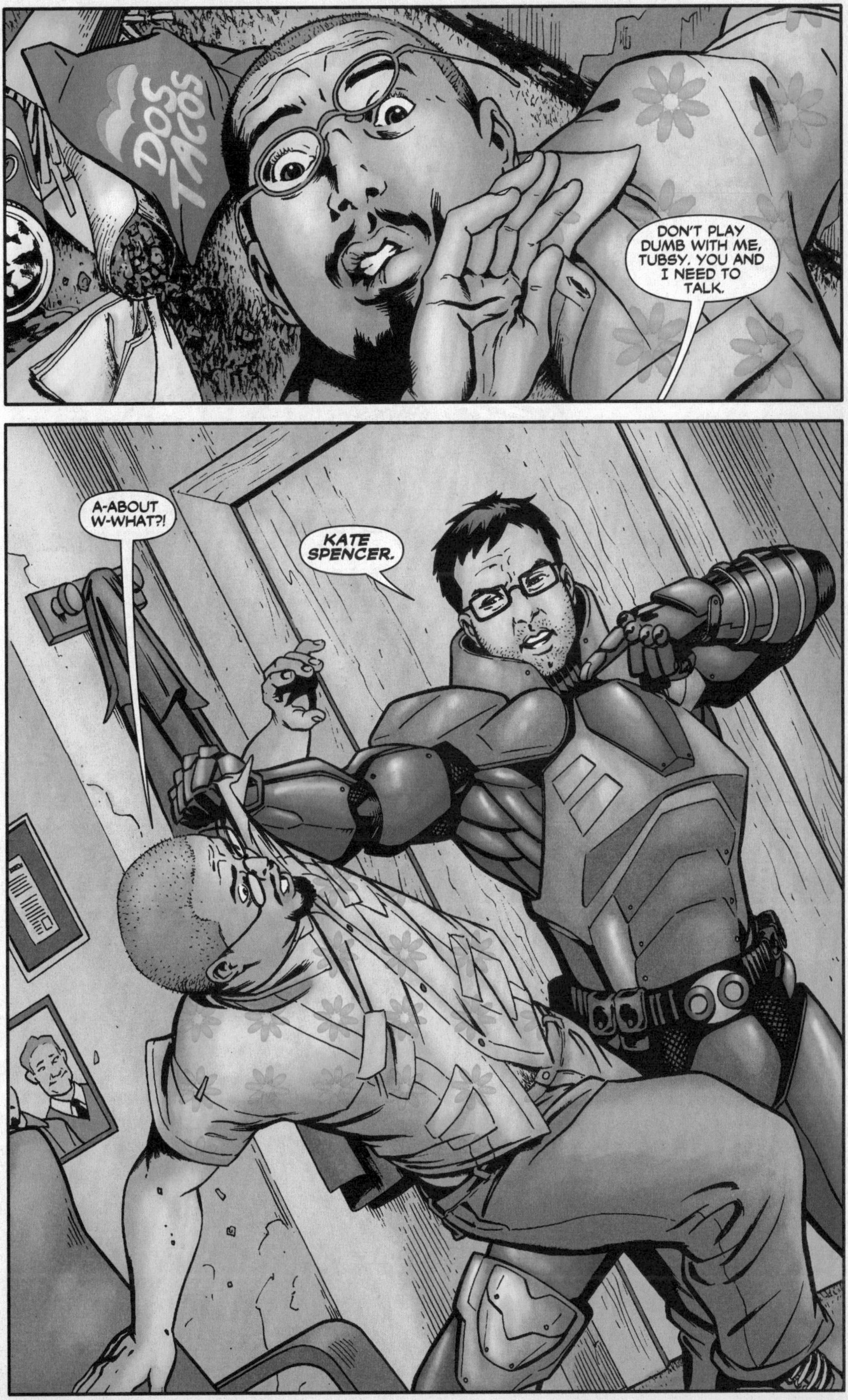
DOS TACOS
DON'T PLAY DUMB WITH ME, TUBSY. YOU AND I NEED TO TALK.
A-ABOUT W-WHAT?!
KATE SPENCER.

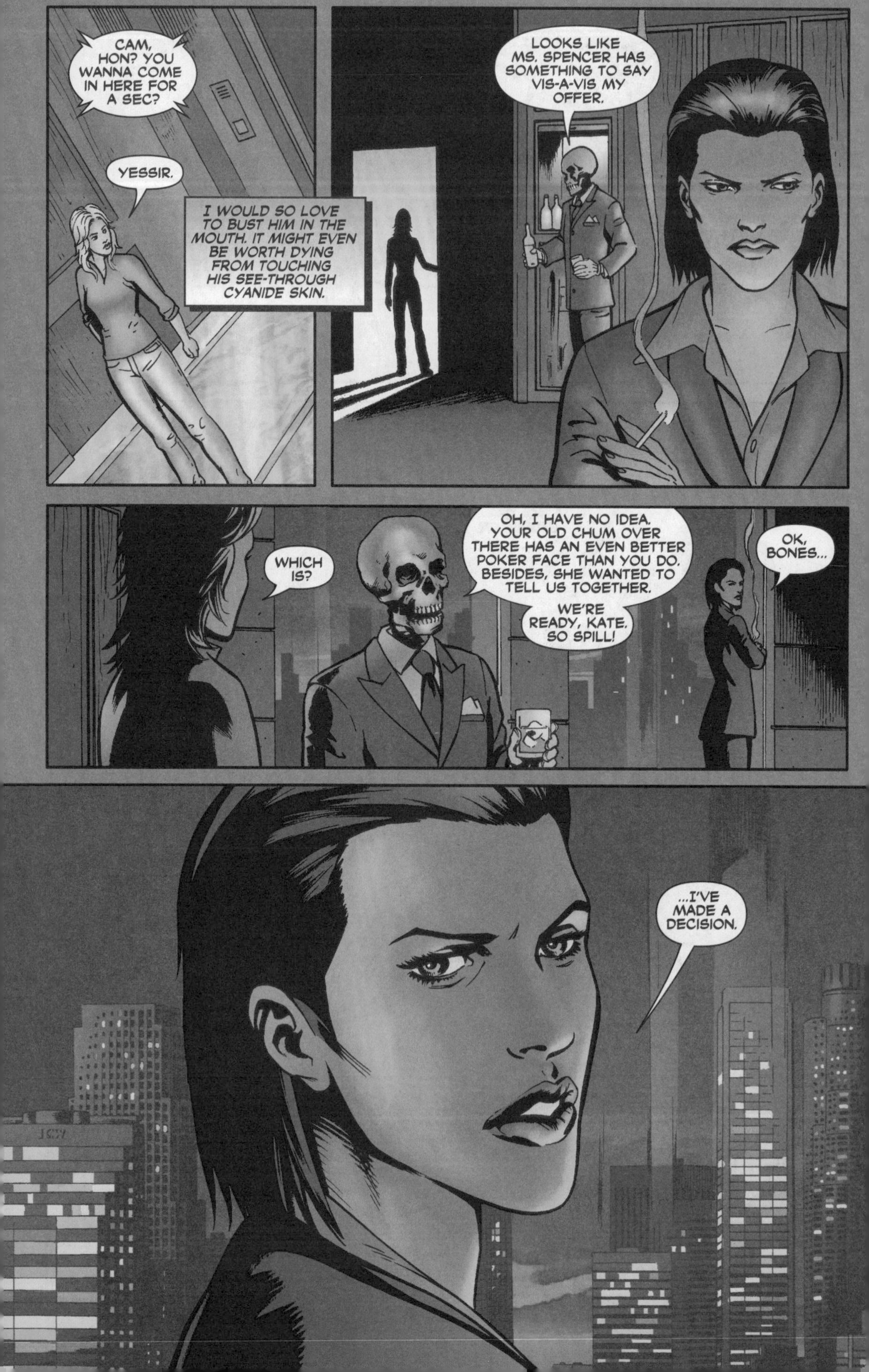
CAM, HON? YOU WANNA COME IN HERE FOR A SEC?
YESSIR.
I WOULD SO LOVE TO BUST HIM IN THE MOUTH. IT MIGHT EVEN BE WORTH DYING FROM TOUCHING HIS SEE-THROUGH CYANIDE SKIN.
LOOKS LIKE MS. SPENCER HAS SOMETHING TO SAY VIS-A-VIS MY OFFER.
WHICH IS?
OH, I HAVE NO IDEA. YOUR OLD CHUM OVER THERE HAS AN EVEN BETTER POKER FACE THAN YOU DO. BESIDES, SHE WANTED TO TELL US TOGETHER.
WE'RE READY, KATE. SO SPILL!
OK, BONES...
...I'VE MADE A DECISION.

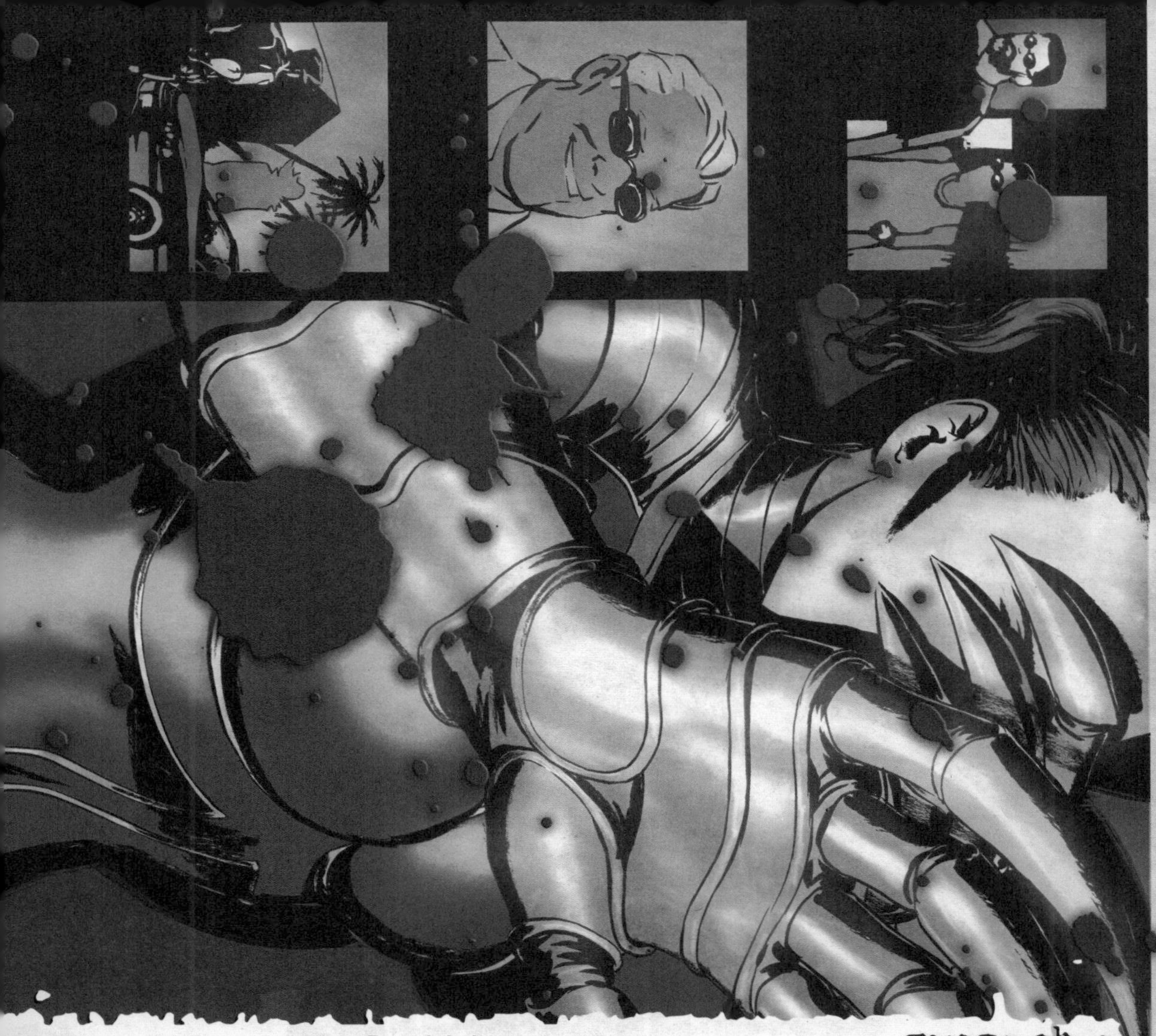

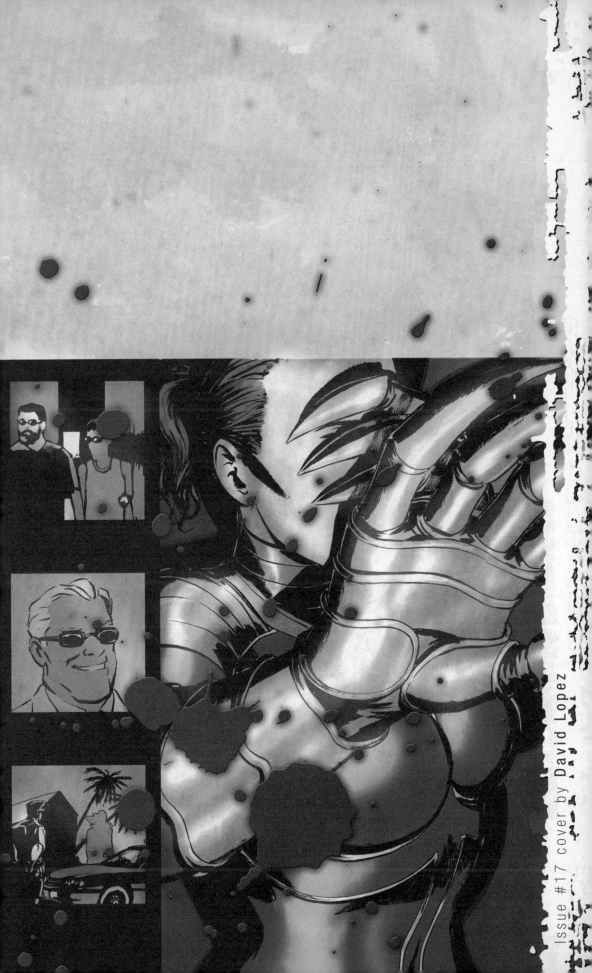

Issue #17 cover by **David Lopez**

Interior art by Javier Pina & Fernando Blanco

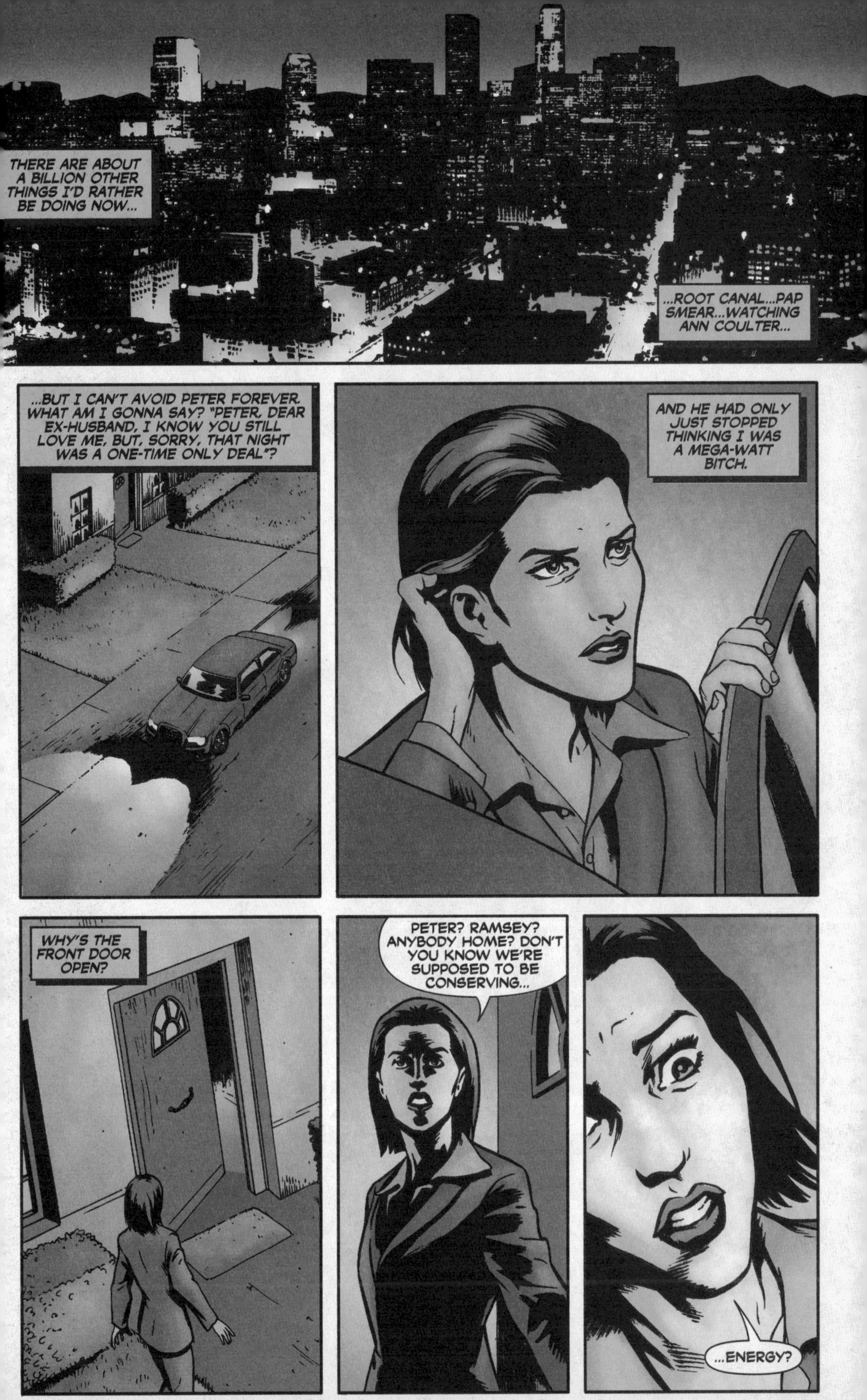
THERE ARE ABOUT A BILLION OTHER THINGS I'D RATHER BE DOING NOW...
...ROOT CANAL...PAP SMEAR...WATCHING ANN COULTER...
...BUT I CAN'T AVOID PETER FOREVER. WHAT AM I GONNA SAY? "PETER, DEAR EX-HUSBAND, I KNOW YOU STILL LOVE ME, BUT, SORRY, THAT NIGHT WAS A ONE-TIME ONLY DEAL"?
AND HE HAD ONLY JUST STOPPED THINKING I WAS A MEGA-WATT BITCH.
WHY'S THE FRONT DOOR OPEN?
PETER? RAMSEY? ANYBODY HOME? DON'T YOU KNOW WE'RE SUPPOSED TO BE CONSERVING...
...ENERGY?

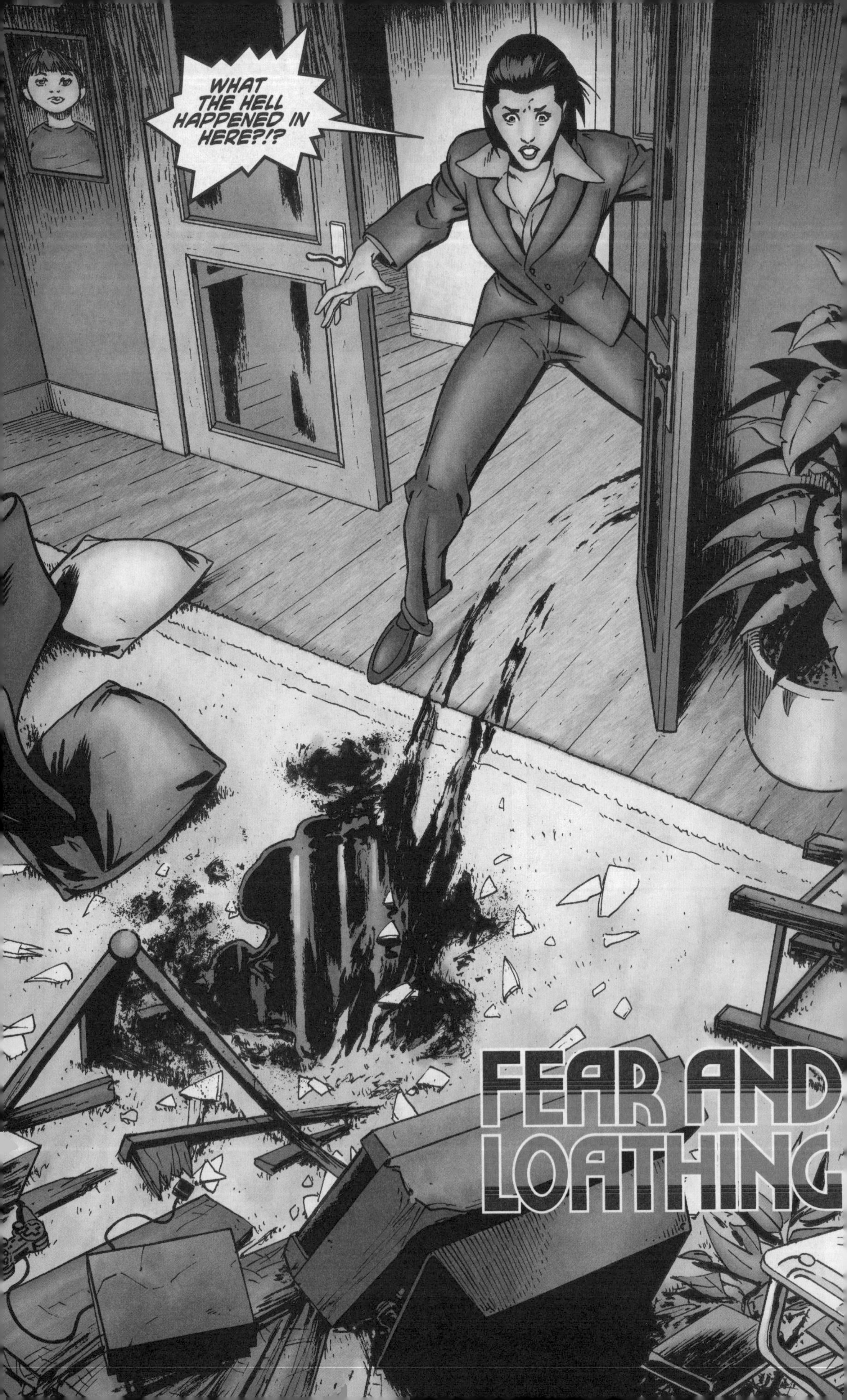
WHAT THE HELL HAPPENED IN HERE?!?
FEAR AND LOATHING

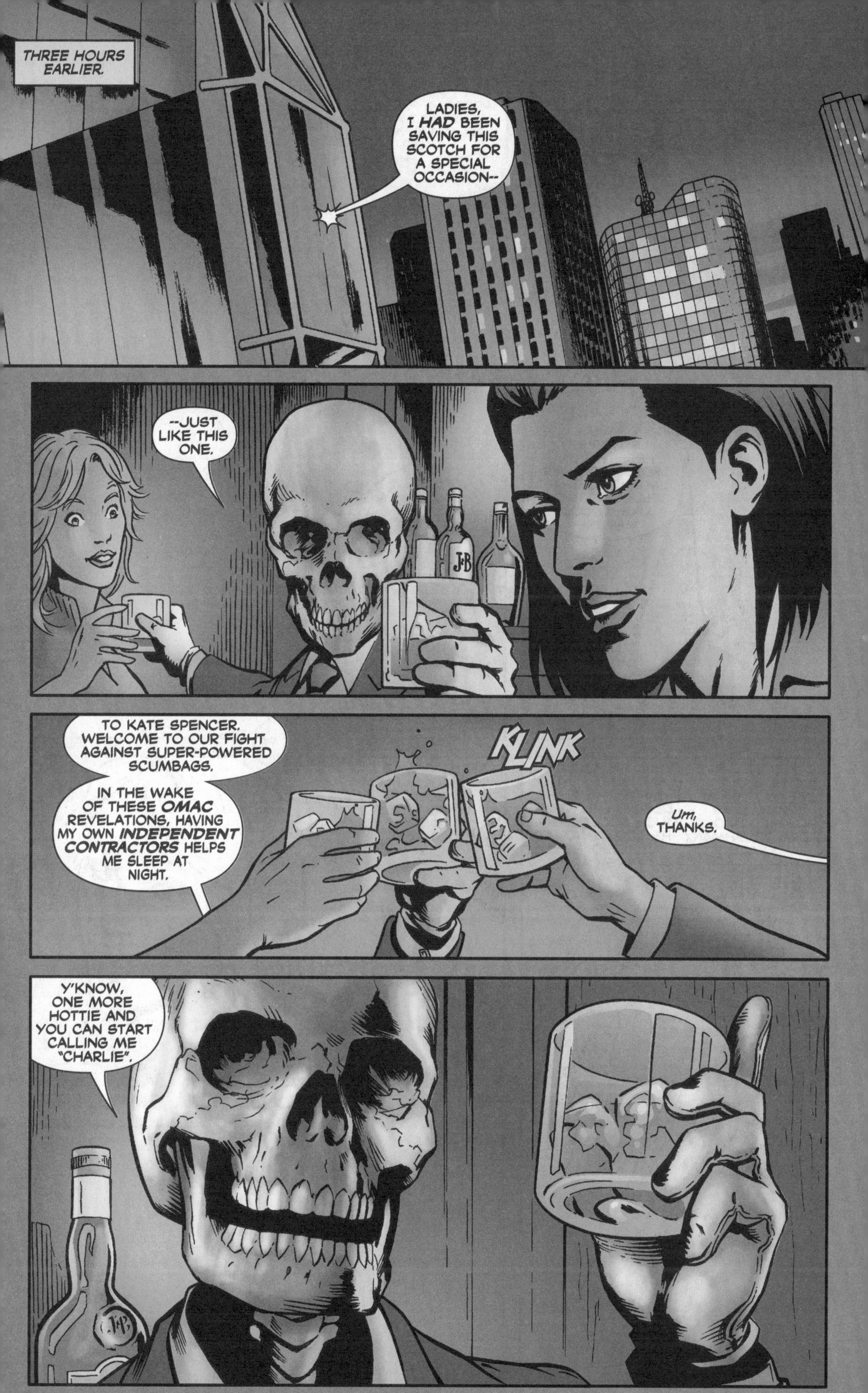
THREE HOURS EARLIER.
LADIES, I HAD BEEN SAVING THIS SCOTCH FOR A SPECIAL OCCASION--
--JUST LIKE THIS ONE.
TO KATE SPENCER. WELCOME TO OUR FIGHT AGAINST SUPER-POWERED SCUMBAGS.
IN THE WAKE OF THESE OMAC REVELATIONS, HAVING MY OWN INDEPENDENT CONTRACTORS HELPS ME SLEEP AT NIGHT.
KLINK
Um, THANKS.
Y'KNOW, ONE MORE HOTTIE AND YOU CAN START CALLING ME "CHARLIE".

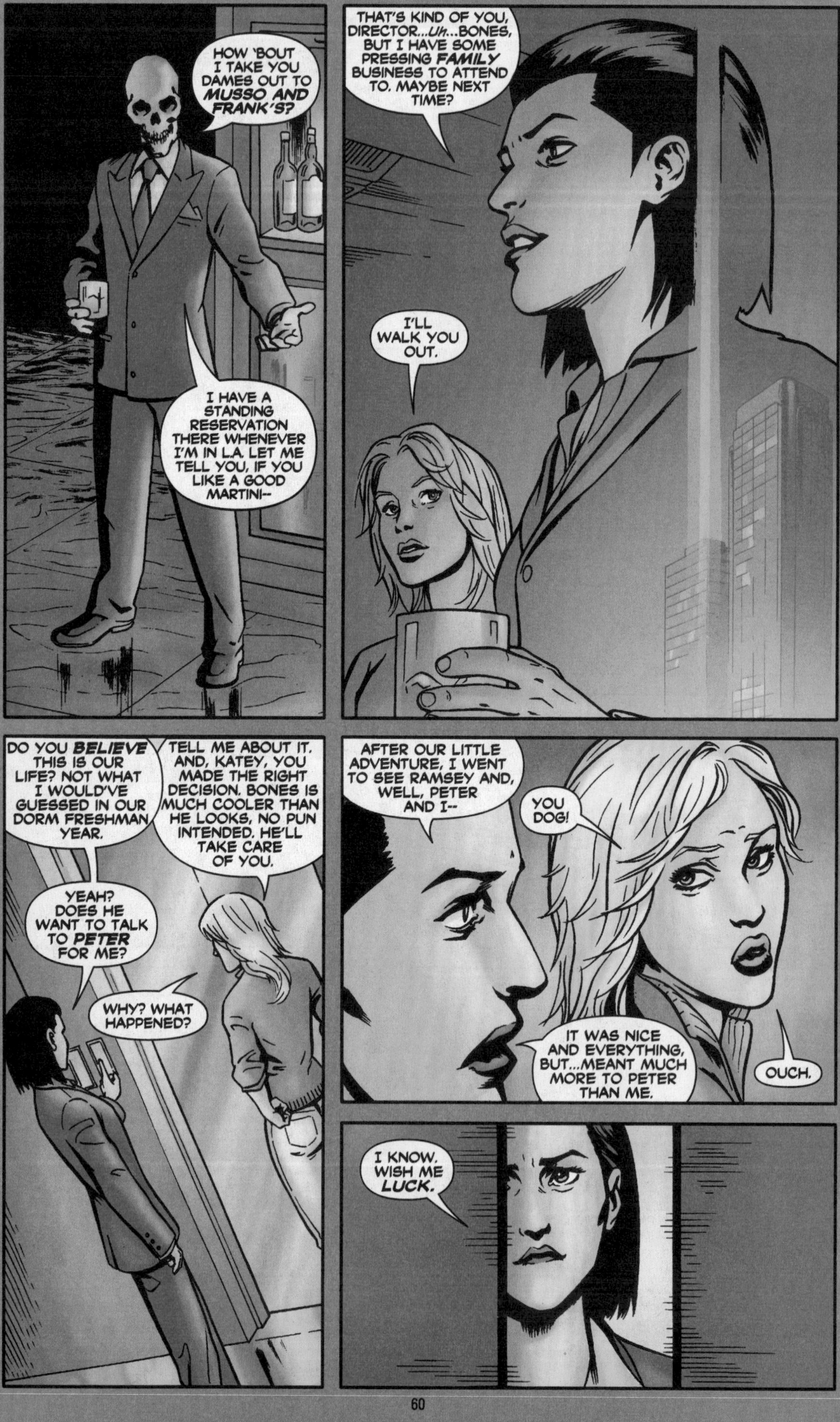
HOW 'BOUT I TAKE YOU DAMES OUT TO MUSSO AND FRANK'S?
I HAVE A STANDING RESERVATION THERE WHENEVER I'M IN L.A. LET ME TELL YOU, IF YOU LIKE A GOOD MARTINI--
THAT'S KIND OF YOU, DIRECTOR...Uh...BONES, BUT I HAVE SOME PRESSING FAMILY BUSINESS TO ATTEND TO. MAYBE NEXT TIME?
I'LL WALK YOU OUT.
DO YOU BELIEVE THIS IS OUR LIFE? NOT WHAT I WOULD'VE GUESSED IN OUR DORM FRESHMAN YEAR.
TELL ME ABOUT IT. AND, KATEY, YOU MADE THE RIGHT DECISION. BONES IS MUCH COOLER THAN HE LOOKS, NO PUN INTENDED. HE'LL TAKE CARE OF YOU.
YEAH? DOES HE WANT TO TALK TO PETER FOR ME?
WHY? WHAT HAPPENED?
AFTER OUR LITTLE ADVENTURE, I WENT TO SEE RAMSEY AND, WELL, PETER AND I--
YOU DOG!
IT WAS NICE AND EVERYTHING, BUT...MEANT MUCH MORE TO PETER THAN ME.
OUCH.
I KNOW. WISH ME LUCK.

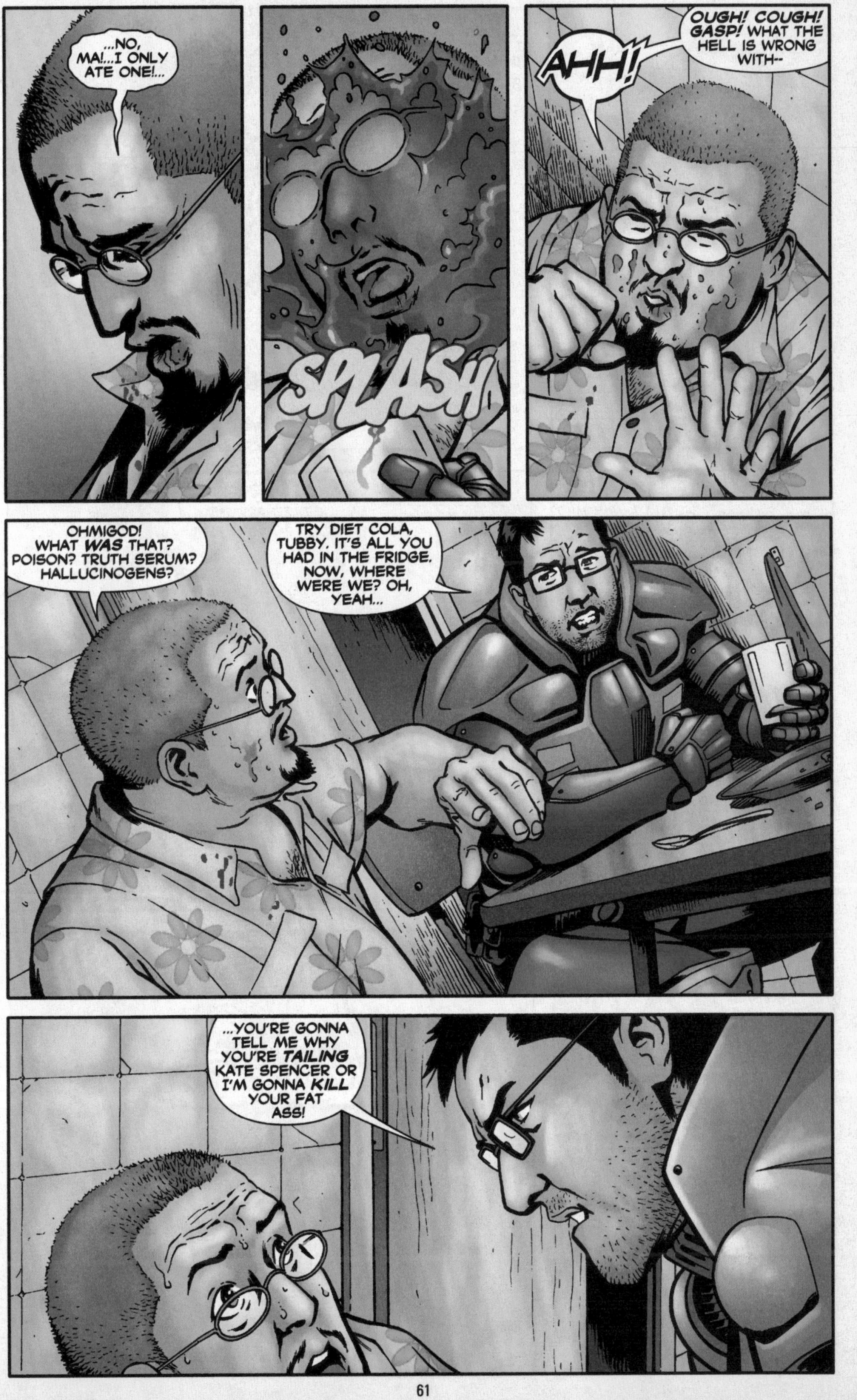
...NO, MA!...I ONLY ATE ONE!...
SPLASH
AHH!
OUGH! COUGH! GASP! WHAT THE HELL IS WRONG WITH--
OHMIGOD! WHAT WAS THAT? POISON? TRUTH SERUM? HALLUCINOGENS?
TRY DIET COLA, TUBBY. IT'S ALL YOU HAD IN THE FRIDGE. NOW, WHERE WERE WE? OH, YEAH...
...YOU'RE GONNA TELL ME WHY YOU'RE TAILING KATE SPENCER OR I'M GONNA KILL YOUR FAT ASS!

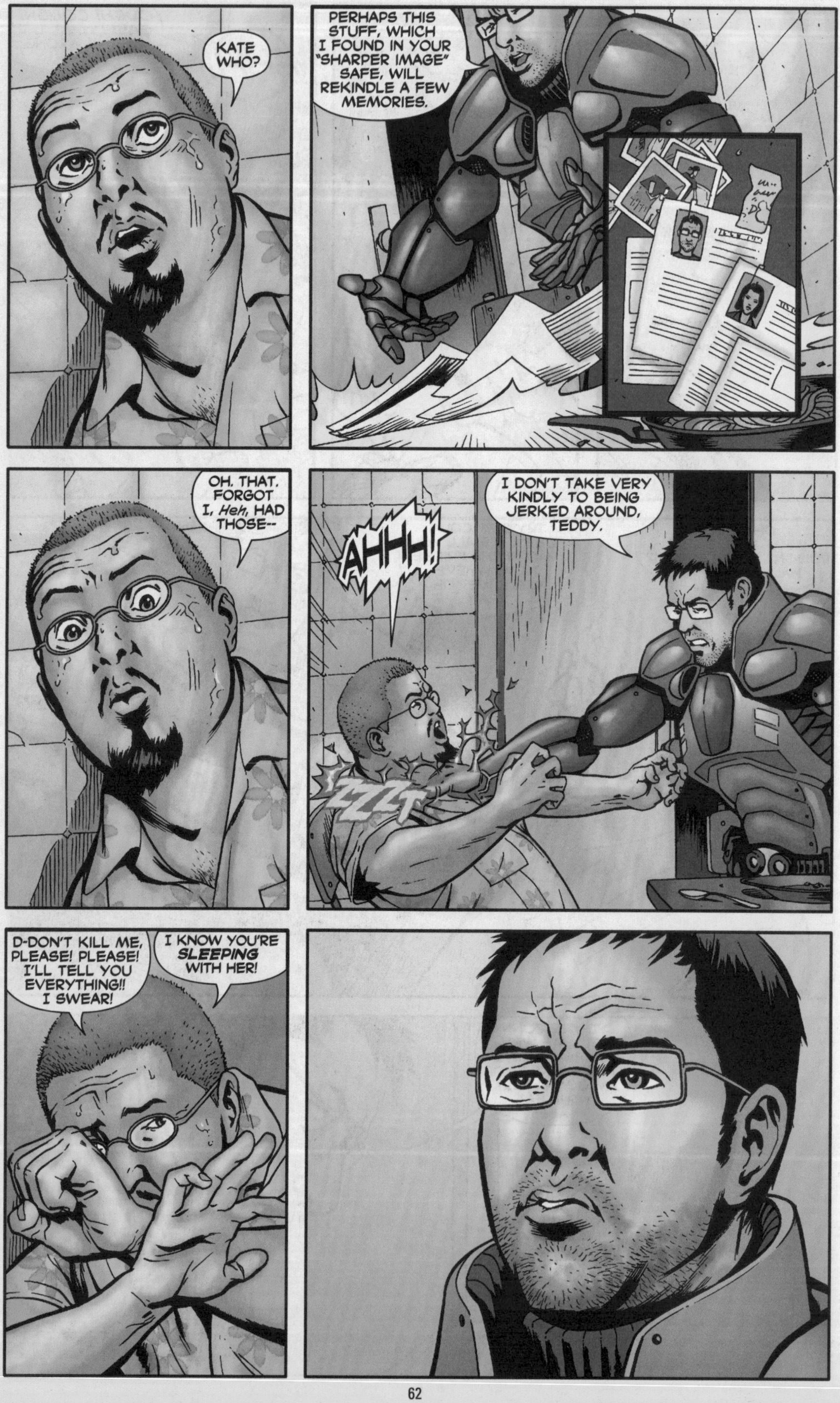
KATE WHO?
PERHAPS THIS STUFF, WHICH I FOUND IN YOUR "SHARPER IMAGE" SAFE, WILL REKINDLE A FEW MEMORIES.
OH. THAT. FORGOT I, *Heh*, HAD THOSE--
I DON'T TAKE VERY KINDLY TO BEING JERKED AROUND, TEDDY.
AHHH!
ZZZT
D-DON'T KILL ME, PLEASE! PLEASE! I'LL TELL YOU EVERYTHING!! I SWEAR!
I KNOW YOU'RE *SLEEPING* WITH HER!

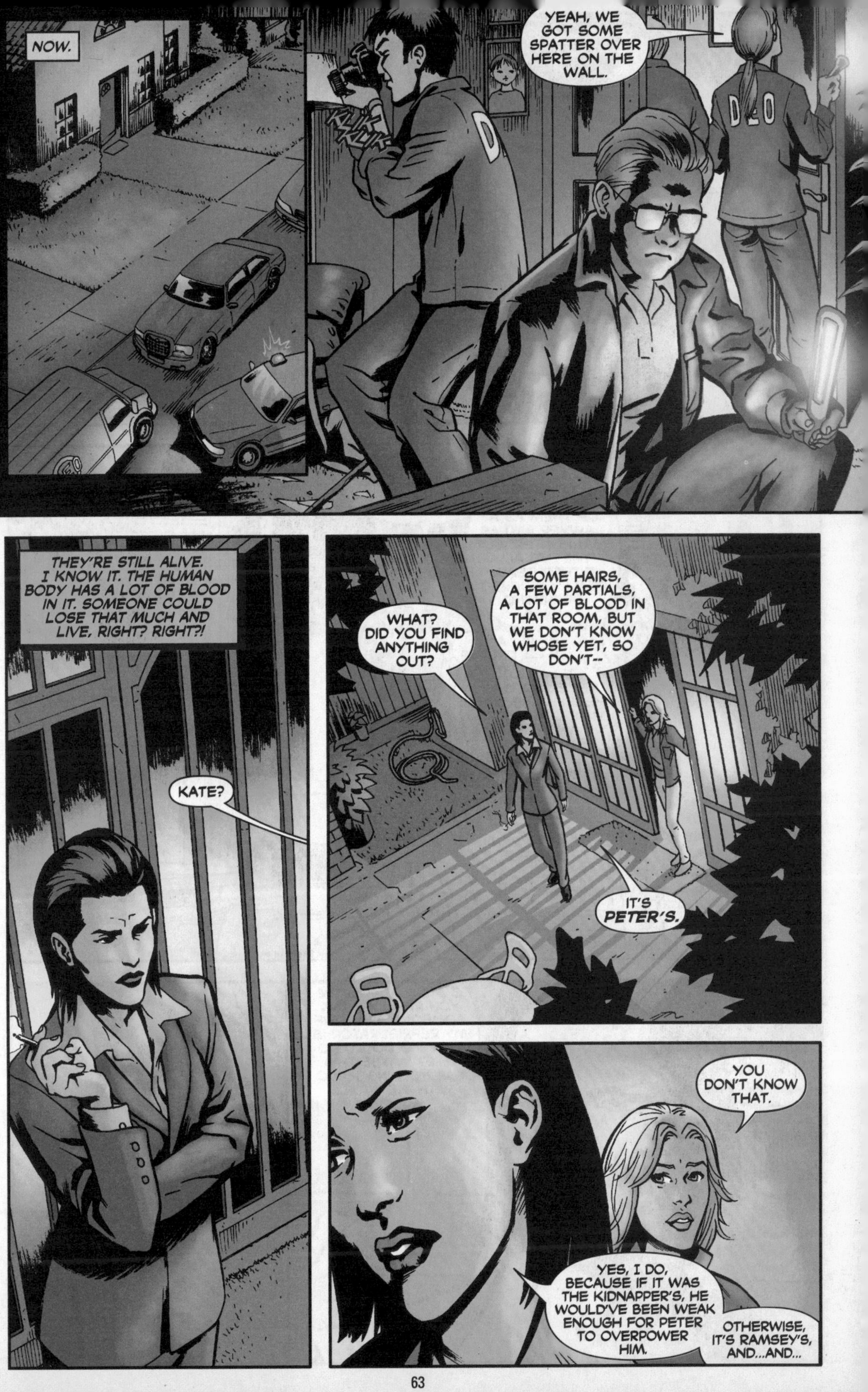
NOW.
KLIK KLIK
YEAH, WE GOT SOME SPATTER OVER HERE ON THE WALL.
DEO
THEY'RE STILL ALIVE. I KNOW IT. THE HUMAN BODY HAS A LOT OF BLOOD IN IT. SOMEONE COULD LOSE THAT MUCH AND LIVE, RIGHT? RIGHT?!
KATE?
WHAT? DID YOU FIND ANYTHING OUT?
SOME HAIRS, A FEW PARTIALS, A LOT OF BLOOD IN THAT ROOM, BUT WE DON'T KNOW WHOSE YET, SO DON'T--
IT'S PETER'S.
YOU DON'T KNOW THAT.
YES, I DO, BECAUSE IF IT WAS THE KIDNAPPER'S, HE WOULD'VE BEEN WEAK ENOUGH FOR PETER TO OVERPOWER HIM.
OTHERWISE, IT'S RAMSEY'S, AND...AND...

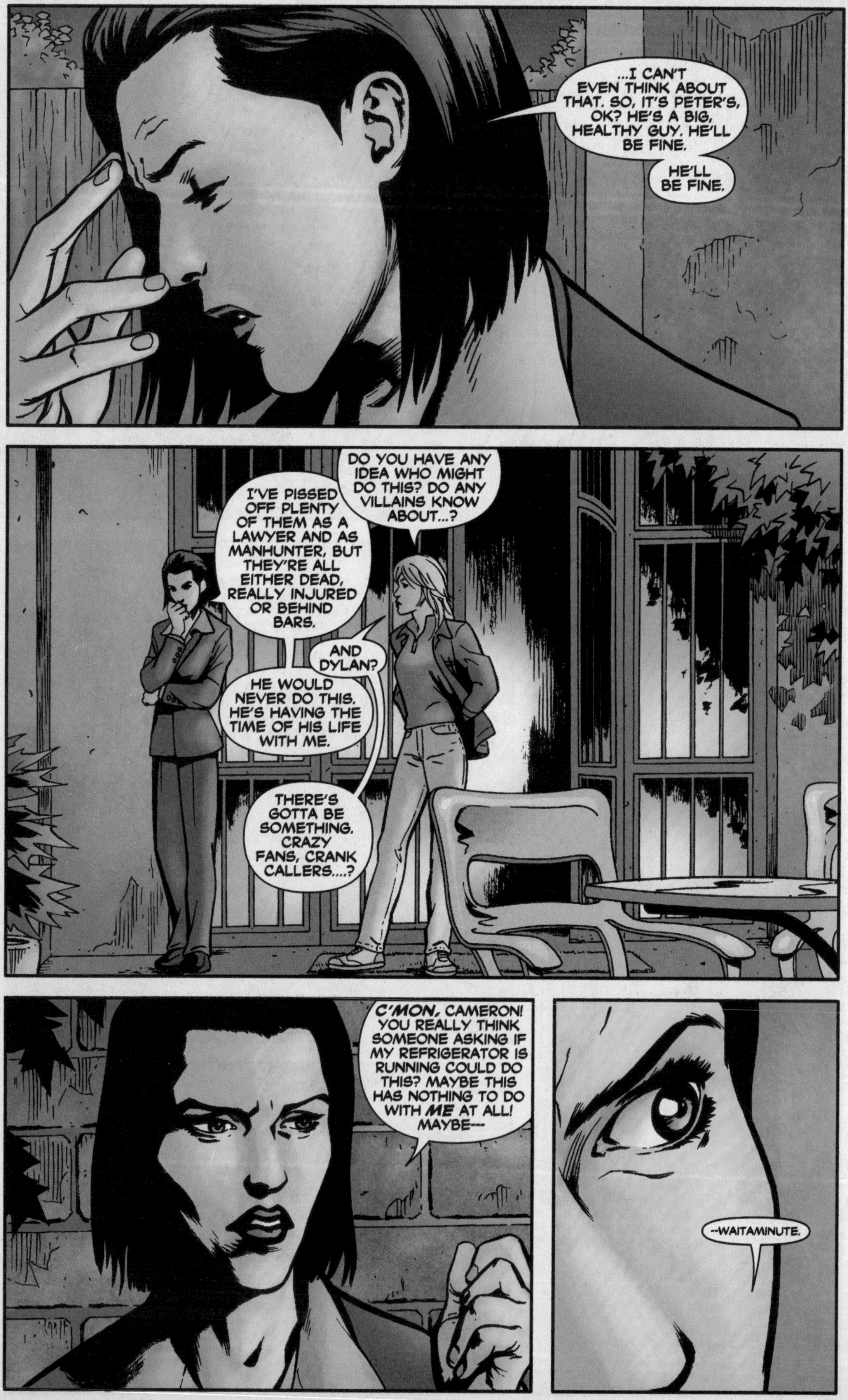
...I CAN'T EVEN THINK ABOUT THAT. SO, IT'S PETER'S, OK? HE'S A BIG, HEALTHY GUY. HE'LL BE FINE.
HE'LL BE FINE.
DO YOU HAVE ANY IDEA WHO MIGHT DO THIS? DO ANY VILLAINS KNOW ABOUT...?
I'VE PISSED OFF PLENTY OF THEM AS A LAWYER AND AS MANHUNTER, BUT THEY'RE ALL EITHER DEAD, REALLY INJURED OR BEHIND BARS.
AND DYLAN?
HE WOULD NEVER DO THIS. HE'S HAVING THE TIME OF HIS LIFE WITH ME.
THERE'S GOTTA BE SOMETHING. CRAZY FANS, CRANK CALLERS....?
C'MON, CAMERON! YOU REALLY THINK SOMEONE ASKING IF MY REFRIGERATOR IS RUNNING COULD DO THIS? MAYBE THIS HAS NOTHING TO DO WITH ME AT ALL! MAYBE---
--WAITAMINUTE.

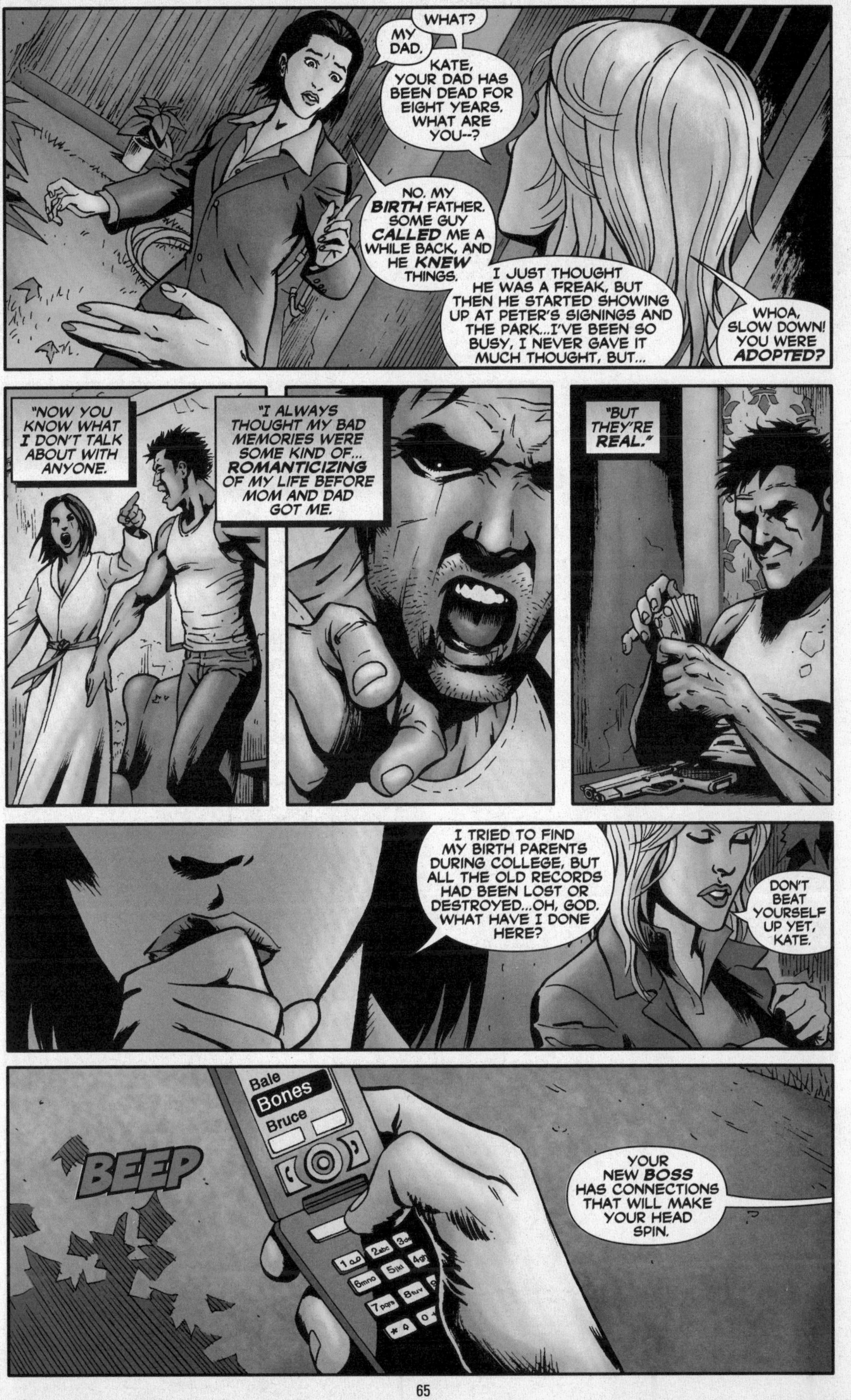
WHAT?
MY DAD.
KATE, YOUR DAD HAS BEEN DEAD FOR EIGHT YEARS. WHAT ARE YOU--?
NO. MY BIRTH FATHER. SOME GUY CALLED ME A WHILE BACK, AND HE KNEW THINGS.
I JUST THOUGHT HE WAS A FREAK, BUT THEN HE STARTED SHOWING UP AT PETER'S SIGNINGS AND THE PARK...I'VE BEEN SO BUSY, I NEVER GAVE IT MUCH THOUGHT, BUT...
WHOA, SLOW DOWN! YOU WERE ADOPTED?
"NOW YOU KNOW WHAT I DON'T TALK ABOUT WITH ANYONE.
"I ALWAYS THOUGHT MY BAD MEMORIES WERE SOME KIND OF... ROMANTICIZING OF MY LIFE BEFORE MOM AND DAD GOT ME.
"BUT THEY'RE REAL."
I TRIED TO FIND MY BIRTH PARENTS DURING COLLEGE, BUT ALL THE OLD RECORDS HAD BEEN LOST OR DESTROYED...OH, GOD. WHAT HAVE I DONE HERE?
DON'T BEAT YOURSELF UP YET, KATE.
Bale
Bones
Bruce
BEEP
YOUR NEW BOSS HAS CONNECTIONS THAT WILL MAKE YOUR HEAD SPIN.

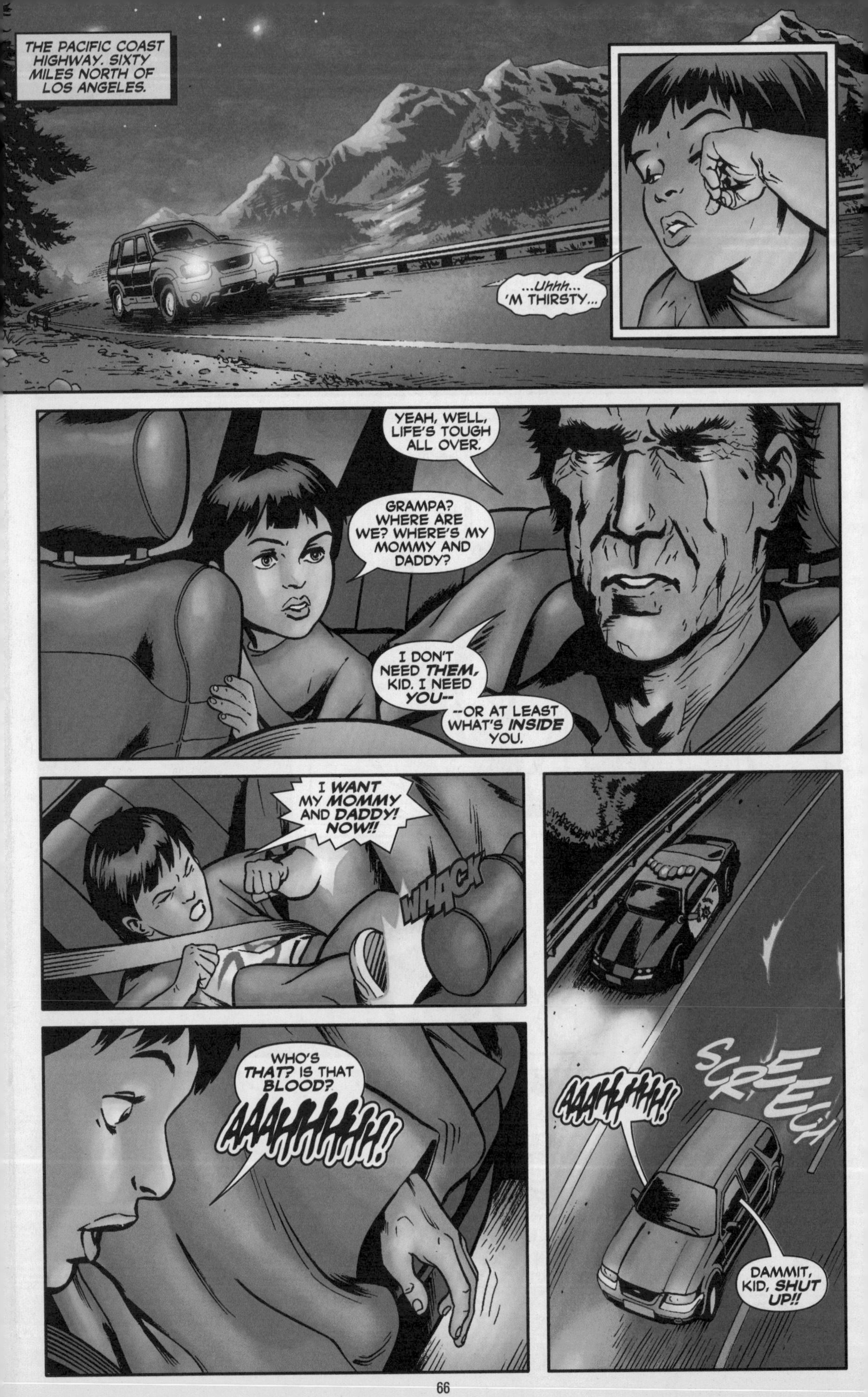
THE PACIFIC COAST HIGHWAY. SIXTY MILES NORTH OF LOS ANGELES.
...Uhhh... 'M THIRSTY...
YEAH, WELL, LIFE'S TOUGH ALL OVER.
GRAMPA? WHERE ARE WE? WHERE'S MY MOMMY AND DADDY?
I DON'T NEED THEM, KID. I NEED YOU--
--OR AT LEAST WHAT'S INSIDE YOU.
I WANT MY MOMMY AND DADDY! NOW!!
WHACK
WHO'S THAT? IS THAT BLOOD?
AAAHHHHH!
SCREEECH
AAAHHHHH!
DAMMIT, KID, SHUT UP!!

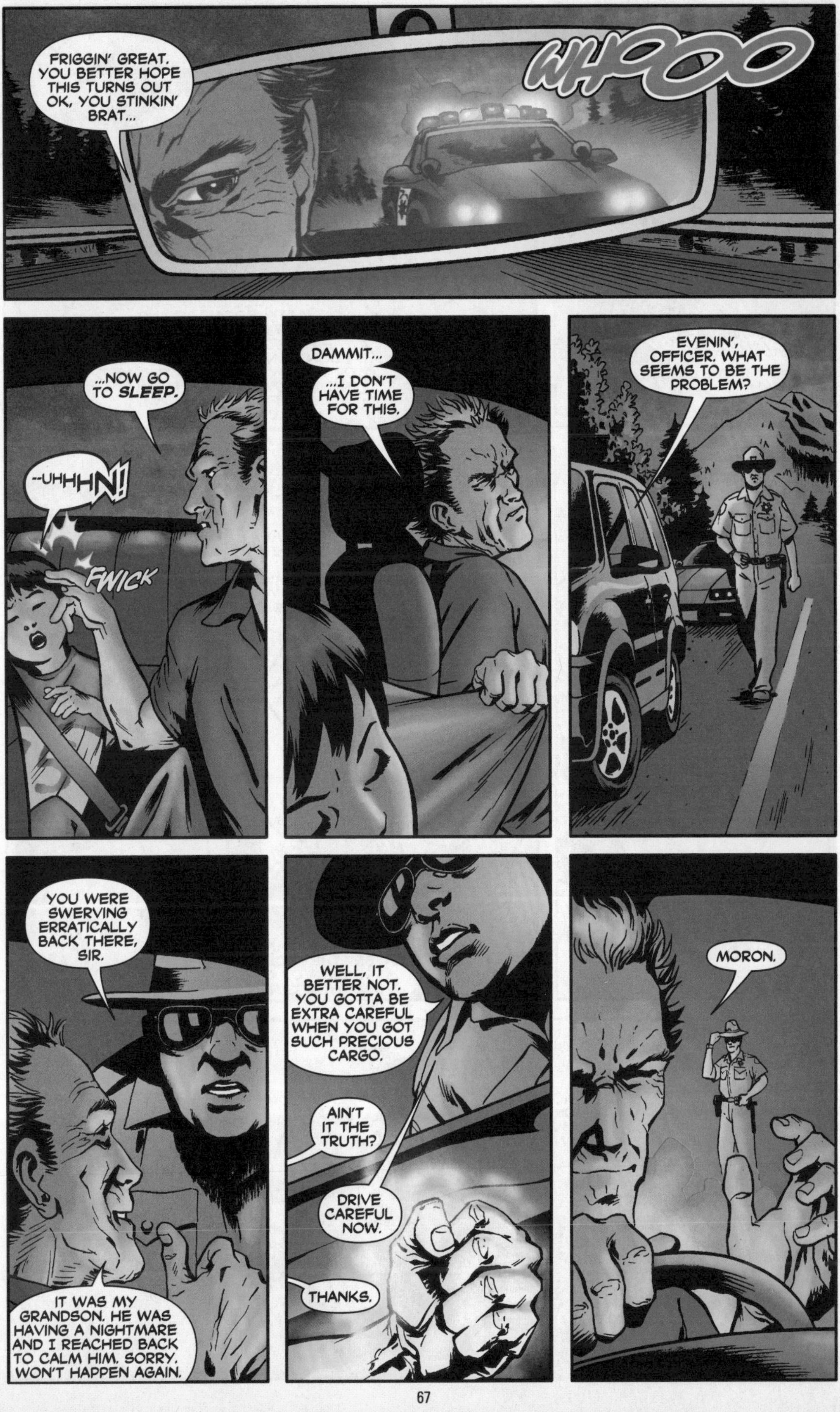
FRIGGIN' GREAT. YOU BETTER HOPE THIS TURNS OUT OK, YOU STINKIN' BRAT...
WHOOO
...NOW GO TO SLEEP.
--UHHHN!
FWICK
DAMMIT...
...I DON'T HAVE TIME FOR THIS.
EVENIN', OFFICER. WHAT SEEMS TO BE THE PROBLEM?
YOU WERE SWERVING ERRATICALLY BACK THERE, SIR.
IT WAS MY GRANDSON. HE WAS HAVING A NIGHTMARE AND I REACHED BACK TO CALM HIM. SORRY. WON'T HAPPEN AGAIN.
WELL, IT BETTER NOT. YOU GOTTA BE EXTRA CAREFUL WHEN YOU GOT SUCH PRECIOUS CARGO.
AIN'T IT THE TRUTH?
DRIVE CAREFUL NOW.
THANKS.
MORON.

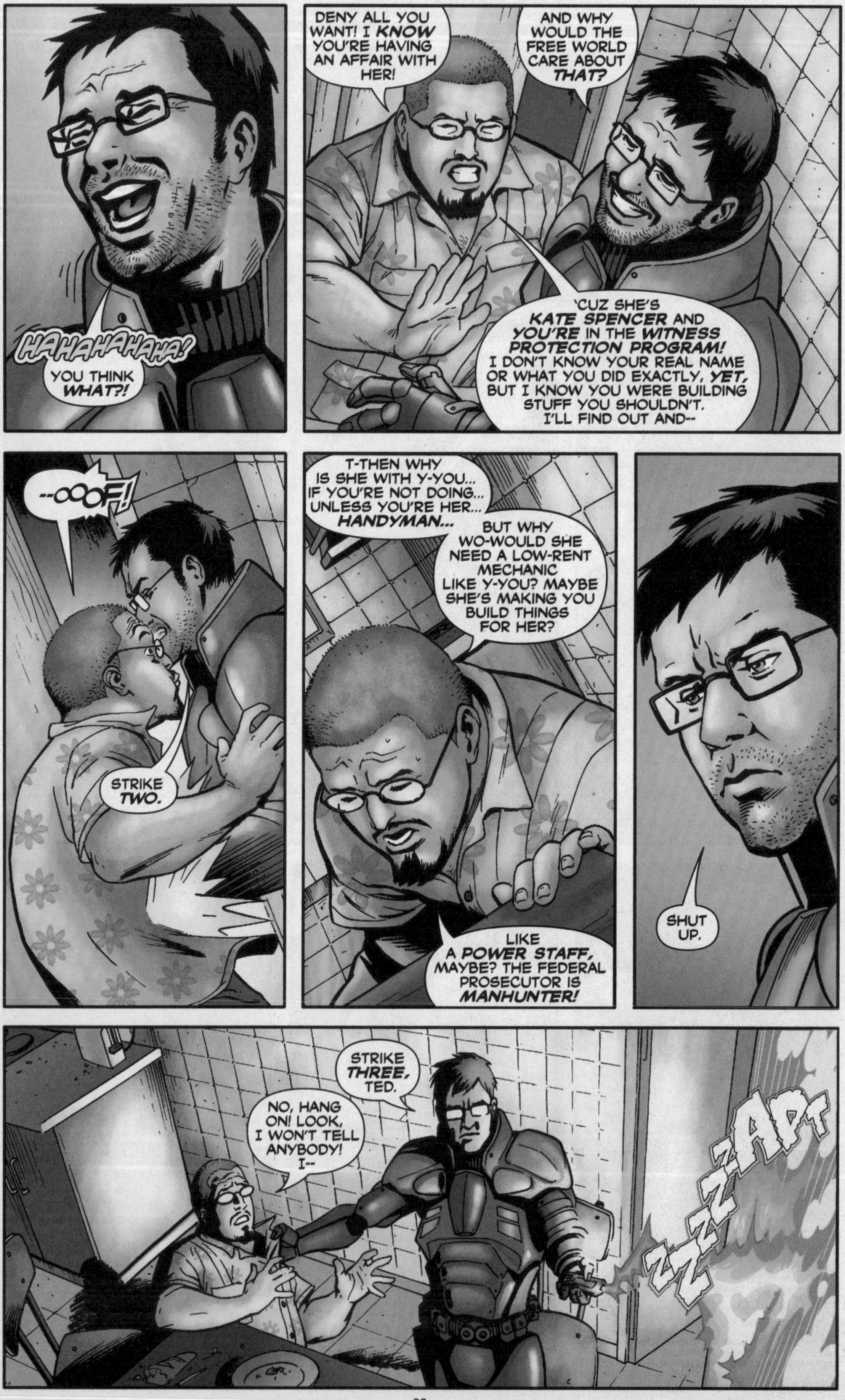
HAHAHAHAHA!
YOU THINK WHAT?!
DENY ALL YOU WANT! I KNOW YOU'RE HAVING AN AFFAIR WITH HER!
AND WHY WOULD THE FREE WORLD CARE ABOUT THAT?
'CUZ SHE'S KATE SPENCER AND YOU'RE IN THE WITNESS PROTECTION PROGRAM! I DON'T KNOW YOUR REAL NAME OR WHAT YOU DID EXACTLY, YET, BUT I KNOW YOU WERE BUILDING STUFF YOU SHOULDN'T. I'LL FIND OUT AND--
--OOOF!
STRIKE TWO.
T-THEN WHY IS SHE WITH Y-YOU... IF YOU'RE NOT DOING... UNLESS YOU'RE HER... HANDYMAN...
BUT WHY WO-WOULD SHE NEED A LOW-RENT MECHANIC LIKE Y-YOU? MAYBE SHE'S MAKING YOU BUILD THINGS FOR HER?
LIKE A POWER STAFF, MAYBE? THE FEDERAL PROSECUTOR IS MANHUNTER!
SHUT UP.
STRIKE THREE, TED.
NO, HANG ON! LOOK, I WON'T TELL ANYBODY! I--
ZZZZZAPT

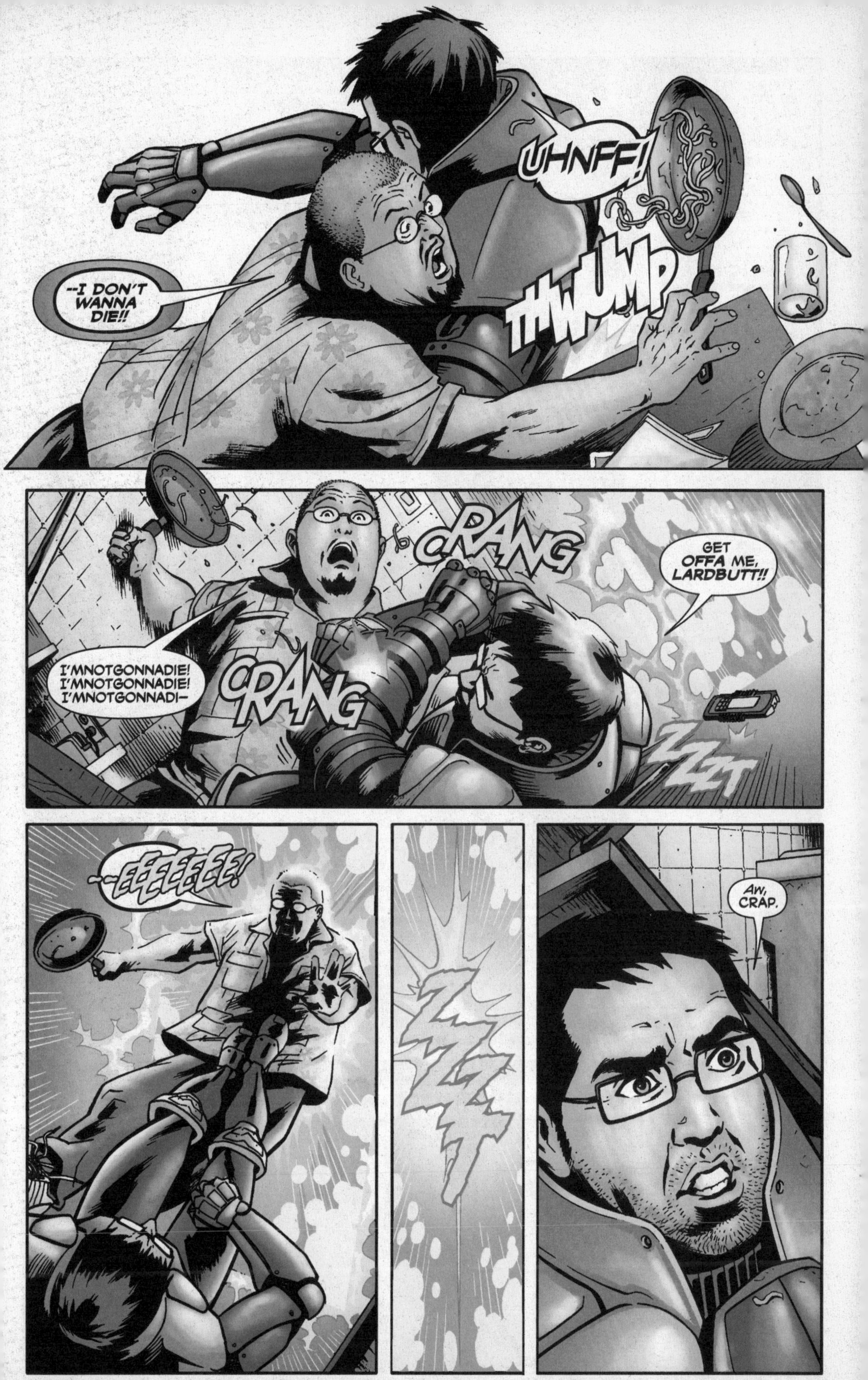
--I DON'T WANNA DIE!!
UHNFF!
THWUMP
CRANG
GET OFFA ME, LARDBUTT!!
I'MNOTGONNADIE! I'MNOTGONNADIE! I'MNOTGONNADI—
CRANG
ZZZT
--EEEEEEEE!
ZZZT
AW, CRAP.

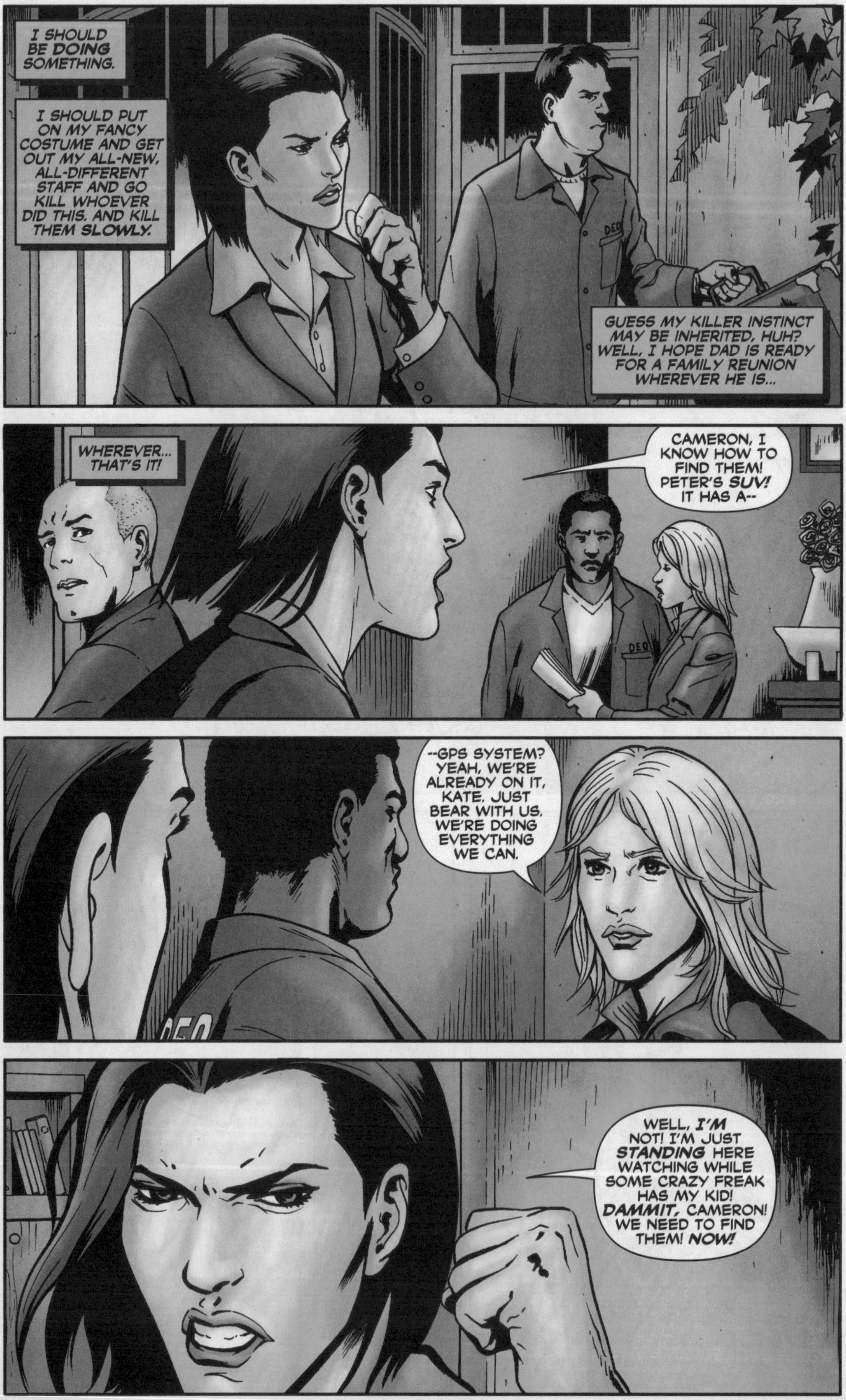
I SHOULD BE DOING SOMETHING.
I SHOULD PUT ON MY FANCY COSTUME AND GET OUT MY ALL-NEW, ALL-DIFFERENT STAFF AND GO KILL WHOEVER DID THIS. AND KILL THEM SLOWLY.
DEO
GUESS MY KILLER INSTINCT MAY BE INHERITED, HUH? WELL, I HOPE DAD IS READY FOR A FAMILY REUNION WHEREVER HE IS...
WHEREVER... THAT'S IT!
CAMERON, I KNOW HOW TO FIND THEM! PETER'S SUV! IT HAS A--
DEO
--GPS SYSTEM? YEAH, WE'RE ALREADY ON IT, KATE. JUST BEAR WITH US. WE'RE DOING EVERYTHING WE CAN.
WELL, I'M NOT! I'M JUST STANDING HERE WATCHING WHILE SOME CRAZY FREAK HAS MY KID! DAMMIT, CAMERON! WE NEED TO FIND THEM! NOW!

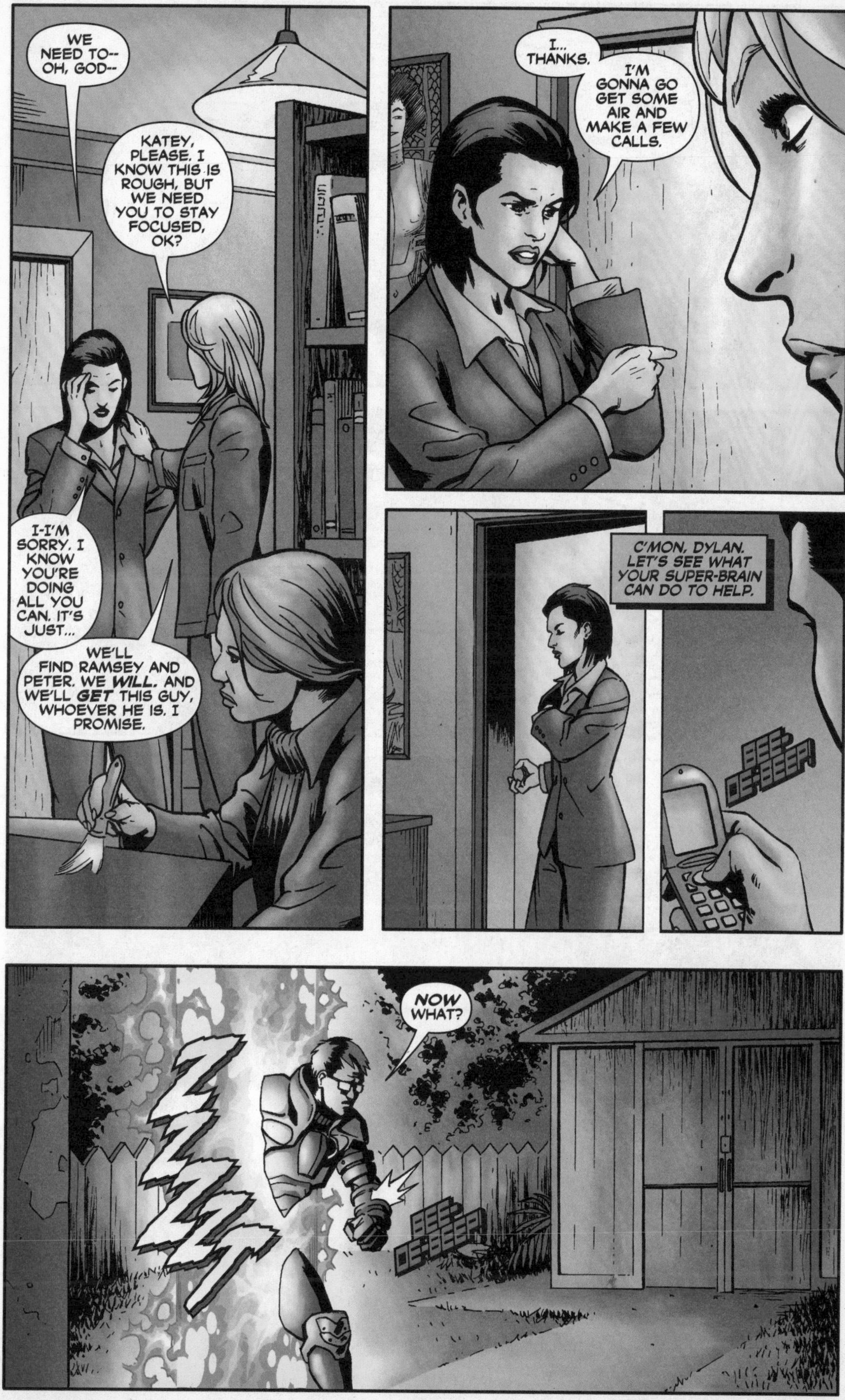
WE NEED TO-- OH, GOD--
KATEY, PLEASE. I KNOW THIS IS ROUGH, BUT WE NEED YOU TO STAY FOCUSED, OK?
I-I'M SORRY. I KNOW YOU'RE DOING ALL YOU CAN. IT'S JUST...
WE'LL FIND RAMSEY AND PETER. WE *WILL*. AND WE'LL *GET* THIS GUY, WHOEVER HE IS. I PROMISE.
I... THANKS.
I'M GONNA GO GET SOME AIR AND MAKE A FEW CALLS.
C'MON, DYLAN. LET'S SEE WHAT YOUR SUPER-BRAIN CAN DO TO HELP.
BEE-DE-BEEP!
NOW WHAT?
ZZZZZT
BEE-DE-BEEP

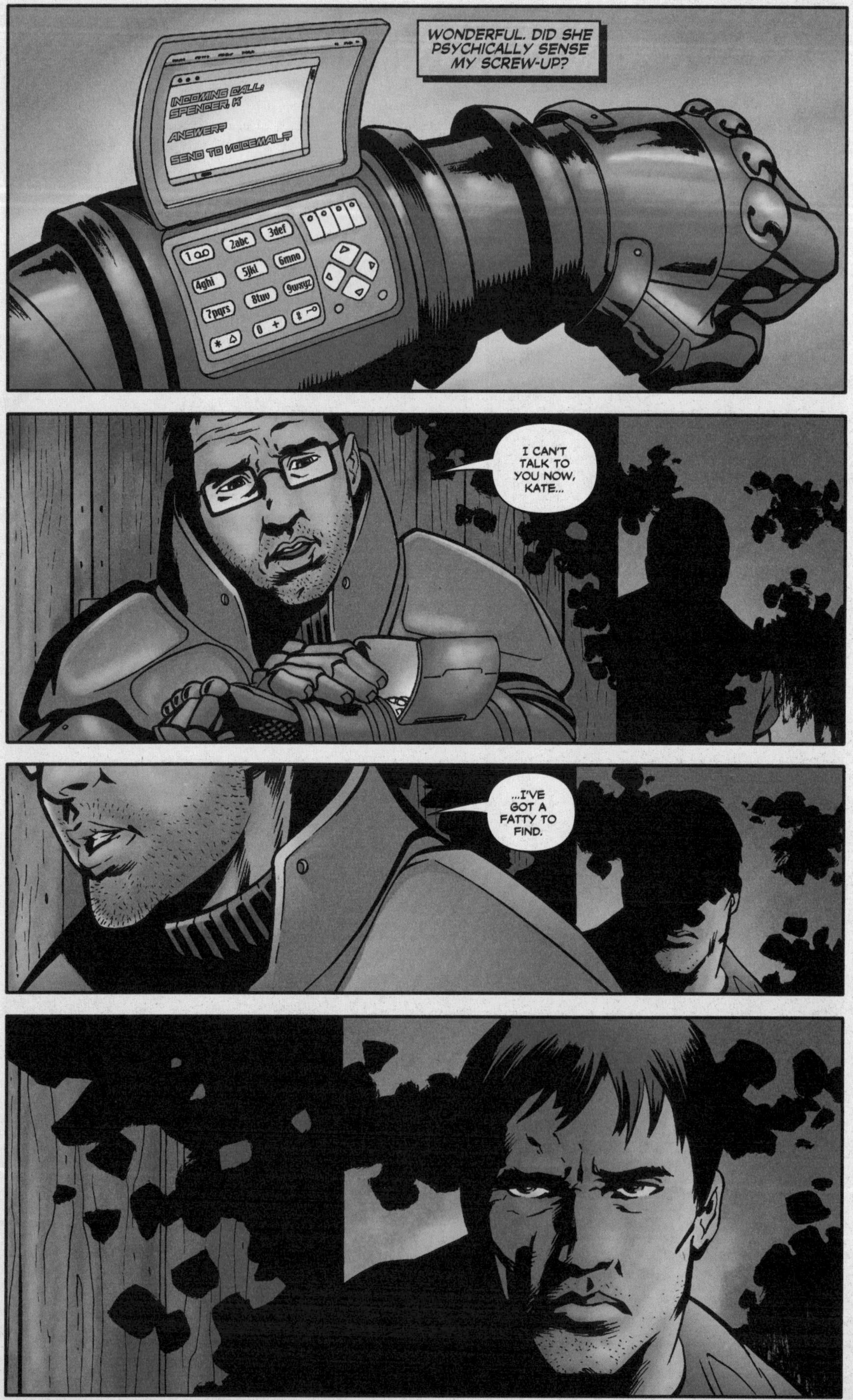
WONDERFUL. DID SHE PSYCHICALLY SENSE MY SCREW-UP?
INCOMING CALL: SPENCER, K
ANSWER?
SEND TO VOICEMAIL?
I CAN'T TALK TO YOU NOW, KATE...
...I'VE GOT A FATTY TO FIND.

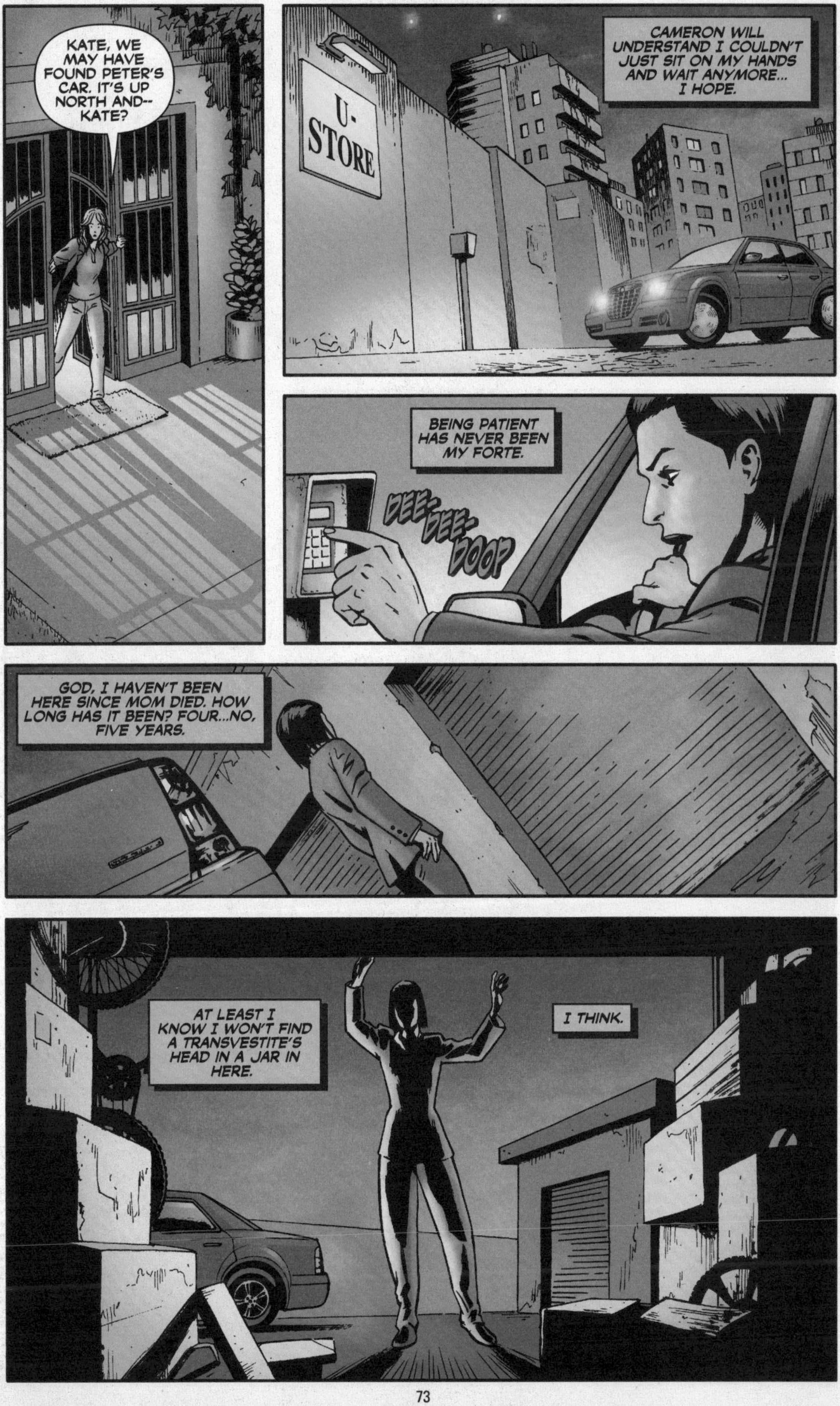
KATE, WE MAY HAVE FOUND PETER'S CAR. IT'S UP NORTH AND-- KATE?
U-STORE
CAMERON WILL UNDERSTAND I COULDN'T JUST SIT ON MY HANDS AND WAIT ANYMORE... I HOPE.
BEING PATIENT HAS NEVER BEEN MY FORTE.
DEE-DEE-DOOP
GOD, I HAVEN'T BEEN HERE SINCE MOM DIED. HOW LONG HAS IT BEEN? FOUR...NO, FIVE YEARS.
AT LEAST I KNOW I WON'T FIND A TRANSVESTITE'S HEAD IN A JAR IN HERE.
I THINK.

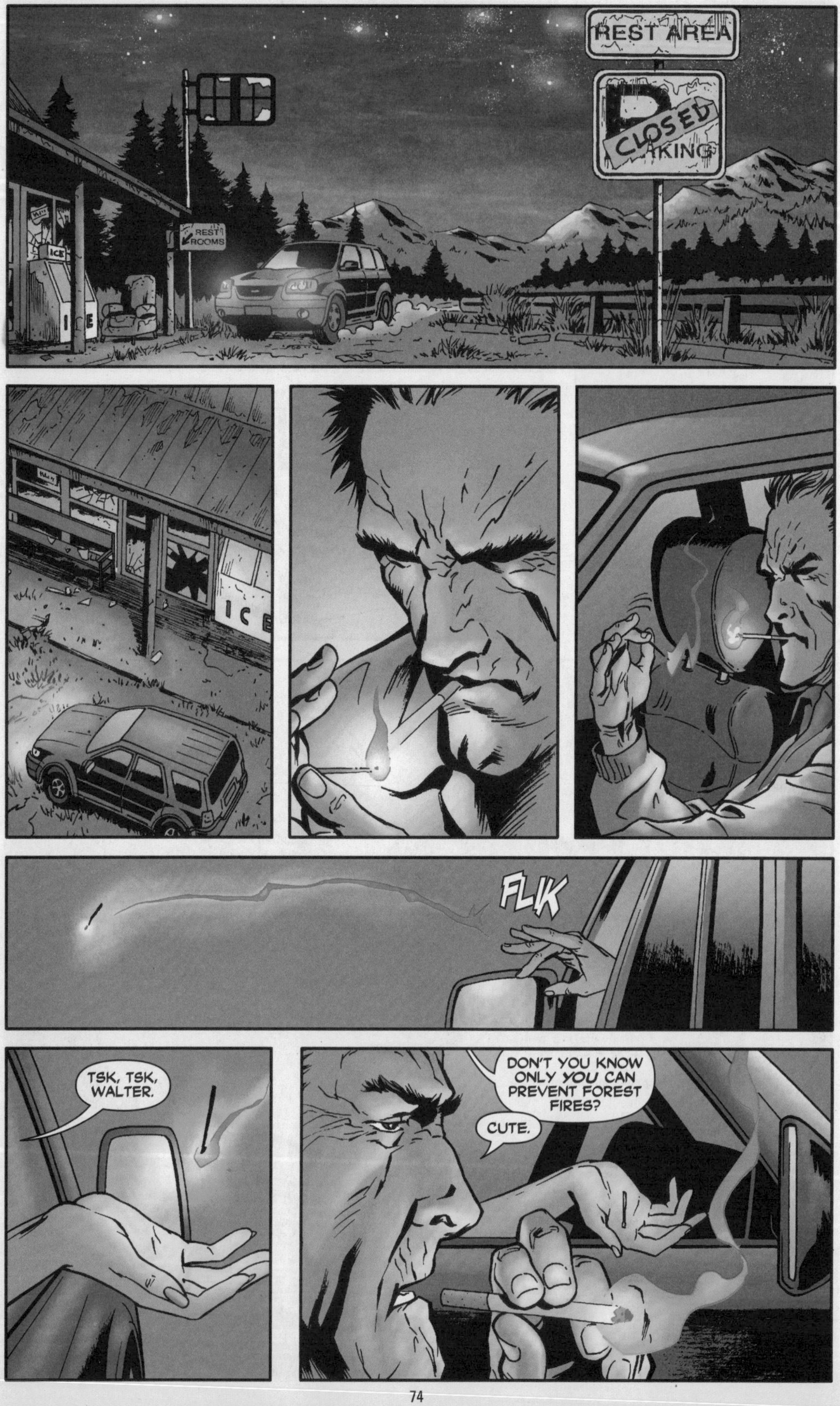
REST AREA
CLOSED
REST ROOMS
ICE
FLIK
TSK, TSK, WALTER.
DON'T YOU KNOW ONLY *YOU* CAN PREVENT FOREST FIRES?
CUTE.

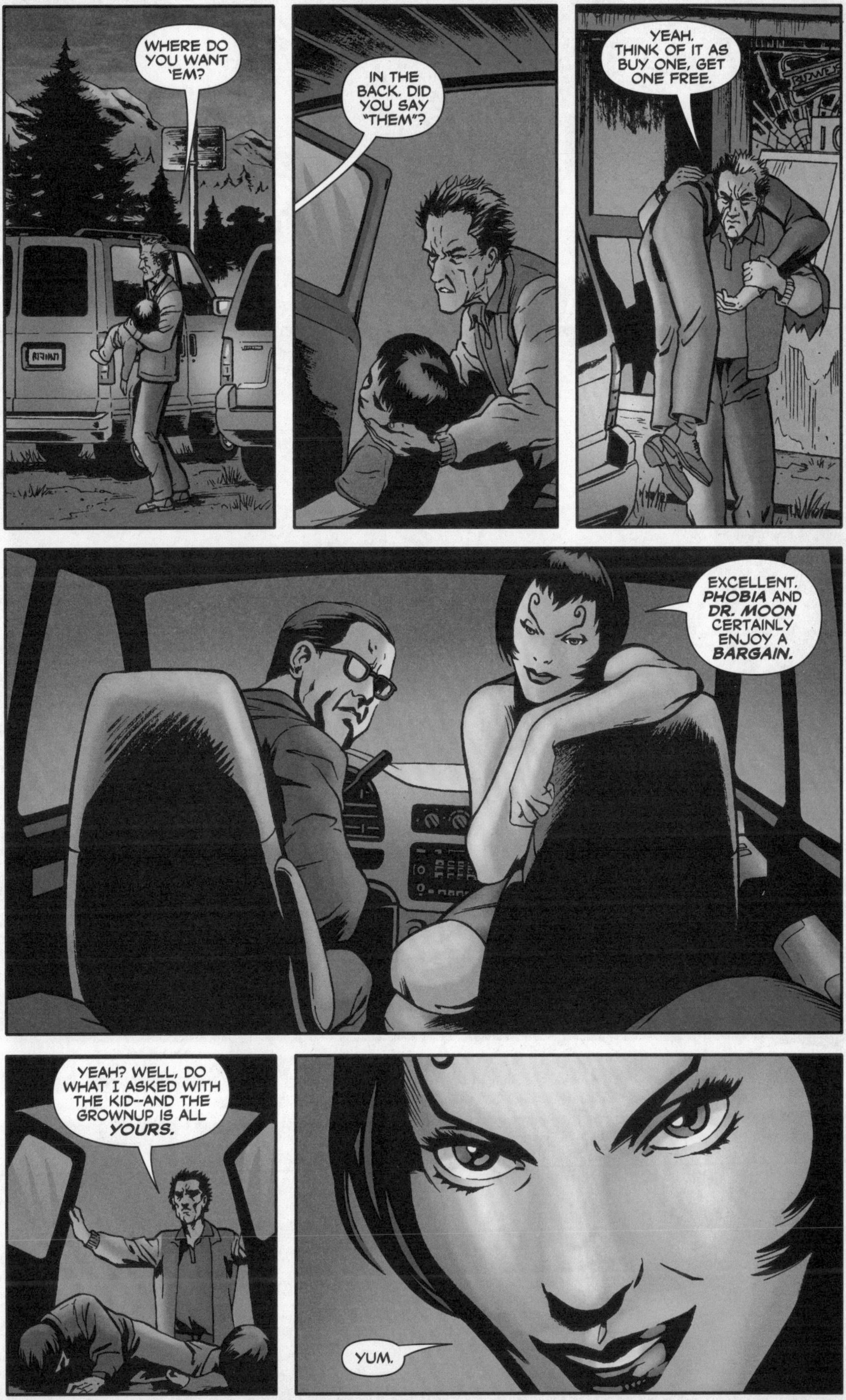

WHERE DO YOU WANT 'EM?
IN THE BACK. DID YOU SAY "THEM"?
YEAH. THINK OF IT AS BUY ONE, GET ONE FREE.
EXCELLENT. PHOBIA AND DR. MOON CERTAINLY ENJOY A BARGAIN.
YEAH? WELL, DO WHAT I ASKED WITH THE KID--AND THE GROWNUP IS ALL YOURS.
YUM.

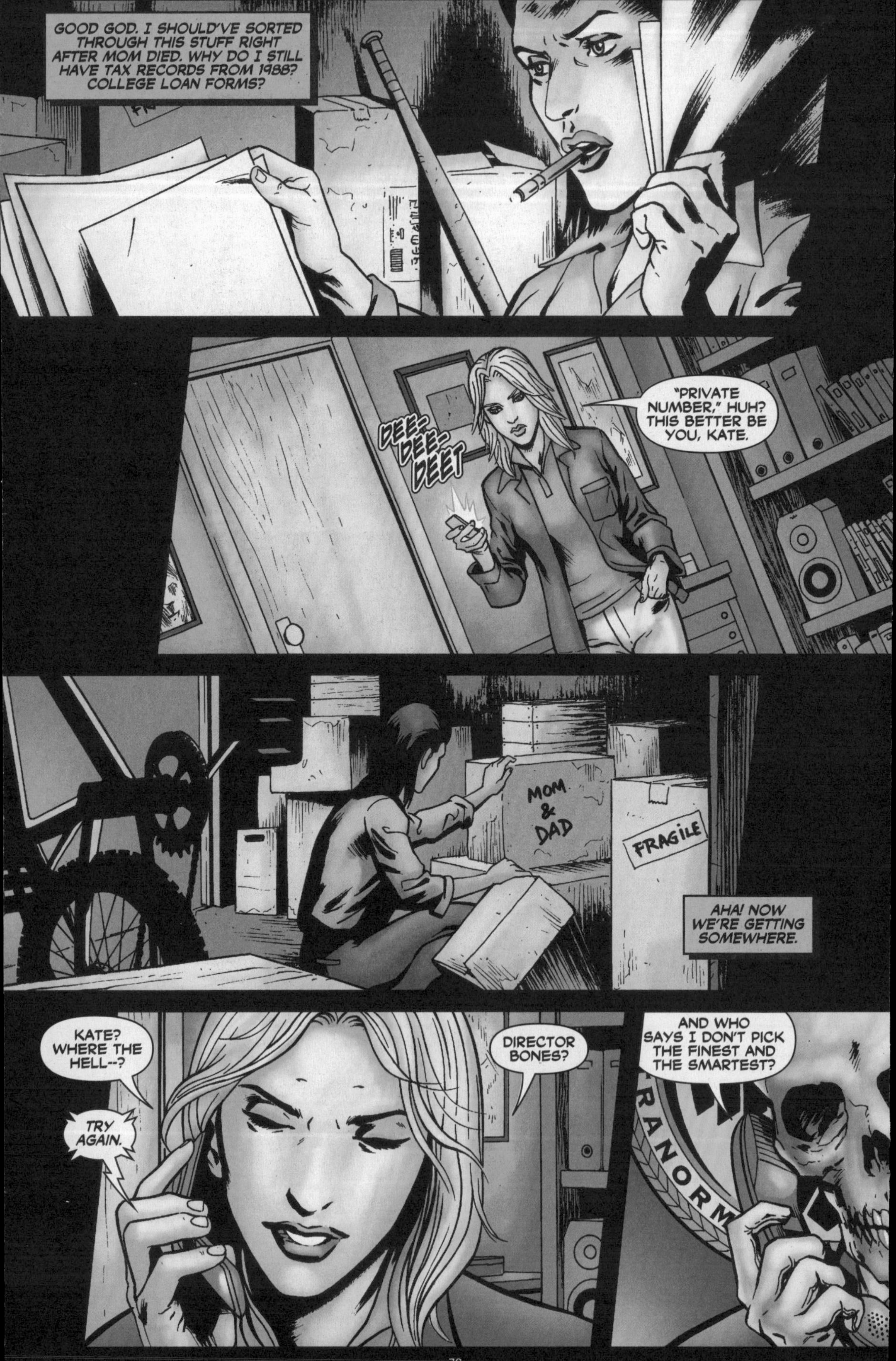
GOOD GOD. I SHOULD'VE SORTED THROUGH THIS STUFF RIGHT AFTER MOM DIED. WHY DO I STILL HAVE TAX RECORDS FROM 1988? COLLEGE LOAN FORMS?
DEE-DEE-DEET
"PRIVATE NUMBER," HUH? THIS BETTER BE YOU, KATE.
MOM & DAD
FRAGILE
AHA! NOW WE'RE GETTING SOMEWHERE.
KATE? WHERE THE HELL--?
TRY AGAIN.
DIRECTOR BONES?
AND WHO SAYS I DON'T PICK THE FINEST AND THE SMARTEST?

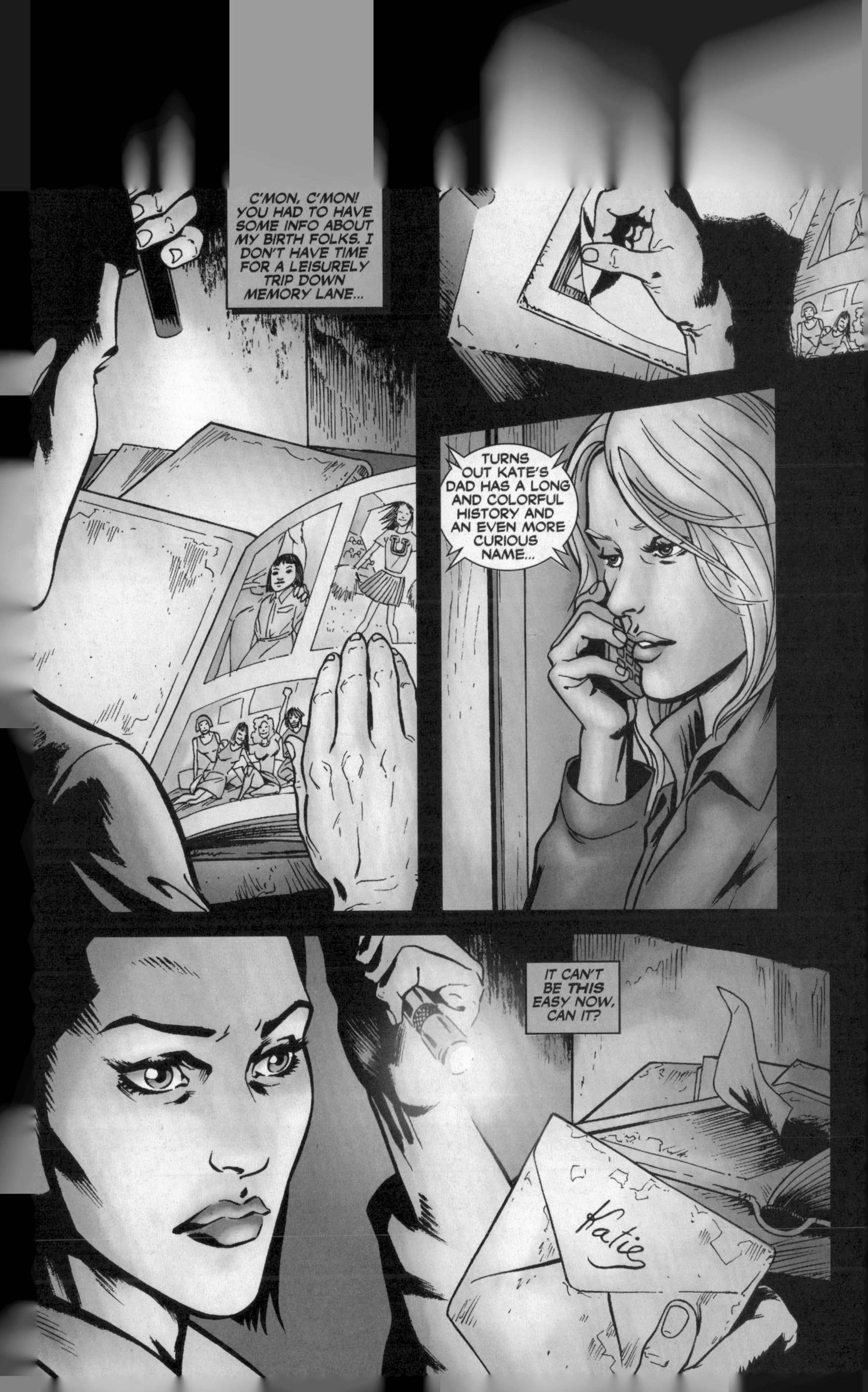
C'MON, C'MON! YOU HAD TO HAVE SOME INFO ABOUT MY BIRTH FOLKS. I DON'T HAVE TIME FOR A LEISURELY TRIP DOWN MEMORY LANE...
TURNS OUT KATE'S DAD HAS A LONG AND COLORFUL HISTORY AND AN EVEN MORE CURIOUS NAME...
IT CAN'T BE THIS EASY NOW, CAN IT?
Katie

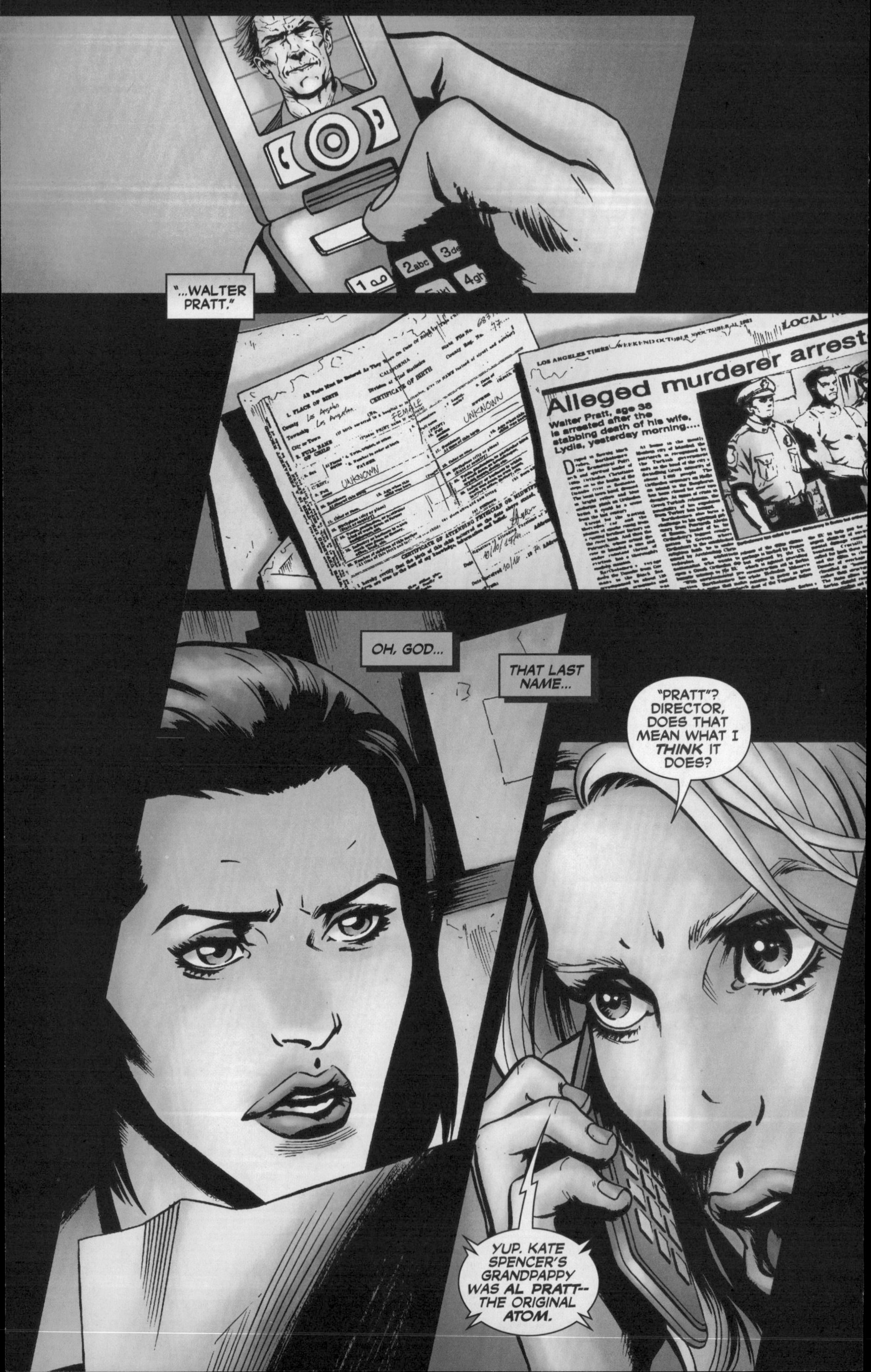
"...WALTER PRATT."
LOS ANGELES TIMES
Alleged murderer arrest
Walter Pratt, age 38 is arrested after the stabbing death of his wife, Lydia, yesterday morning....
OH, GOD...
THAT LAST NAME...
"PRATT"? DIRECTOR, DOES THAT MEAN WHAT I THINK IT DOES?
YUP. KATE SPENCER'S GRANDPAPPY WAS AL PRATT-- THE ORIGINAL ATOM.

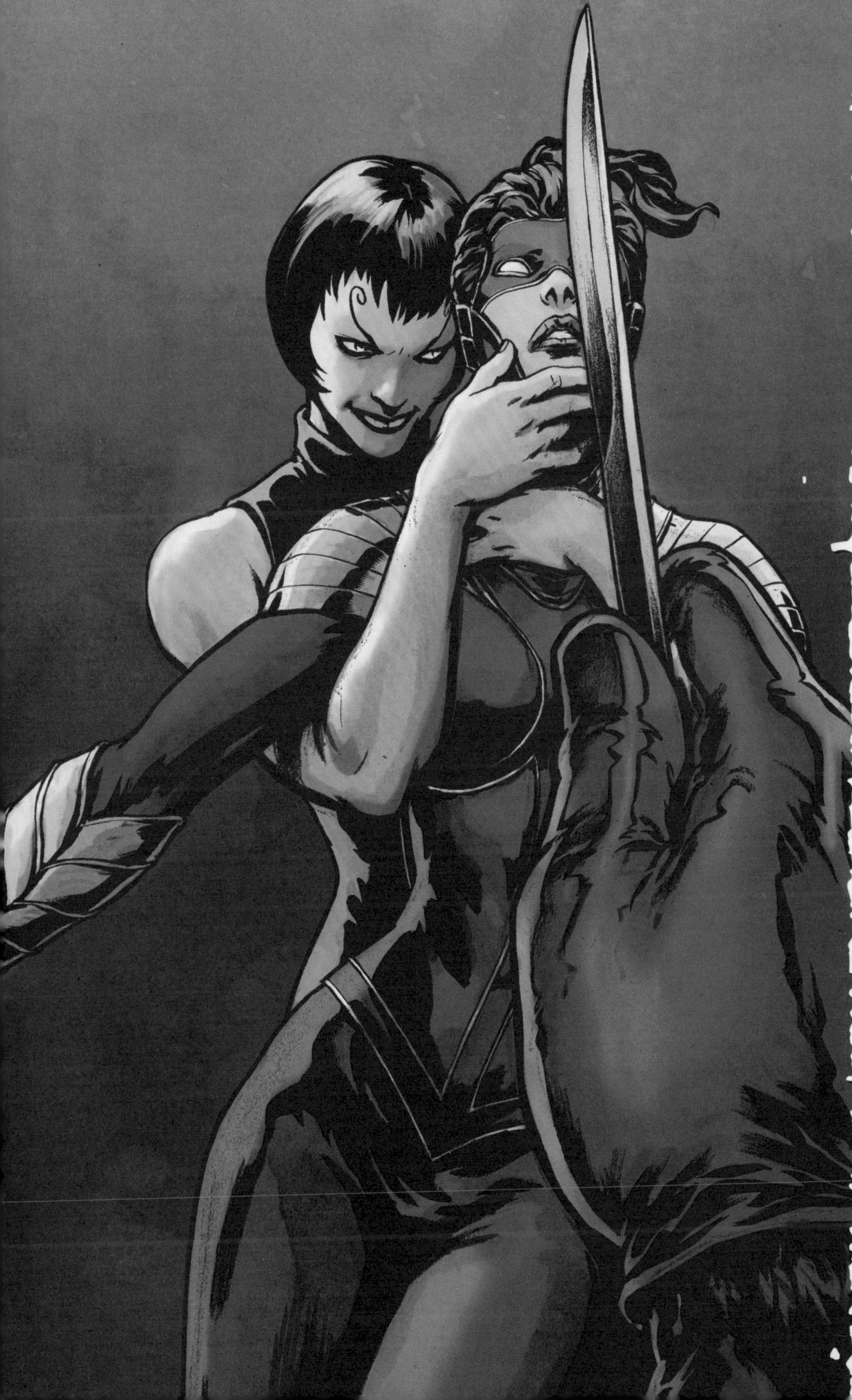

Issue #18 cover by Jesus Saiz & Jose Villarrubia

Interior art by Javier Pina & Fernando Blanco

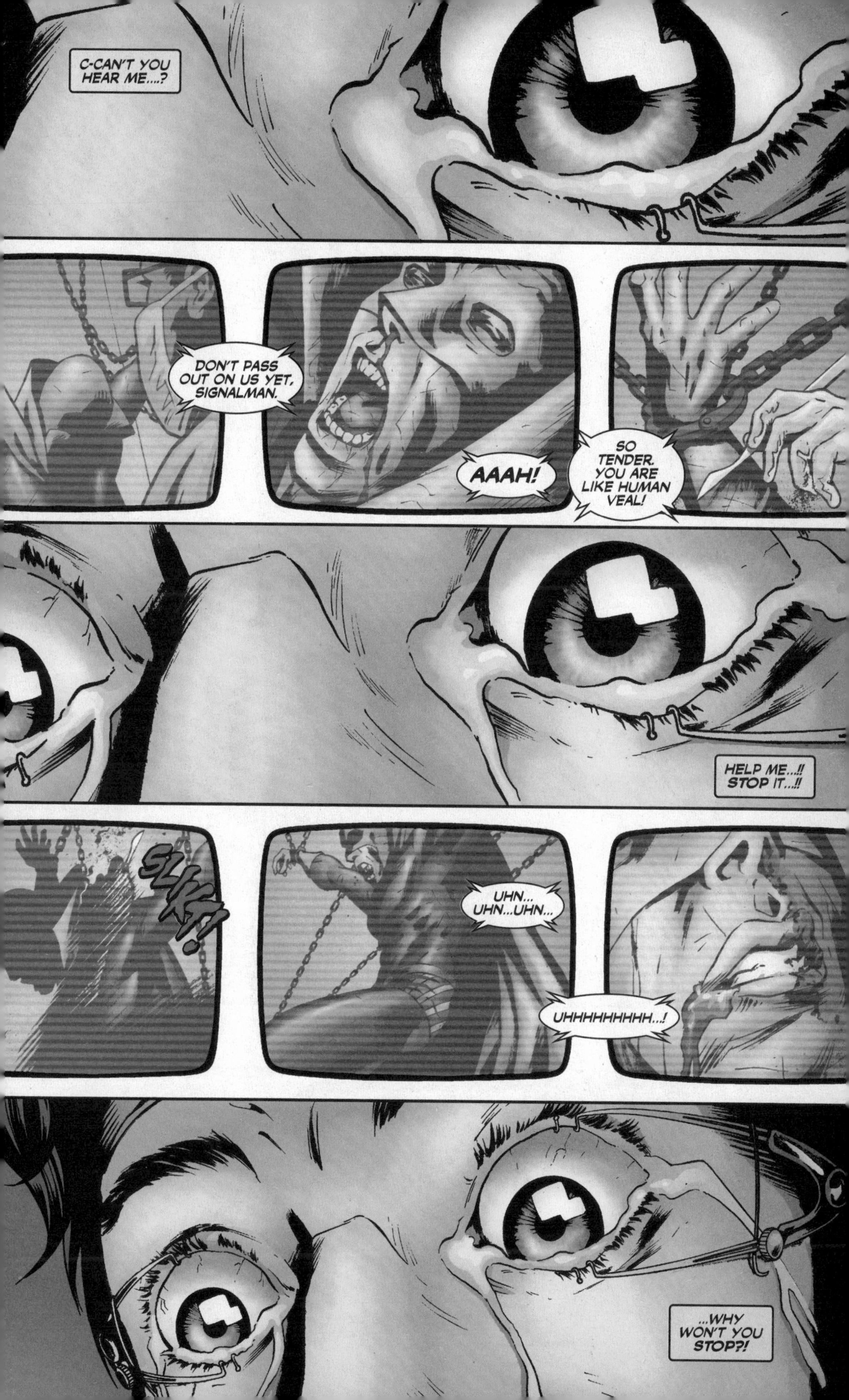
C-CAN'T YOU HEAR ME....?
DON'T PASS OUT ON US YET, SIGNALMAN.
AAAH!
SO TENDER. YOU ARE LIKE HUMAN VEAL!
HELP ME...!! STOP IT...!!
SLIKK!
UHN... UHN...UHN...
UHHHHHHHHH...!
...WHY WON'T YOU STOP?!

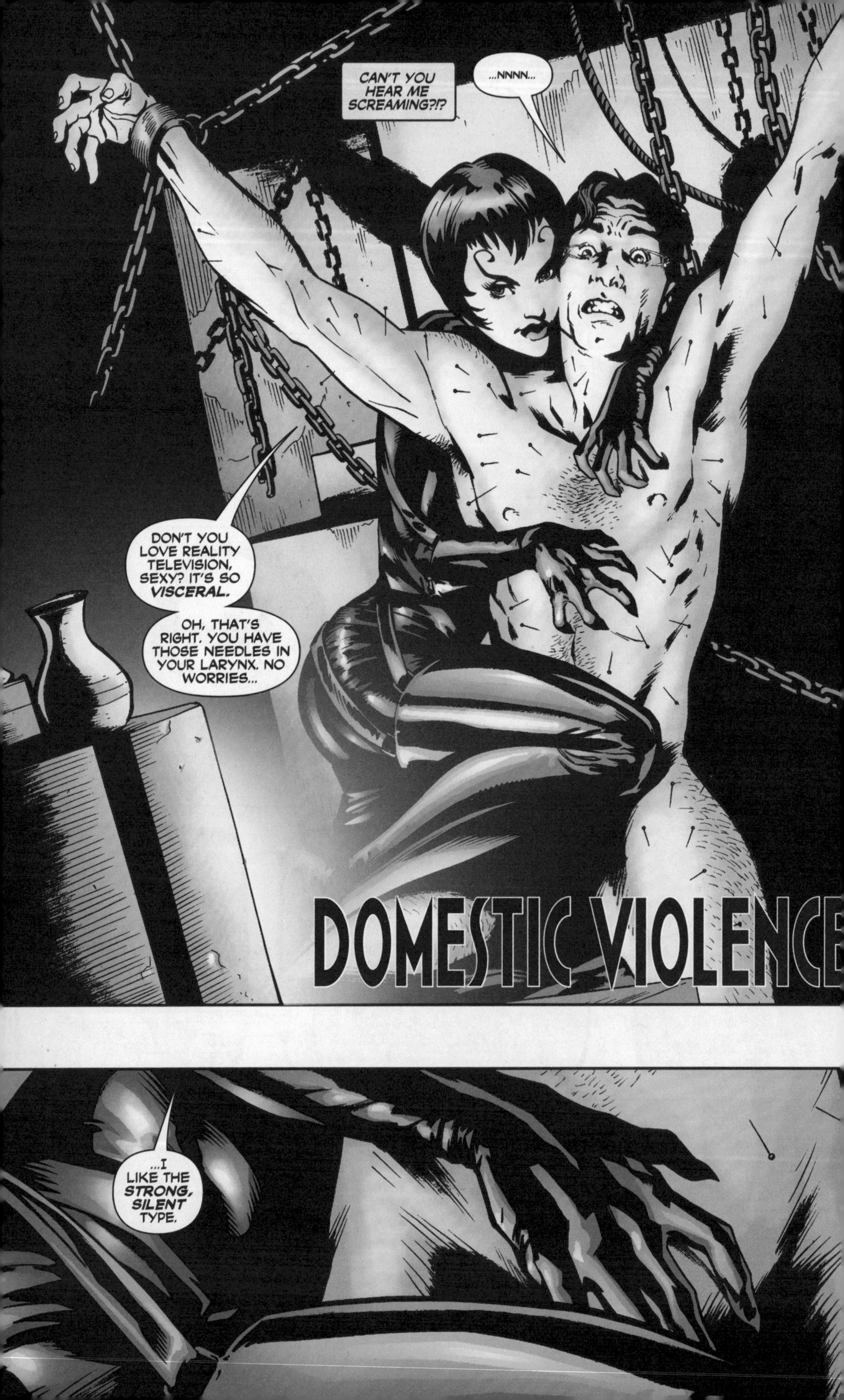
CAN'T YOU HEAR ME SCREAMING?!?
...NNNN...
DON'T YOU LOVE REALITY TELEVISION, SEXY? IT'S SO VISCERAL.
OH, THAT'S RIGHT. YOU HAVE THOSE NEEDLES IN YOUR LARYNX. NO WORRIES...
DOMESTIC VIOLENCE
...I LIKE THE STRONG, SILENT TYPE.

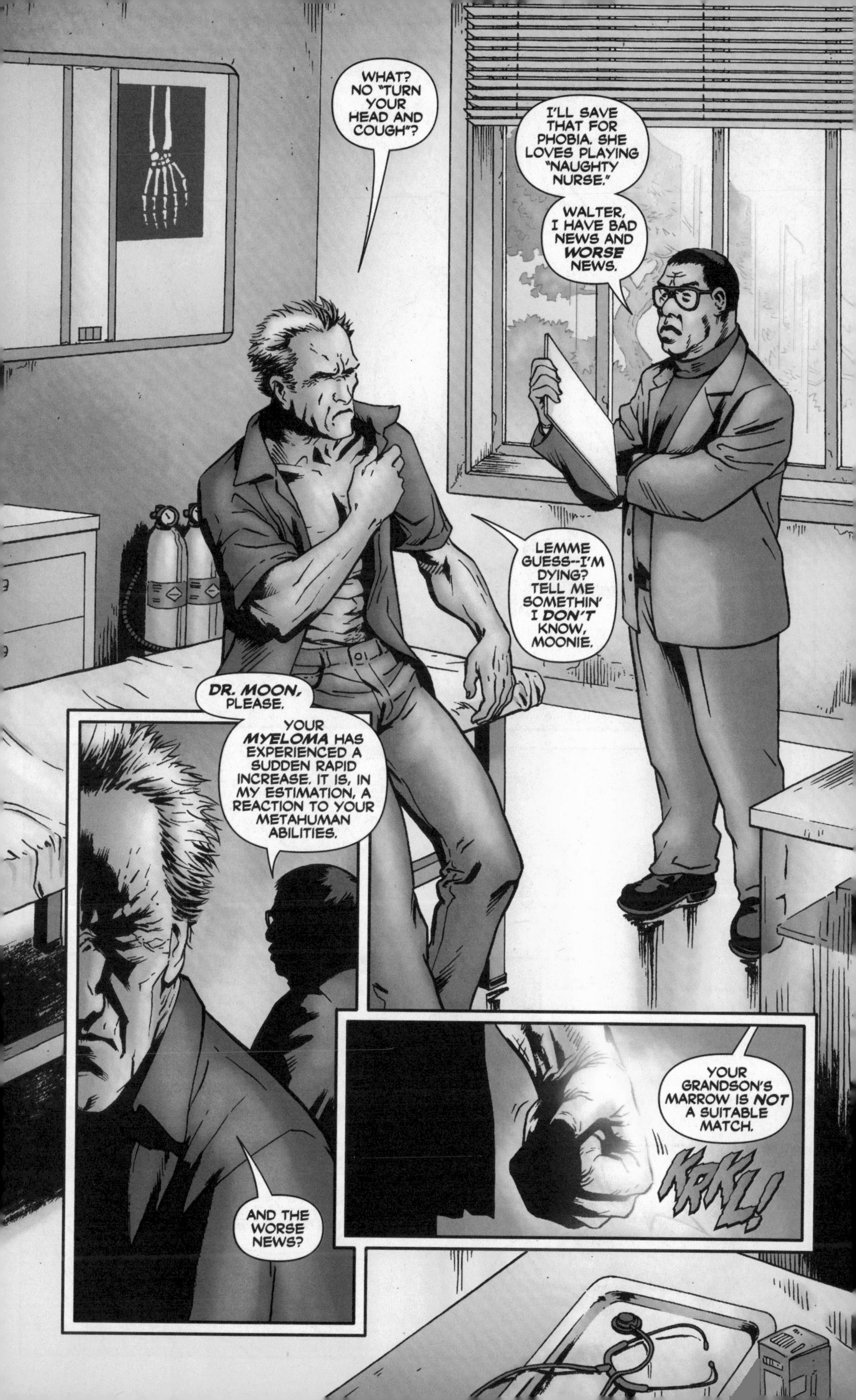
WHAT? NO "TURN YOUR HEAD AND COUGH"?
I'LL SAVE THAT FOR PHOBIA. SHE LOVES PLAYING "NAUGHTY NURSE."
WALTER, I HAVE BAD NEWS AND WORSE NEWS.
LEMME GUESS--I'M DYING? TELL ME SOMETHIN' I DON'T KNOW, MOONIE.
DR. MOON, PLEASE.
YOUR MYELOMA HAS EXPERIENCED A SUDDEN RAPID INCREASE. IT IS, IN MY ESTIMATION, A REACTION TO YOUR METAHUMAN ABILITIES.
AND THE WORSE NEWS?
YOUR GRANDSON'S MARROW IS NOT A SUITABLE MATCH.
KRKL!

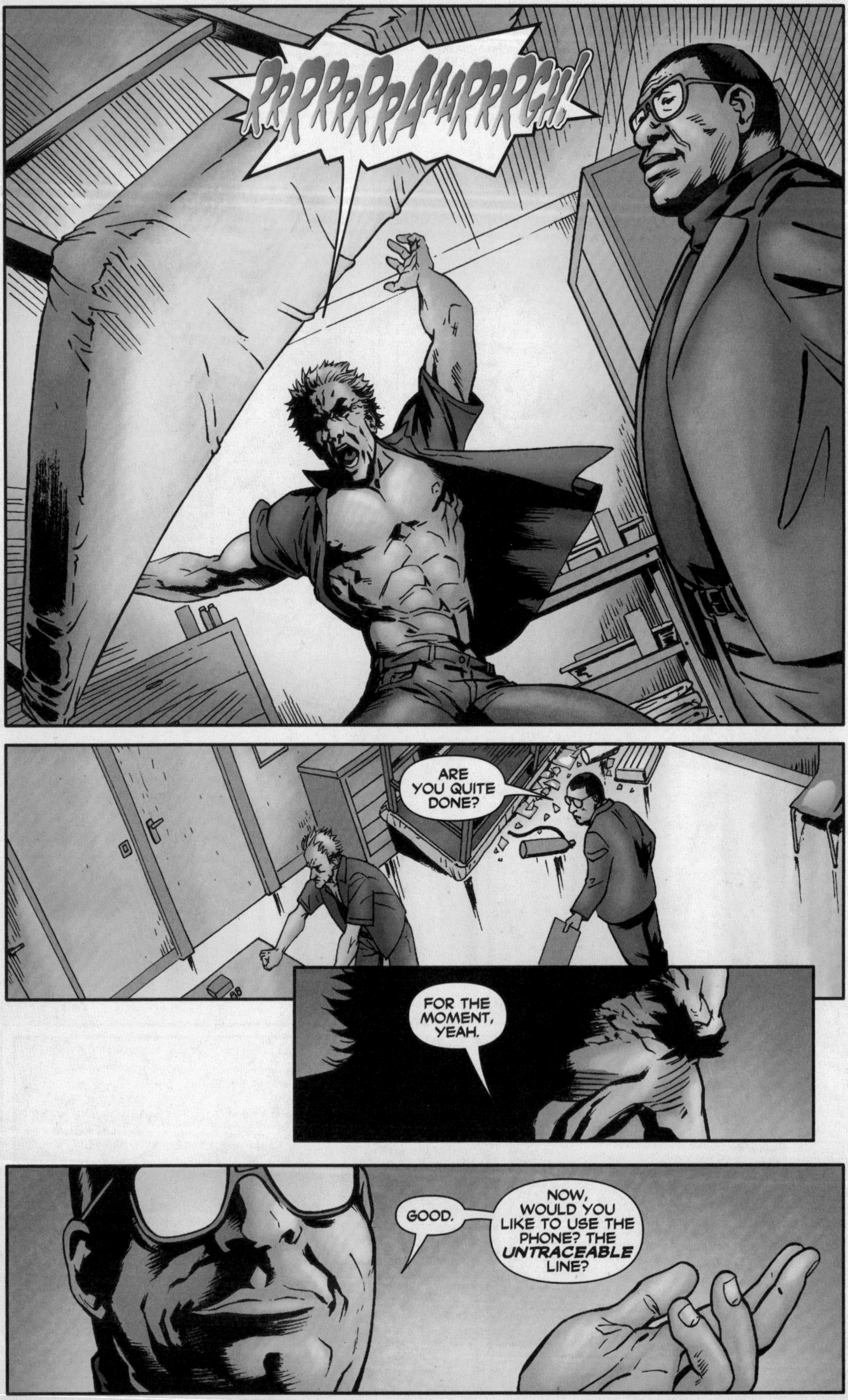
RRRRRRAAARRRGH!
ARE YOU QUITE DONE?
FOR THE MOMENT, YEAH.
GOOD.
NOW, WOULD YOU LIKE TO USE THE PHONE? THE *UNTRACEABLE* LINE?

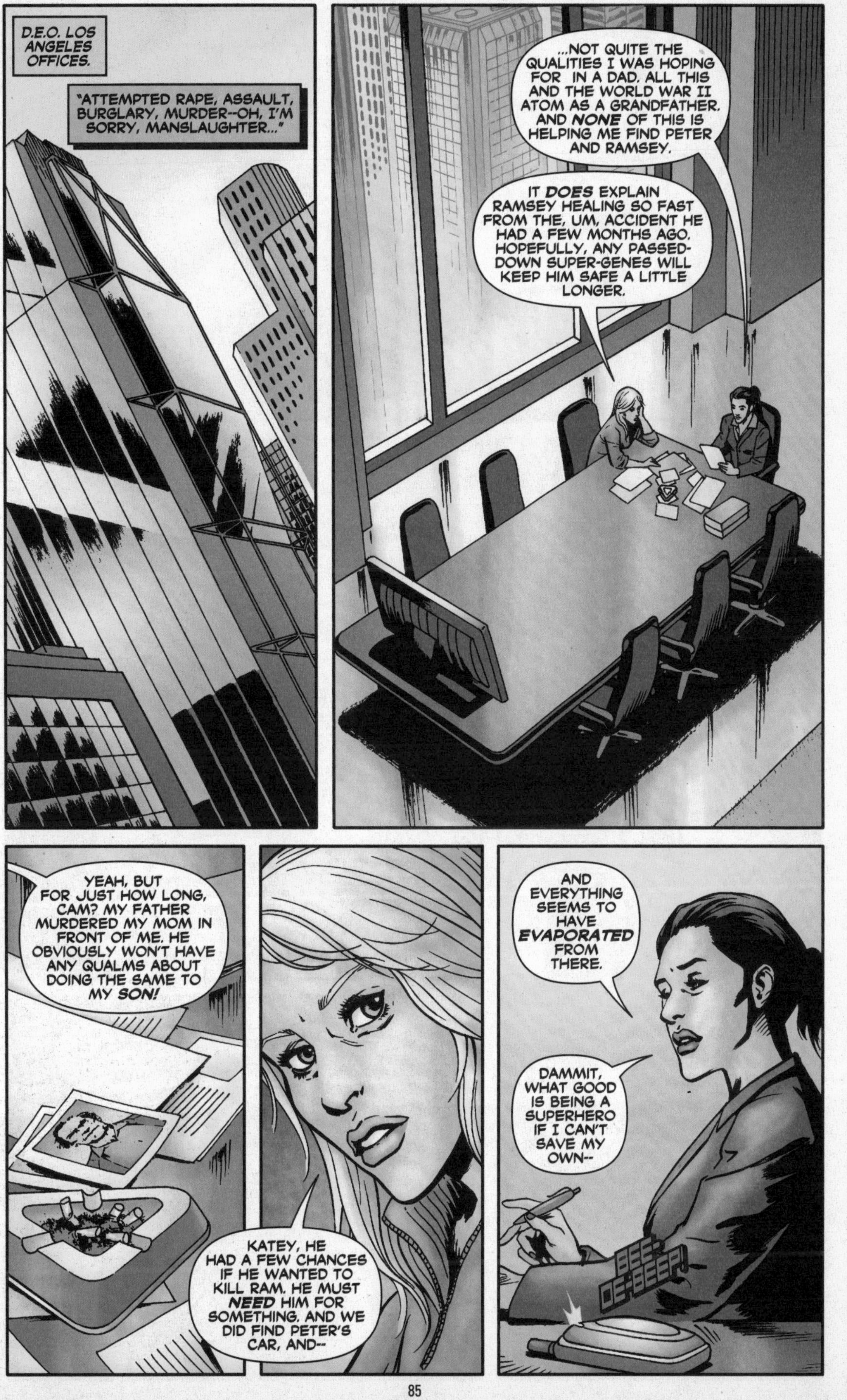
D.E.O. LOS ANGELES OFFICES.
"ATTEMPTED RAPE, ASSAULT, BURGLARY, MURDER--OH, I'M SORRY, MANSLAUGHTER..."
...NOT QUITE THE QUALITIES I WAS HOPING FOR IN A DAD. ALL THIS AND THE WORLD WAR II ATOM AS A GRANDFATHER. AND NONE OF THIS IS HELPING ME FIND PETER AND RAMSEY.
IT DOES EXPLAIN RAMSEY HEALING SO FAST FROM THE, UM, ACCIDENT HE HAD A FEW MONTHS AGO. HOPEFULLY, ANY PASSED-DOWN SUPER-GENES WILL KEEP HIM SAFE A LITTLE LONGER.
YEAH, BUT FOR JUST HOW LONG, CAM? MY FATHER MURDERED MY MOM IN FRONT OF ME. HE OBVIOUSLY WON'T HAVE ANY QUALMS ABOUT DOING THE SAME TO MY SON!
KATEY, HE HAD A FEW CHANCES IF HE WANTED TO KILL RAM. HE MUST NEED HIM FOR SOMETHING. AND WE DID FIND PETER'S CAR, AND--
AND EVERYTHING SEEMS TO HAVE EVAPORATED FROM THERE.
DAMMIT, WHAT GOOD IS BEING A SUPERHERO IF I CAN'T SAVE MY OWN--
BEE-DE-BEEP!

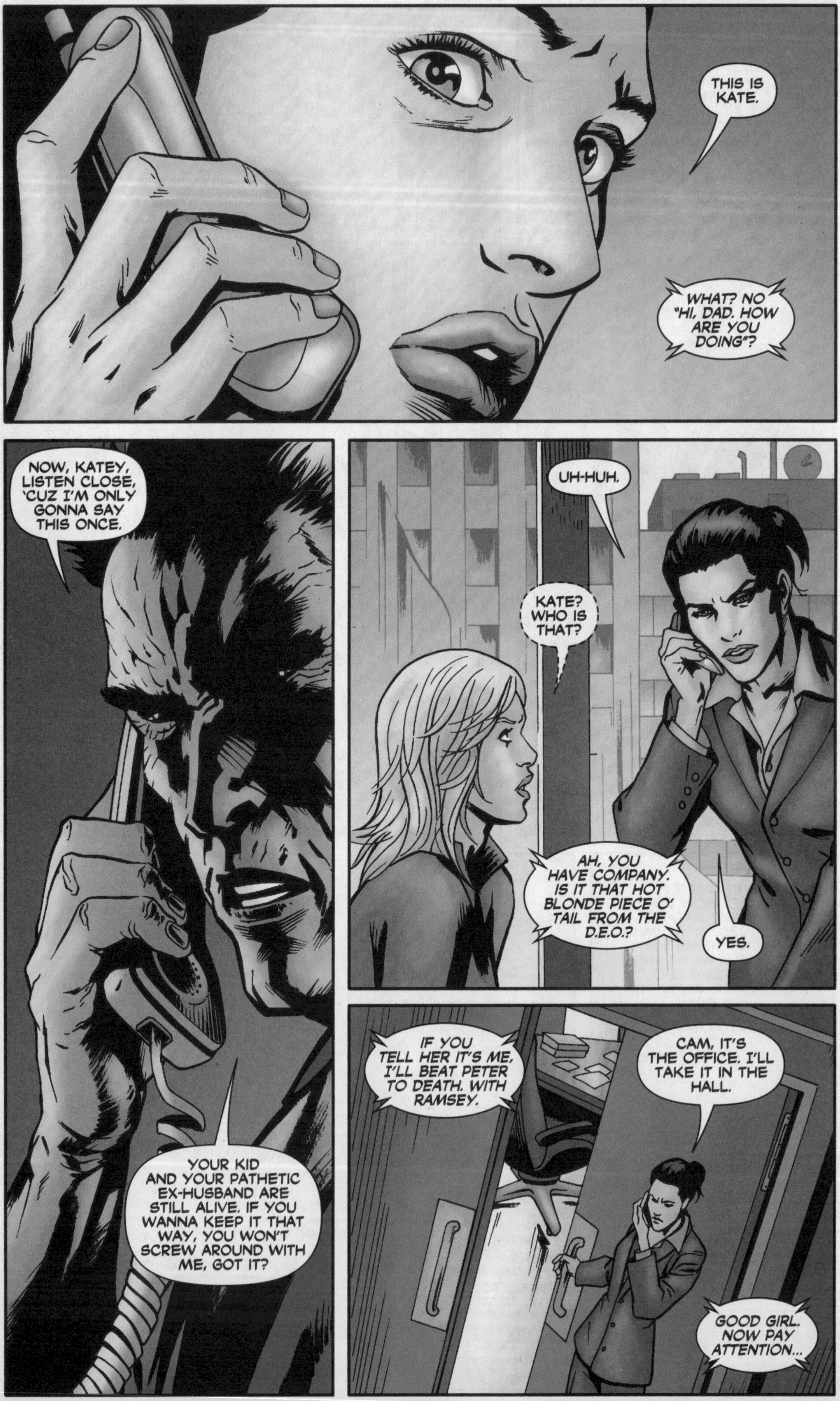
THIS IS KATE.
WHAT? NO "HI, DAD. HOW ARE YOU DOING"?
NOW, KATEY, LISTEN CLOSE, 'CUZ I'M ONLY GONNA SAY THIS ONCE.
YOUR KID AND YOUR PATHETIC EX-HUSBAND ARE STILL ALIVE. IF YOU WANNA KEEP IT THAT WAY, YOU WON'T SCREW AROUND WITH ME, GOT IT?
UH-HUH.
KATE? WHO IS THAT?
AH, YOU HAVE COMPANY. IS IT THAT HOT BLONDE PIECE O' TAIL FROM THE D.E.O.?
YES.
IF YOU TELL HER IT'S ME, I'LL BEAT PETER TO DEATH. WITH RAMSEY.
CAM, IT'S THE OFFICE. I'LL TAKE IT IN THE HALL.
GOOD GIRL. NOW PAY ATTENTION...

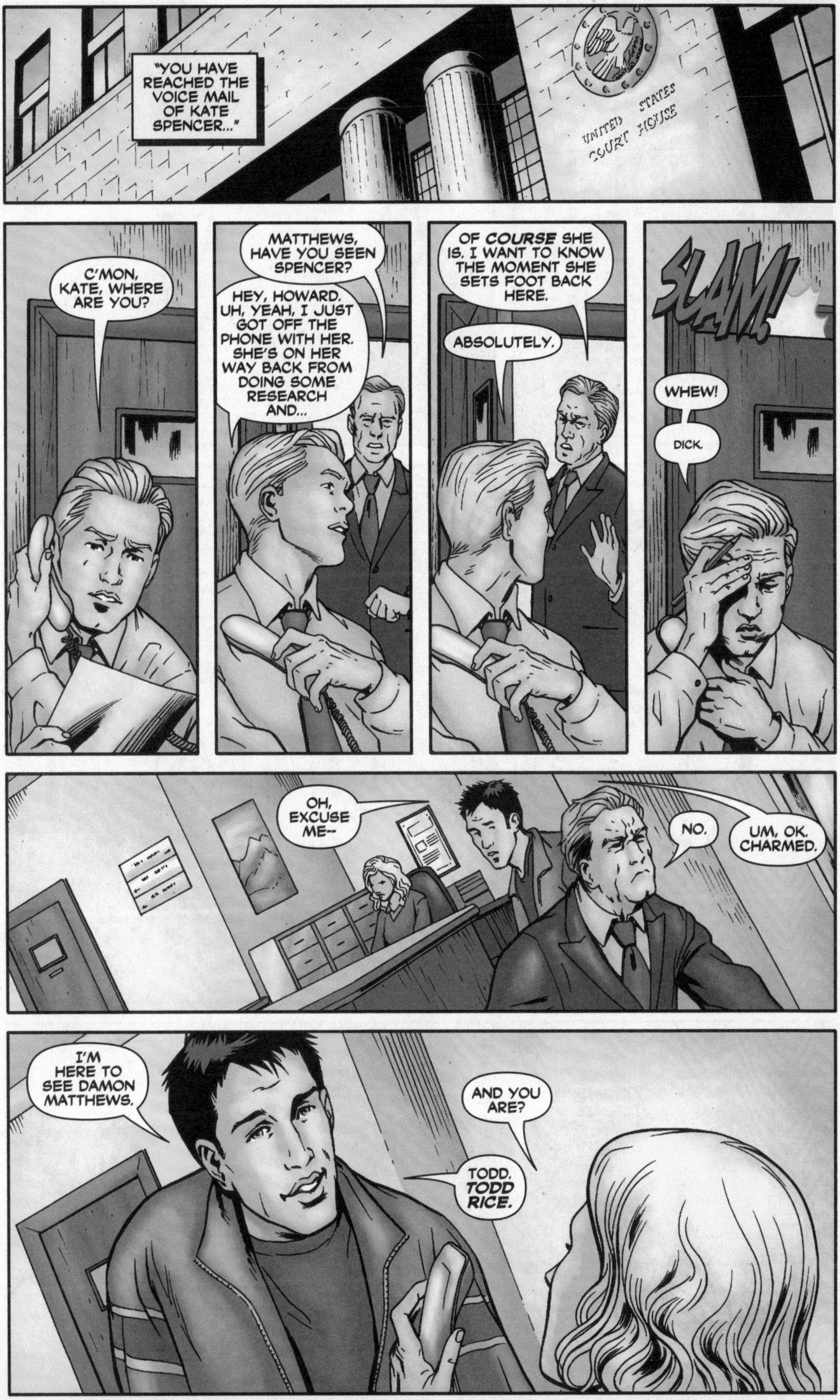
"YOU HAVE REACHED THE VOICE MAIL OF KATE SPENCER..."
UNITED STATES COURT HOUSE
C'MON, KATE, WHERE ARE YOU?
MATTHEWS, HAVE YOU SEEN SPENCER?
HEY, HOWARD. UH, YEAH, I JUST GOT OFF THE PHONE WITH HER. SHE'S ON HER WAY BACK FROM DOING SOME RESEARCH AND...
OF COURSE SHE IS. I WANT TO KNOW THE MOMENT SHE SETS FOOT BACK HERE.
ABSOLUTELY.
SLAM!
WHEW!
DICK.
OH, EXCUSE ME--
NO.
UM, OK. CHARMED.
I'M HERE TO SEE DAMON MATTHEWS.
AND YOU ARE?
TODD. TODD RICE.

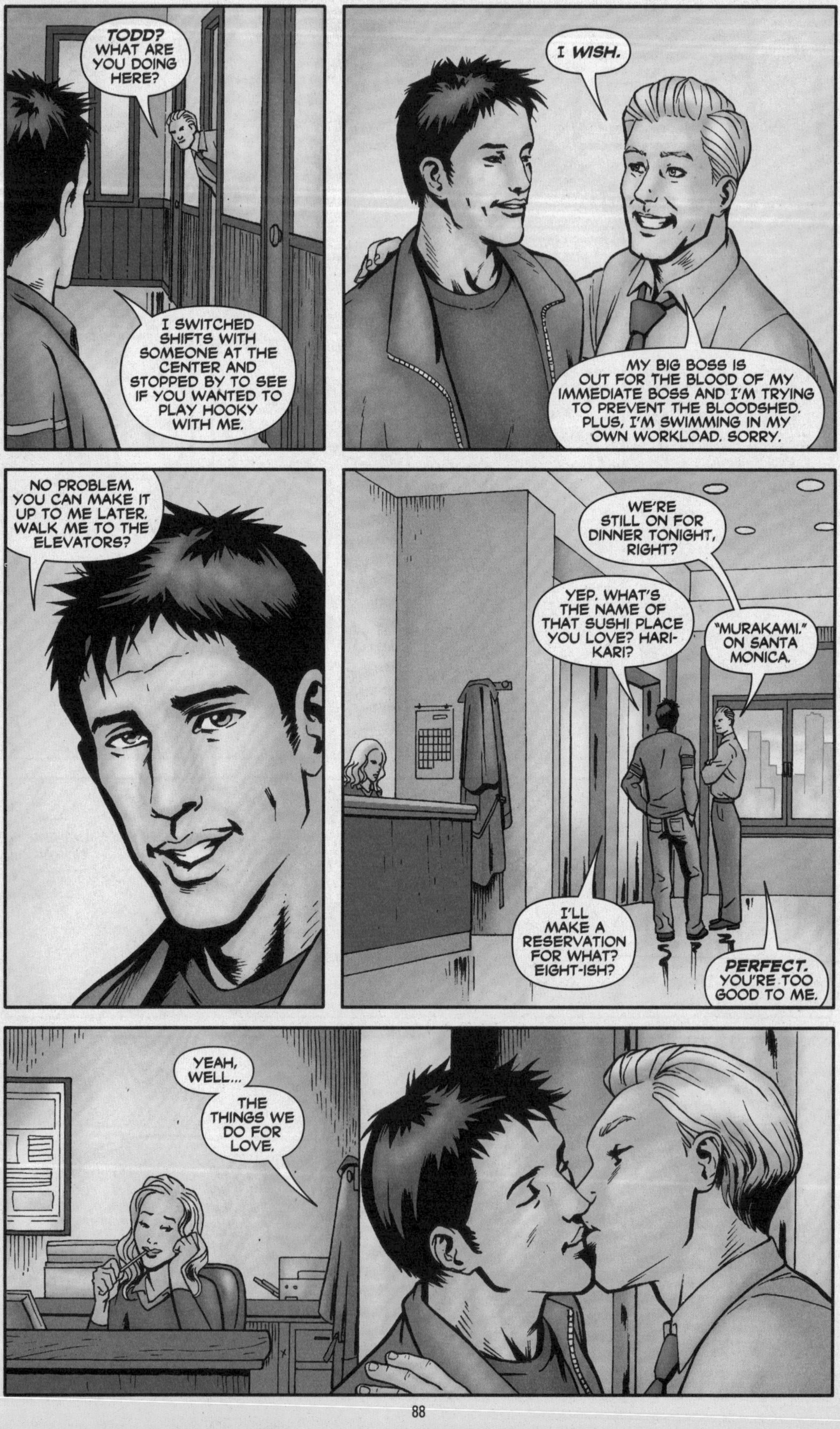
TODD? WHAT ARE YOU DOING HERE?
I SWITCHED SHIFTS WITH SOMEONE AT THE CENTER AND STOPPED BY TO SEE IF YOU WANTED TO PLAY HOOKY WITH ME.
I WISH.
MY BIG BOSS IS OUT FOR THE BLOOD OF MY IMMEDIATE BOSS AND I'M TRYING TO PREVENT THE BLOODSHED. PLUS, I'M SWIMMING IN MY OWN WORKLOAD. SORRY.
NO PROBLEM. YOU CAN MAKE IT UP TO ME LATER. WALK ME TO THE ELEVATORS?
WE'RE STILL ON FOR DINNER TONIGHT, RIGHT?
YEP. WHAT'S THE NAME OF THAT SUSHI PLACE YOU LOVE? HARI-KARI?
"MURAKAMI." ON SANTA MONICA.
I'LL MAKE A RESERVATION FOR WHAT? EIGHT-ISH?
PERFECT. YOU'RE TOO GOOD TO ME.
YEAH, WELL...
THE THINGS WE DO FOR LOVE.

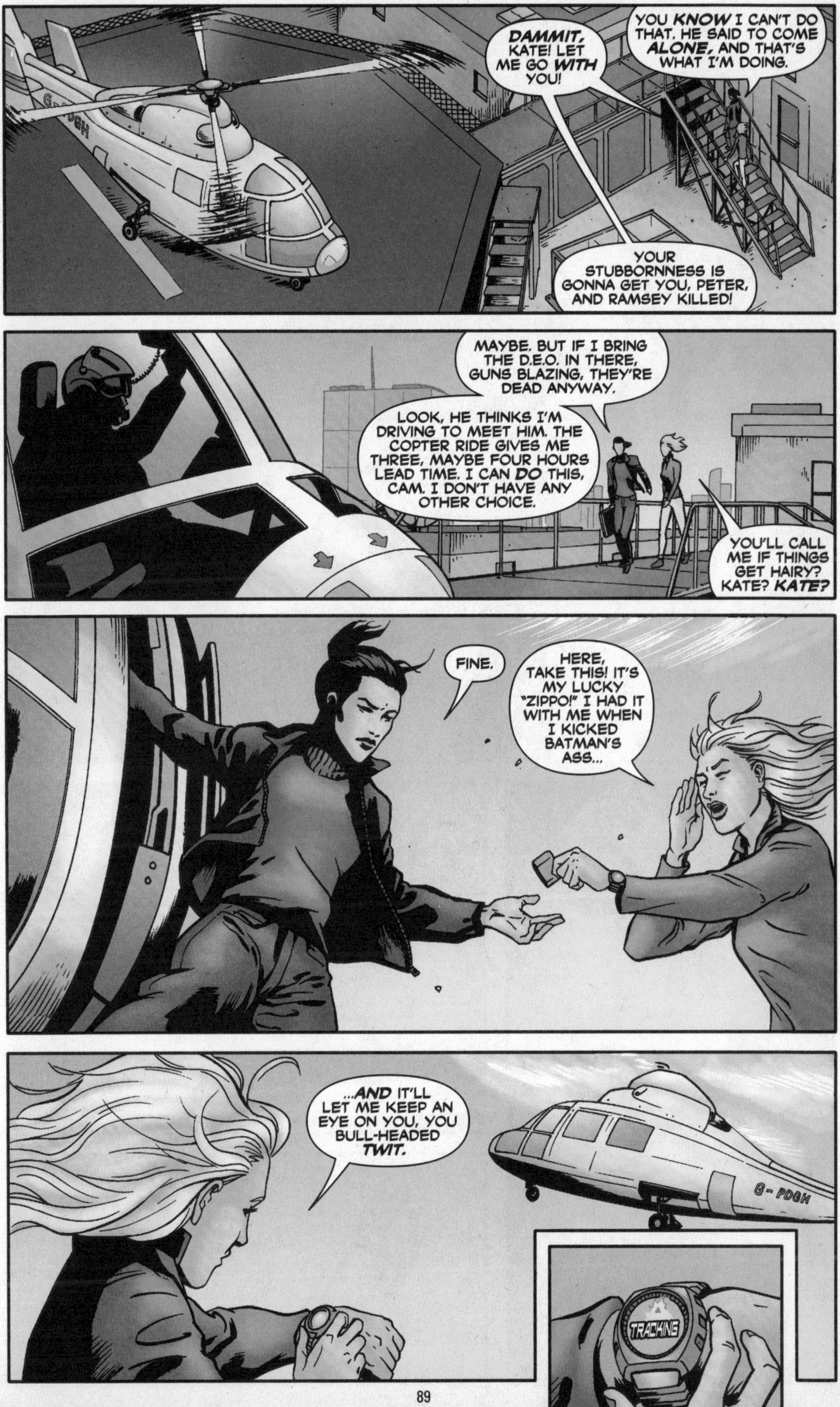
DAMMIT, KATE! LET ME GO WITH YOU!
YOU KNOW I CAN'T DO THAT. HE SAID TO COME ALONE, AND THAT'S WHAT I'M DOING.
YOUR STUBBORNNESS IS GONNA GET YOU, PETER, AND RAMSEY KILLED!
MAYBE. BUT IF I BRING THE D.E.O. IN THERE, GUNS BLAZING, THEY'RE DEAD ANYWAY.
LOOK, HE THINKS I'M DRIVING TO MEET HIM. THE COPTER RIDE GIVES ME THREE, MAYBE FOUR HOURS LEAD TIME. I CAN DO THIS, CAM. I DON'T HAVE ANY OTHER CHOICE.
YOU'LL CALL ME IF THINGS GET HAIRY? KATE? KATE?
FINE.
HERE, TAKE THIS! IT'S MY LUCKY "ZIPPO!" I HAD IT WITH ME WHEN I KICKED BATMAN'S ASS...
...AND IT'LL LET ME KEEP AN EYE ON YOU, YOU BULL-HEADED TWIT.
TRACKING

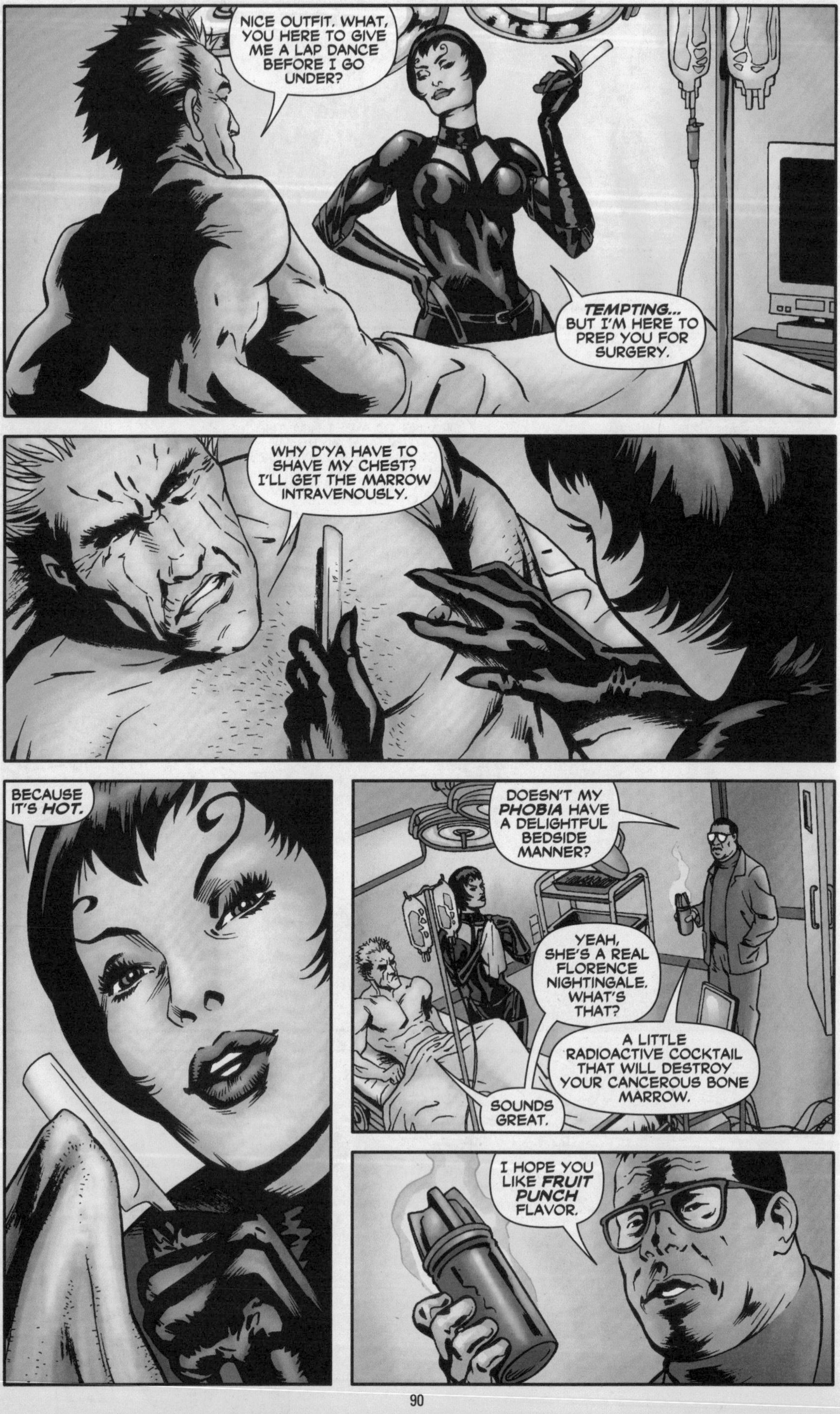
NICE OUTFIT. WHAT, YOU HERE TO GIVE ME A LAP DANCE BEFORE I GO UNDER?
TEMPTING... BUT I'M HERE TO PREP YOU FOR SURGERY.
WHY D'YA HAVE TO SHAVE MY CHEST? I'LL GET THE MARROW INTRAVENOUSLY.
BECAUSE IT'S HOT.
DOESN'T MY PHOBIA HAVE A DELIGHTFUL BEDSIDE MANNER?
YEAH, SHE'S A REAL FLORENCE NIGHTINGALE. WHAT'S THAT?
A LITTLE RADIOACTIVE COCKTAIL THAT WILL DESTROY YOUR CANCEROUS BONE MARROW.
SOUNDS GREAT.
I HOPE YOU LIKE FRUIT PUNCH FLAVOR.

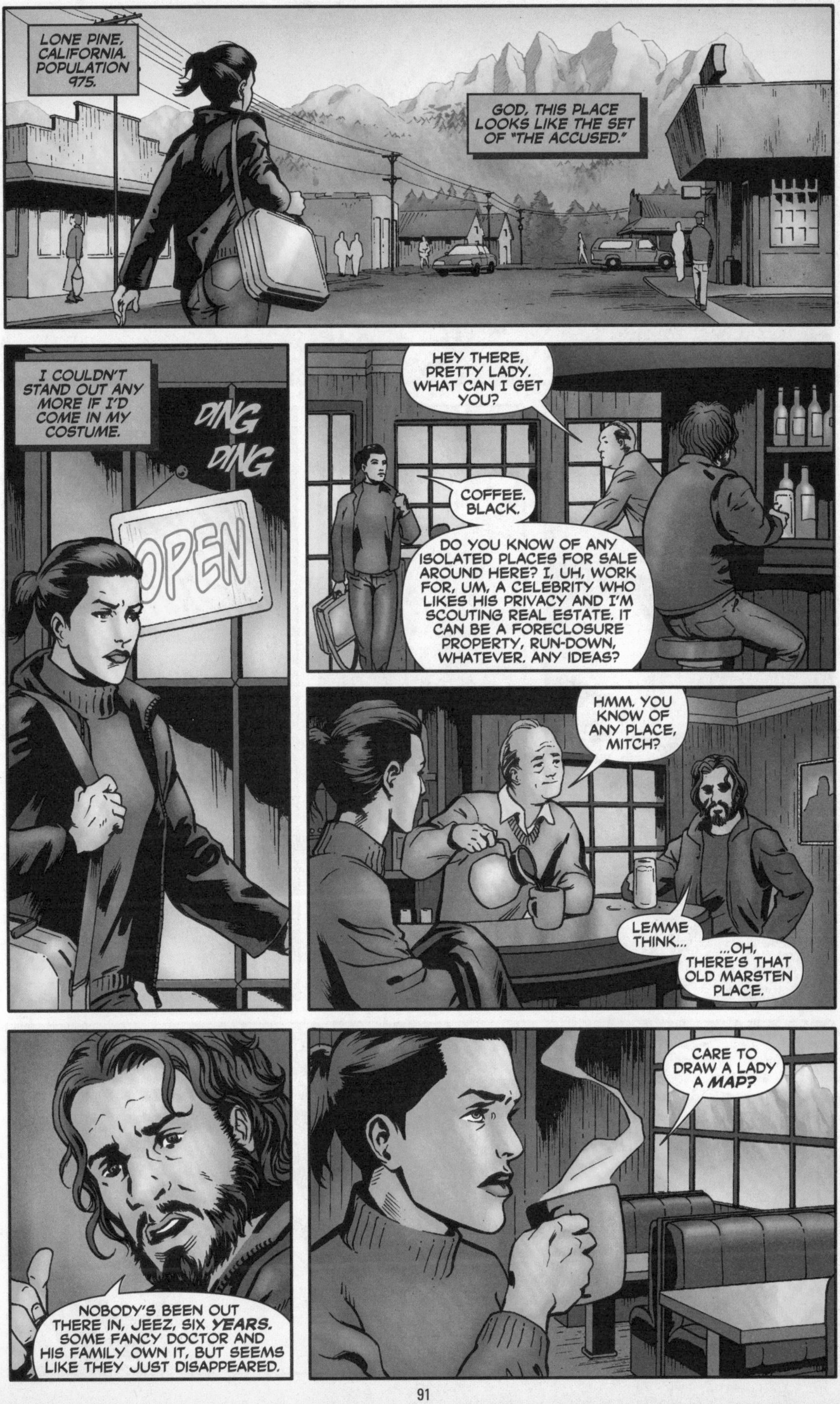
LONE PINE, CALIFORNIA. POPULATION 975.
GOD, THIS PLACE LOOKS LIKE THE SET OF "THE ACCUSED."
I COULDN'T STAND OUT ANY MORE IF I'D COME IN MY COSTUME.
DING DING
OPEN
HEY THERE, PRETTY LADY. WHAT CAN I GET YOU?
COFFEE. BLACK.
DO YOU KNOW OF ANY ISOLATED PLACES FOR SALE AROUND HERE? I, UH, WORK FOR, UM, A CELEBRITY WHO LIKES HIS PRIVACY AND I'M SCOUTING REAL ESTATE. IT CAN BE A FORECLOSURE PROPERTY, RUN-DOWN, WHATEVER. ANY IDEAS?
HMM. YOU KNOW OF ANY PLACE, MITCH?
LEMME THINK...
...OH, THERE'S THAT OLD MARSTEN PLACE.
NOBODY'S BEEN OUT THERE IN, JEEZ, SIX YEARS. SOME FANCY DOCTOR AND HIS FAMILY OWN IT, BUT SEEMS LIKE THEY JUST DISAPPEARED.
CARE TO DRAW A LADY A MAP?

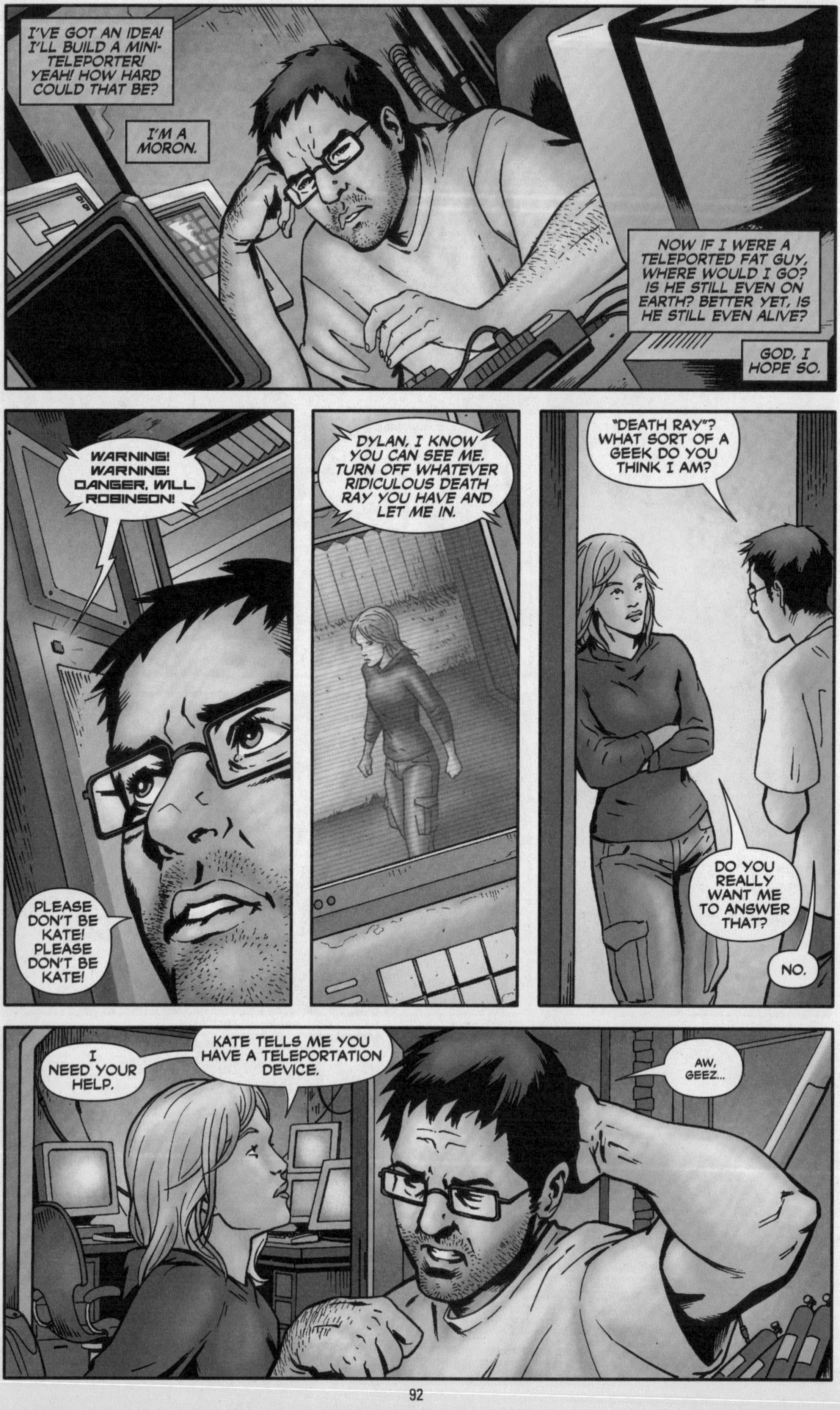
I'VE GOT AN IDEA! I'LL BUILD A MINI-TELEPORTER! YEAH! HOW HARD COULD THAT BE?
I'M A MORON.
NOW IF I WERE A TELEPORTED FAT GUY, WHERE WOULD I GO? IS HE STILL EVEN ON EARTH? BETTER YET, IS HE STILL EVEN ALIVE?
GOD, I HOPE SO.
WARNING! WARNING! DANGER, WILL ROBINSON!
PLEASE DON'T BE KATE! PLEASE DON'T BE KATE!
DYLAN, I KNOW YOU CAN SEE ME. TURN OFF WHATEVER RIDICULOUS DEATH RAY YOU HAVE AND LET ME IN.
"DEATH RAY"? WHAT SORT OF A GEEK DO YOU THINK I AM?
DO YOU REALLY WANT ME TO ANSWER THAT?
NO.
I NEED YOUR HELP.
KATE TELLS ME YOU HAVE A TELEPORTATION DEVICE.
AW, GEEZ...

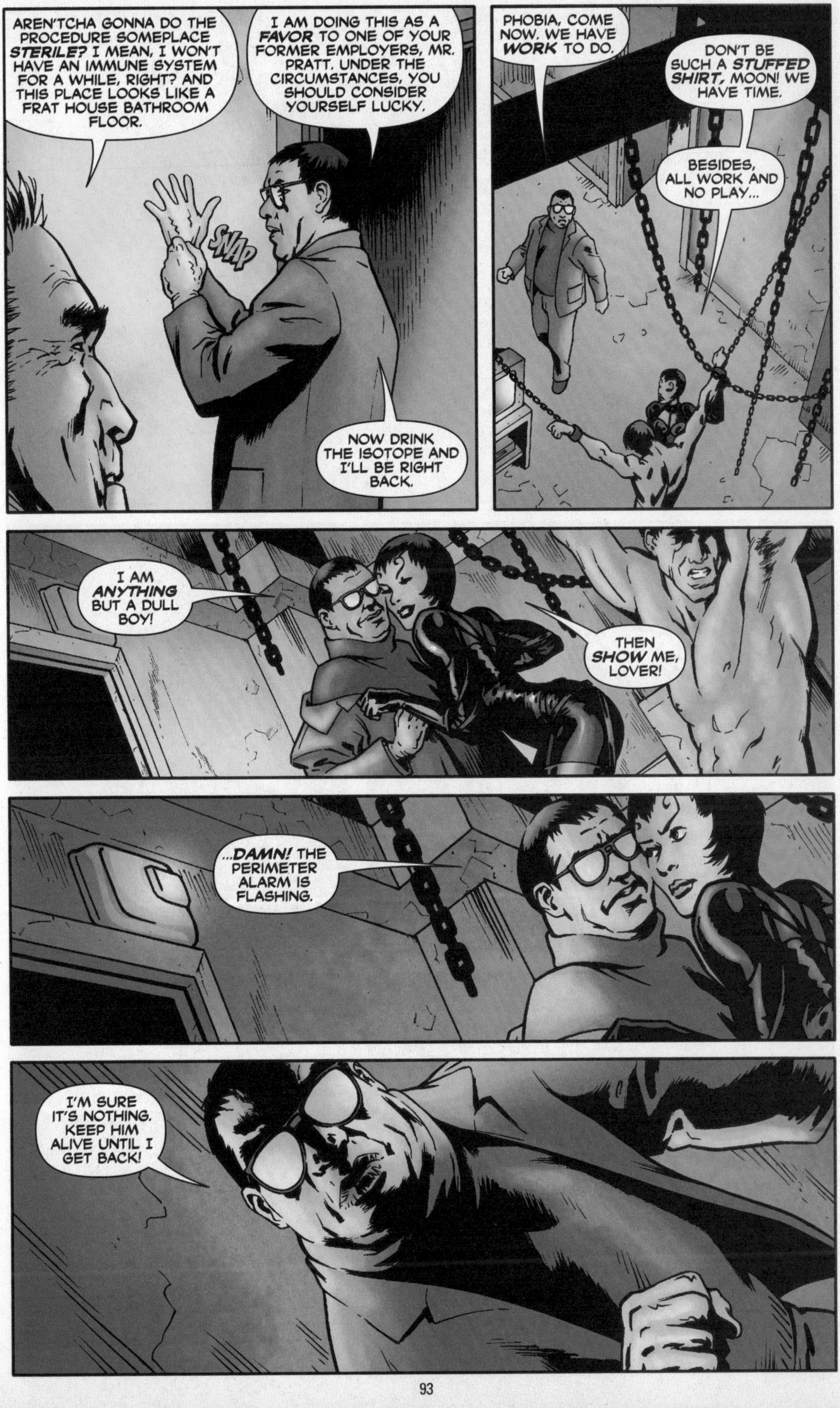
AREN'TCHA GONNA DO THE PROCEDURE SOMEPLACE STERILE? I MEAN, I WON'T HAVE AN IMMUNE SYSTEM FOR A WHILE, RIGHT? AND THIS PLACE LOOKS LIKE A FRAT HOUSE BATHROOM FLOOR.
I AM DOING THIS AS A FAVOR TO ONE OF YOUR FORMER EMPLOYERS, MR. PRATT. UNDER THE CIRCUMSTANCES, YOU SHOULD CONSIDER YOURSELF LUCKY.
SNAP
NOW DRINK THE ISOTOPE AND I'LL BE RIGHT BACK.
PHOBIA, COME NOW. WE HAVE WORK TO DO.
DON'T BE SUCH A STUFFED SHIRT, MOON! WE HAVE TIME.
BESIDES, ALL WORK AND NO PLAY...
I AM ANYTHING BUT A DULL BOY!
THEN SHOW ME, LOVER!
...DAMN! THE PERIMETER ALARM IS FLASHING.
I'M SURE IT'S NOTHING. KEEP HIM ALIVE UNTIL I GET BACK!

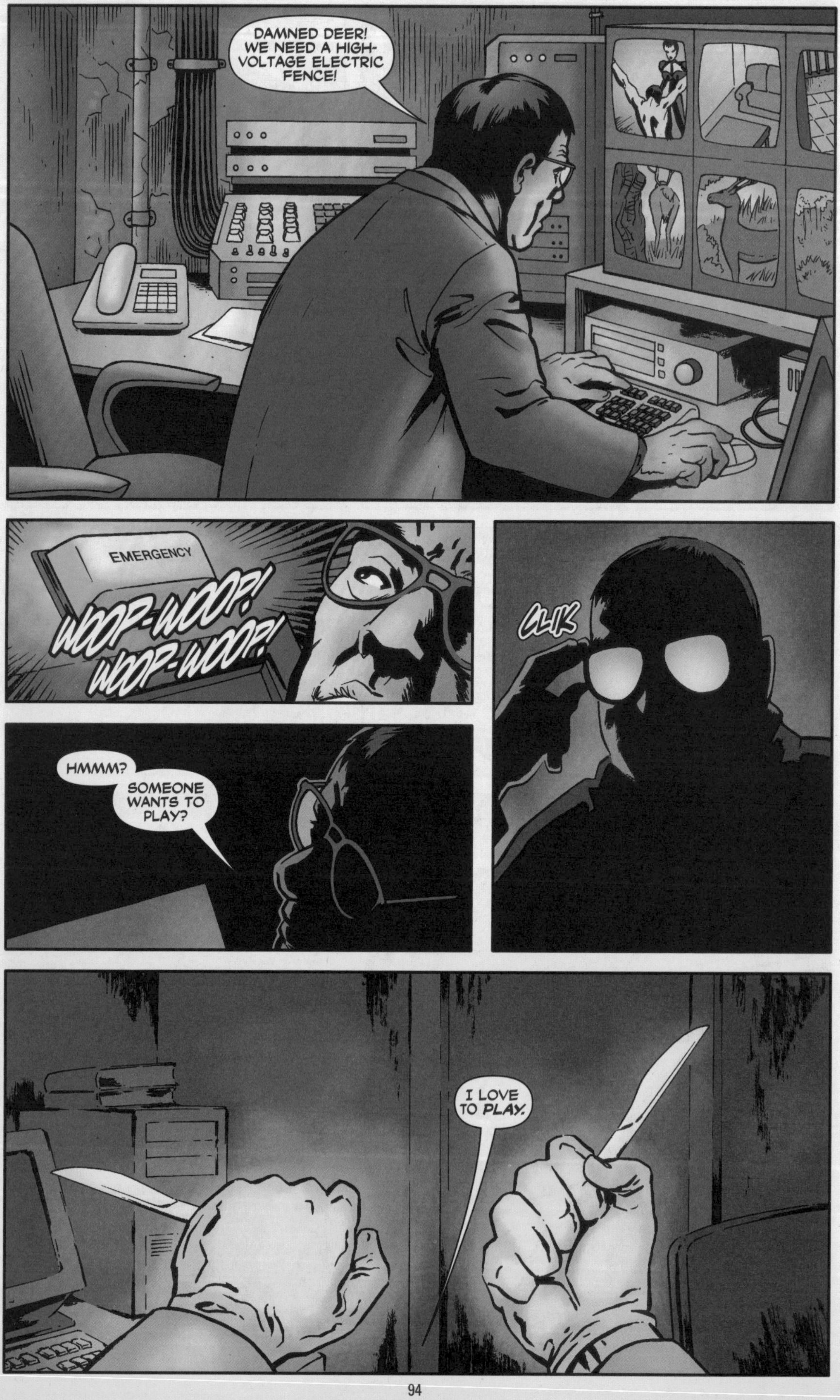
DAMNED DEER! WE NEED A HIGH-VOLTAGE ELECTRIC FENCE!
EMERGENCY
WOOP-WOOP! WOOP-WOOP!
CLIK
HMMM? SOMEONE WANTS TO PLAY?
I LOVE TO PLAY.

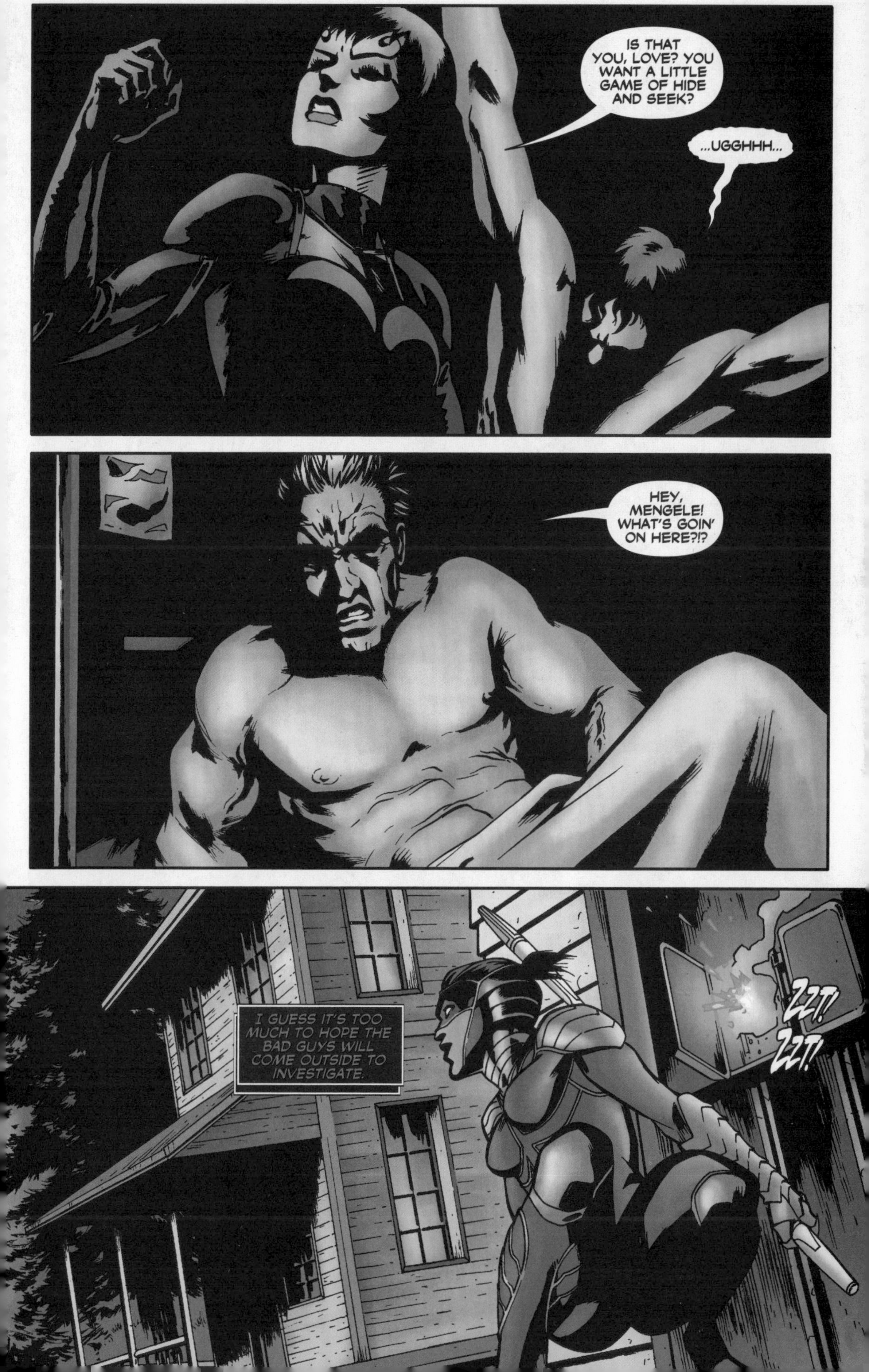
IS THAT YOU, LOVE? YOU WANT A LITTLE GAME OF HIDE AND SEEK?
...UGGHHH...
HEY, MENGELE! WHAT'S GOIN' ON HERE?!?
I GUESS IT'S TOO MUCH TO HOPE THE BAD GUYS WILL COME OUTSIDE TO INVESTIGATE.
ZZT!
ZZT!

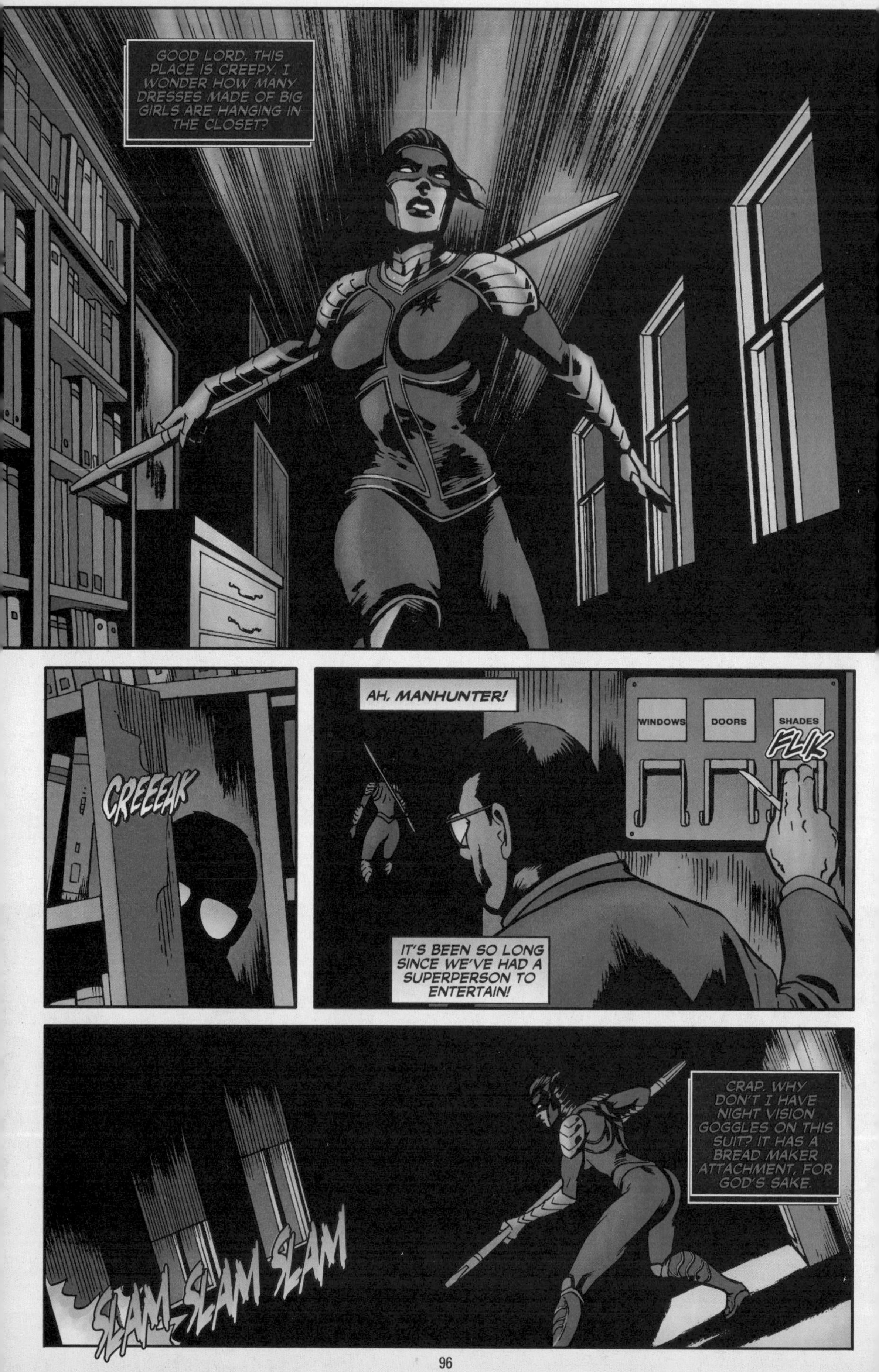
GOOD LORD. THIS PLACE IS CREEPY. I WONDER HOW MANY DRESSES MADE OF BIG GIRLS ARE HANGING IN THE CLOSET?
CREEEAK
AH, MANHUNTER!
WINDOWS
DOORS
SHADES
FLIK
IT'S BEEN SO LONG SINCE WE'VE HAD A SUPERPERSON TO ENTERTAIN!
CRAP. WHY DON'T I HAVE NIGHT VISION GOGGLES ON THIS SUIT? IT HAS A BREAD MAKER ATTACHMENT, FOR GOD'S SAKE.
SLAM SLAM SLAM

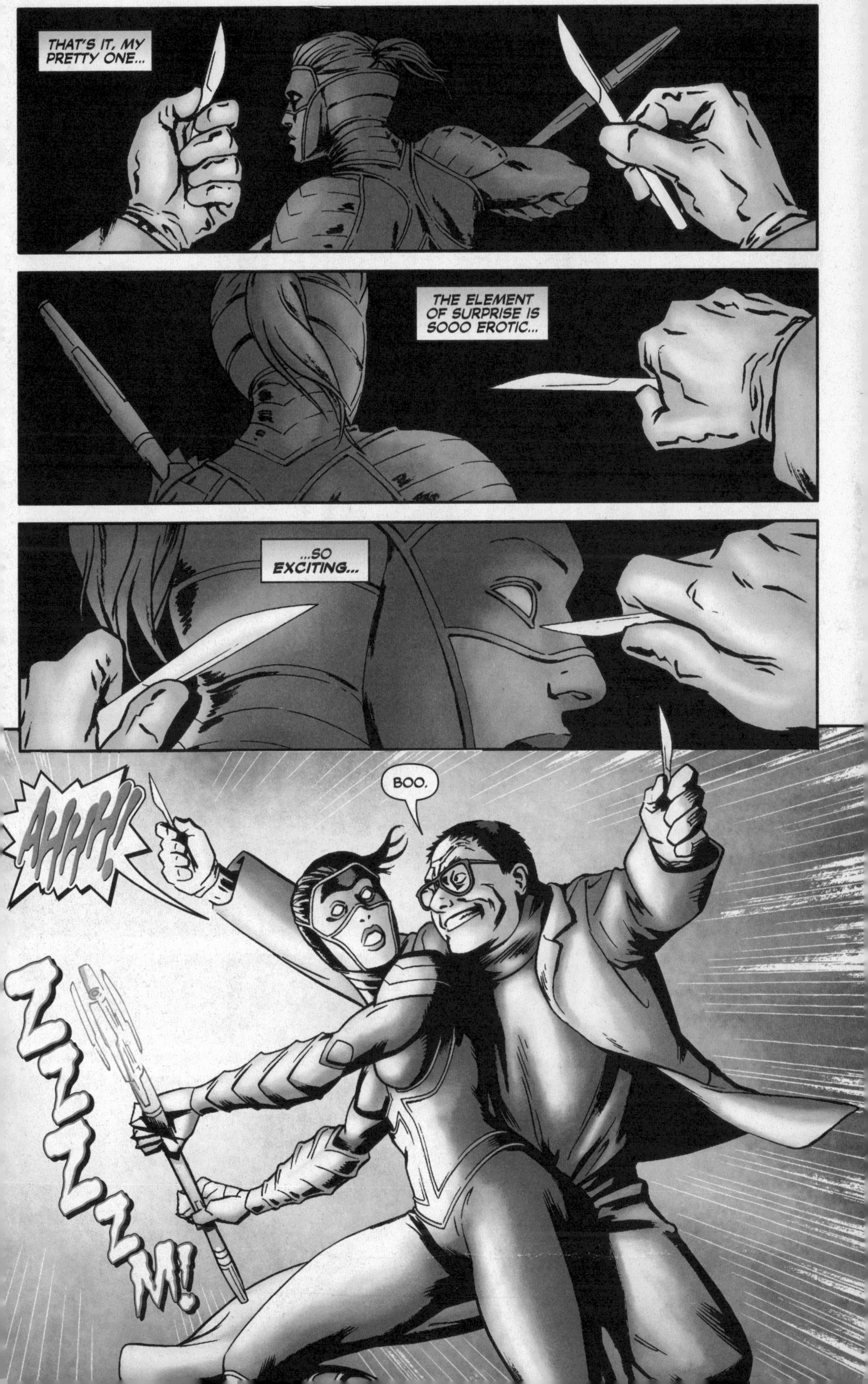
THAT'S IT, MY PRETTY ONE...
THE ELEMENT OF SURPRISE IS SOOO EROTIC...
...SO EXCITING...
AHHH!
BOO.
ZZZZZM!

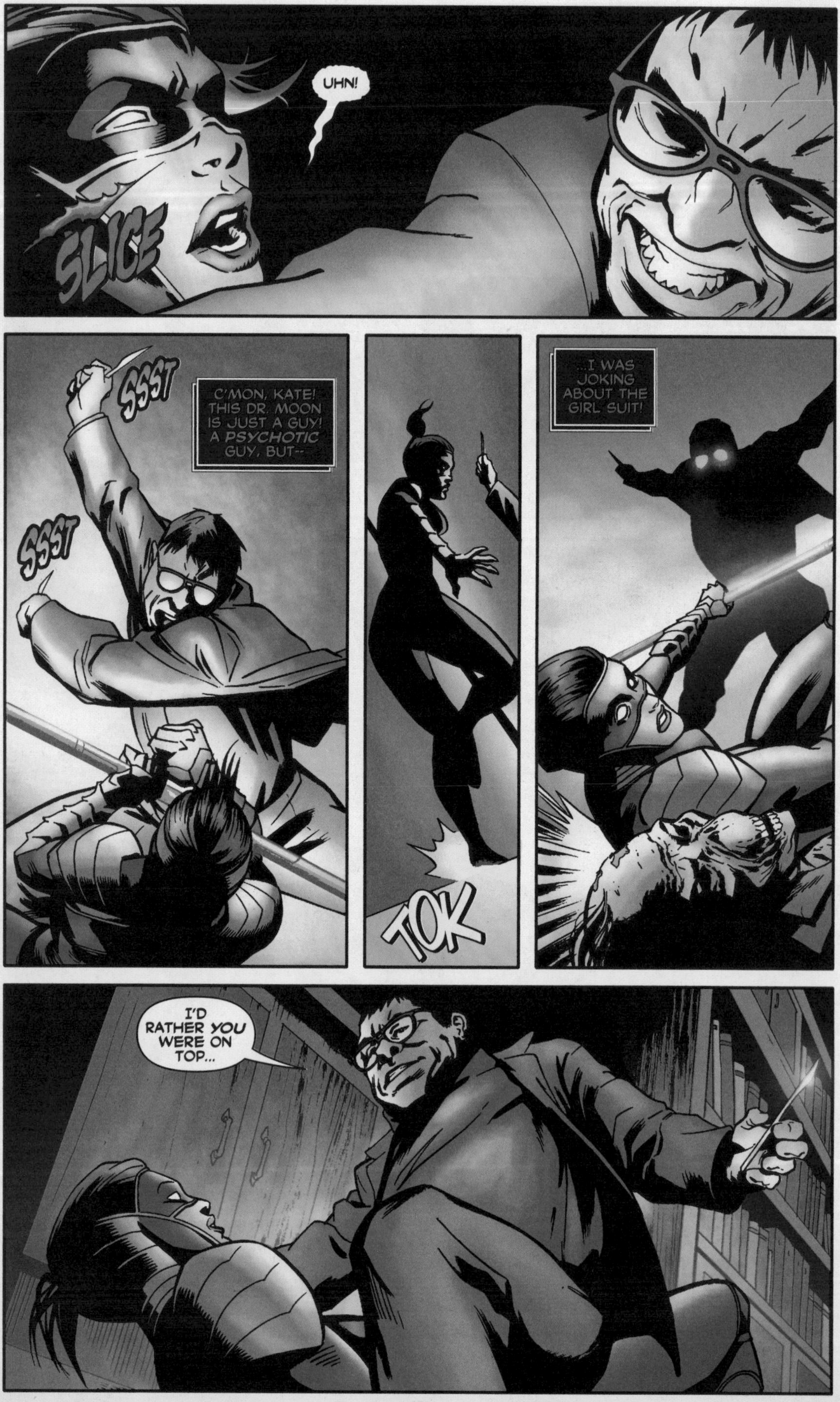
UHN!
SLICE
SSST
C'MON, KATE! THIS DR. MOON IS JUST A GUY! A PSYCHOTIC GUY, BUT--
SSST
TOK
...I WAS JOKING ABOUT THE GIRL SUIT!
I'D RATHER YOU WERE ON TOP...

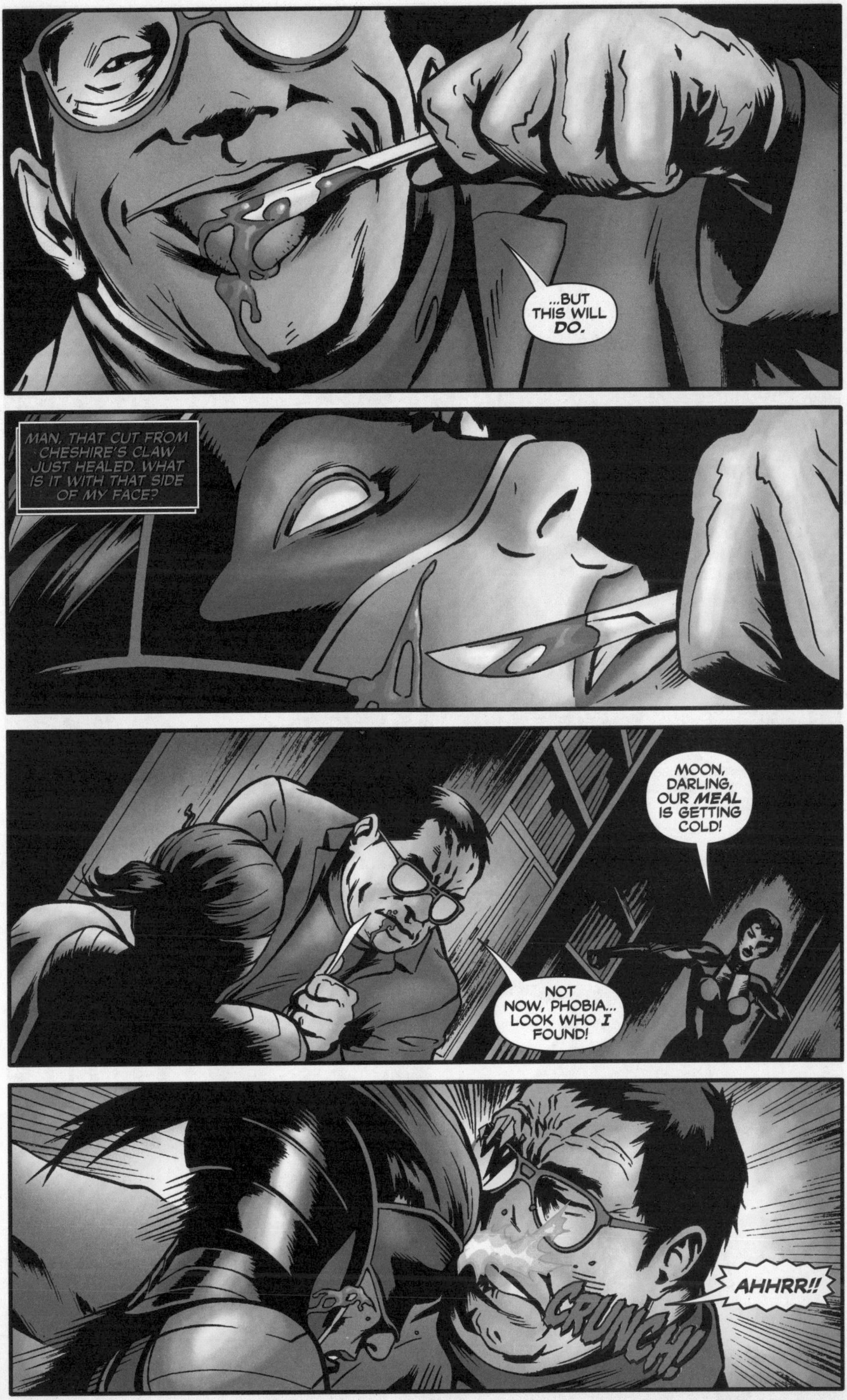
...BUT THIS WILL DO.
MAN, THAT CUT FROM CHESHIRE'S CLAW JUST HEALED. WHAT IS IT WITH THAT SIDE OF MY FACE?
MOON, DARLING, OUR MEAL IS GETTING COLD!
NOT NOW, PHOBIA... LOOK WHO I FOUND!
AHHRR!!
CRUNCH!

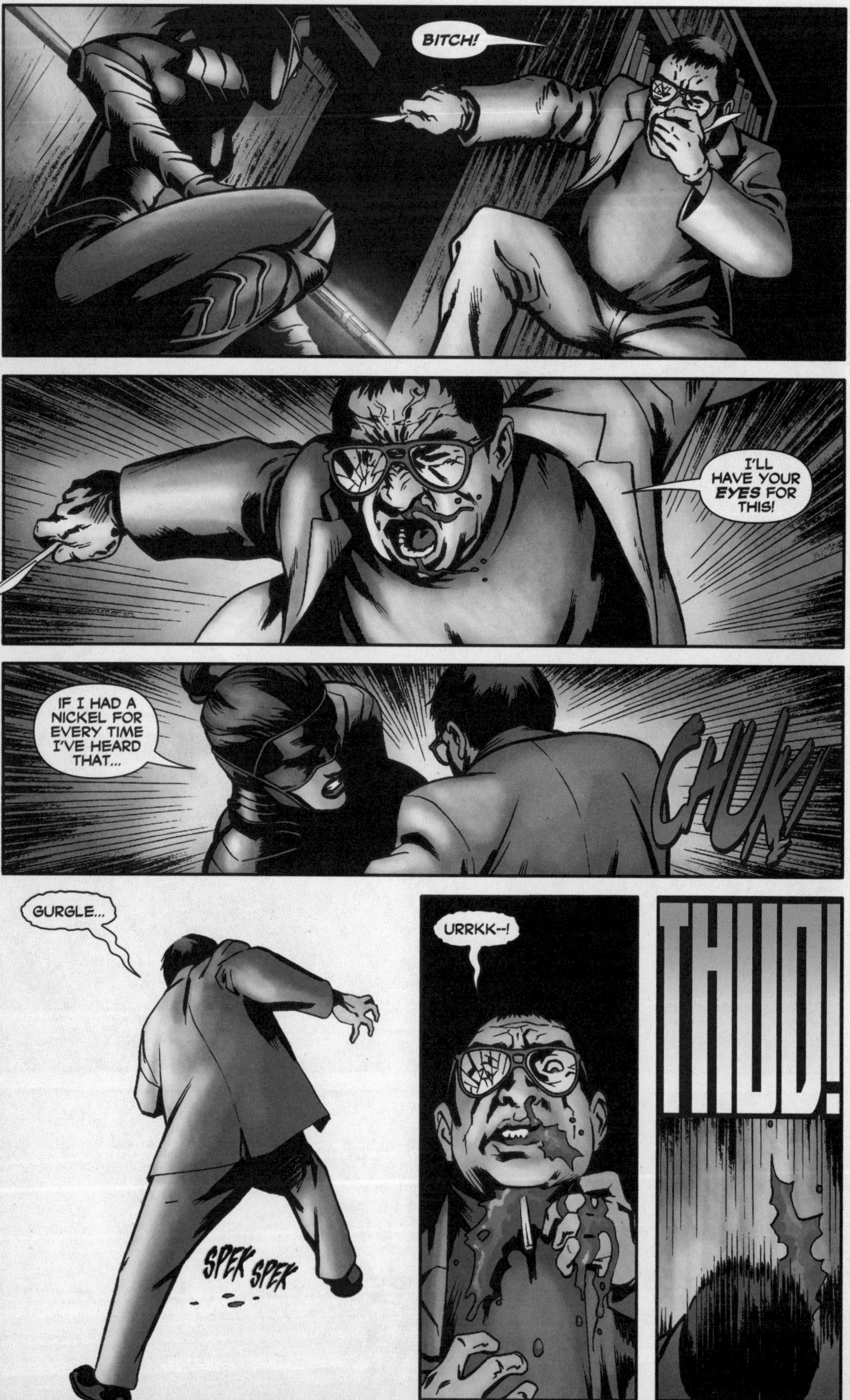
BITCH!
I'LL HAVE YOUR EYES FOR THIS!
IF I HAD A NICKEL FOR EVERY TIME I'VE HEARD THAT...
CHUK!
GURGLE...
SPEK SPEK
URRKK--!
THUD!

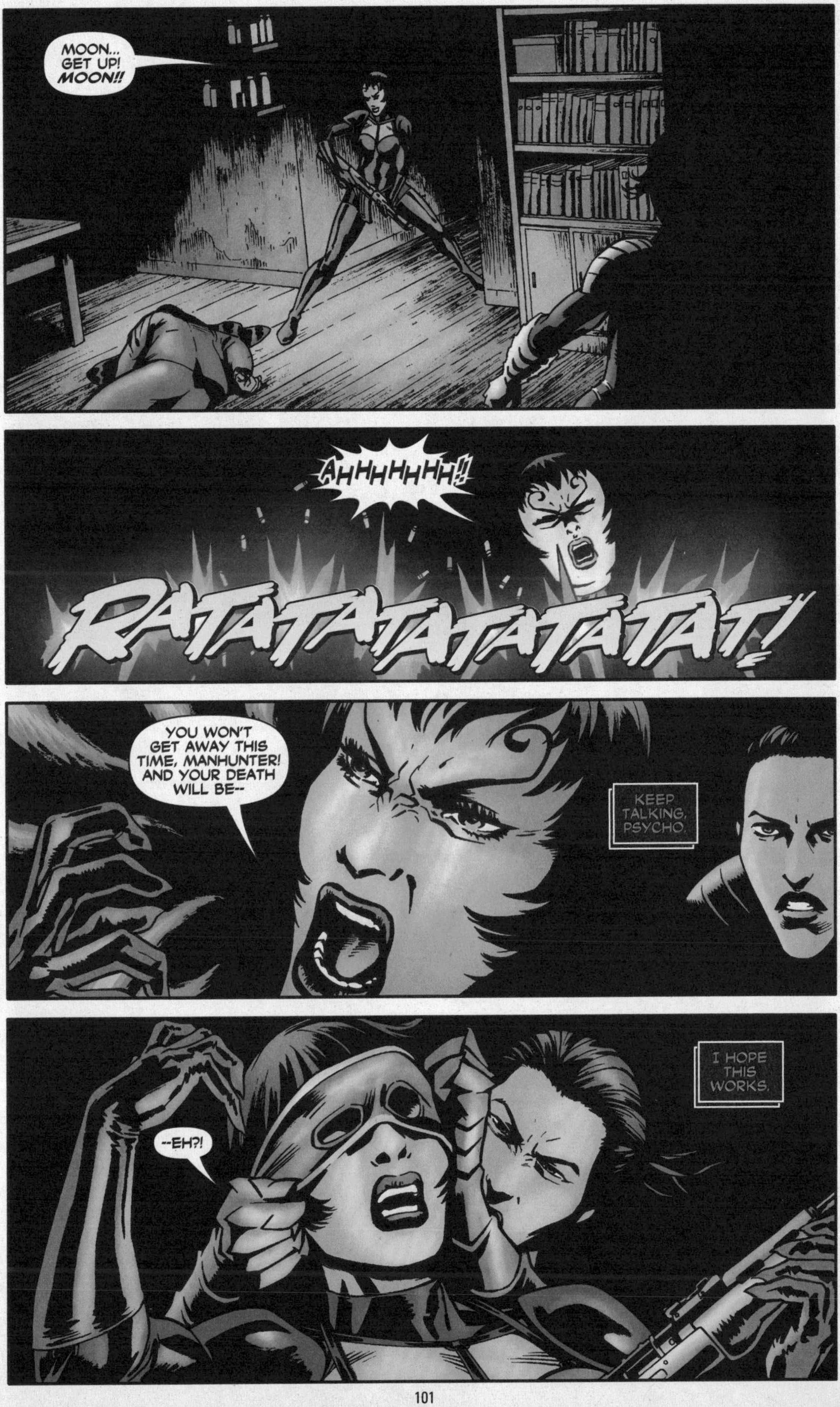
MOON... GET UP! MOON!!
AHHHHHHHH!!
RATATATATATATAT!
YOU WON'T GET AWAY THIS TIME, MANHUNTER! AND YOUR DEATH WILL BE--
KEEP TALKING, PSYCHO.
I HOPE THIS WORKS.
--EH?!

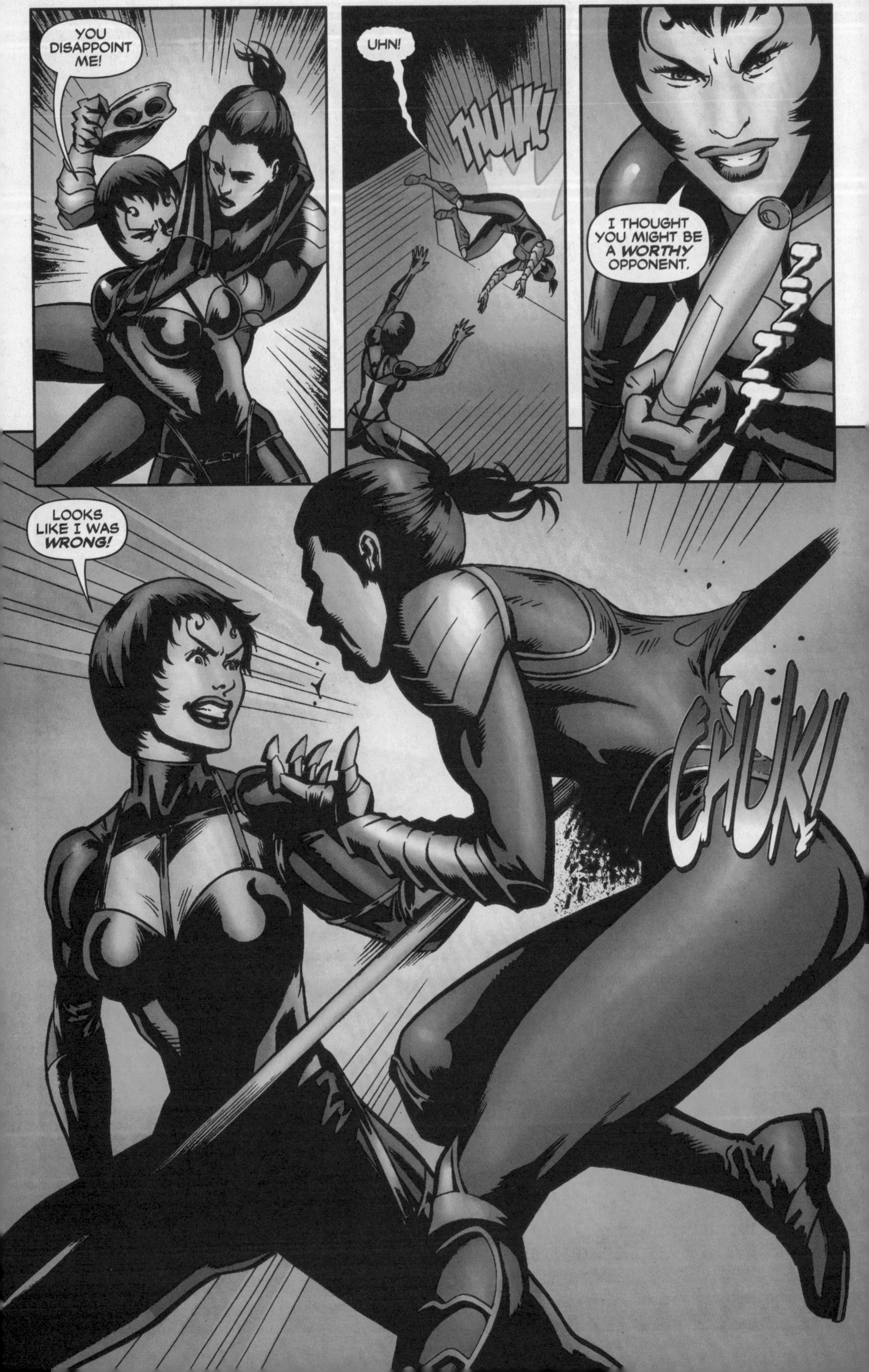

YOU DISAPPOINT ME!
UHN!
THUNK!
I THOUGHT YOU MIGHT BE A *WORTHY* OPPONENT.
ZZZZT
LOOKS LIKE I WAS *WRONG!*
CHUK!

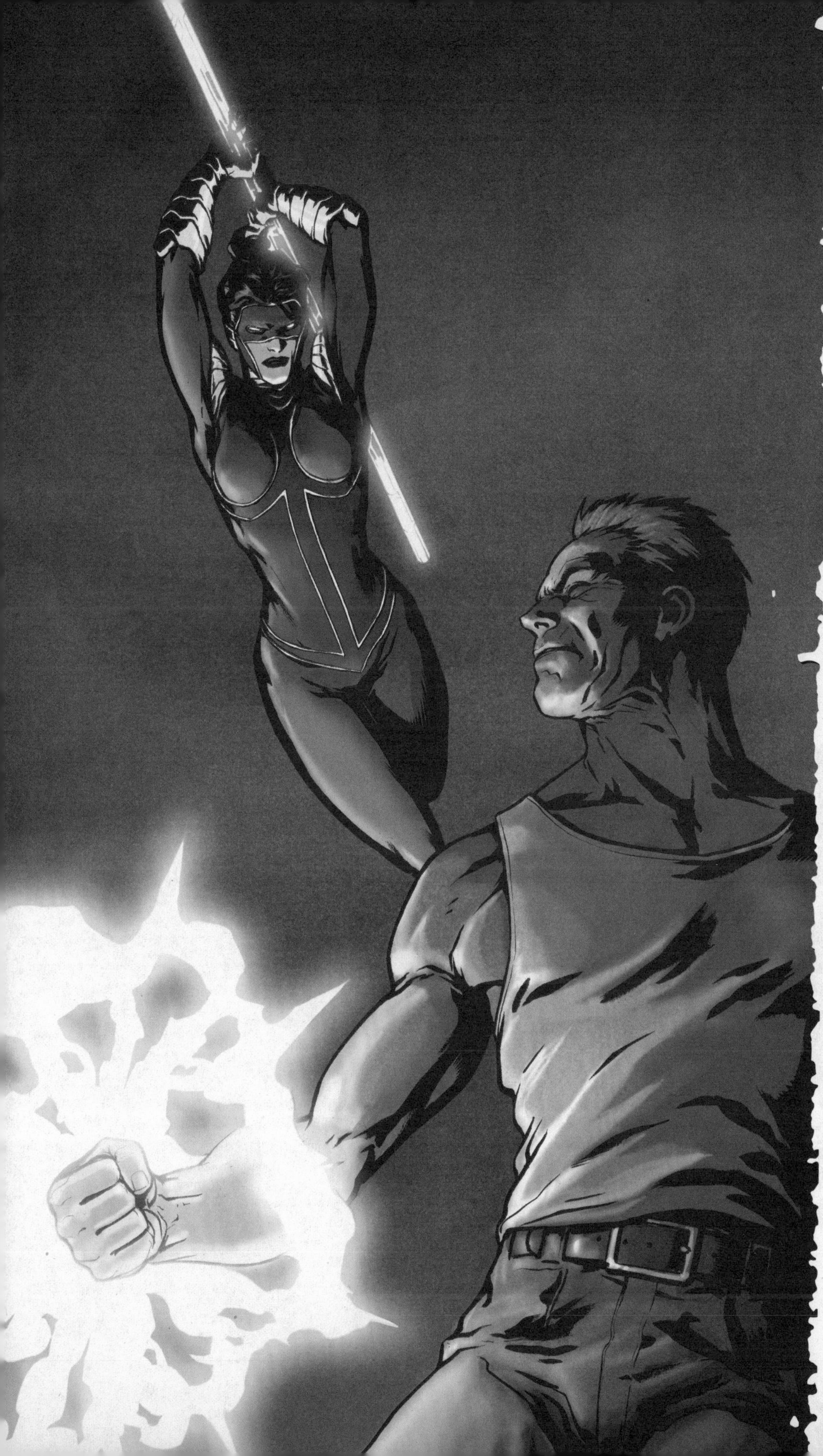

Issue #19 cover by Jesus Saiz & Jose Villarrubia

Interior art by Javier Pina & Fernando Blanco

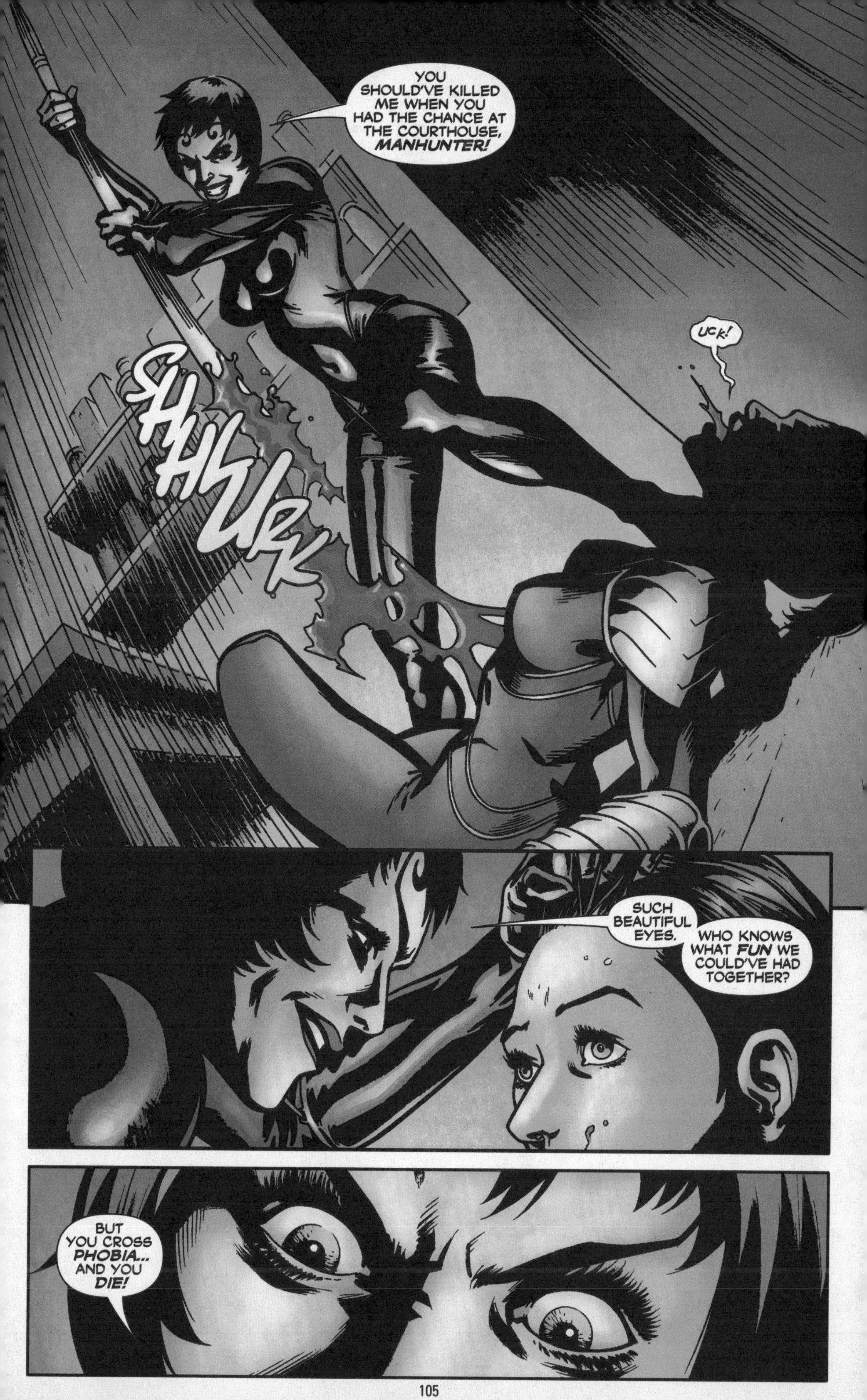
YOU SHOULD'VE KILLED ME WHEN YOU HAD THE CHANCE AT THE COURTHOUSE, *MANHUNTER!*
SHHHURK
UCK!
SUCH BEAUTIFUL EYES.
WHO KNOWS WHAT *FUN* WE COULD'VE HAD TOGETHER?
BUT YOU CROSS *PHOBIA*... AND YOU *DIE!*

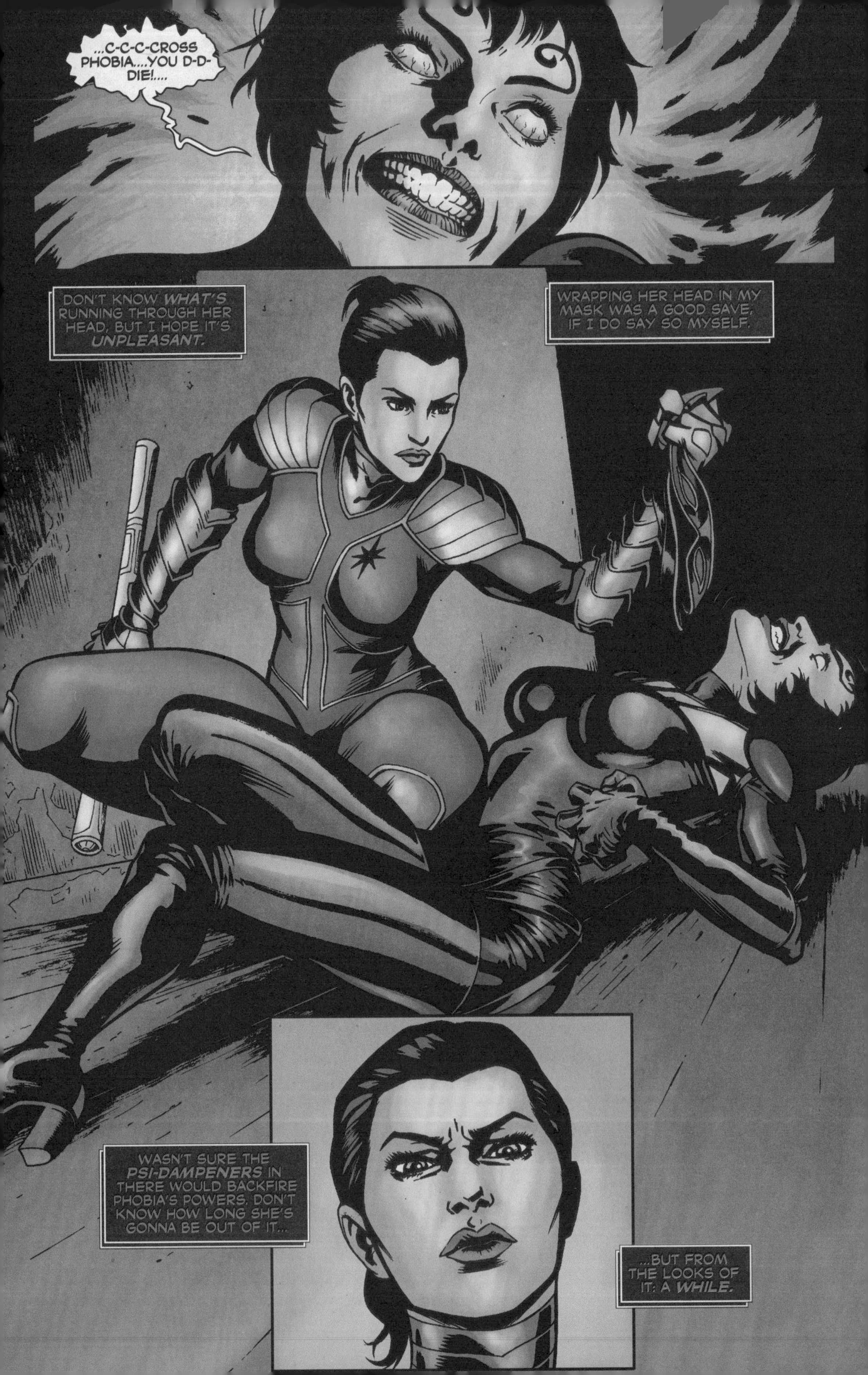
...C-C-C-CROSS PHOBIA....YOU D-D-DIE!....
DON'T KNOW WHAT'S RUNNING THROUGH HER HEAD, BUT I HOPE IT'S UNPLEASANT.
WRAPPING HER HEAD IN MY MASK WAS A GOOD SAVE, IF I DO SAY SO MYSELF.
WASN'T SURE THE PSI-DAMPENERS IN THERE WOULD BACKFIRE PHOBIA'S POWERS. DON'T KNOW HOW LONG SHE'S GONNA BE OUT OF IT...
...BUT FROM THE LOOKS OF IT: A WHILE.

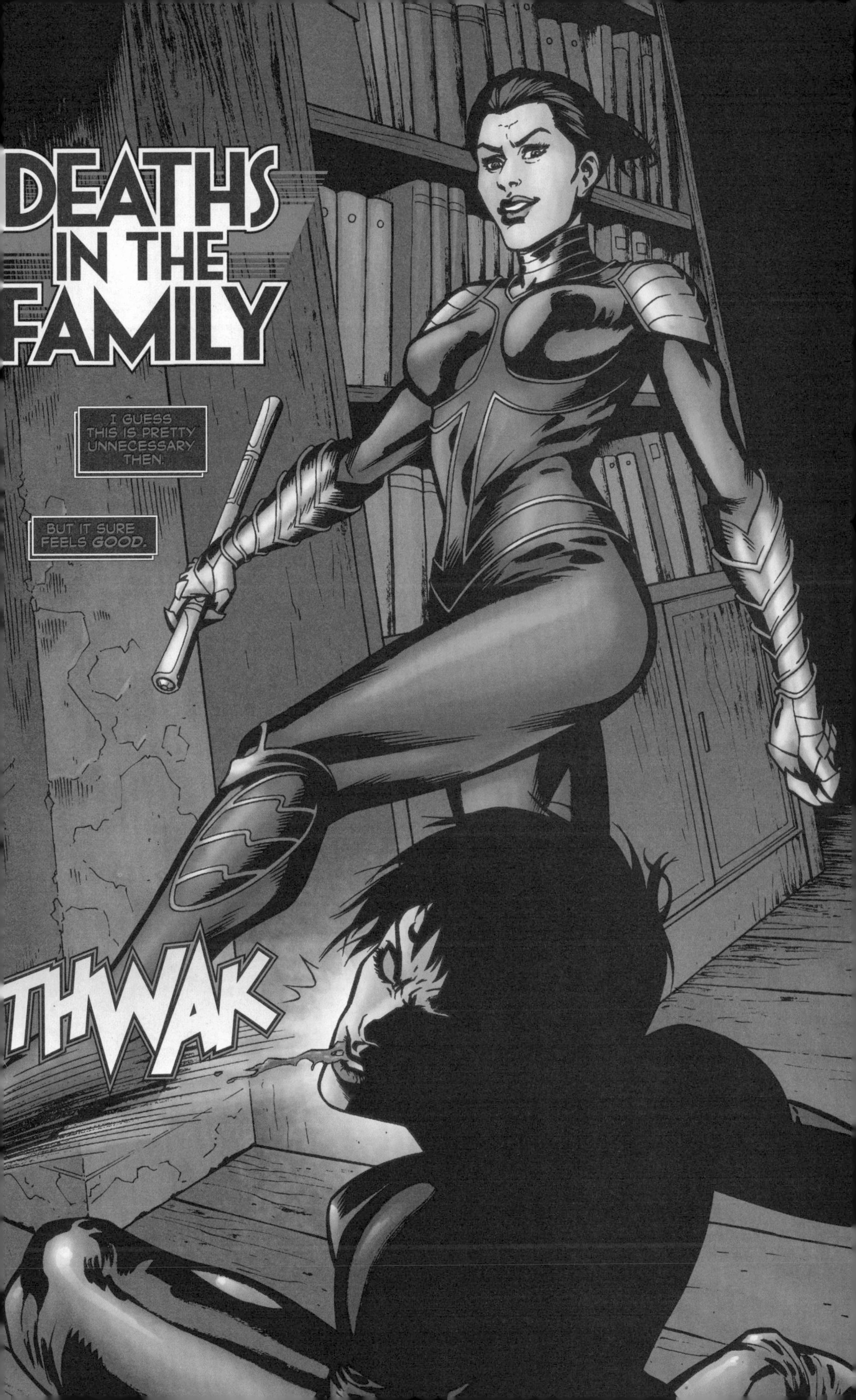
DEATHS IN THE FAMILY
I GUESS THIS IS PRETTY UNNECESSARY THEN.
BUT IT SURE FEELS *GOOD.*
THWAK

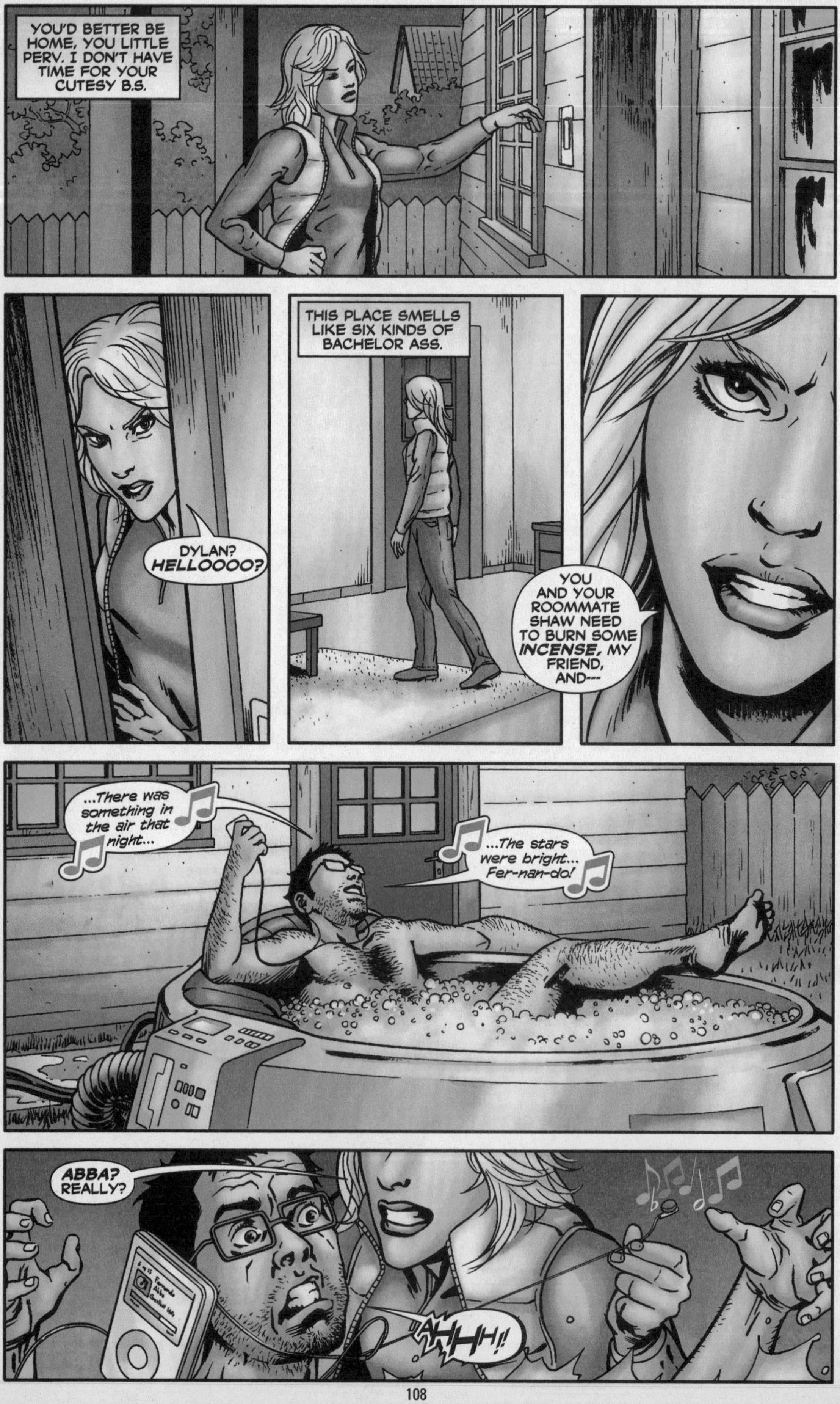
YOU'D BETTER BE HOME, YOU LITTLE PERV. I DON'T HAVE TIME FOR YOUR CUTESY B.S.
DYLAN? **HELLOOOO?**
THIS PLACE SMELLS LIKE SIX KINDS OF BACHELOR ASS.
YOU AND YOUR ROOMMATE SHAW NEED TO BURN SOME **INCENSE,** MY FRIEND, AND---
...There was something in the air that night...
...The stars were bright... Fer-nan-do!
ABBA? REALLY?
AHHHH!!

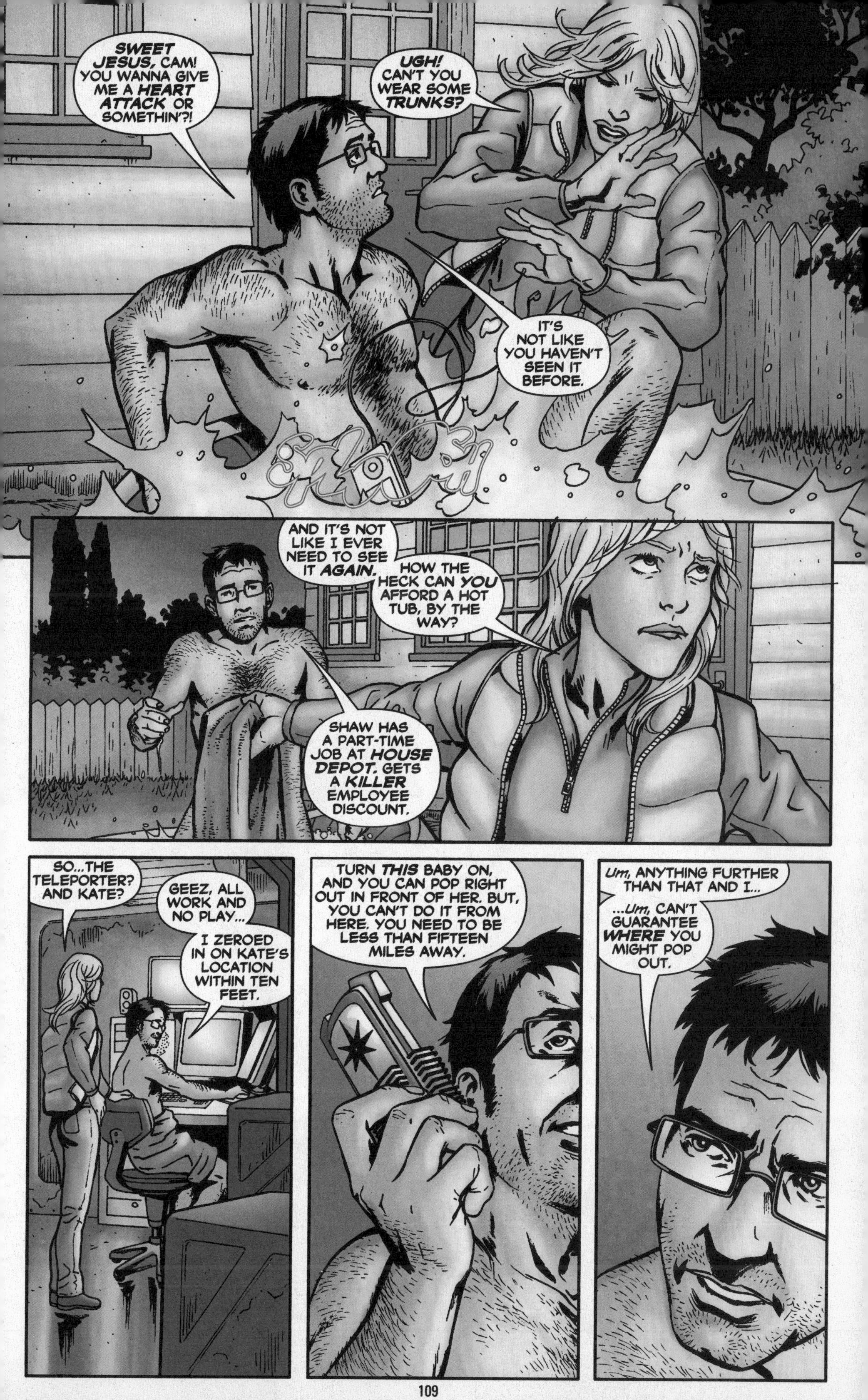
SWEET JESUS, CAM! YOU WANNA GIVE ME A HEART ATTACK OR SOMETHIN'?!
UGH! CAN'T YOU WEAR SOME TRUNKS?
IT'S NOT LIKE YOU HAVEN'T SEEN IT BEFORE.
AND IT'S NOT LIKE I EVER NEED TO SEE IT AGAIN.
HOW THE HECK CAN YOU AFFORD A HOT TUB, BY THE WAY?
SHAW HAS A PART-TIME JOB AT HOUSE DEPOT. GETS A KILLER EMPLOYEE DISCOUNT.
SO...THE TELEPORTER? AND KATE?
GEEZ, ALL WORK AND NO PLAY...
I ZEROED IN ON KATE'S LOCATION WITHIN TEN FEET.
TURN THIS BABY ON, AND YOU CAN POP RIGHT OUT IN FRONT OF HER. BUT, YOU CAN'T DO IT FROM HERE. YOU NEED TO BE LESS THAN FIFTEEN MILES AWAY.
Um, ANYTHING FURTHER THAN THAT AND I...
...Um, CAN'T GUARANTEE WHERE YOU MIGHT POP OUT.

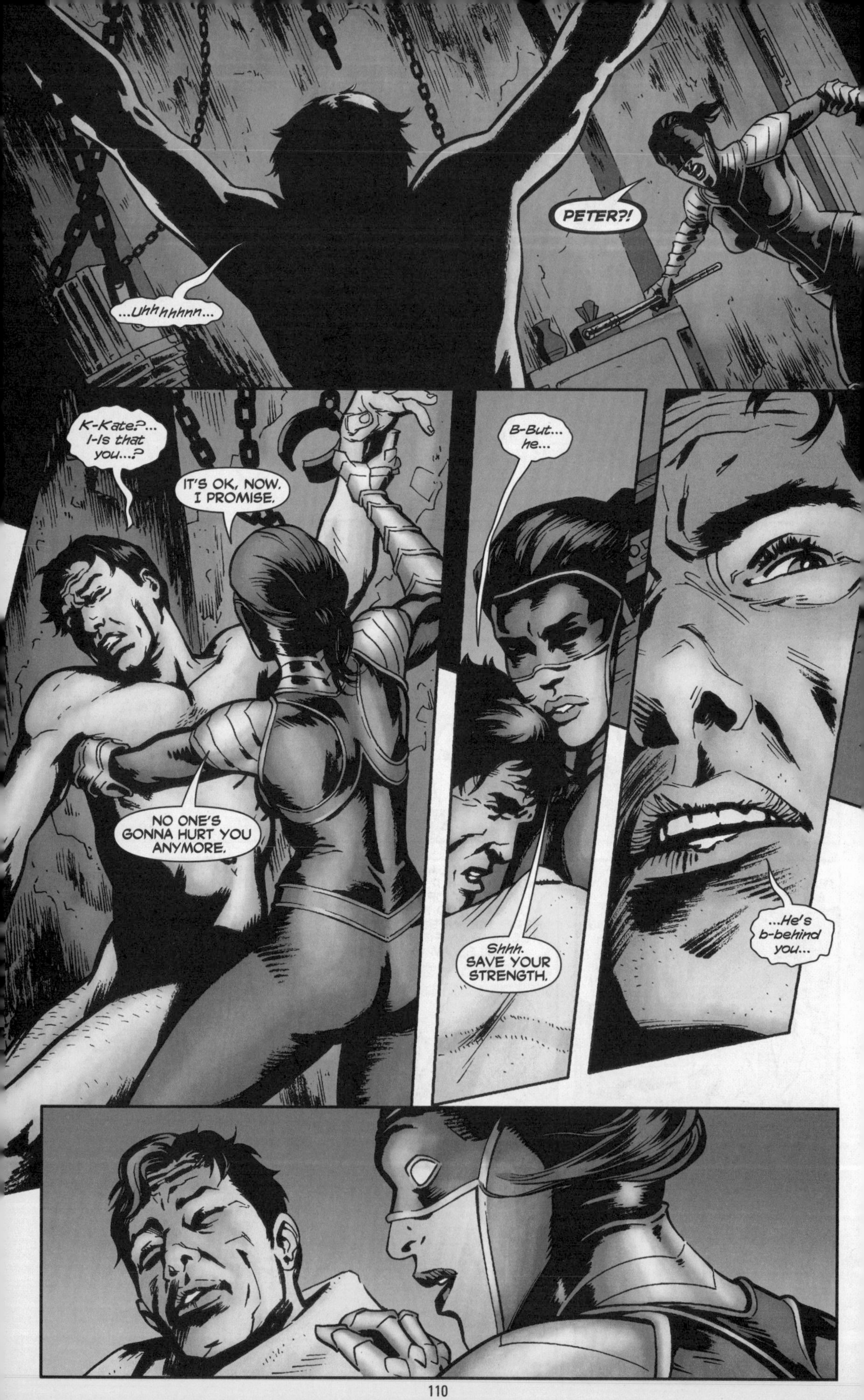
PETER?!
...Uhhhhhhn...
K-Kate?... I-Is that you...?
IT'S OK, NOW. I PROMISE.
NO ONE'S GONNA HURT YOU ANYMORE.
B-But... he...
Shhh. SAVE YOUR STRENGTH.
...He's b-behind you...

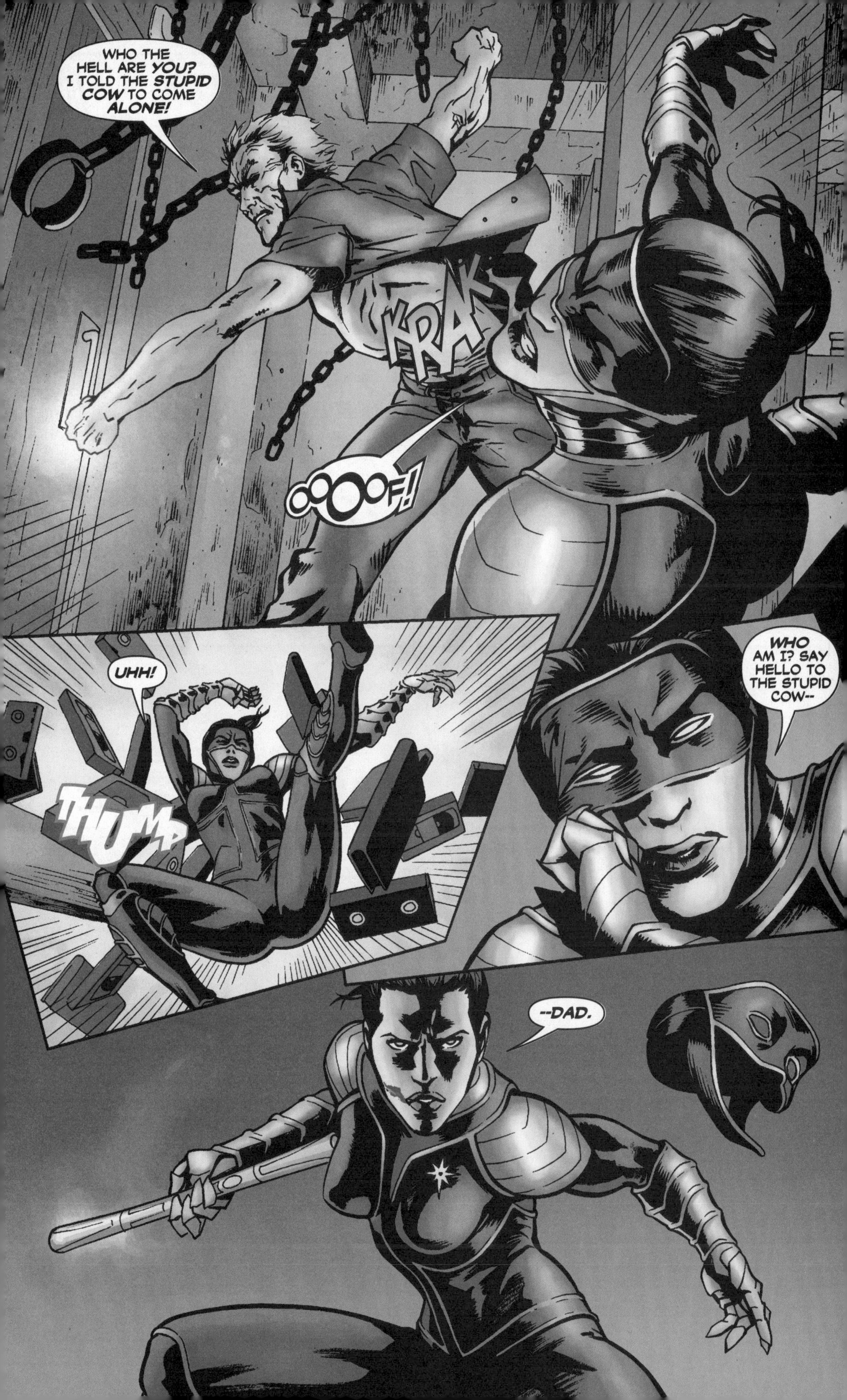
WHO THE HELL ARE YOU? I TOLD THE STUPID COW TO COME ALONE!
KRAK
OOOOF!
UHH!
THUMP
WHO AM I? SAY HELLO TO THE STUPID COW--
--DAD.

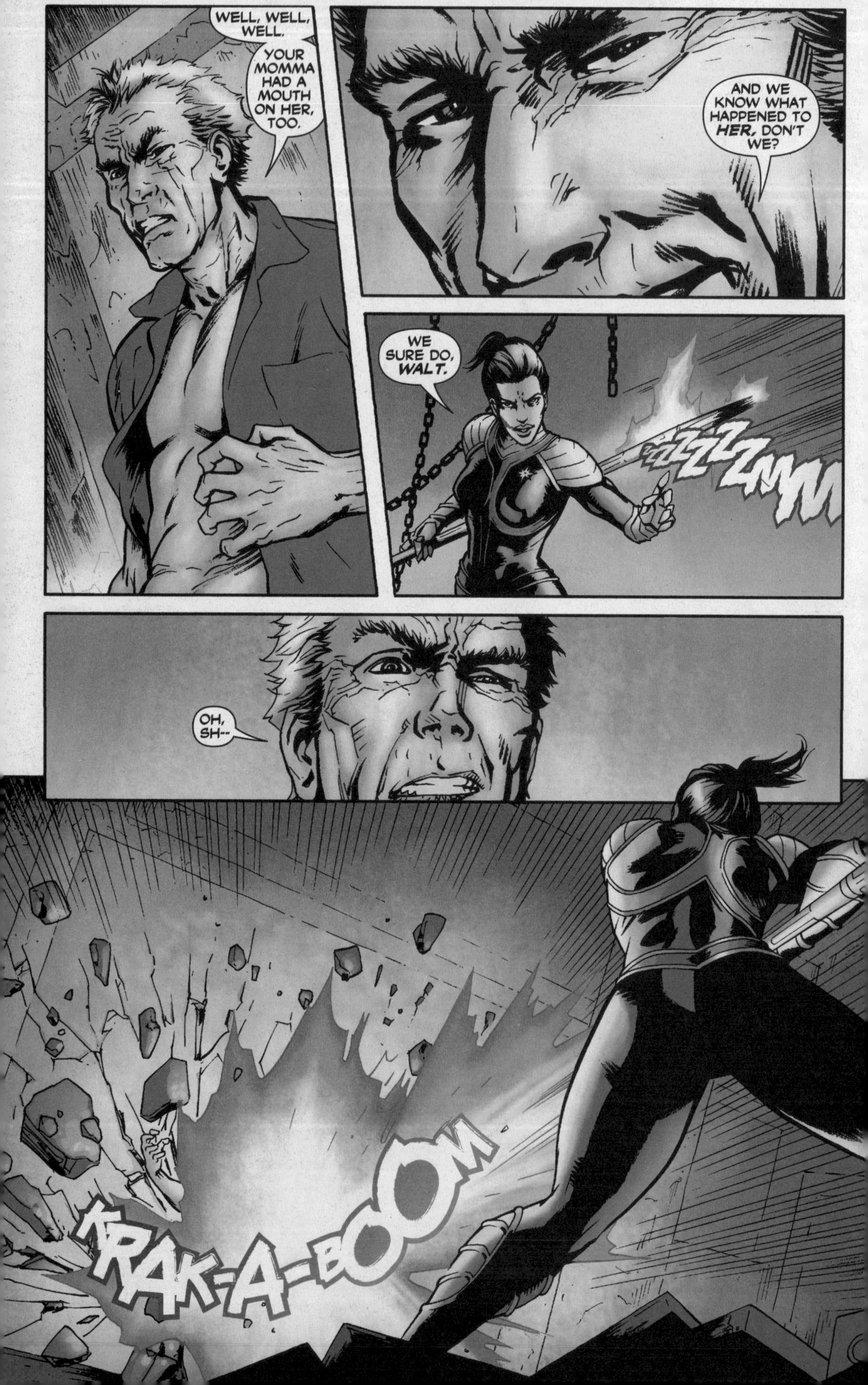
WELL, WELL, WELL.
YOUR MOMMA HAD A MOUTH ON HER, TOO.
AND WE KNOW WHAT HAPPENED TO HER, DON'T WE?
WE SURE DO, WALT.
ZZZZZNMM
OH, SH--
KRAK-A-BOOM

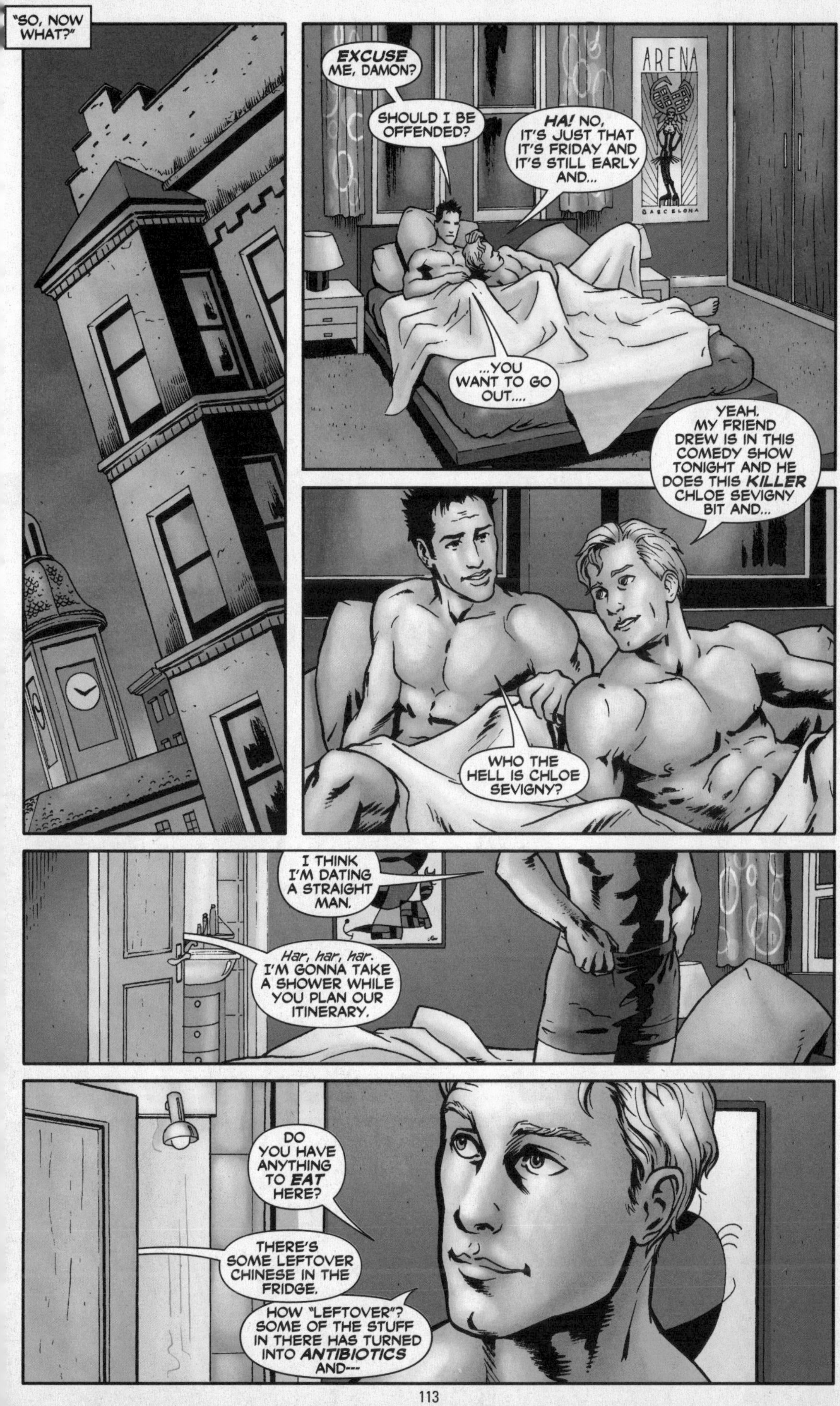
"SO, NOW WHAT?"
EXCUSE ME, DAMON?
SHOULD I BE OFFENDED?
HA! NO, IT'S JUST THAT IT'S FRIDAY AND IT'S STILL EARLY AND...
ARENA
BARCELONA
...YOU WANT TO GO OUT....
YEAH. MY FRIEND DREW IS IN THIS COMEDY SHOW TONIGHT AND HE DOES THIS KILLER CHLOE SEVIGNY BIT AND...
WHO THE HELL IS CHLOE SEVIGNY?
I THINK I'M DATING A STRAIGHT MAN.
Har, har, har. I'M GONNA TAKE A SHOWER WHILE YOU PLAN OUR ITINERARY.
DO YOU HAVE ANYTHING TO EAT HERE?
THERE'S SOME LEFTOVER CHINESE IN THE FRIDGE.
HOW "LEFTOVER"? SOME OF THE STUFF IN THERE HAS TURNED INTO ANTIBIOTICS AND---

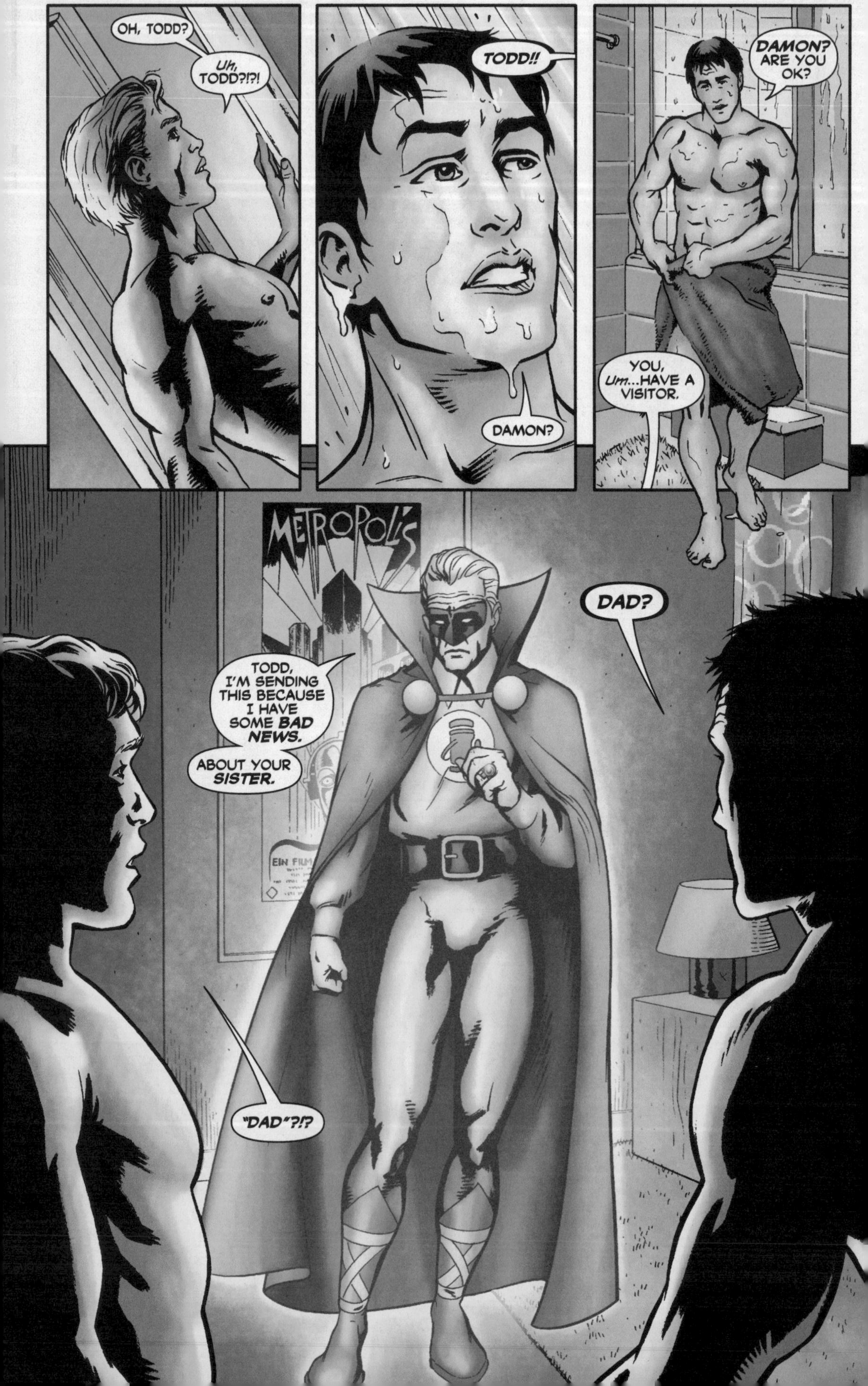
OH, TODD?
Uh, TODD?!?!
TODD!!
DAMON?
DAMON? ARE YOU OK?
YOU, Um...HAVE A VISITOR.
DAD?
TODD, I'M SENDING THIS BECAUSE I HAVE SOME BAD NEWS.
ABOUT YOUR SISTER.
"DAD"?!?
METROPOLIS
EIN FILM

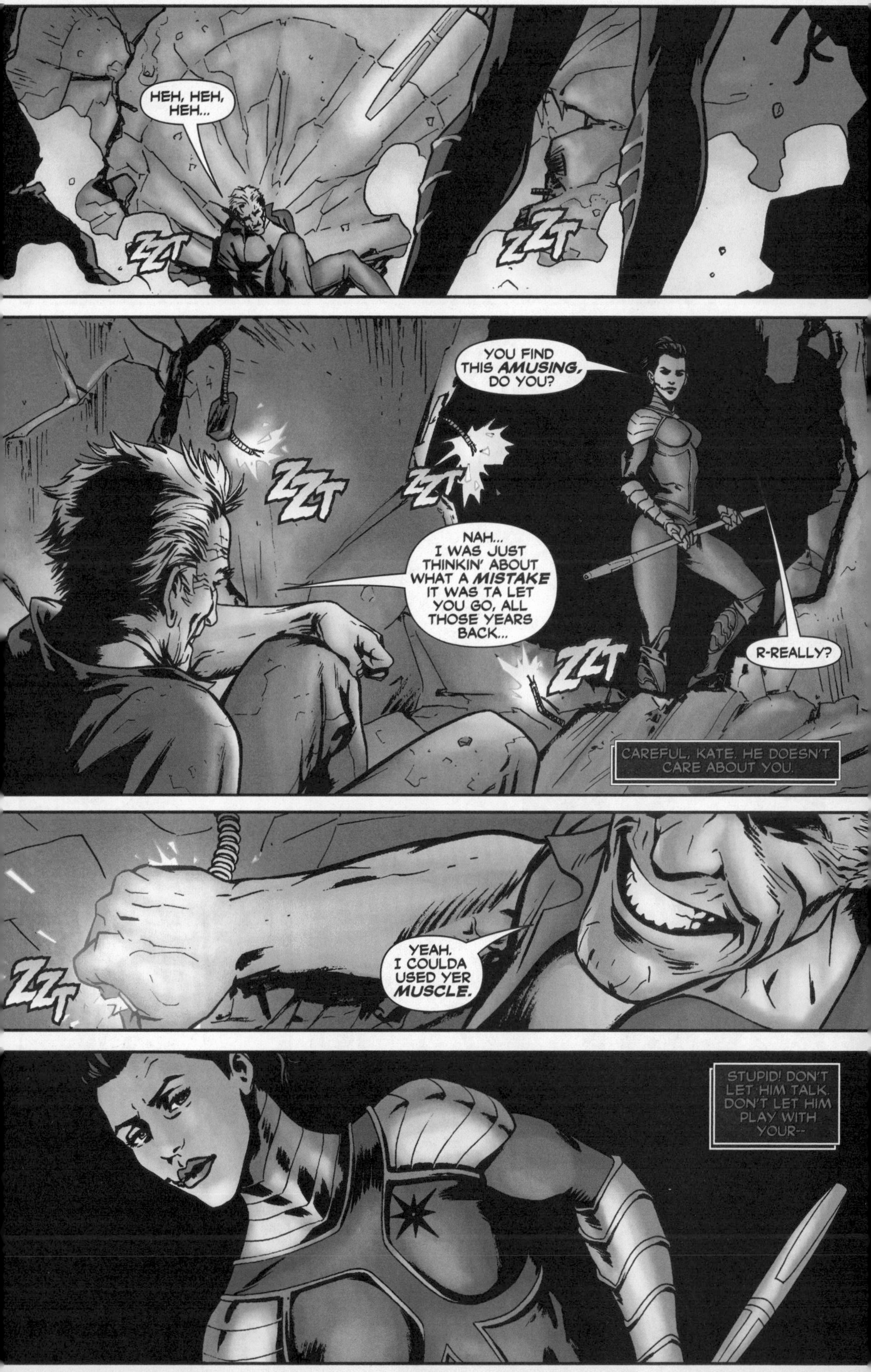
HEH, HEH, HEH...
ZZT
ZZT
YOU FIND THIS AMUSING, DO YOU?
ZZT
ZZT
NAH... I WAS JUST THINKIN' ABOUT WHAT A MISTAKE IT WAS TA LET YOU GO, ALL THOSE YEARS BACK...
ZZT
R-REALLY?
CAREFUL, KATE. HE DOESN'T CARE ABOUT YOU.
YEAH. I COULDA USED YER MUSCLE.
ZZT
STUPID! DON'T LET HIM TALK. DON'T LET HIM PLAY WITH YOUR--

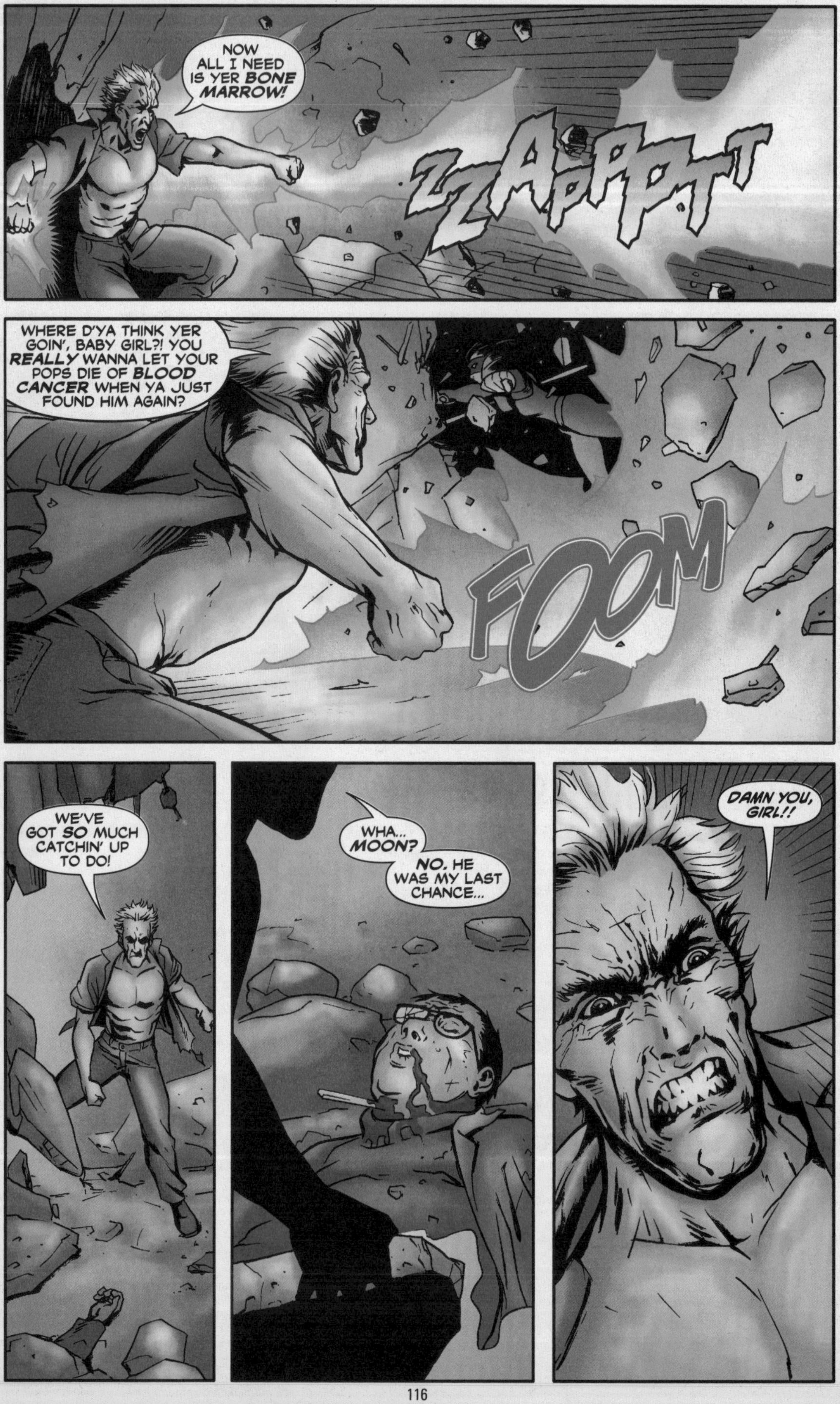
NOW ALL I NEED IS YER BONE MARROW!
ZZAPPPTT
WHERE D'YA THINK YER GOIN', BABY GIRL?! YOU REALLY WANNA LET YOUR POPS DIE OF BLOOD CANCER WHEN YA JUST FOUND HIM AGAIN?
FOOM
WE'VE GOT SO MUCH CATCHIN' UP TO DO!
WHA... MOON?
NO. HE WAS MY LAST CHANCE...
DAMN YOU, GIRL!!

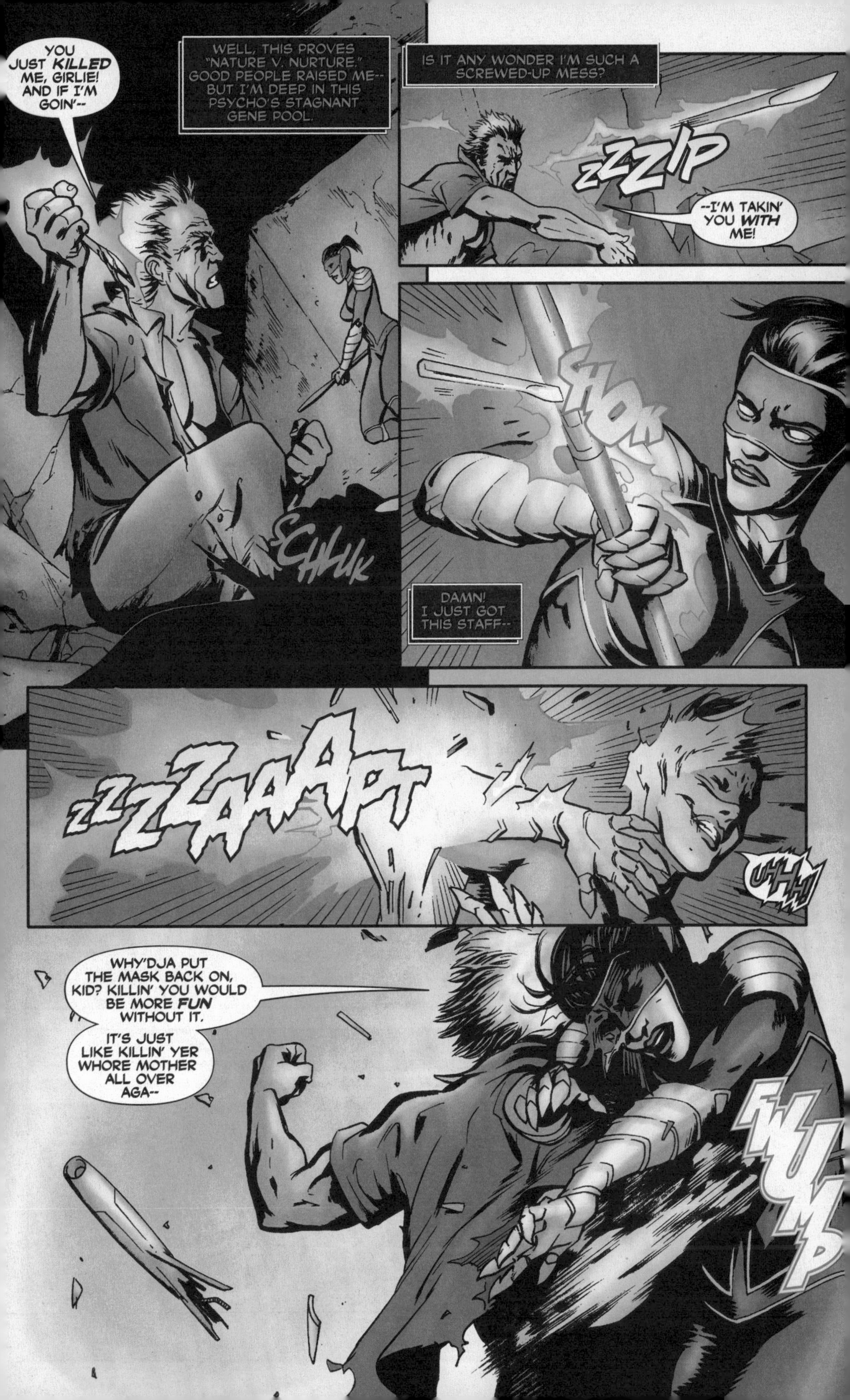
YOU JUST KILLED ME, GIRLIE! AND IF I'M GOIN'--
WELL, THIS PROVES "NATURE V. NURTURE." GOOD PEOPLE RAISED ME-- BUT I'M DEEP IN THIS PSYCHO'S STAGNANT GENE POOL.
SCHHUK
IS IT ANY WONDER I'M SUCH A SCREWED-UP MESS?
ZZZIP
--I'M TAKIN' YOU WITH ME!
SHOK
DAMN! I JUST GOT THIS STAFF--
ZZZAAAPT
UHH
WHY'DJA PUT THE MASK BACK ON, KID? KILLIN' YOU WOULD BE MORE FUN WITHOUT IT.
IT'S JUST LIKE KILLIN' YER WHORE MOTHER ALL OVER AGA--
FWUMP

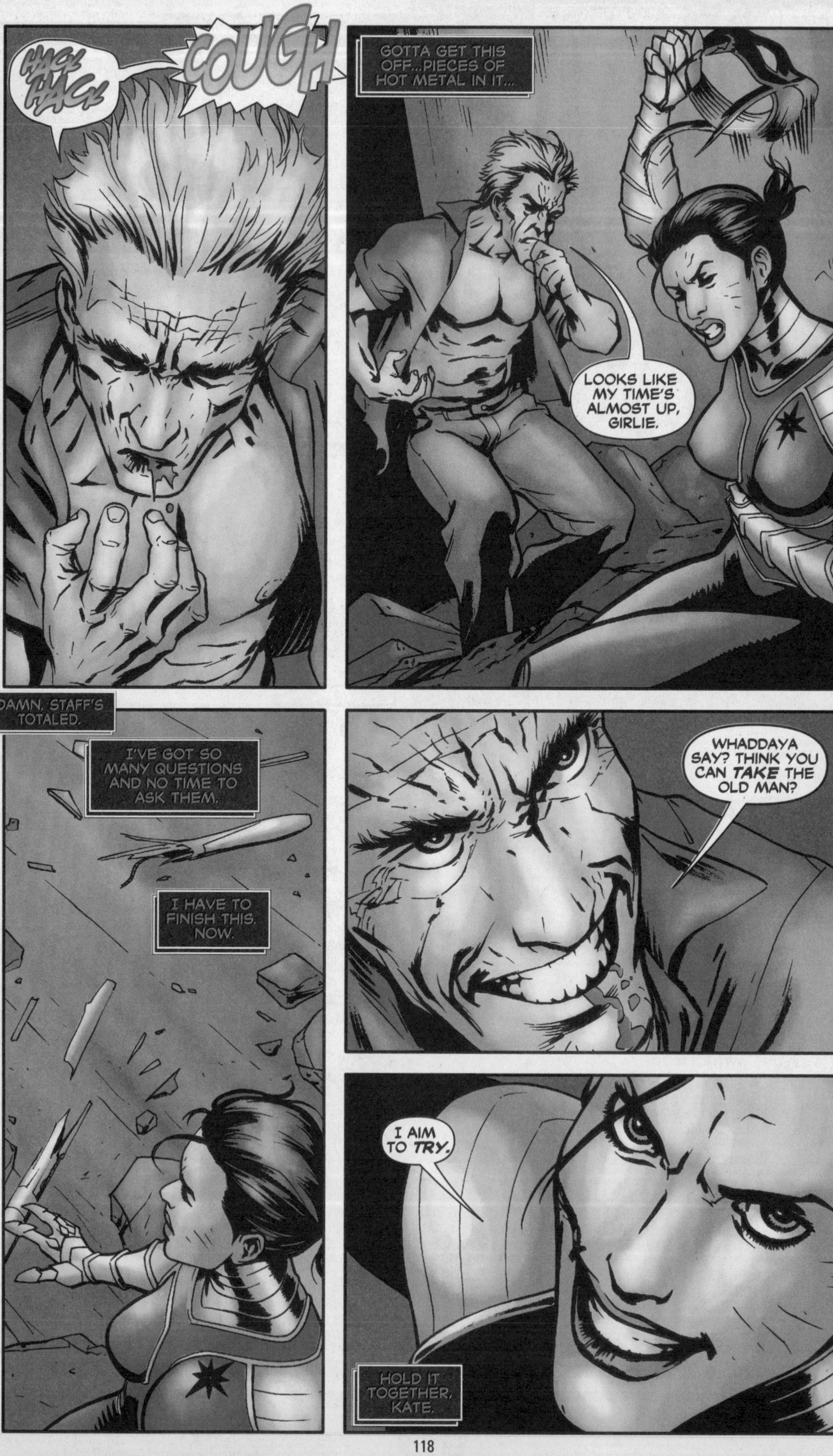
HACK HACK
COUGH
GOTTA GET THIS OFF...PIECES OF HOT METAL IN IT...
LOOKS LIKE MY TIME'S ALMOST UP, GIRLIE.
DAMN. STAFF'S TOTALED.
I'VE GOT SO MANY QUESTIONS AND NO TIME TO ASK THEM.
I HAVE TO FINISH THIS. NOW.
WHADDAYA SAY? THINK YOU CAN TAKE THE OLD MAN?
I AIM TO TRY.
HOLD IT TOGETHER, KATE.

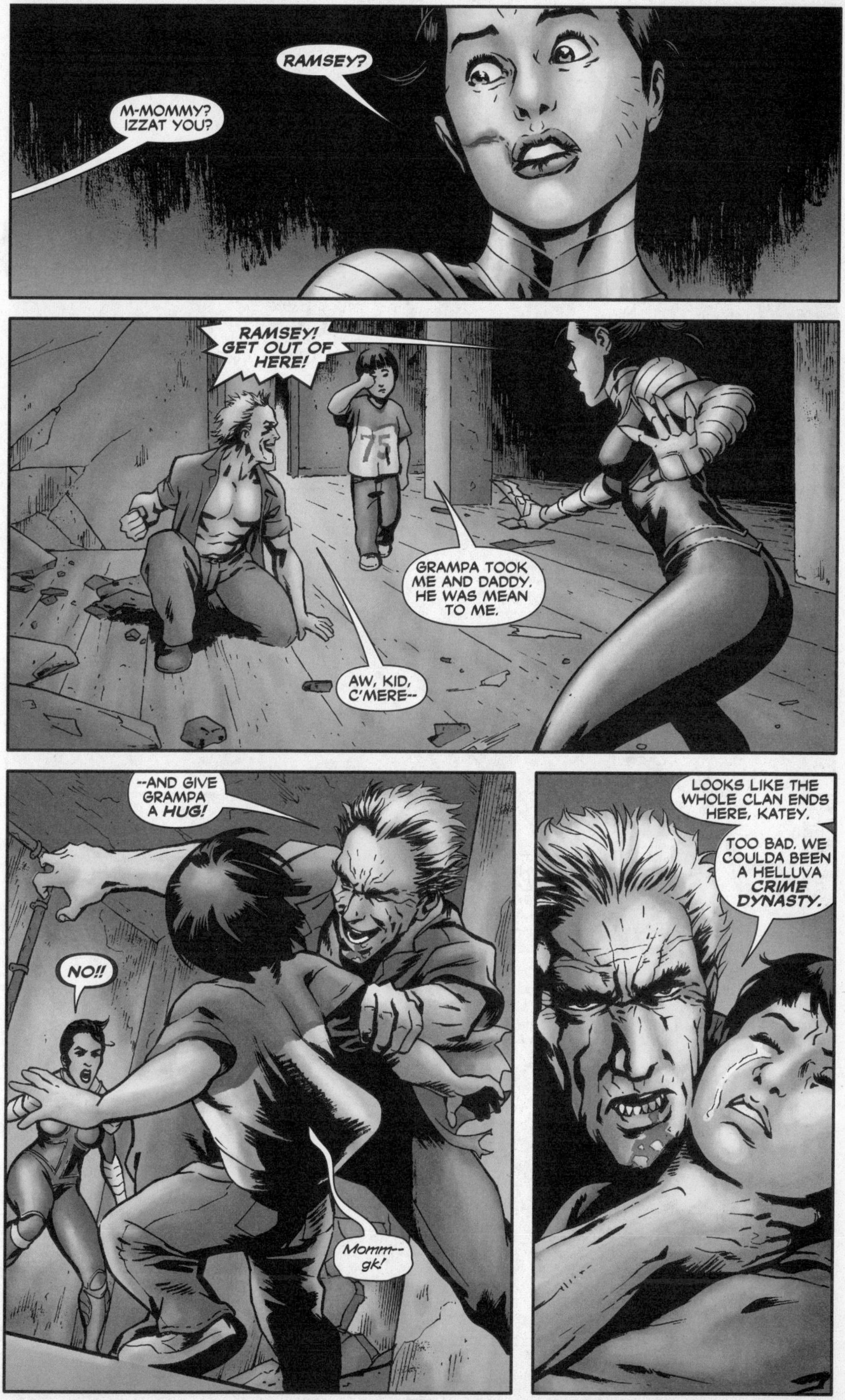

M-MOMMY? IZZAT YOU?
RAMSEY?
RAMSEY! GET OUT OF HERE!
GRAMPA TOOK ME AND DADDY. HE WAS MEAN TO ME.
AW, KID, C'MERE--
--AND GIVE GRAMPA A *HUG!*
NO!!
Momm-- gk!
LOOKS LIKE THE WHOLE CLAN ENDS HERE, KATEY.
TOO BAD. WE COULDA BEEN A HELLUVA *CRIME DYNASTY.*

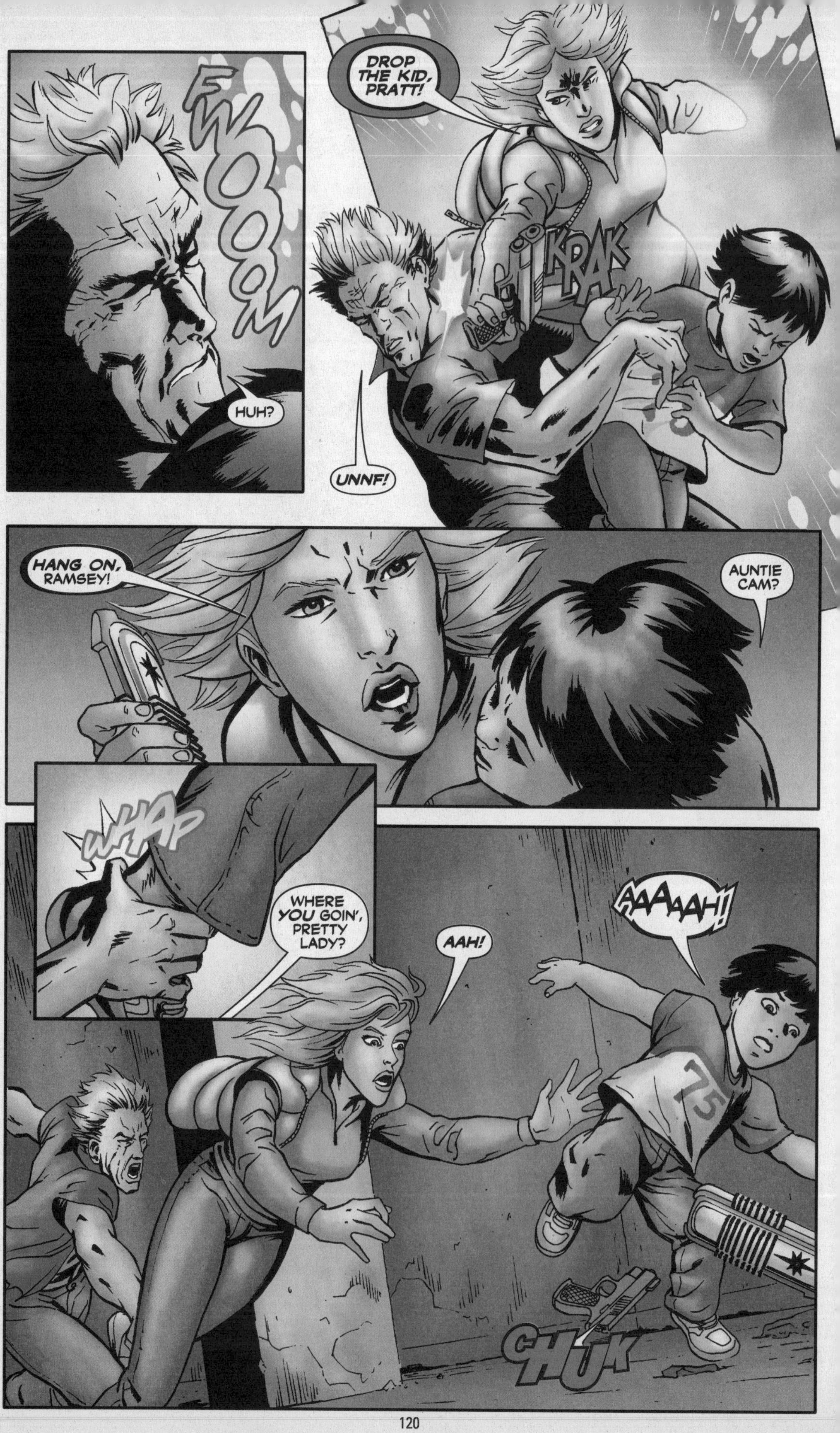
FWOOOM
HUH?
DROP THE KID, PRATT!
KRAK
UNNF!
HANG ON, RAMSEY!
AUNTIE CAM?
WHAP
WHERE YOU GOIN', PRETTY LADY?
AAH!
AAAAAH!!
CHUK

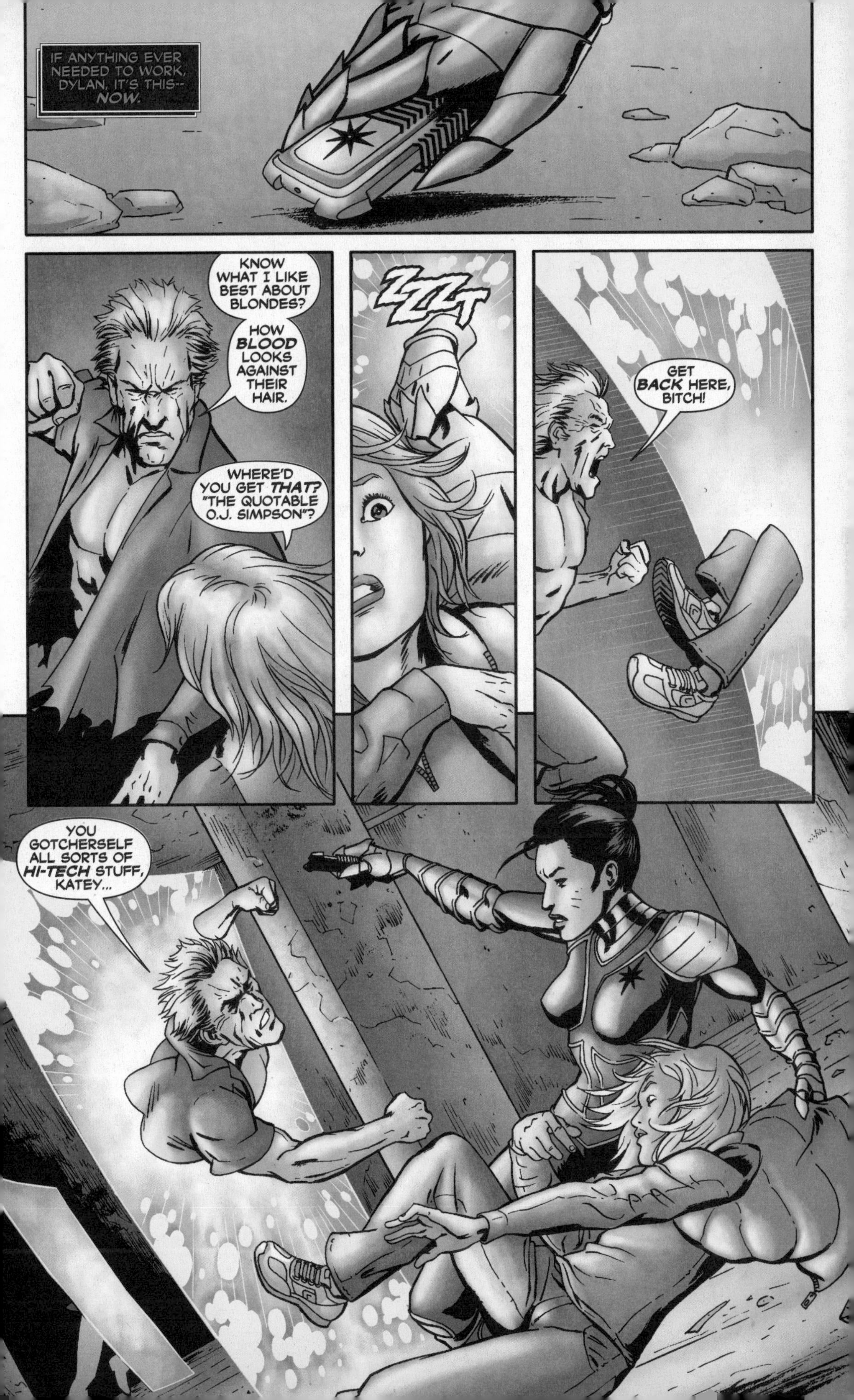

IF ANYTHING EVER NEEDED TO WORK, DYLAN, IT'S THIS-- NOW.
KNOW WHAT I LIKE BEST ABOUT BLONDES?
HOW BLOOD LOOKS AGAINST THEIR HAIR.
WHERE'D YOU GET THAT? "THE QUOTABLE O.J. SIMPSON"?
ZZZT
GET BACK HERE, BITCH!
YOU GOTCHERSELF ALL SORTS OF HI-TECH STUFF, KATEY...

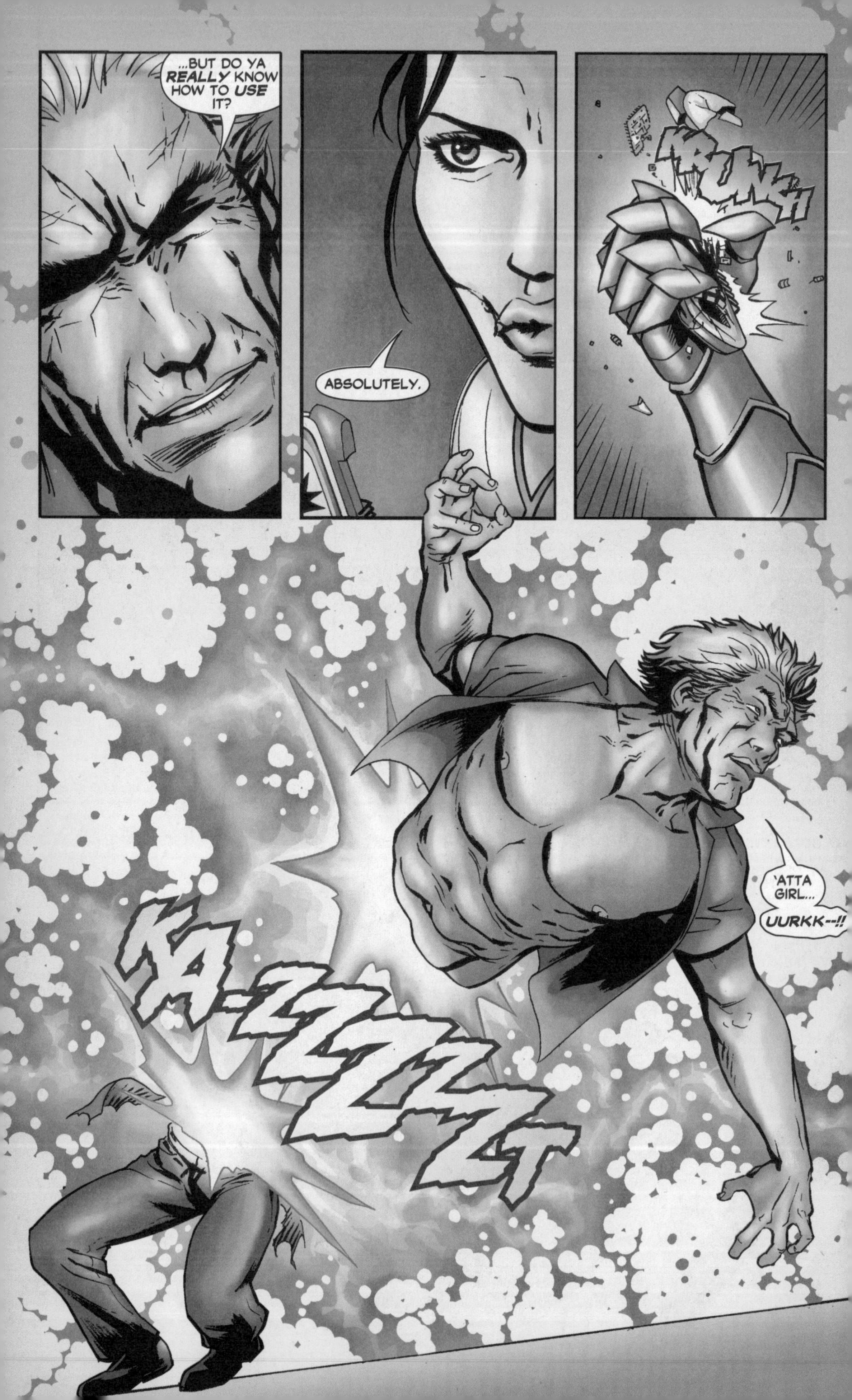
...BUT DO YA REALLY KNOW HOW TO USE IT?
ABSOLUTELY.
KRUNCH
KA-ZZZZZT
'ATTA GIRL...
UURKK--!!

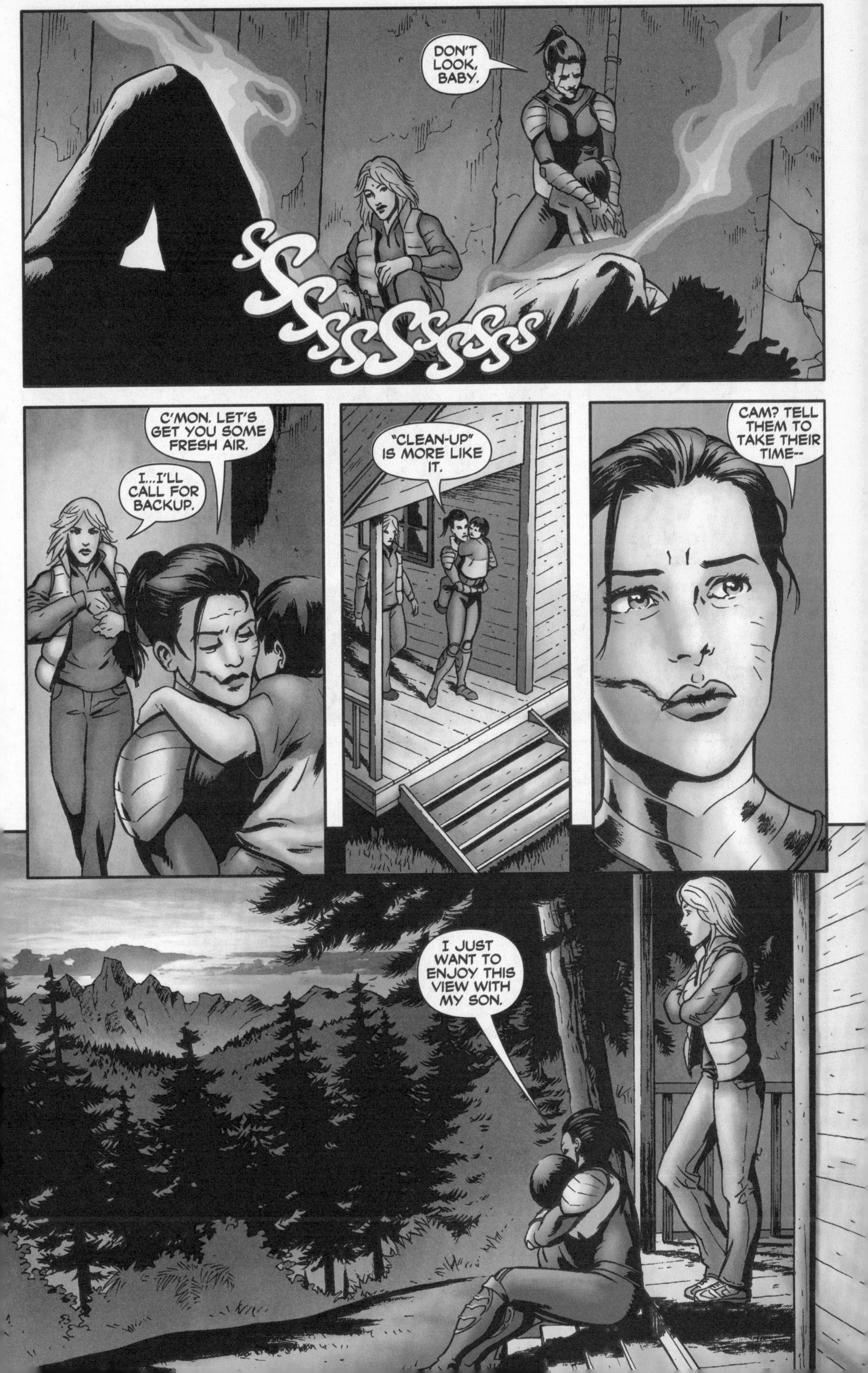
DON'T LOOK, BABY.
SSSSSSSSSS
C'MON. LET'S GET YOU SOME FRESH AIR.
I...I'LL CALL FOR BACKUP.
"CLEAN-UP" IS MORE LIKE IT.
CAM? TELL THEM TO TAKE THEIR TIME--
I JUST WANT TO ENJOY THIS VIEW WITH MY SON.

"SO, THEY'LL BOTH BE OK?"

YES, YOUR HUSBAND REQUIRED A TRANSFUSION, BUT MOST OF HIS INJURIES WERE MINOR. AND YOUR SON IS SUFFERING FROM SHOCK AND A MILD CONCUSSION. HE SHOULD BOUNCE BACK QUICKLY.

BUT, HE HAD A CONCUSSION BEFORE AND NEEDED--

NURSE, WE NEED A WHEELCHAIR HERE! NOW!

KATE?! WHAT IS IT?

MS. SPENCER?

CAN YOU HEAR ME?

HI, THERE. YOU HAD US SCARED FOR A BIT. I'M DR. LEWIS.

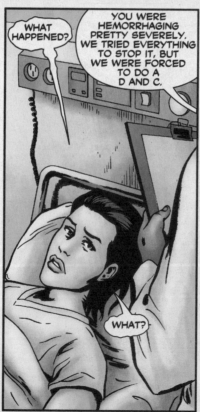

WHAT HAPPENED?

YOU WERE HEMORRHAGING PRETTY SEVERELY. WE TRIED EVERYTHING TO STOP IT, BUT WE WERE FORCED TO DO A D AND C.

WHAT?

YOU HAD A MISCARRIAGE, MS. SPENCER. I'M SORRY.

124

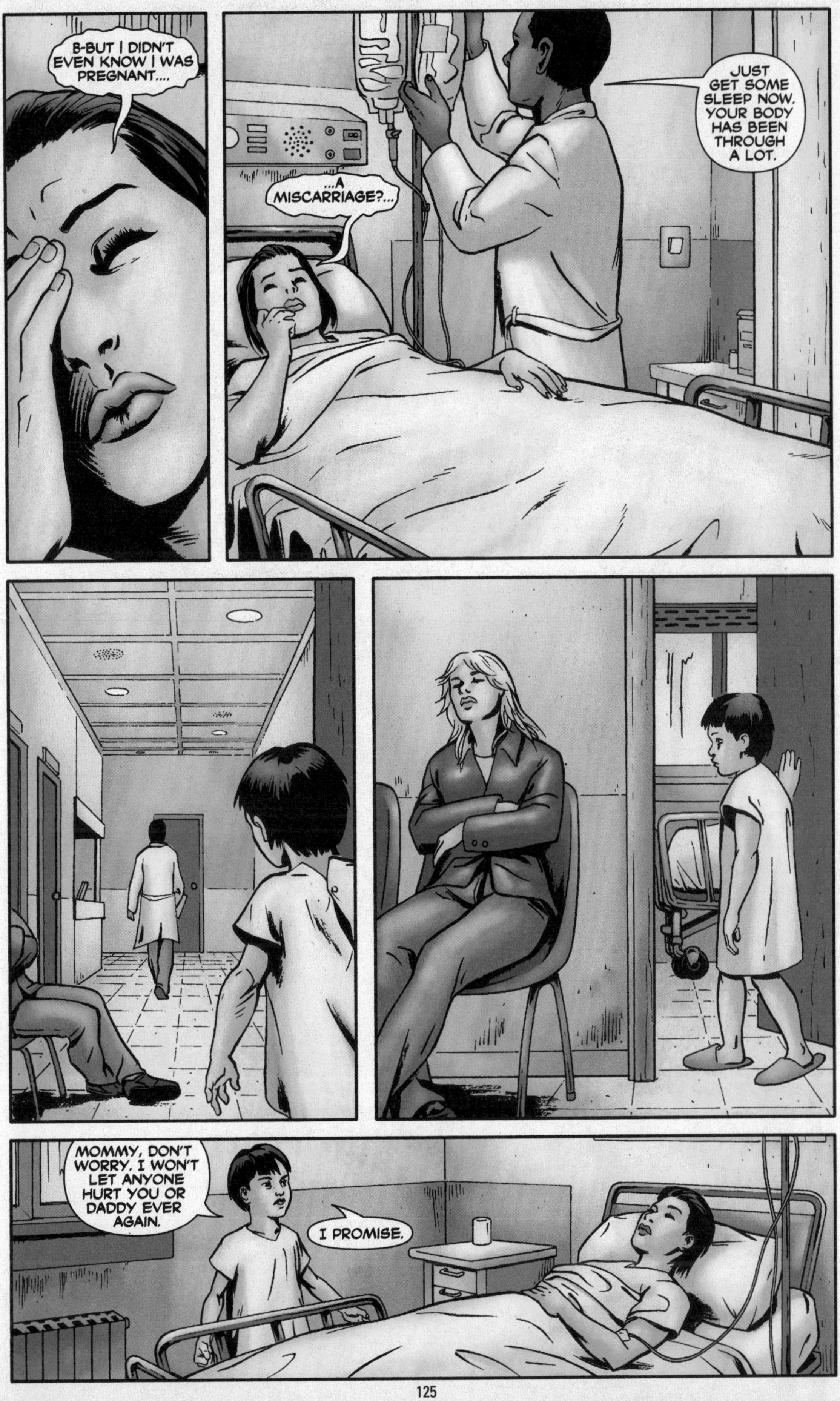
B-BUT I DIDN'T EVEN KNOW I WAS PREGNANT....
...A MISCARRIAGE?...
JUST GET SOME SLEEP NOW. YOUR BODY HAS BEEN THROUGH A LOT.
MOMMY, DON'T WORRY. I WON'T LET ANYONE HURT YOU OR DADDY EVER AGAIN.
I PROMISE.

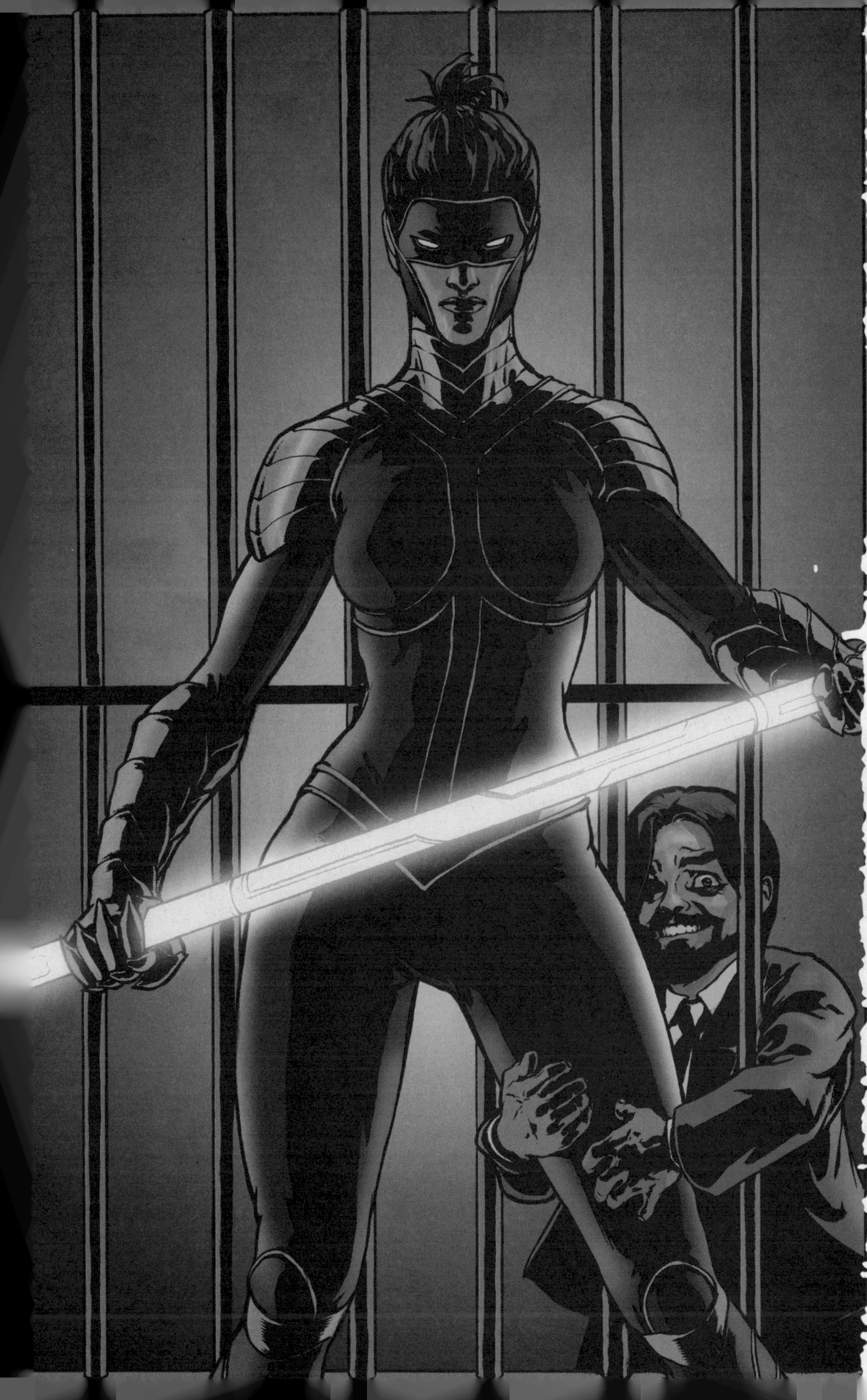

e #20 cover by Jesus Saiz & Jose Villarrubia

Interior art by Javier Pina & Fernando Blanco

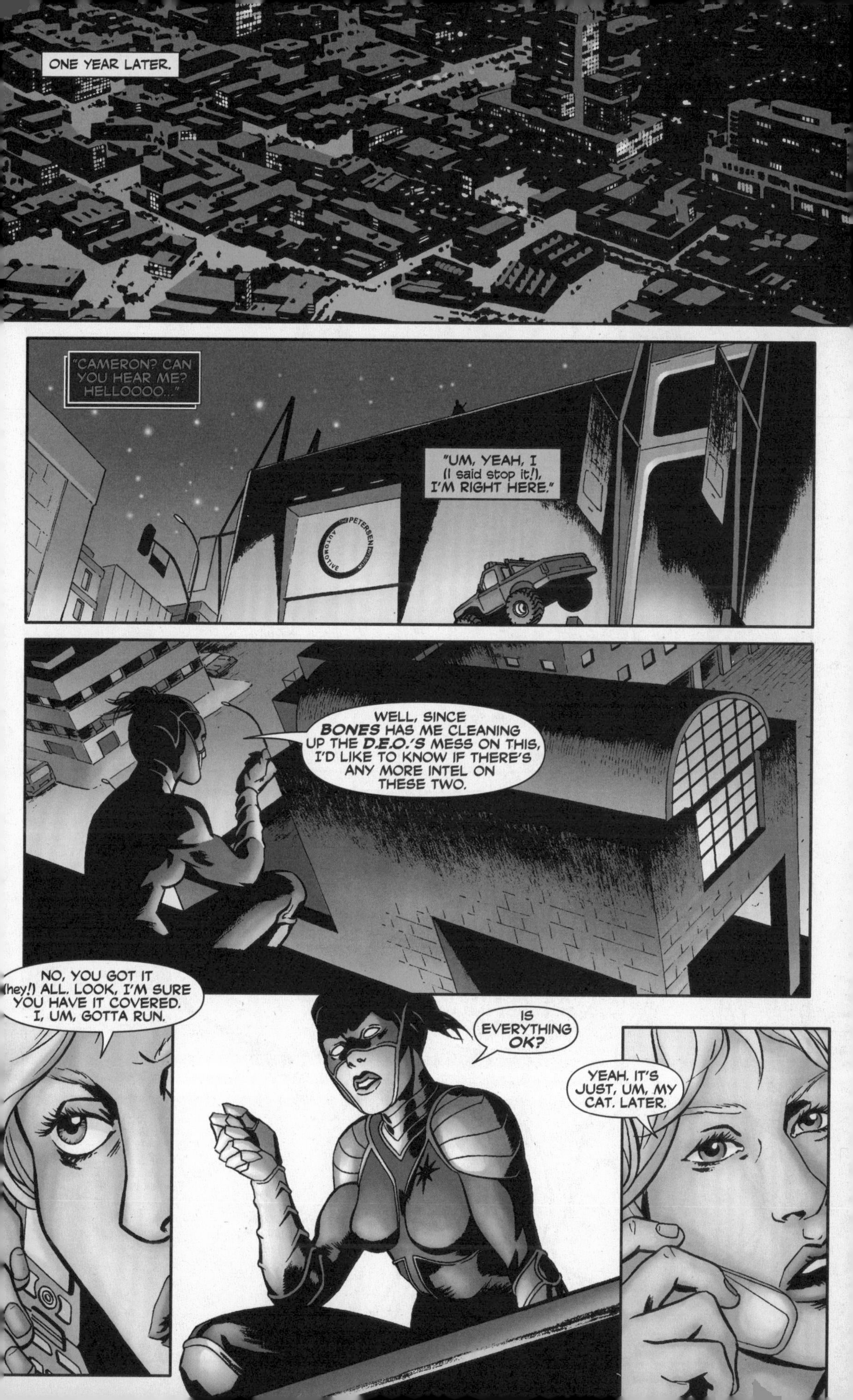
ONE YEAR LATER.
"CAMERON? CAN YOU HEAR ME? HELLOOOO..."
PETERSEN AUTOMOTIVE MUSEUM
"UM, YEAH, I (I said stop it!), I'M RIGHT HERE."
WELL, SINCE BONES HAS ME CLEANING UP THE D.E.O.'S MESS ON THIS, I'D LIKE TO KNOW IF THERE'S ANY MORE INTEL ON THESE TWO.
NO, YOU GOT IT (hey!) ALL. LOOK, I'M SURE YOU HAVE IT COVERED. I, UM, GOTTA RUN.
IS EVERYTHING OK?
YEAH. IT'S JUST, UM, MY CAT. LATER.

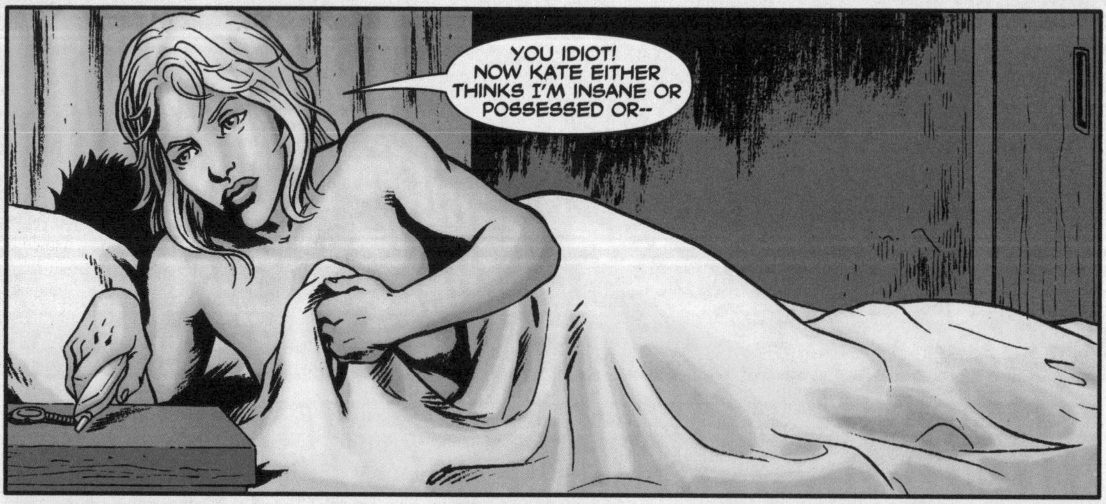
YOU IDIOT! NOW KATE EITHER THINKS I'M INSANE OR POSSESSED OR--

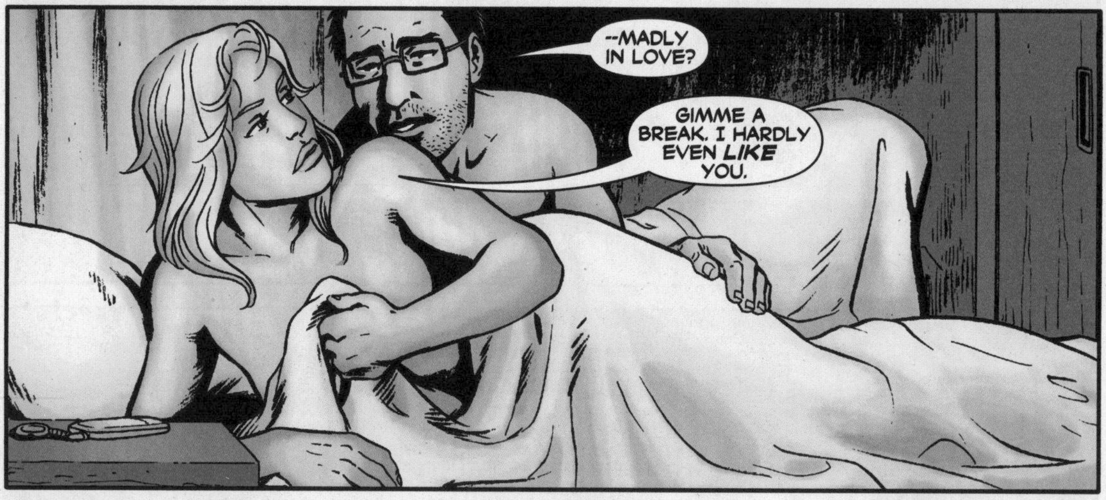
--MADLY IN LOVE?
GIMME A BREAK. I HARDLY EVEN **LIKE** YOU.

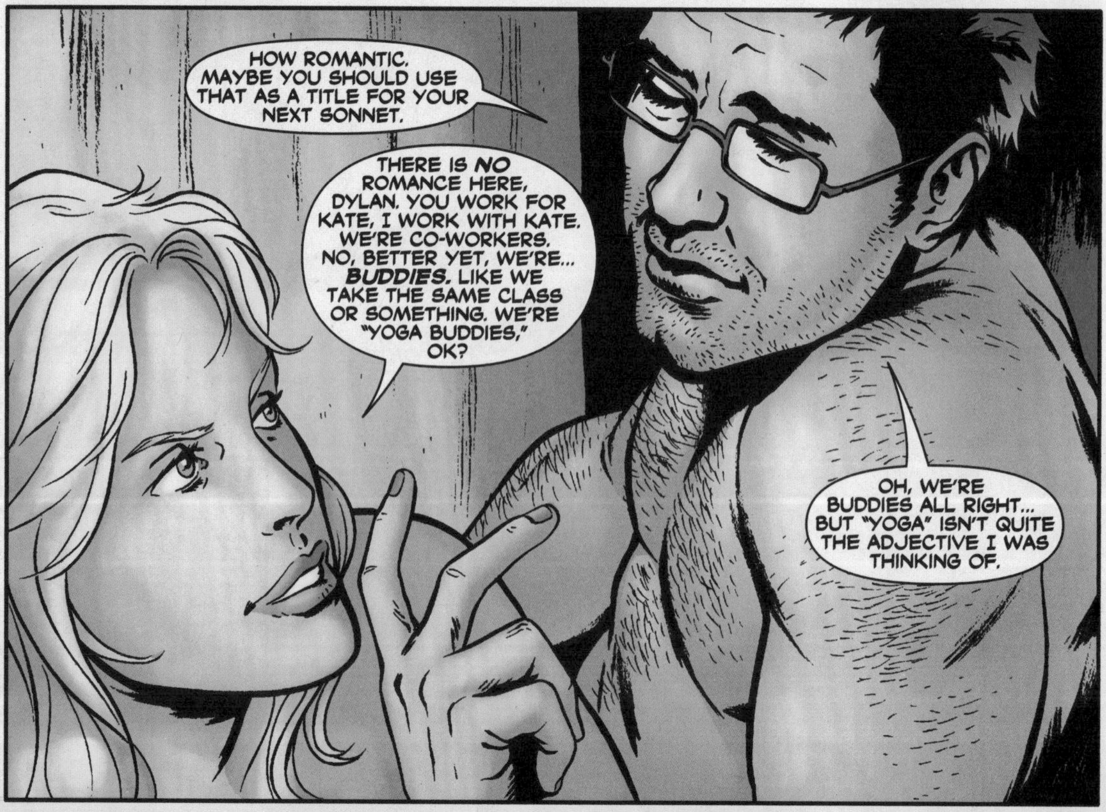
HOW ROMANTIC. MAYBE YOU SHOULD USE THAT AS A TITLE FOR YOUR NEXT SONNET.
THERE IS **NO** ROMANCE HERE, DYLAN. YOU WORK FOR KATE, I WORK WITH KATE. WE'RE CO-WORKERS. NO, BETTER YET, WE'RE... **BUDDIES.** LIKE WE TAKE THE SAME CLASS OR SOMETHING. WE'RE "YOGA BUDDIES," OK?
OH, WE'RE BUDDIES ALL RIGHT... BUT "YOGA" ISN'T QUITE THE ADJECTIVE I WAS THINKING OF.

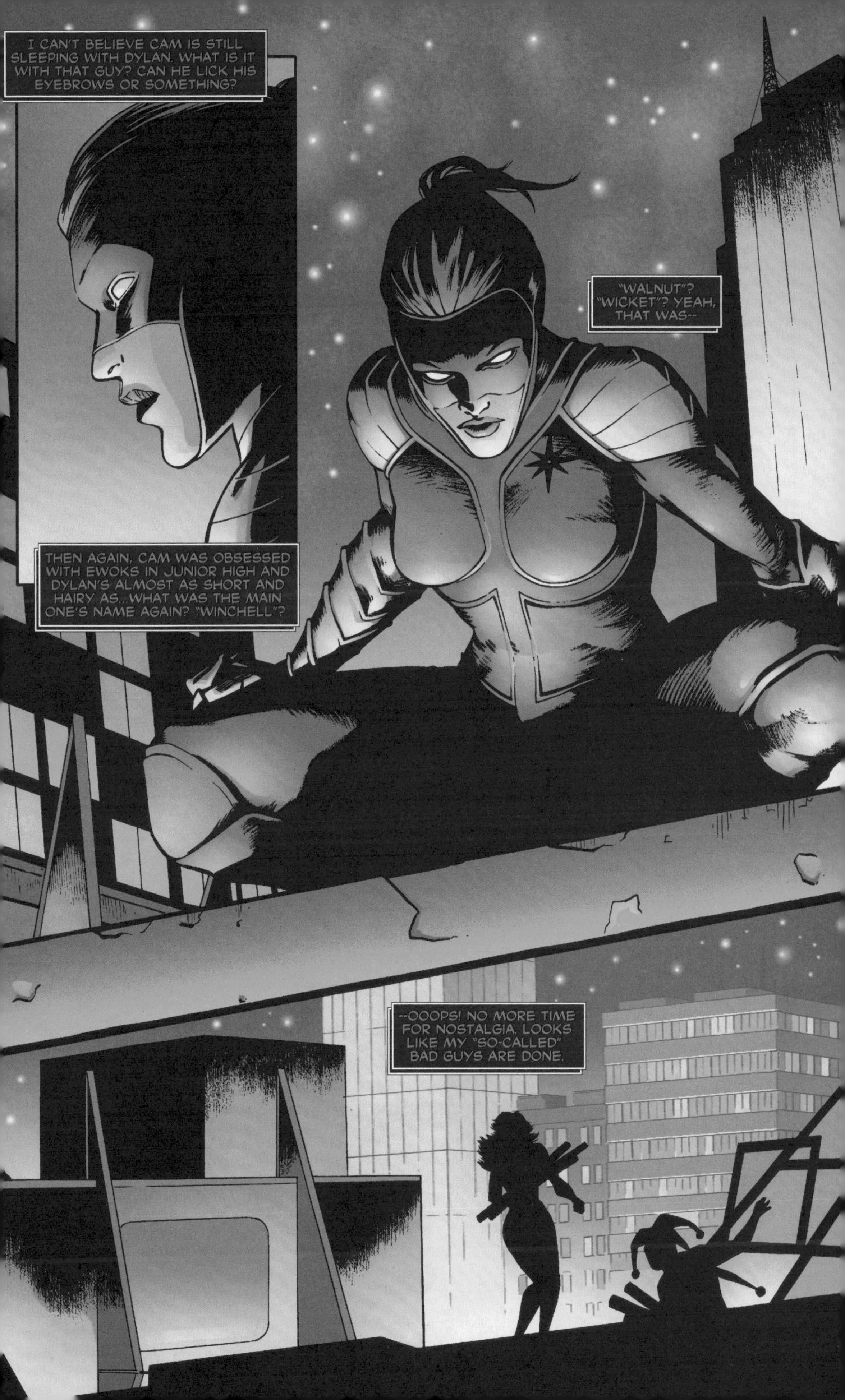
I CAN'T BELIEVE CAM IS STILL SLEEPING WITH DYLAN. WHAT IS IT WITH THAT GUY? CAN HE LICK HIS EYEBROWS OR SOMETHING?
THEN AGAIN, CAM WAS OBSESSED WITH EWOKS IN JUNIOR HIGH AND DYLAN'S ALMOST AS SHORT AND HAIRY AS...WHAT WAS THE MAIN ONE'S NAME AGAIN? "WINCHELL"?
"WALNUT"? "WICKET"? YEAH, THAT WAS--
--OOOPS! NO MORE TIME FOR NOSTALGIA. LOOKS LIKE MY "SO-CALLED" BAD GUYS ARE DONE.

JUST TAKING THOSE PAINTINGS OUT FOR SOME FRESH AIR, RIGHT?
UGH. I SHOULD JUST BE THE "SILENT SUPERHERO."
PUNCH, LOOK!
AW, CRAP! IT'S MANHUNTER!
EVEN THAT'S A BETTER ENTRANCE LINE.
PSYCHOBABBLE

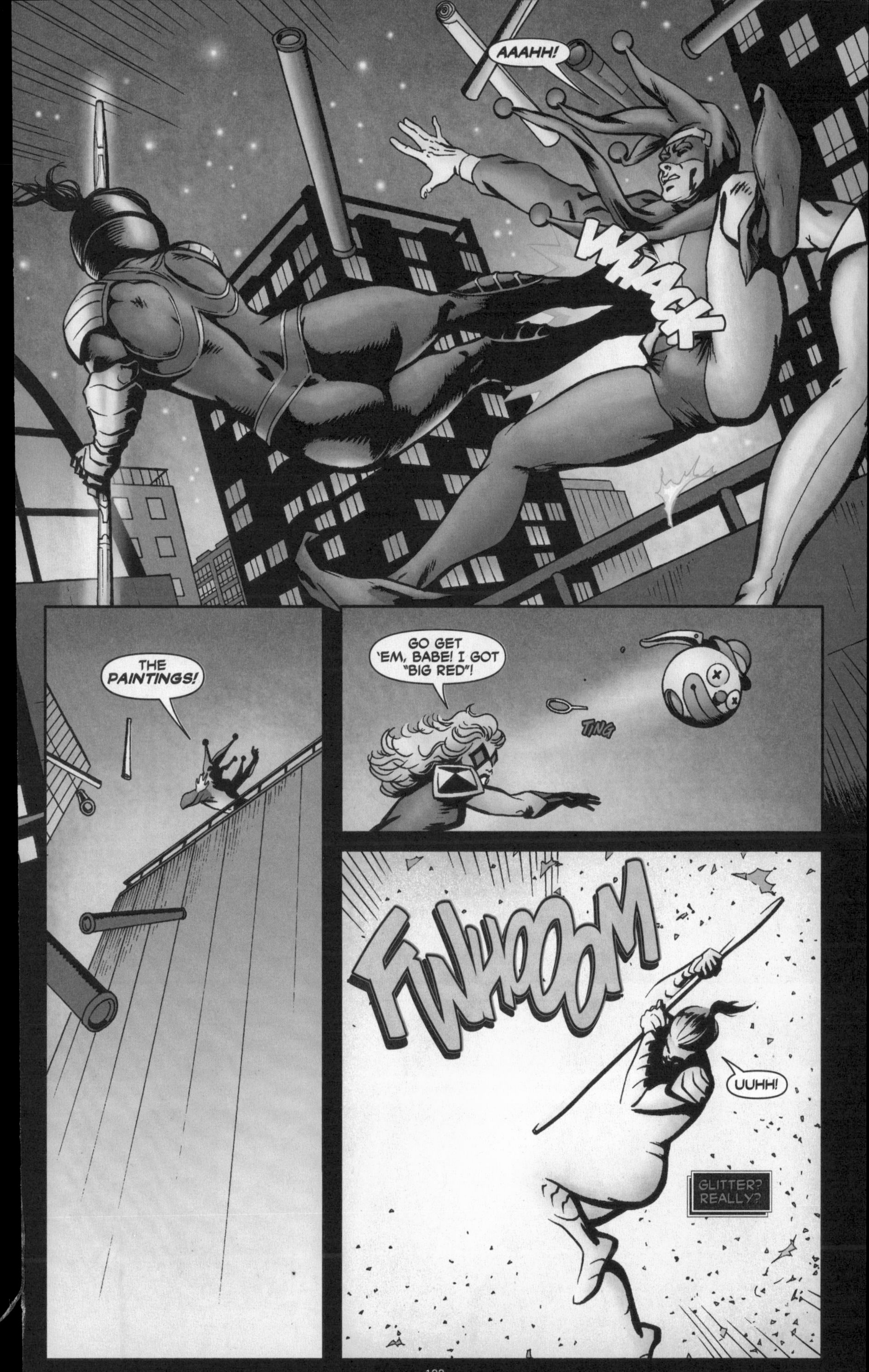
AAAHH!
WHACK
THE PAINTINGS!
GO GET 'EM, BABE! I GOT "BIG RED"!
TING
FWHOOOM
UUHH!
GLITTER? REALLY?

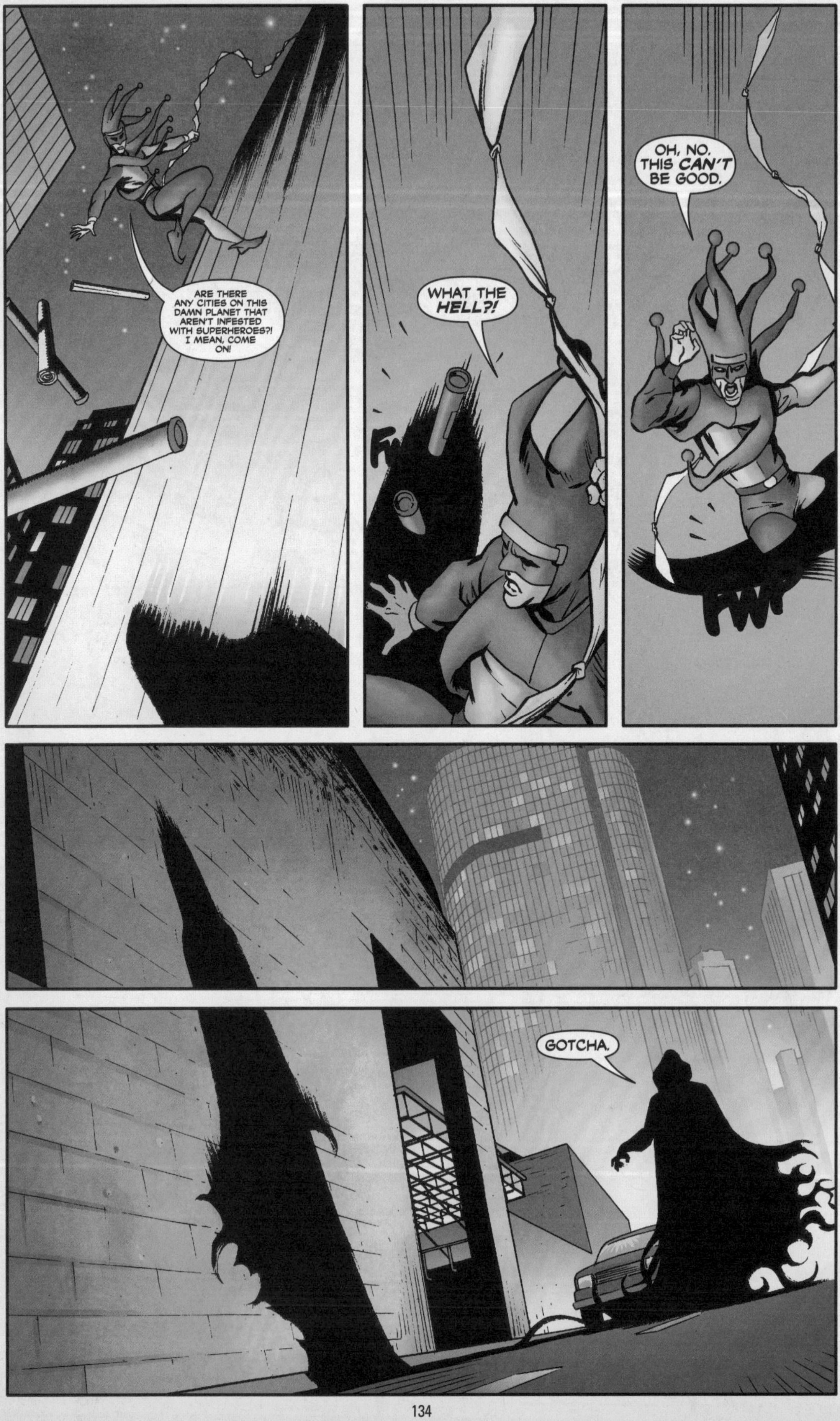
ARE THERE ANY CITIES ON THIS DAMN PLANET THAT AREN'T INFESTED WITH SUPERHEROES?! I MEAN, COME ON!
WHAT THE HELL?!
OH, NO. THIS CAN'T BE GOOD.
GOTCHA.

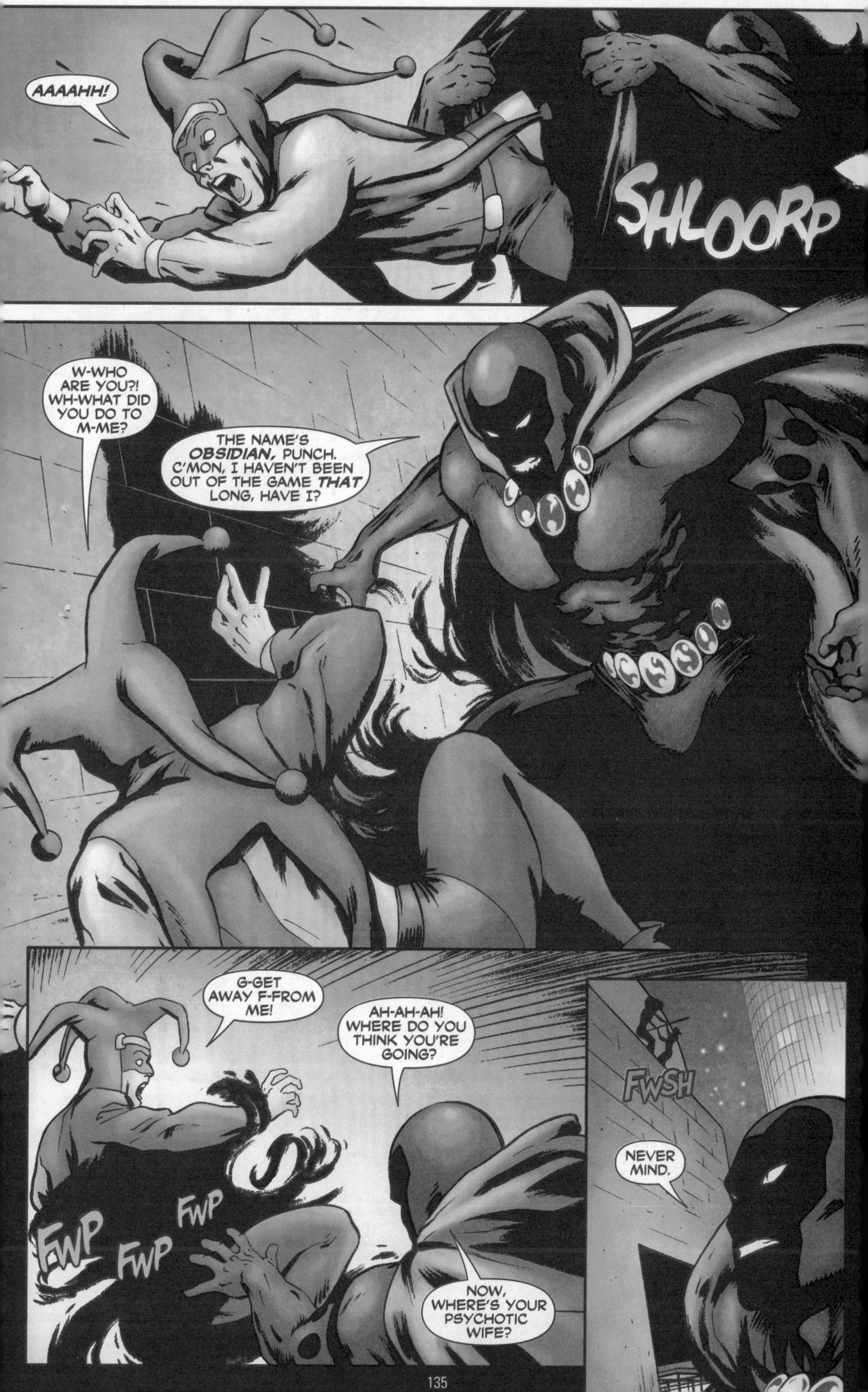
AAAAHH!
SHLOORP
W-WHO ARE YOU?! WH-WHAT DID YOU DO TO M-ME?
THE NAME'S OBSIDIAN, PUNCH. C'MON, I HAVEN'T BEEN OUT OF THE GAME THAT LONG, HAVE I?
G-GET AWAY F-FROM ME!
AH-AH-AH! WHERE DO YOU THINK YOU'RE GOING?
FWP
FWP
FWP
NOW, WHERE'S YOUR PSYCHOTIC WIFE?
FWSH
NEVER MIND.

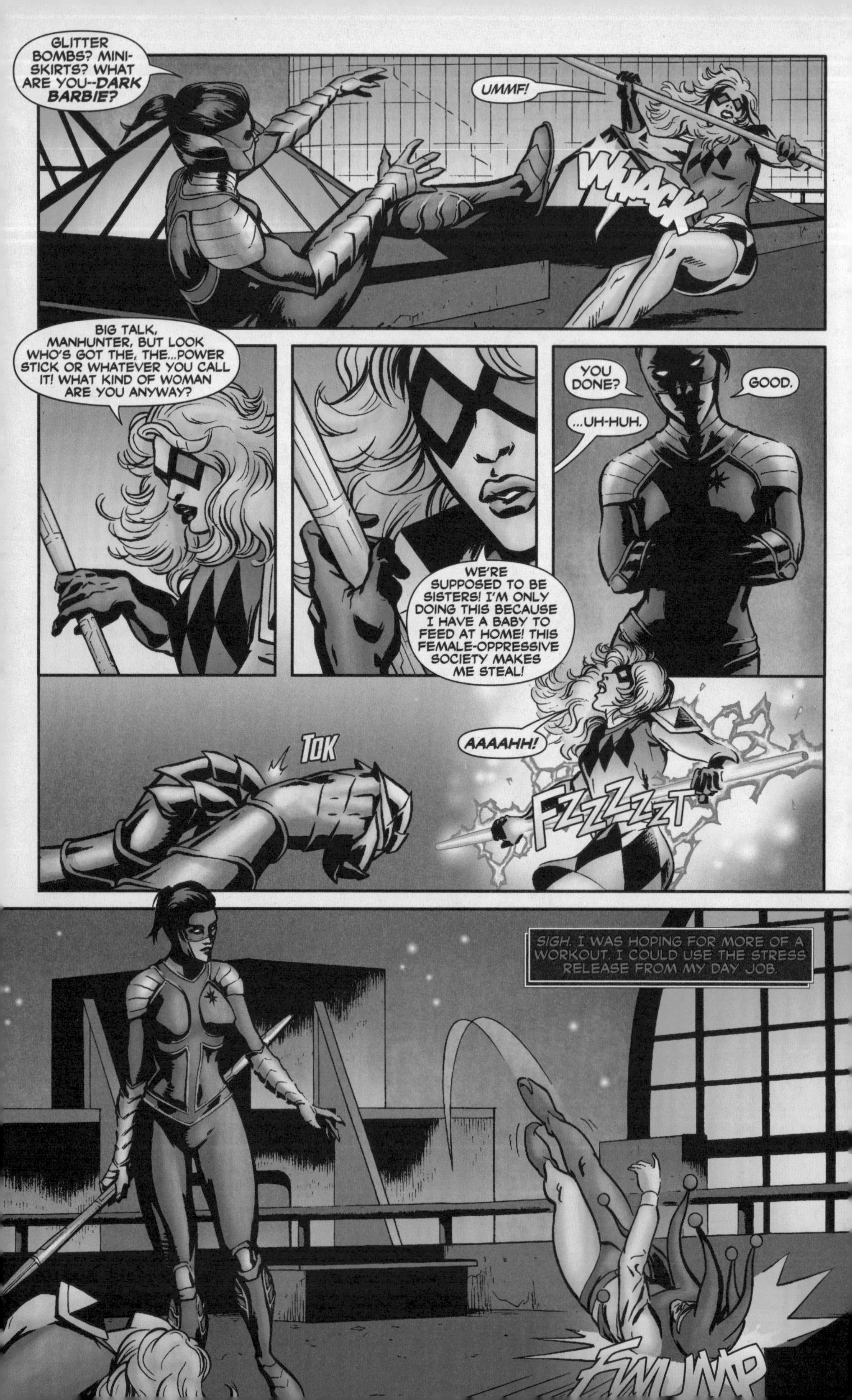
GLITTER BOMBS? MINI-SKIRTS? WHAT ARE YOU--DARK BARBIE?
UMMF!
WHACK
BIG TALK, MANHUNTER, BUT LOOK WHO'S GOT THE, THE...POWER STICK OR WHATEVER YOU CALL IT! WHAT KIND OF WOMAN ARE YOU ANYWAY?
WE'RE SUPPOSED TO BE SISTERS! I'M ONLY DOING THIS BECAUSE I HAVE A BABY TO FEED AT HOME! THIS FEMALE-OPPRESSIVE SOCIETY MAKES ME STEAL!
YOU DONE?
...UH-HUH.
GOOD.
TOK
AAAAHH!
FZZZZZZT
SIGH. I WAS HOPING FOR MORE OF A WORKOUT. I COULD USE THE STRESS RELEASE FROM MY DAY JOB.
FWUMP

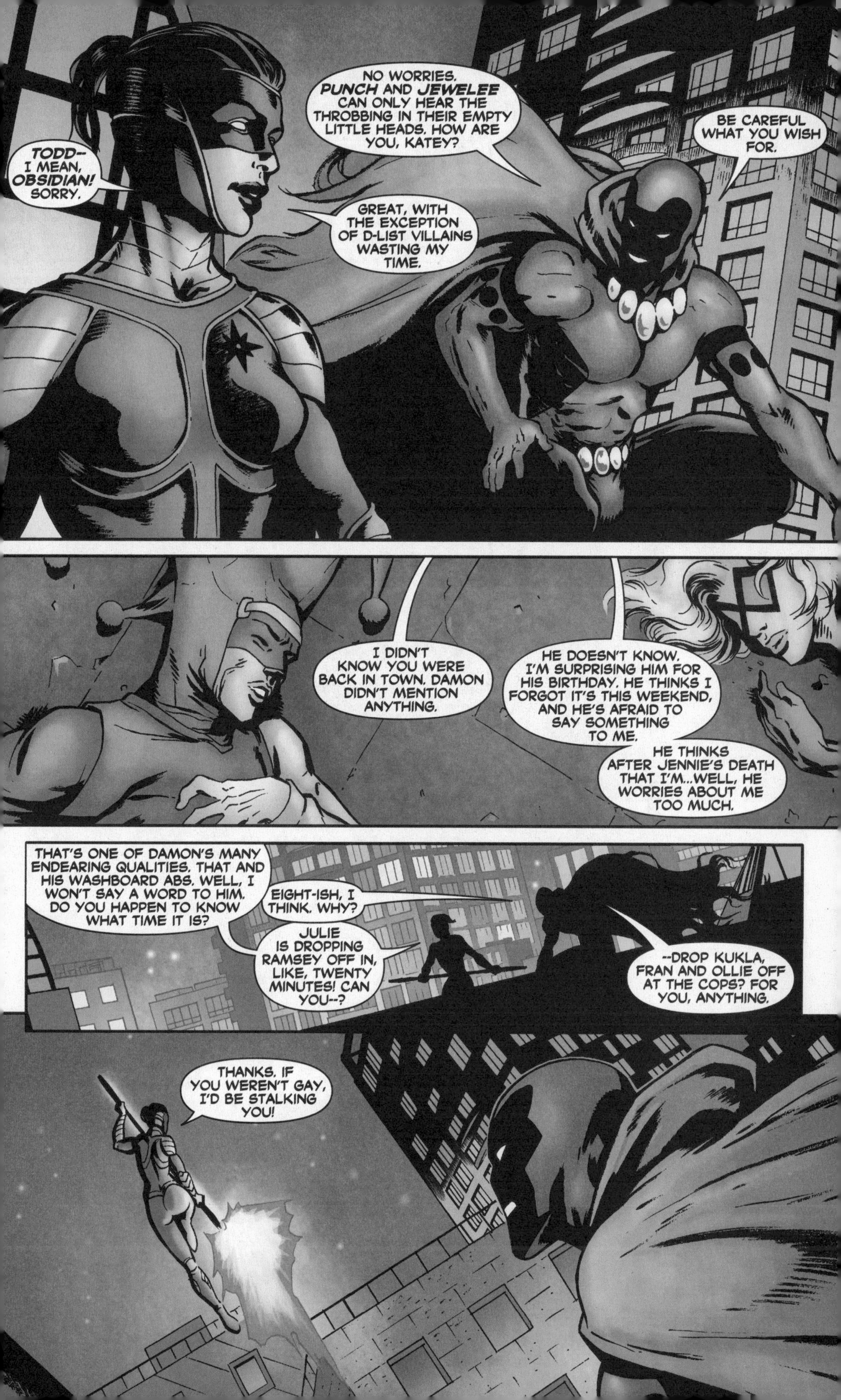
TODD-- I MEAN, OBSIDIAN! SORRY.
NO WORRIES. PUNCH AND JEWELEE CAN ONLY HEAR THE THROBBING IN THEIR EMPTY LITTLE HEADS. HOW ARE YOU, KATEY?
GREAT, WITH THE EXCEPTION OF D-LIST VILLAINS WASTING MY TIME.
BE CAREFUL WHAT YOU WISH FOR.
I DIDN'T KNOW YOU WERE BACK IN TOWN. DAMON DIDN'T MENTION ANYTHING.
HE DOESN'T KNOW. I'M SURPRISING HIM FOR HIS BIRTHDAY. HE THINKS I FORGOT IT'S THIS WEEKEND, AND HE'S AFRAID TO SAY SOMETHING TO ME.
HE THINKS AFTER JENNIE'S DEATH THAT I'M...WELL, HE WORRIES ABOUT ME TOO MUCH.
THAT'S ONE OF DAMON'S MANY ENDEARING QUALITIES. THAT AND HIS WASHBOARD ABS. WELL, I WON'T SAY A WORD TO HIM. DO YOU HAPPEN TO KNOW WHAT TIME IT IS?
EIGHT-ISH, I THINK. WHY?
JULIE IS DROPPING RAMSEY OFF IN, LIKE, TWENTY MINUTES! CAN YOU--?
--DROP KUKLA, FRAN AND OLLIE OFF AT THE COPS? FOR YOU, ANYTHING.
THANKS. IF YOU WEREN'T GAY, I'D BE STALKING YOU!

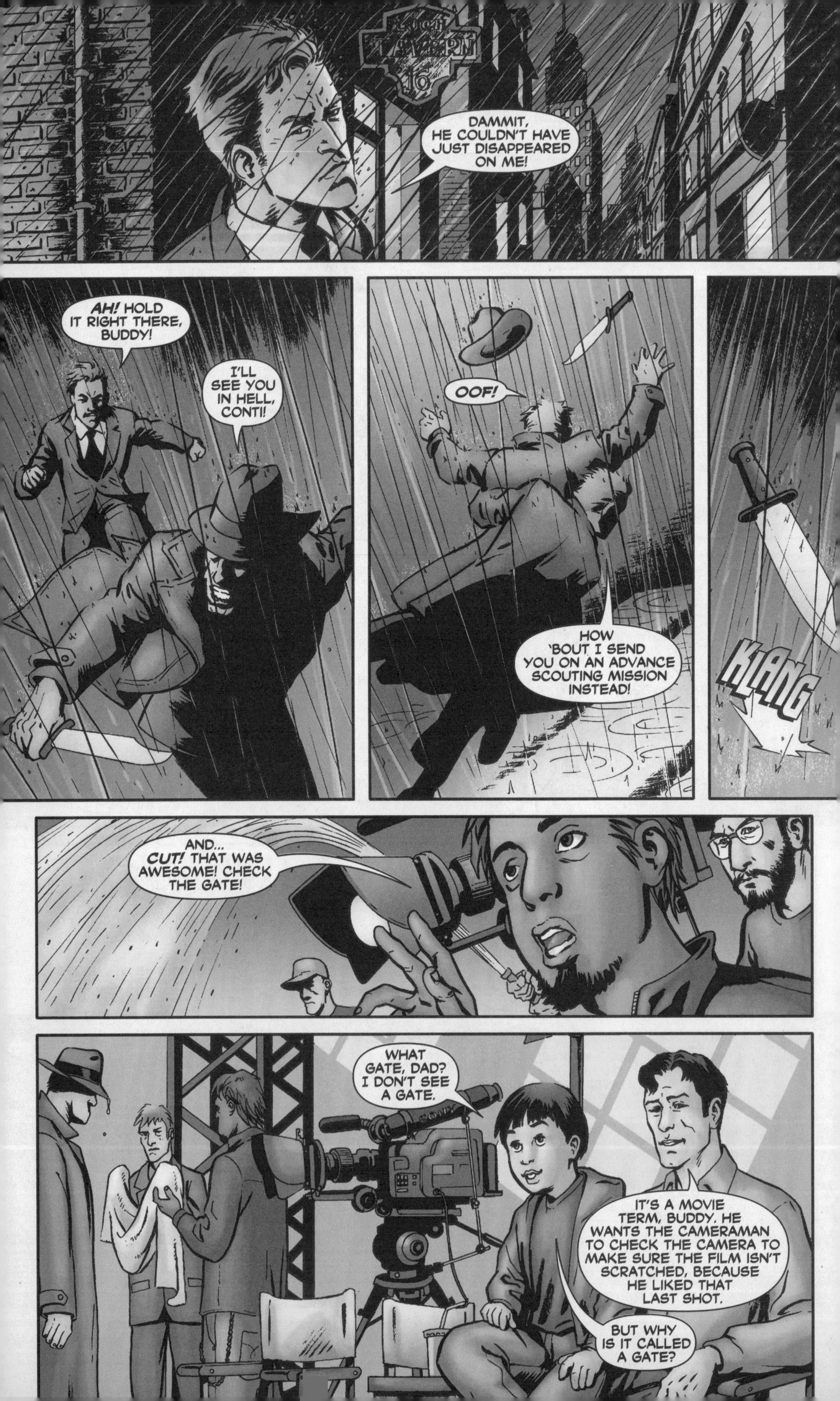

DAMMIT, HE COULDN'T HAVE JUST DISAPPEARED ON ME!
AH! HOLD IT RIGHT THERE, BUDDY!
I'LL SEE YOU IN HELL, CONTI!
OOF!
HOW 'BOUT I SEND YOU ON AN ADVANCE SCOUTING MISSION INSTEAD!
KLANG
AND... *CUT!* THAT WAS AWESOME! CHECK THE GATE!
WHAT GATE, DAD? I DON'T SEE A GATE.
IT'S A MOVIE TERM, BUDDY. HE WANTS THE CAMERAMAN TO CHECK THE CAMERA TO MAKE SURE THE FILM ISN'T SCRATCHED, BECAUSE HE LIKED THAT LAST SHOT.
BUT WHY IS IT CALLED A GATE?

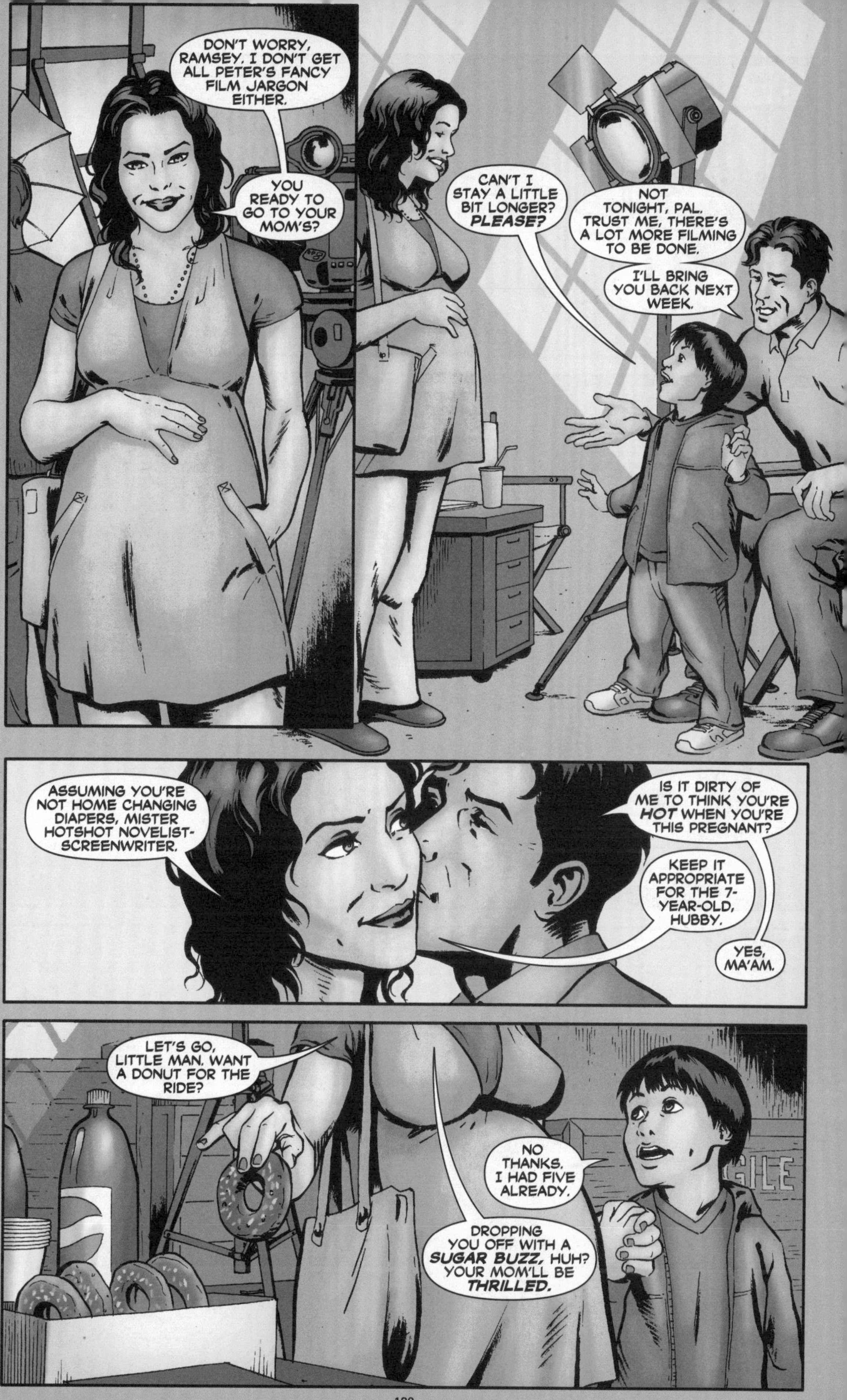

DON'T WORRY, RAMSEY. I DON'T GET ALL PETER'S FANCY FILM JARGON EITHER.
YOU READY TO GO TO YOUR MOM'S?
CAN'T I STAY A LITTLE BIT LONGER? *PLEASE?*
NOT TONIGHT, PAL. TRUST ME, THERE'S A LOT MORE FILMING TO BE DONE.
I'LL BRING YOU BACK NEXT WEEK.
ASSUMING YOU'RE NOT HOME CHANGING DIAPERS, MISTER HOTSHOT NOVELIST-SCREENWRITER.
IS IT DIRTY OF ME TO THINK YOU'RE *HOT* WHEN YOU'RE THIS PREGNANT?
KEEP IT APPROPRIATE FOR THE 7-YEAR-OLD, HUBBY.
YES, MA'AM.
LET'S GO, LITTLE MAN. WANT A DONUT FOR THE RIDE?
NO THANKS. I HAD FIVE ALREADY.
DROPPING YOU OFF WITH A *SUGAR BUZZ,* HUH? YOUR MOM'LL BE *THRILLED.*

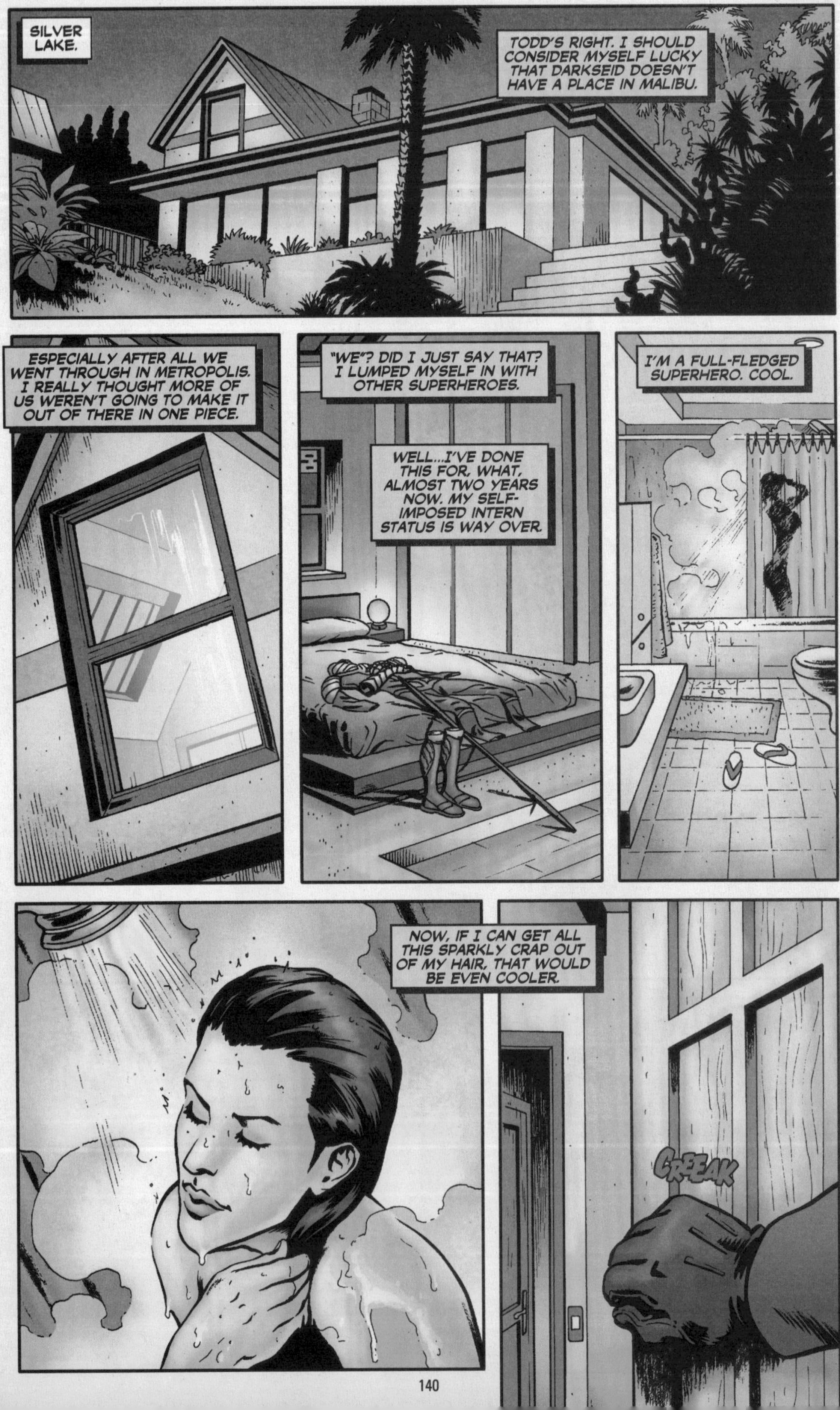
SILVER LAKE.
TODD'S RIGHT. I SHOULD CONSIDER MYSELF LUCKY THAT DARKSEID DOESN'T HAVE A PLACE IN MALIBU.
ESPECIALLY AFTER ALL WE WENT THROUGH IN METROPOLIS. I REALLY THOUGHT MORE OF US WEREN'T GOING TO MAKE IT OUT OF THERE IN ONE PIECE.
"WE"? DID I JUST SAY THAT? I LUMPED MYSELF IN WITH OTHER SUPERHEROES.
WELL...I'VE DONE THIS FOR, WHAT, ALMOST TWO YEARS NOW. MY SELF-IMPOSED INTERN STATUS IS WAY OVER.
I'M A FULL-FLEDGED SUPERHERO. COOL.
NOW, IF I CAN GET ALL THIS SPARKLY CRAP OUT OF MY HAIR, THAT WOULD BE EVEN COOLER.
CREEAK

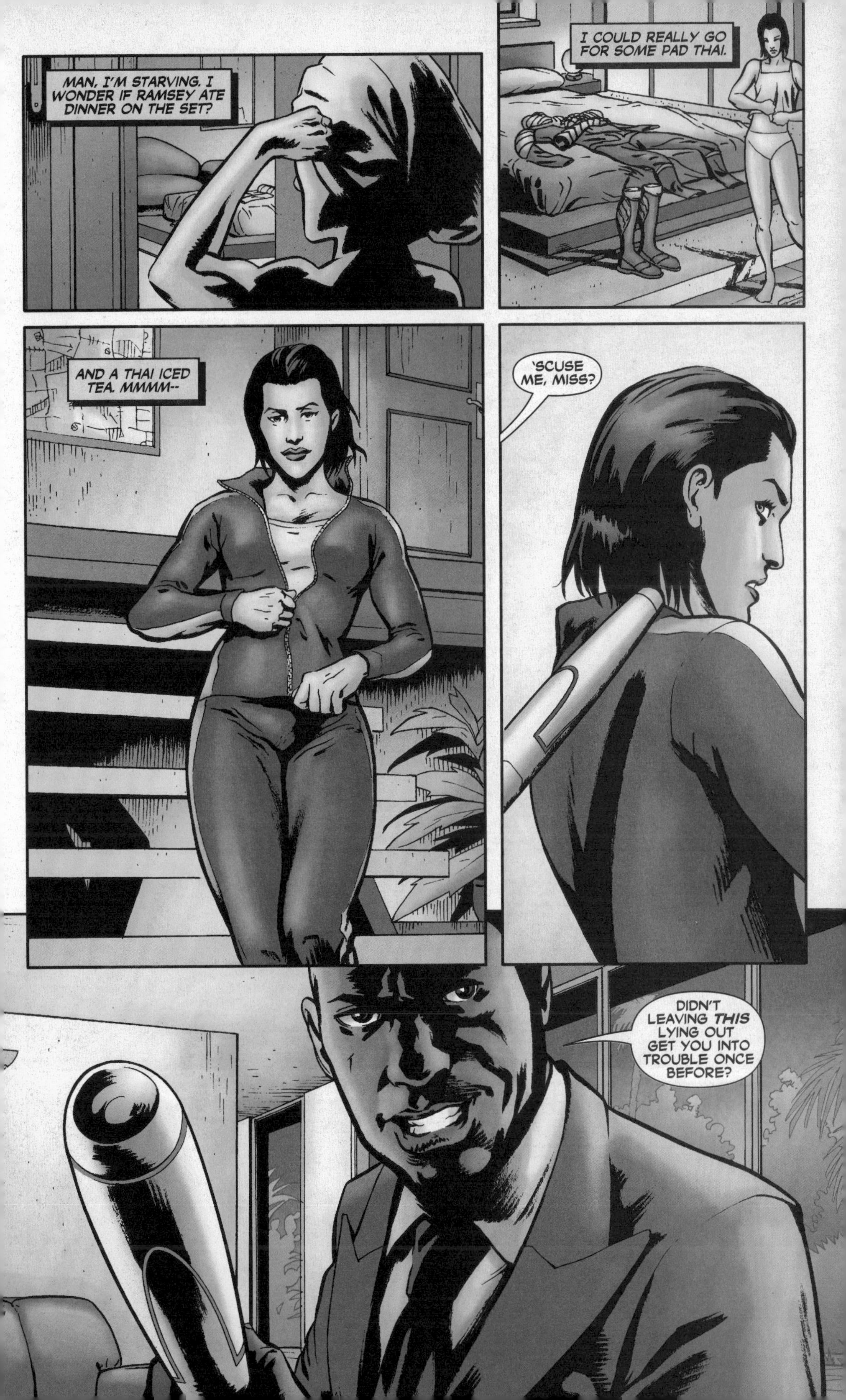
MAN, I'M STARVING. I WONDER IF RAMSEY ATE DINNER ON THE SET?
I COULD REALLY GO FOR SOME PAD THAI.
AND A THAI ICED TEA. MMMM--
'SCUSE ME, MISS?
DIDN'T LEAVING *THIS* LYING OUT GET YOU INTO TROUBLE ONCE BEFORE?

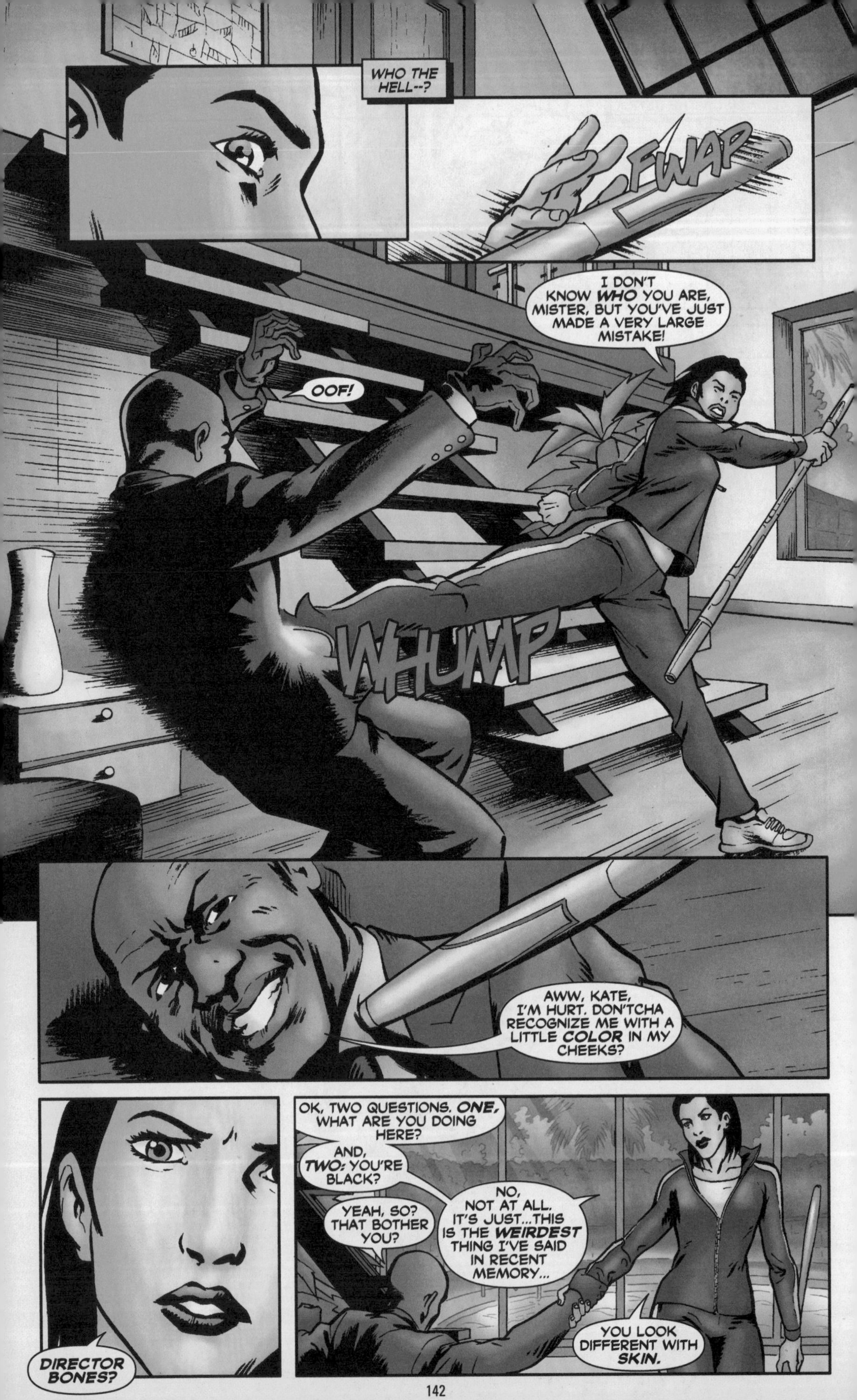
WHO THE HELL--?
FWAP
I DON'T KNOW WHO YOU ARE, MISTER, BUT YOU'VE JUST MADE A VERY LARGE MISTAKE!
OOF!
WHUMP
AWW, KATE, I'M HURT. DON'TCHA RECOGNIZE ME WITH A LITTLE COLOR IN MY CHEEKS?
DIRECTOR BONES?
OK, TWO QUESTIONS. ONE, WHAT ARE YOU DOING HERE?
AND, TWO: YOU'RE BLACK?
YEAH, SO? THAT BOTHER YOU?
NO, NOT AT ALL. IT'S JUST...THIS IS THE WEIRDEST THING I'VE SAID IN RECENT MEMORY...
YOU LOOK DIFFERENT WITH SKIN.

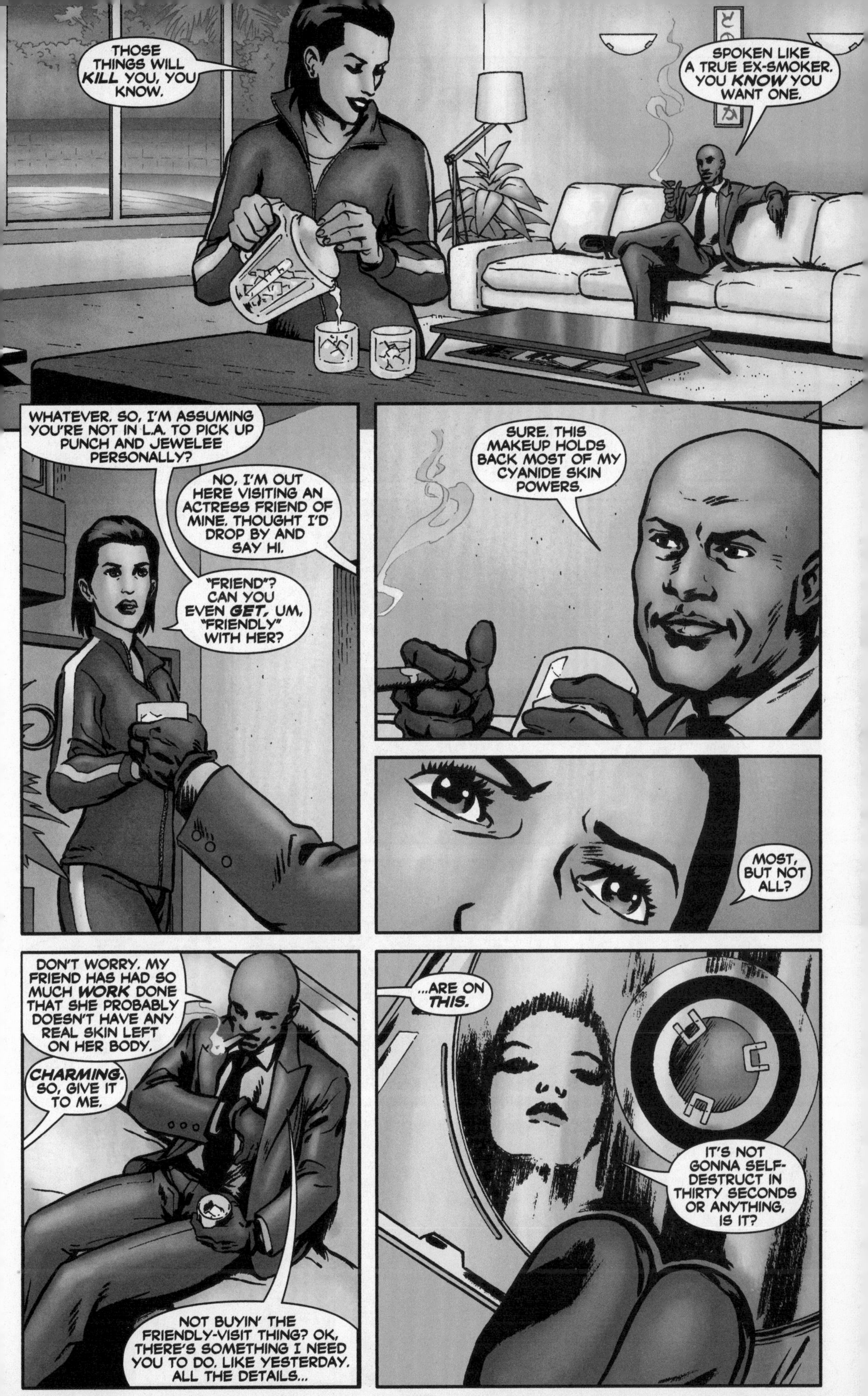
THOSE THINGS WILL KILL YOU, YOU KNOW.
SPOKEN LIKE A TRUE EX-SMOKER. YOU KNOW YOU WANT ONE.
WHATEVER. SO, I'M ASSUMING YOU'RE NOT IN L.A. TO PICK UP PUNCH AND JEWELEE PERSONALLY?
NO, I'M OUT HERE VISITING AN ACTRESS FRIEND OF MINE. THOUGHT I'D DROP BY AND SAY HI.
"FRIEND"? CAN YOU EVEN GET, UM, "FRIENDLY" WITH HER?
SURE. THIS MAKEUP HOLDS BACK MOST OF MY CYANIDE SKIN POWERS.
MOST, BUT NOT ALL?
DON'T WORRY. MY FRIEND HAS HAD SO MUCH WORK DONE THAT SHE PROBABLY DOESN'T HAVE ANY REAL SKIN LEFT ON HER BODY.
CHARMING. SO, GIVE IT TO ME.
NOT BUYIN' THE FRIENDLY-VISIT THING? OK, THERE'S SOMETHING I NEED YOU TO DO. LIKE YESTERDAY. ALL THE DETAILS...
...ARE ON THIS.
IT'S NOT GONNA SELF-DESTRUCT IN THIRTY SECONDS OR ANYTHING, IS IT?

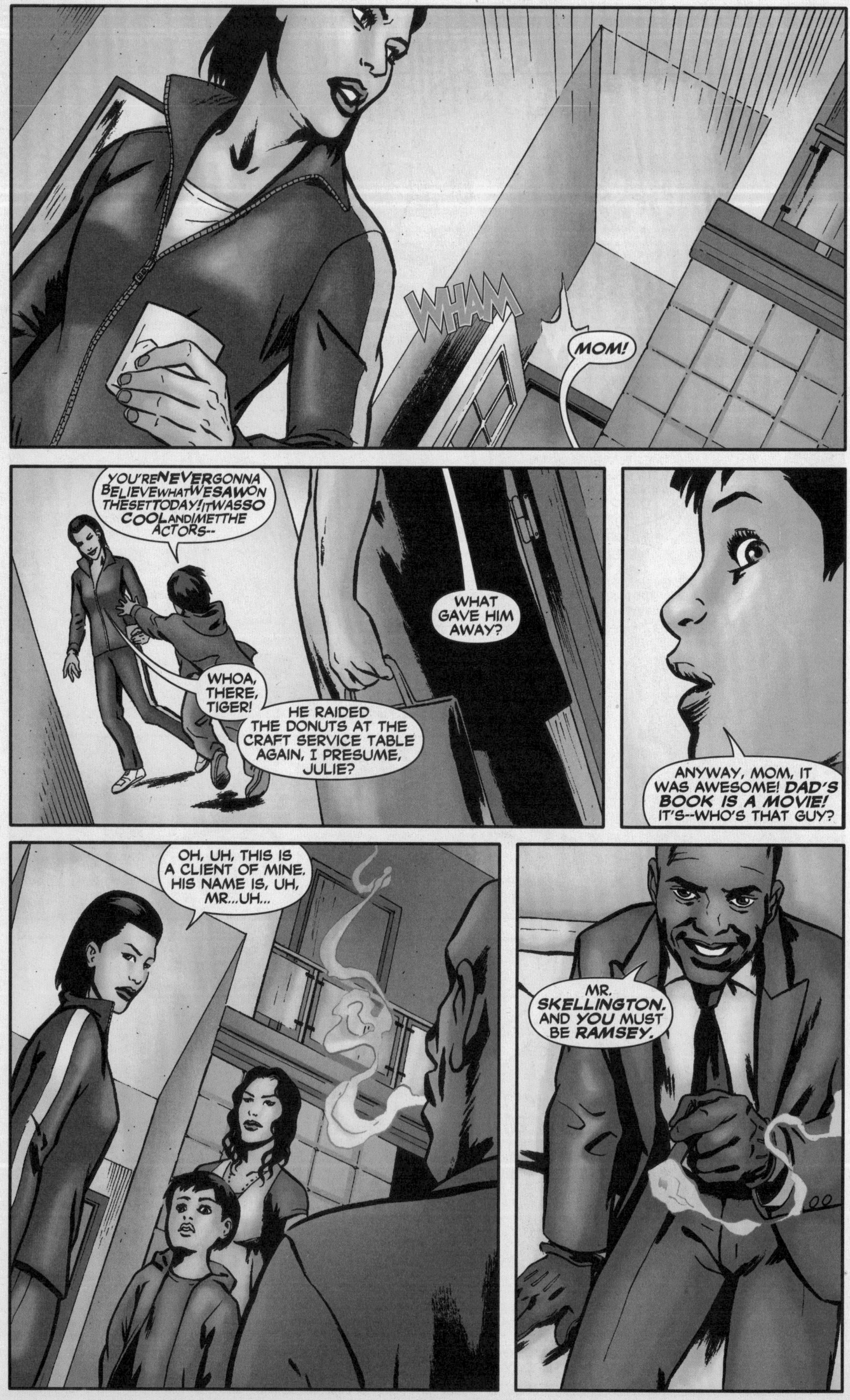
WHAM
MOM!
YOU'RE NEVER GONNA BELIEVE WHAT WE SAW ON THE SET TODAY! IT WAS SO COOL AND I MET THE ACTORS--
WHAT GAVE HIM AWAY?
WHOA, THERE, TIGER!
HE RAIDED THE DONUTS AT THE CRAFT SERVICE TABLE AGAIN, I PRESUME, JULIE?
ANYWAY, MOM, IT WAS AWESOME! DAD'S BOOK IS A MOVIE! IT'S--WHO'S THAT GUY?
OH, UH, THIS IS A CLIENT OF MINE. HIS NAME IS, UH, MR...UH...
MR. SKELLINGTON. AND YOU MUST BE RAMSEY.

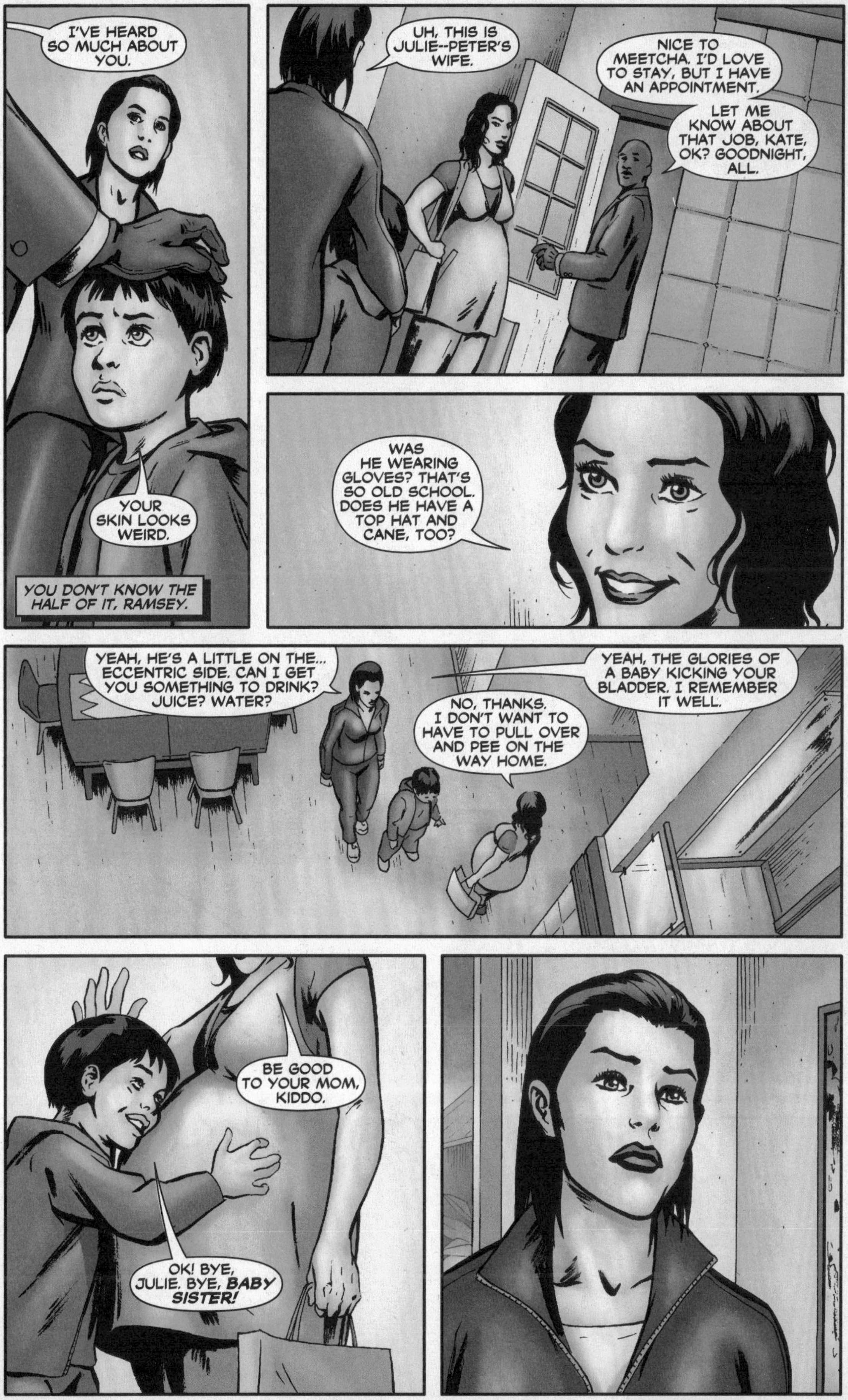
I'VE HEARD SO MUCH ABOUT YOU.
YOUR SKIN LOOKS WEIRD.
YOU DON'T KNOW THE HALF OF IT, RAMSEY.
UH, THIS IS JULIE--PETER'S WIFE.
NICE TO MEETCHA. I'D LOVE TO STAY, BUT I HAVE AN APPOINTMENT.
LET ME KNOW ABOUT THAT JOB, KATE, OK? GOODNIGHT, ALL.
WAS HE WEARING GLOVES? THAT'S SO OLD SCHOOL. DOES HE HAVE A TOP HAT AND CANE, TOO?
YEAH, HE'S A LITTLE ON THE... ECCENTRIC SIDE. CAN I GET YOU SOMETHING TO DRINK? JUICE? WATER?
NO, THANKS. I DON'T WANT TO HAVE TO PULL OVER AND PEE ON THE WAY HOME.
YEAH, THE GLORIES OF A BABY KICKING YOUR BLADDER. I REMEMBER IT WELL.
BE GOOD TO YOUR MOM, KIDDO.
OK! BYE, JULIE. BYE, BABY SISTER!

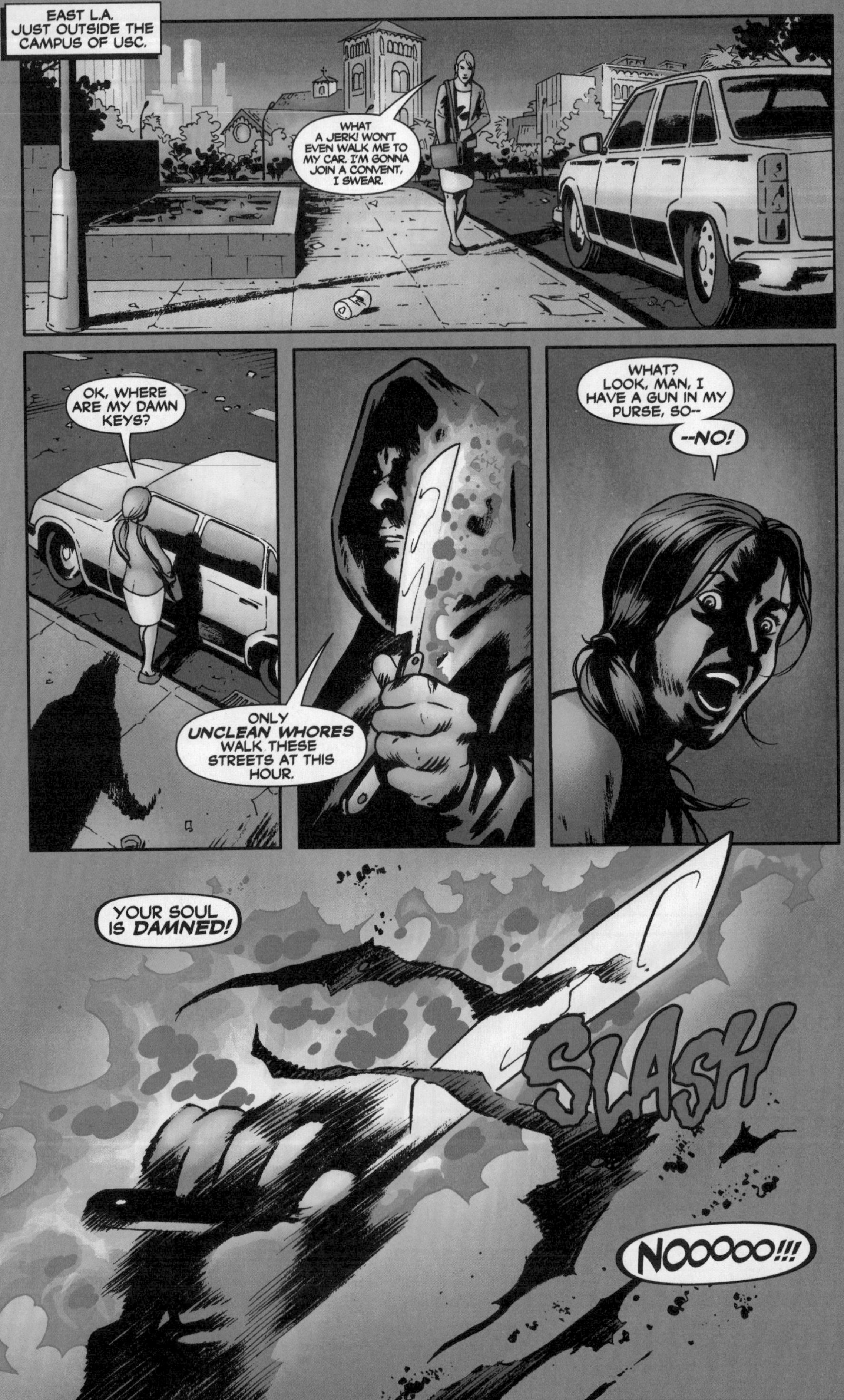
EAST L.A. JUST OUTSIDE THE CAMPUS OF USC.
WHAT A JERK! WON'T EVEN WALK ME TO MY CAR. I'M GONNA JOIN A CONVENT, I SWEAR.
OK, WHERE ARE MY DAMN KEYS?
ONLY UNCLEAN WHORES WALK THESE STREETS AT THIS HOUR.
WHAT? LOOK, MAN, I HAVE A GUN IN MY PURSE, SO--
--NO!
YOUR SOUL IS DAMNED!
SLASH
NOOOOO!!!

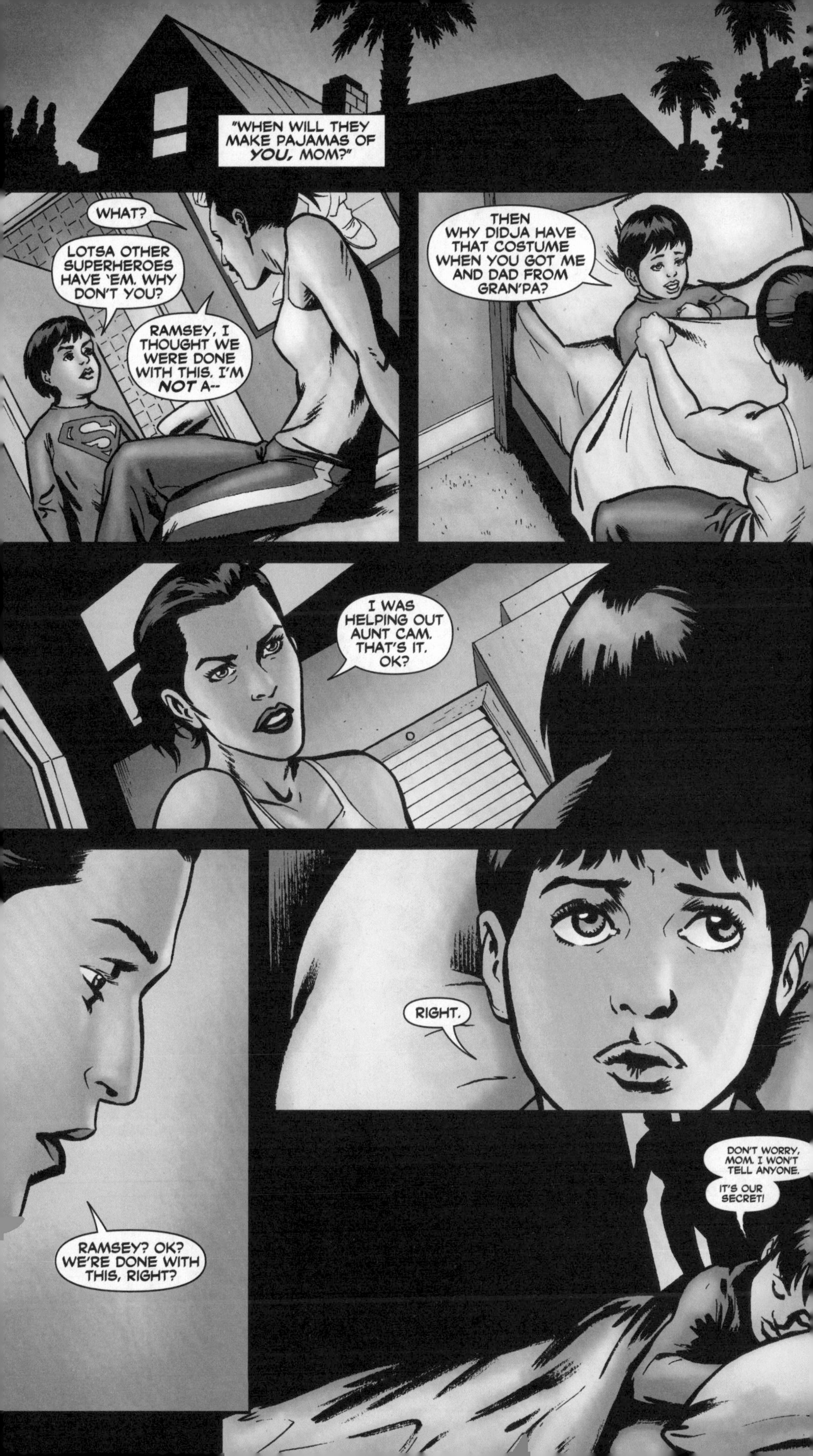
"WHEN WILL THEY MAKE PAJAMAS OF YOU, MOM?"
WHAT?
LOTSA OTHER SUPERHEROES HAVE 'EM. WHY DON'T YOU?
RAMSEY, I THOUGHT WE WERE DONE WITH THIS. I'M NOT A--
THEN WHY DIDJA HAVE THAT COSTUME WHEN YOU GOT ME AND DAD FROM GRAN'PA?
I WAS HELPING OUT AUNT CAM. THAT'S IT. OK?
RAMSEY? OK? WE'RE DONE WITH THIS, RIGHT?
RIGHT.
DON'T WORRY, MOM. I WON'T TELL ANYONE.
IT'S OUR SECRET!

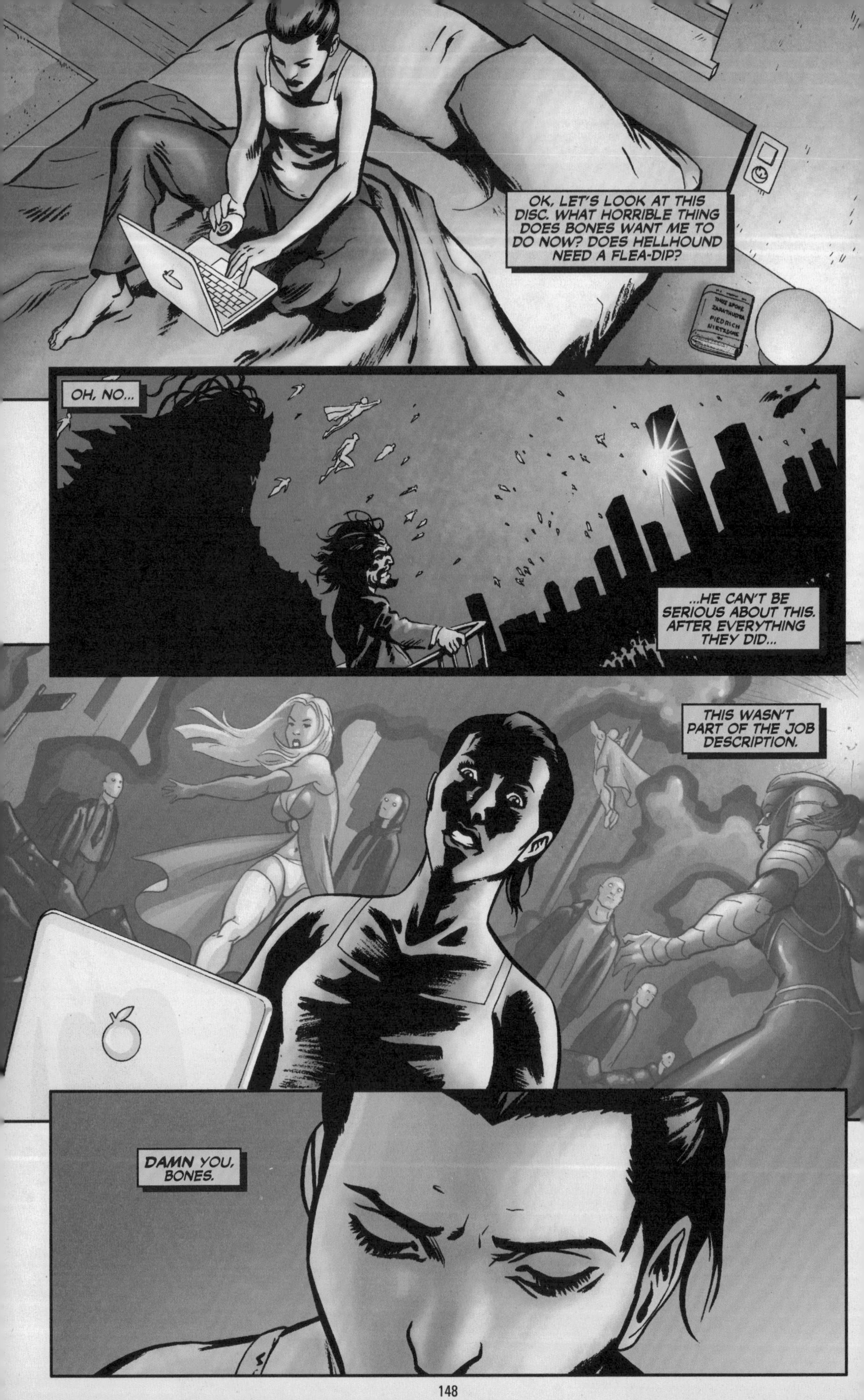
OK, LET'S LOOK AT THIS DISC. WHAT HORRIBLE THING DOES BONES WANT ME TO DO NOW? DOES HELLHOUND NEED A FLEA-DIP?
OH, NO...
...HE CAN'T BE SERIOUS ABOUT THIS. AFTER EVERYTHING THEY DID...
THIS WASN'T PART OF THE JOB DESCRIPTION.
DAMN YOU, BONES.

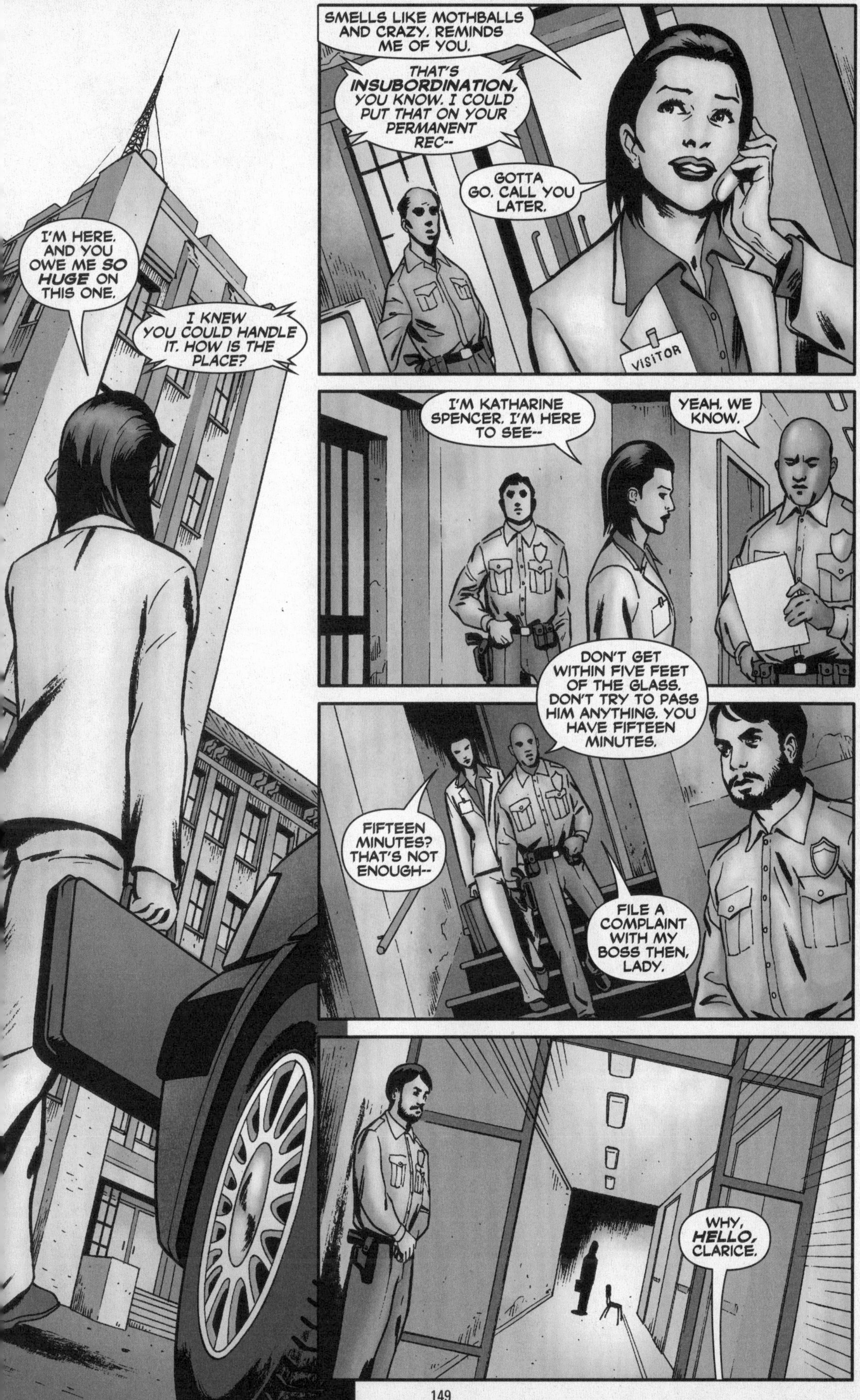

I'M HERE. AND YOU OWE ME SO HUGE ON THIS ONE.
I KNEW YOU COULD HANDLE IT. HOW IS THE PLACE?
SMELLS LIKE MOTHBALLS AND CRAZY. REMINDS ME OF YOU.
THAT'S INSUBORDINATION, YOU KNOW. I COULD PUT THAT ON YOUR PERMANENT REC--
GOTTA GO. CALL YOU LATER.
VISITOR
I'M KATHARINE SPENCER. I'M HERE TO SEE--
YEAH. WE KNOW.
DON'T GET WITHIN FIVE FEET OF THE GLASS. DON'T TRY TO PASS HIM ANYTHING. YOU HAVE FIFTEEN MINUTES.
FIFTEEN MINUTES? THAT'S NOT ENOUGH--
FILE A COMPLAINT WITH MY BOSS THEN, LADY.
WHY, HELLO, CLARICE.

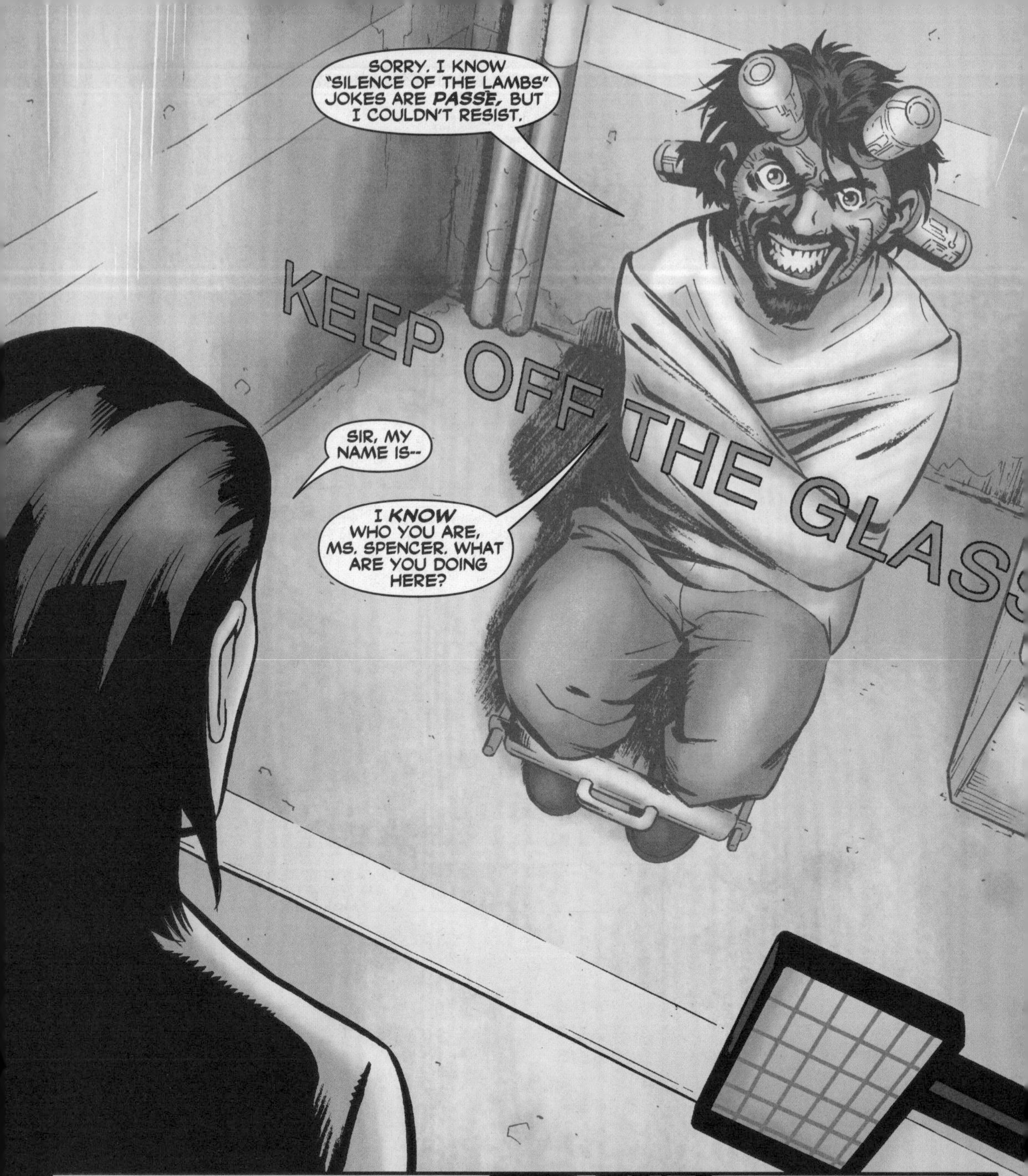
SORRY. I KNOW "SILENCE OF THE LAMBS" JOKES ARE PASSE, BUT I COULDN'T RESIST.
KEEP OFF THE GLASS
SIR, MY NAME IS--
I KNOW WHO YOU ARE, MS. SPENCER. WHAT ARE YOU DOING HERE?

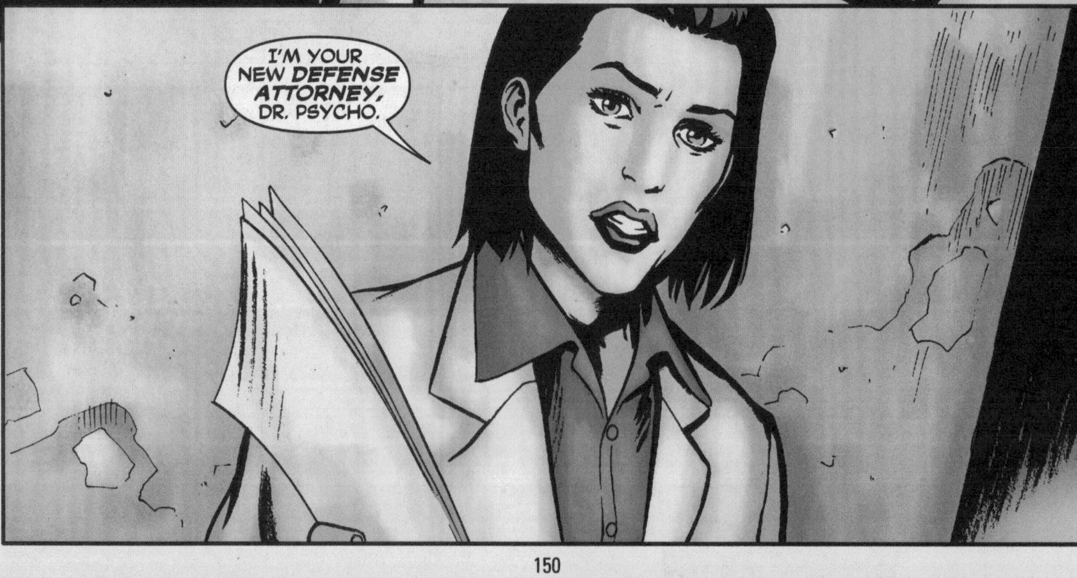
I'M YOUR NEW DEFENSE ATTORNEY, DR. PSYCHO.

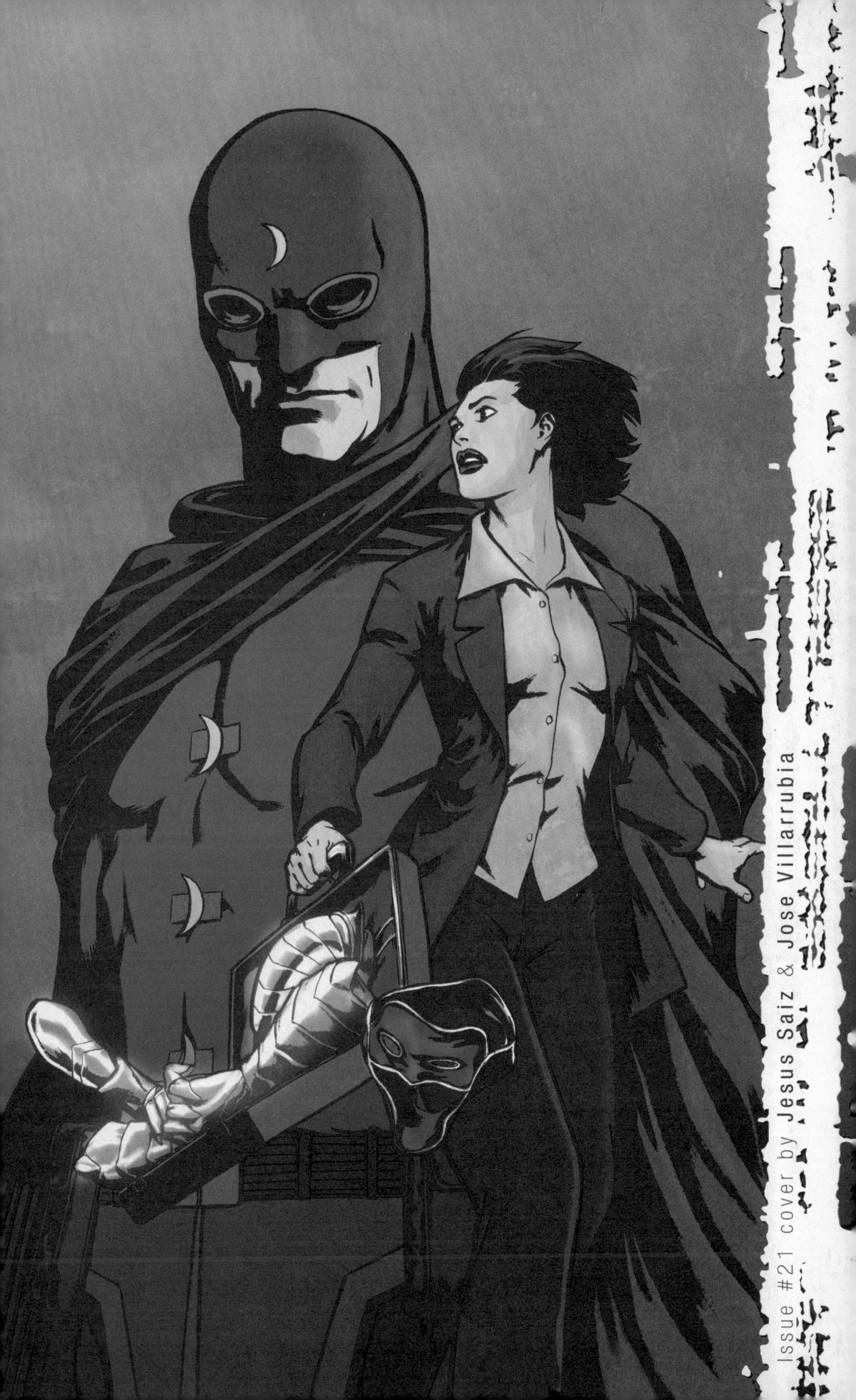

Issue #21 cover by Jesus Saiz & Jose Villarrubia

Interior art by Javier Pina & Fernando Blanco

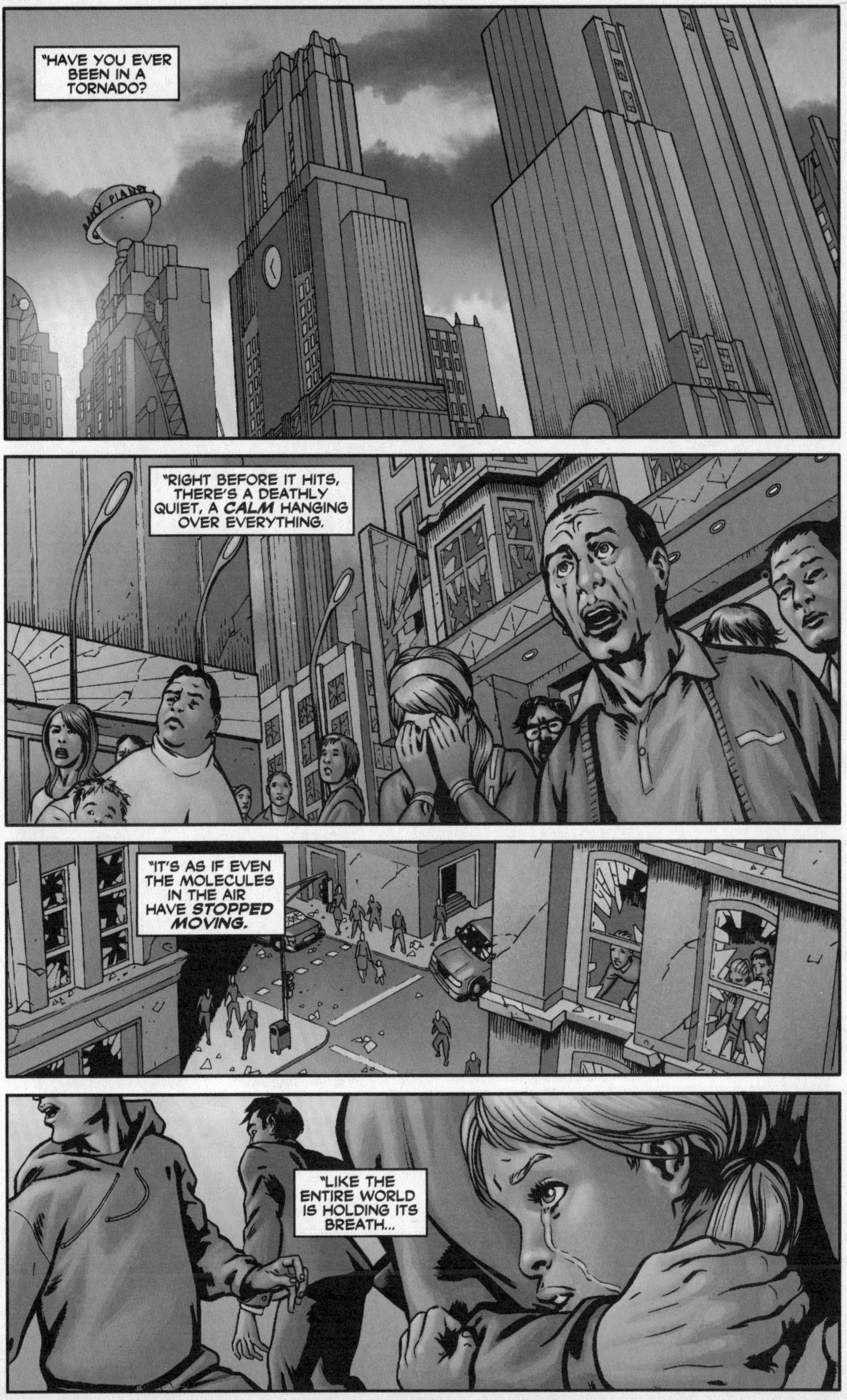
"HAVE YOU EVER BEEN IN A TORNADO?
"RIGHT BEFORE IT HITS, THERE'S A DEATHLY QUIET, A CALM HANGING OVER EVERYTHING.
"IT'S AS IF EVEN THE MOLECULES IN THE AIR HAVE STOPPED MOVING.
"LIKE THE ENTIRE WORLD IS HOLDING ITS BREATH...

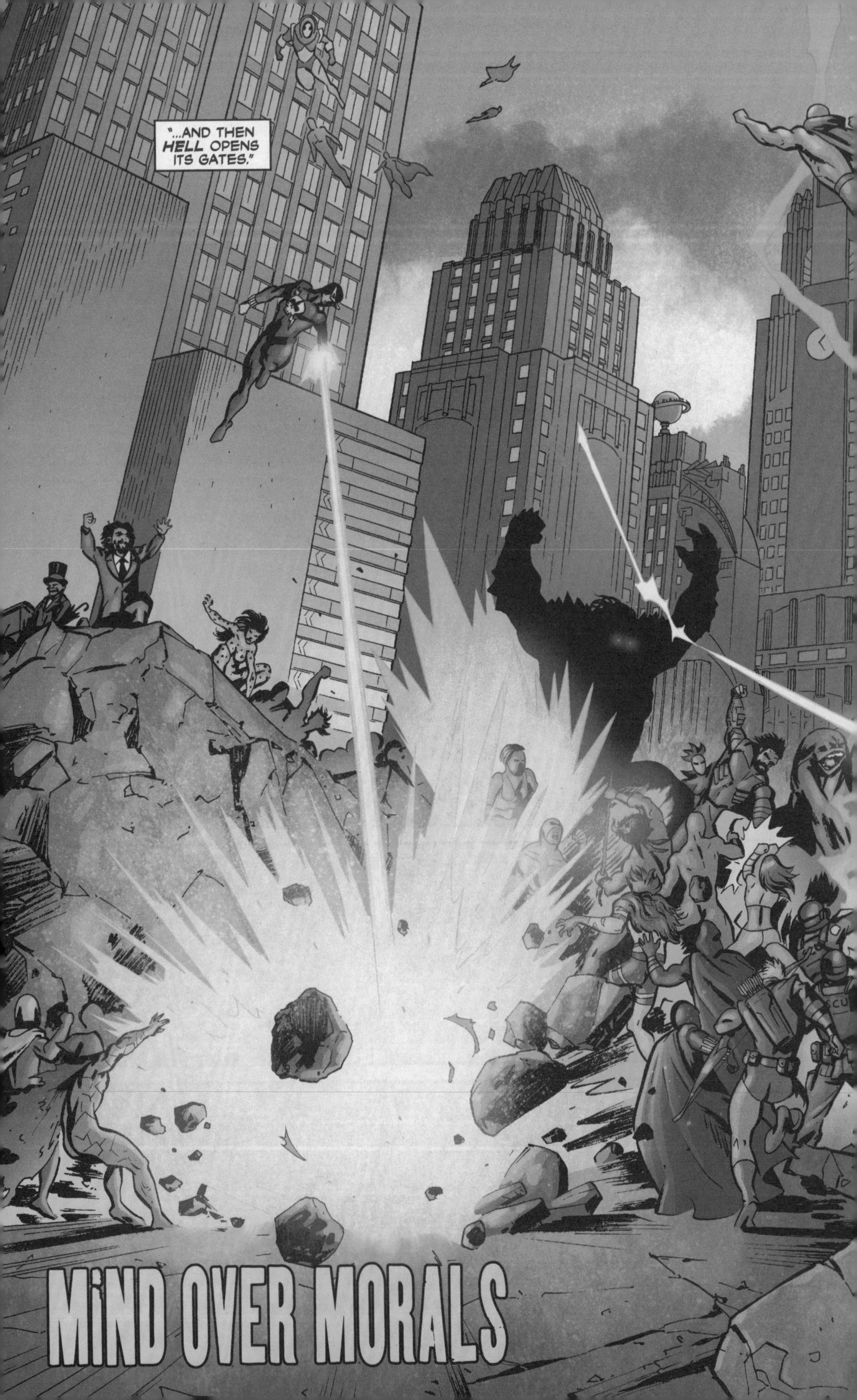
"...AND THEN HELL OPENS ITS GATES."
MIND OVER MORALS

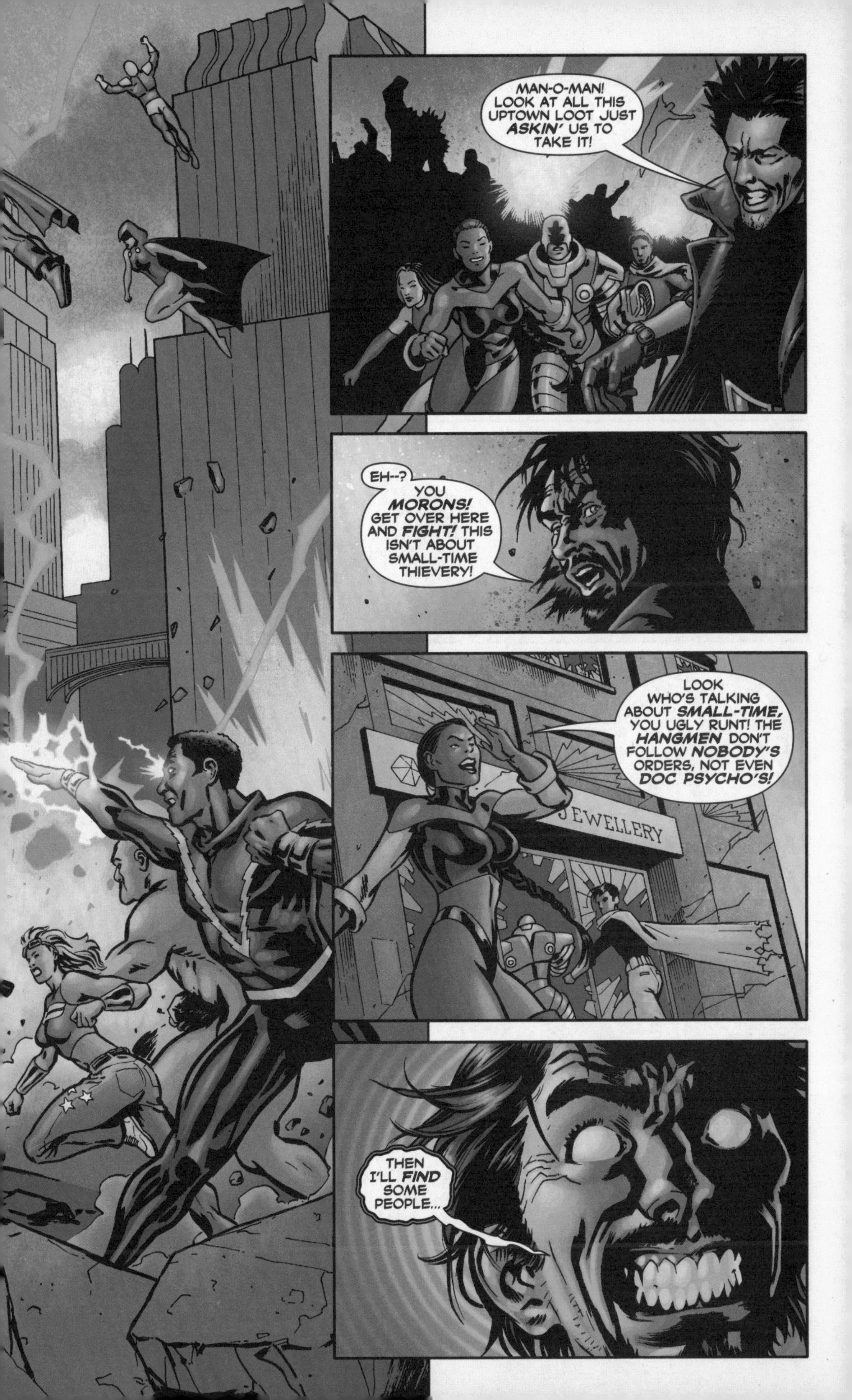

MAN-O-MAN! LOOK AT ALL THIS UPTOWN LOOT JUST ASKIN' US TO TAKE IT!
EH--?
YOU MORONS! GET OVER HERE AND FIGHT! THIS ISN'T ABOUT SMALL-TIME THIEVERY!
LOOK WHO'S TALKING ABOUT SMALL-TIME, YOU UGLY RUNT! THE HANGMEN DON'T FOLLOW NOBODY'S ORDERS, NOT EVEN DOC PSYCHO'S!
JEWELLERY
THEN I'LL FIND SOME PEOPLE...

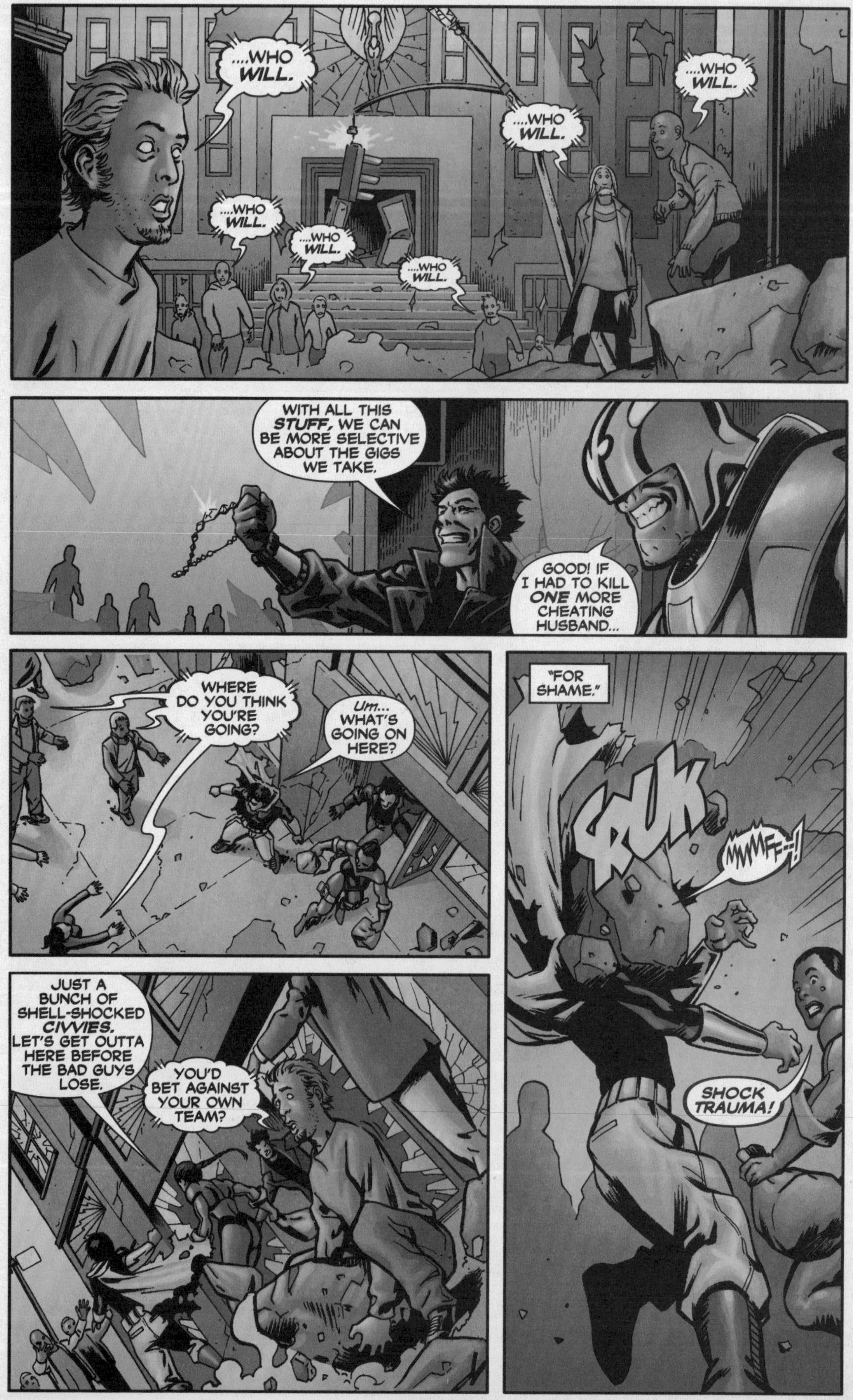

...WHO WILL.
...WHO WILL.
...WHO WILL.
...WHO WILL.
...WHO WILL.
...WHO WILL.
...WHO WILL.
WITH ALL THIS STUFF, WE CAN BE MORE SELECTIVE ABOUT THE GIGS WE TAKE.
GOOD! IF I HAD TO KILL ONE MORE CHEATING HUSBAND...
WHERE DO YOU THINK YOU'RE GOING?
Um... WHAT'S GOING ON HERE?
JUST A BUNCH OF SHELL-SHOCKED CIVVIES. LET'S GET OUTTA HERE BEFORE THE BAD GUYS LOSE.
YOU'D BET AGAINST YOUR OWN TEAM?
"FOR SHAME."
SCHUK
MMMFF--!
SHOCK TRAUMA!

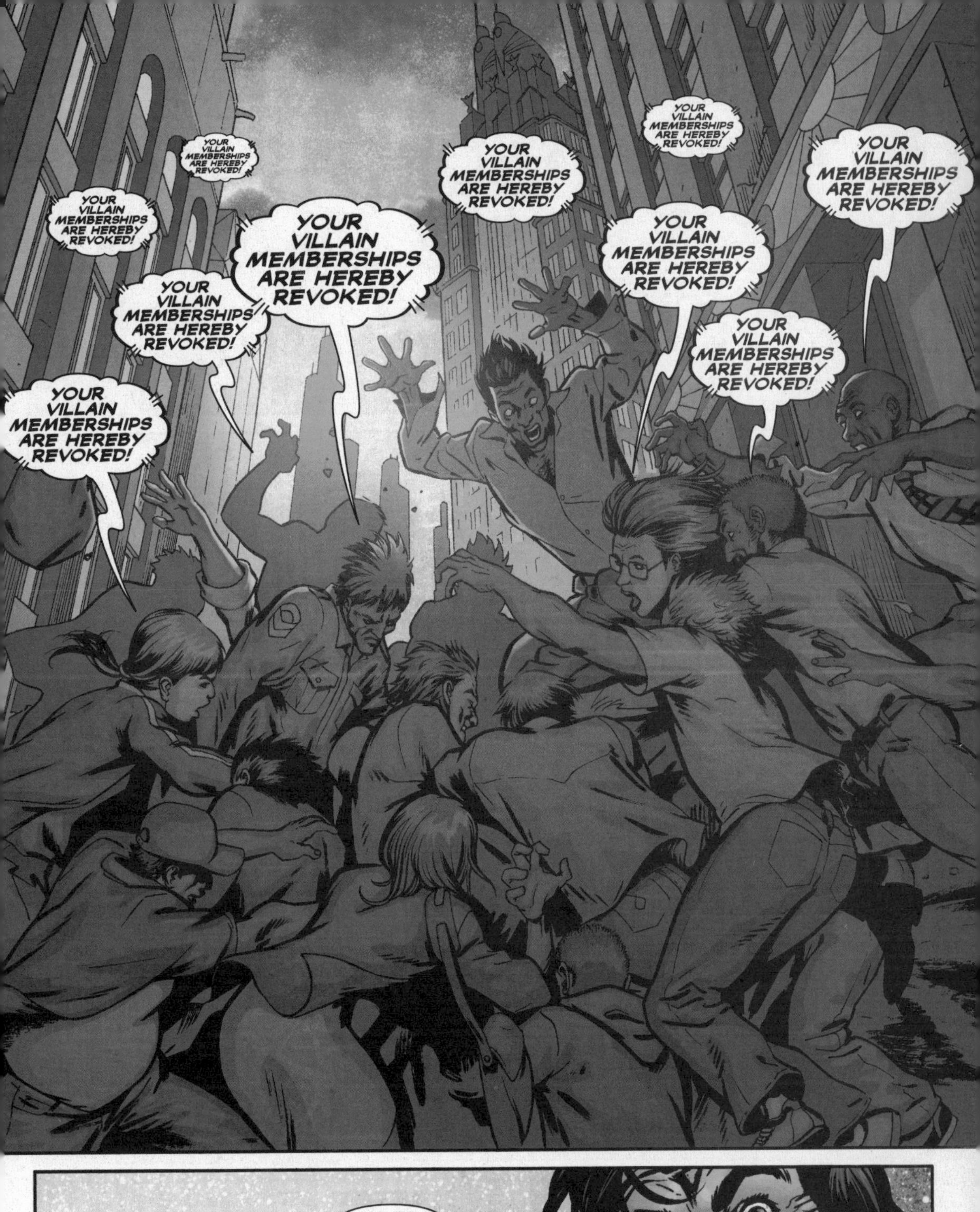
YOUR VILLAIN MEMBERSHIPS ARE HEREBY REVOKED!
YOUR VILLAIN MEMBERSHIPS ARE HEREBY REVOKED!
YOUR VILLAIN MEMBERSHIPS ARE HEREBY REVOKED!
YOUR VILLAIN MEMBERSHIPS ARE HEREBY REVOKED!
YOUR VILLAIN MEMBERSHIPS ARE HEREBY REVOKED!
YOUR VILLAIN MEMBERSHIPS ARE HEREBY REVOKED!
YOUR VILLAIN MEMBERSHIPS ARE HEREBY REVOKED!
YOUR VILLAIN MEMBERSHIPS ARE HEREBY REVOKED!
YOUR VILLAIN MEMBERSHIPS ARE HEREBY REVOKED!
YOUR VILLAIN MEMBERSHIPS ARE HEREBY REVOKED!

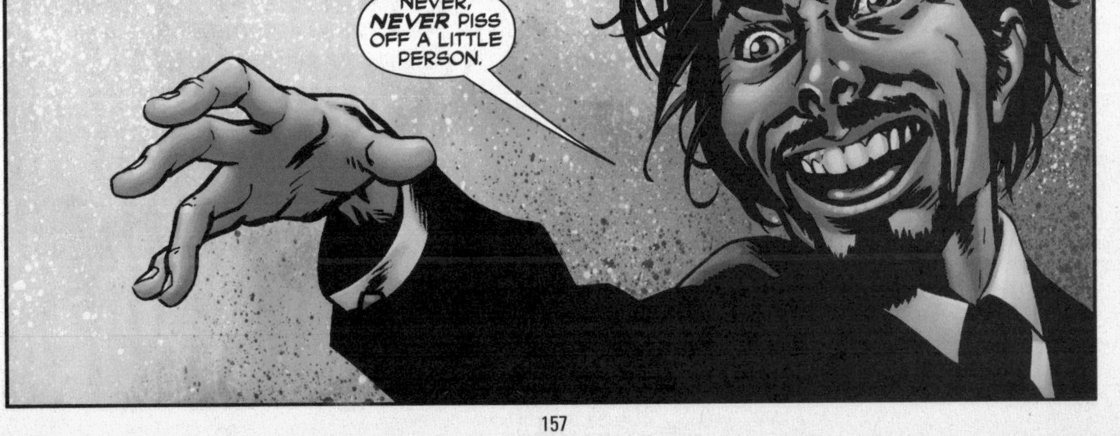
NEVER, **NEVER** PISS OFF A LITTLE PERSON.

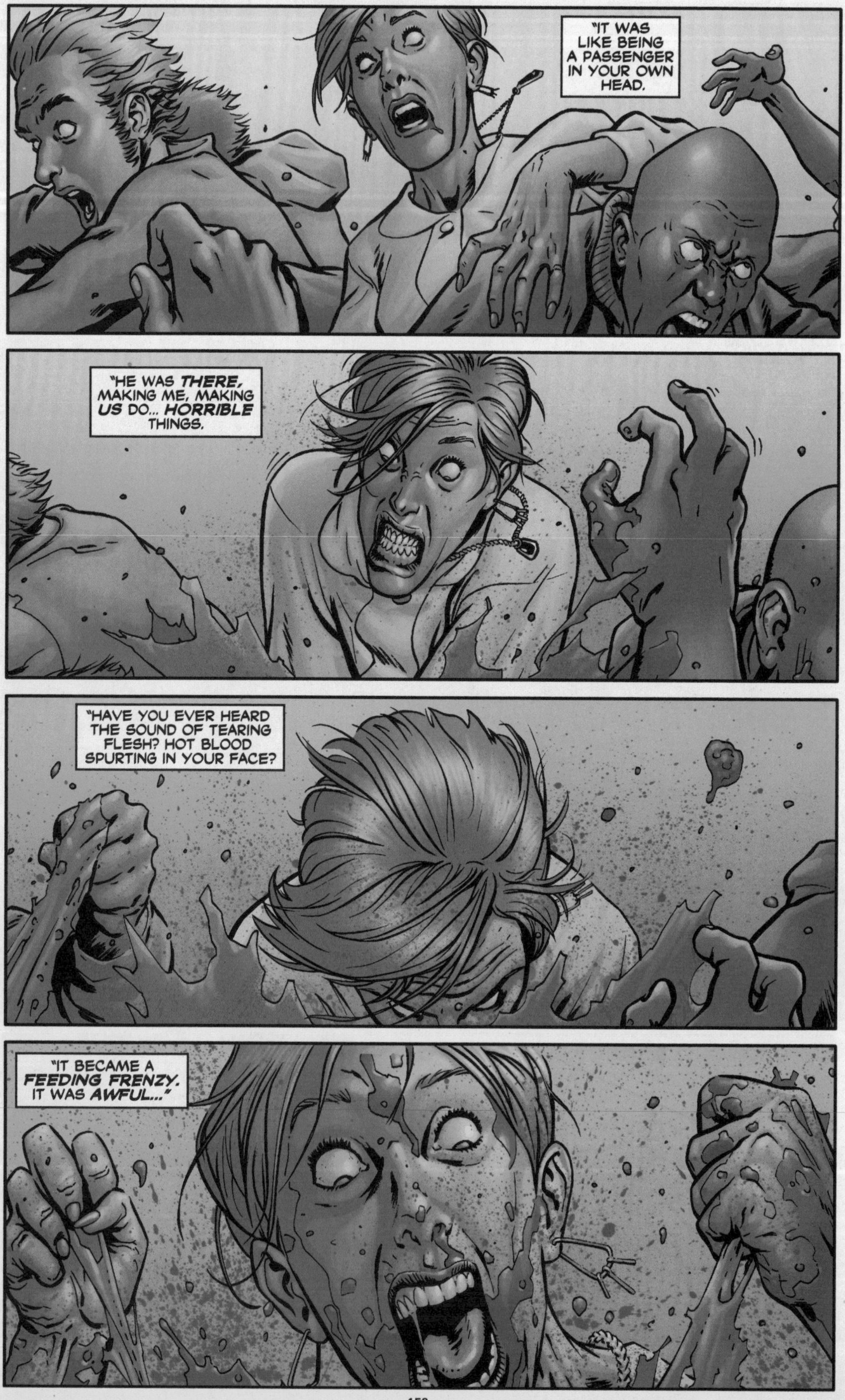
"IT WAS LIKE BEING A PASSENGER IN YOUR OWN HEAD.
"HE WAS THERE, MAKING ME, MAKING US DO... HORRIBLE THINGS.
"HAVE YOU EVER HEARD THE SOUND OF TEARING FLESH? HOT BLOOD SPURTING IN YOUR FACE?
"IT BECAME A FEEDING FRENZY. IT WAS AWFUL..."

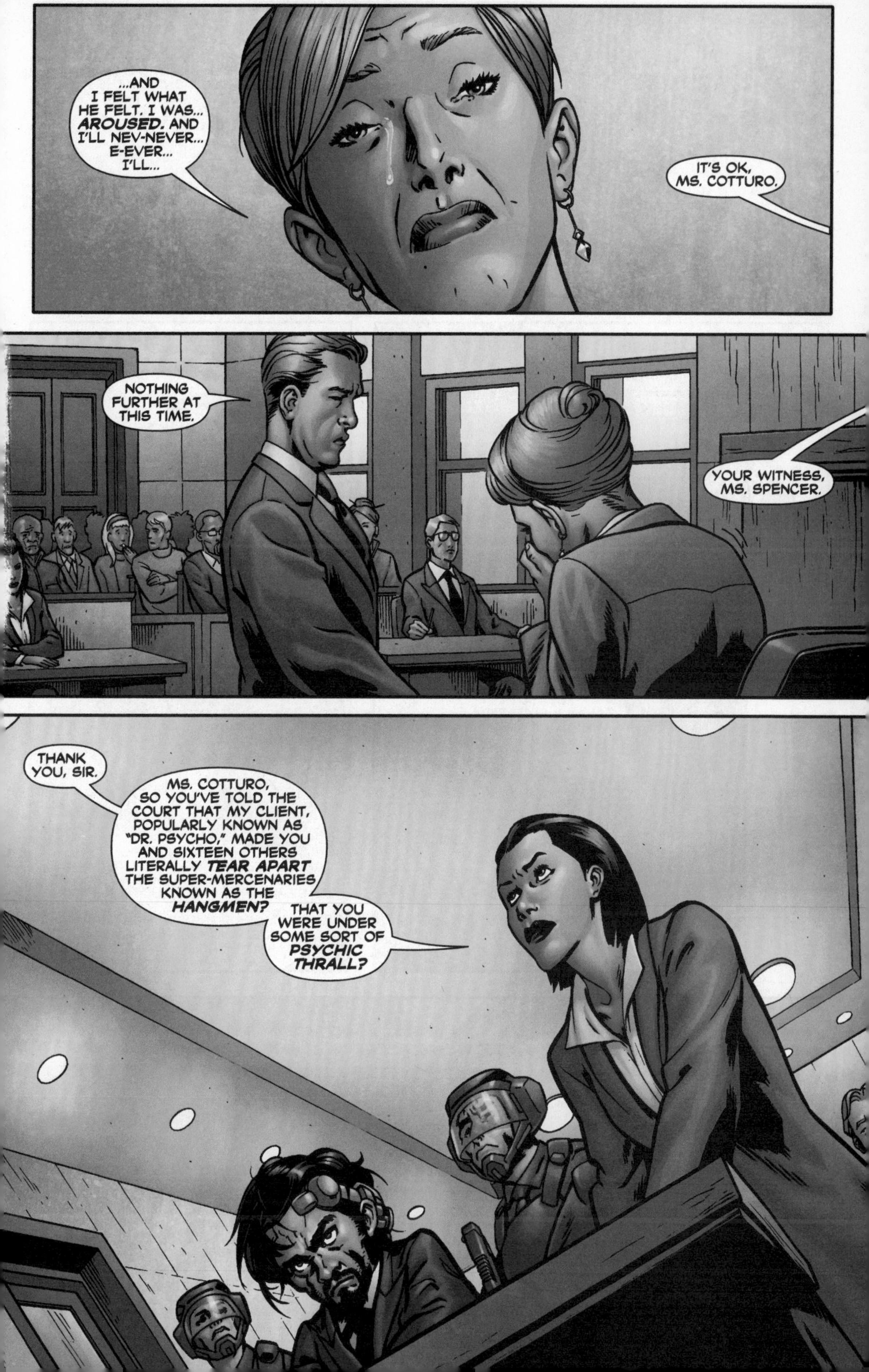
...AND I FELT WHAT HE FELT. I WAS... AROUSED. AND I'LL NEV-NEVER... E-EVER... I'LL...
IT'S OK, MS. COTTURO.
NOTHING FURTHER AT THIS TIME.
YOUR WITNESS, MS. SPENCER.
THANK YOU, SIR.
MS. COTTURO, SO YOU'VE TOLD THE COURT THAT MY CLIENT, POPULARLY KNOWN AS "DR. PSYCHO," MADE YOU AND SIXTEEN OTHERS LITERALLY TEAR APART THE SUPER-MERCENARIES KNOWN AS THE HANGMEN?
THAT YOU WERE UNDER SOME SORT OF PSYCHIC THRALL?

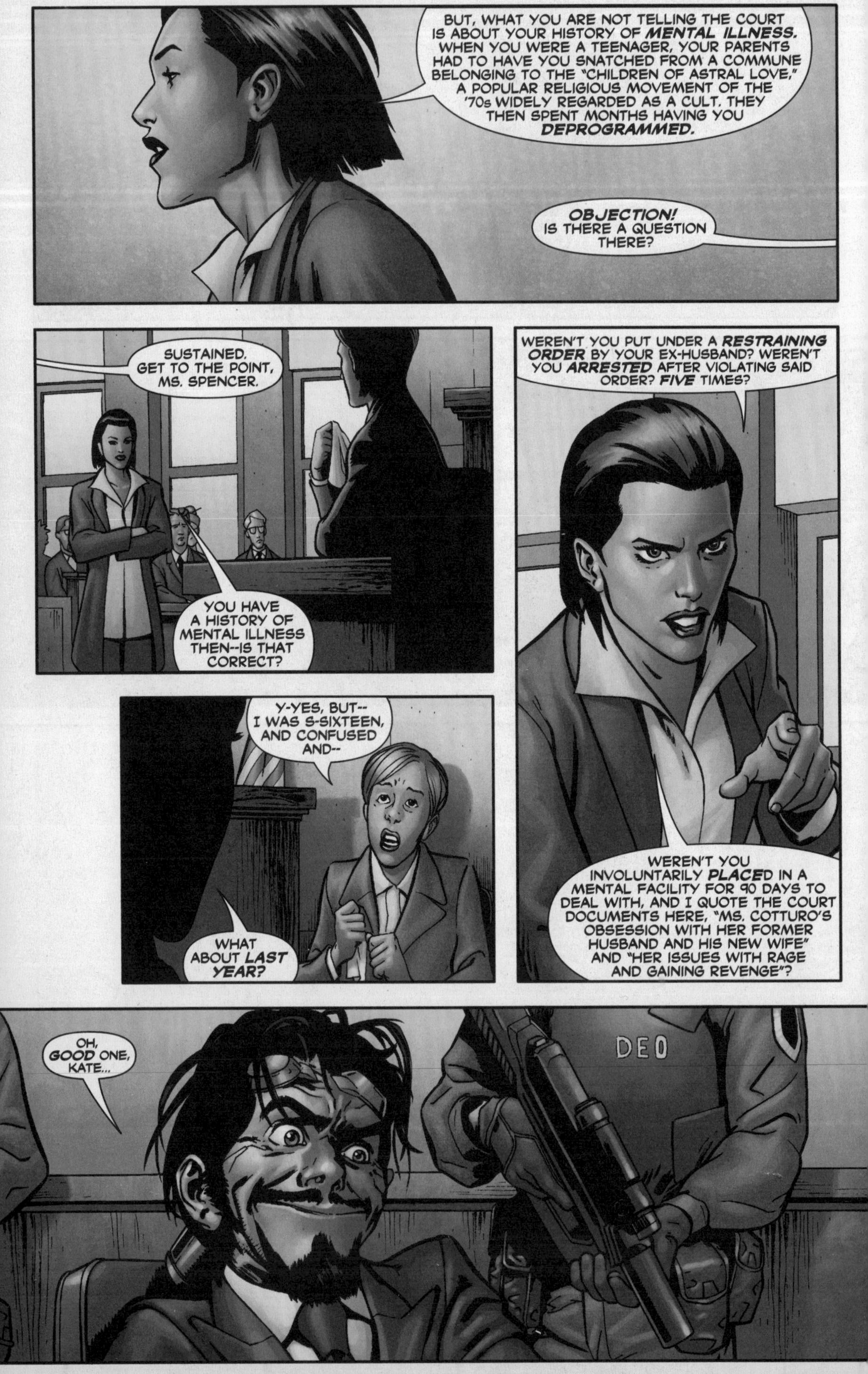
BUT, WHAT YOU ARE NOT TELLING THE COURT IS ABOUT YOUR HISTORY OF MENTAL ILLNESS. WHEN YOU WERE A TEENAGER, YOUR PARENTS HAD TO HAVE YOU SNATCHED FROM A COMMUNE BELONGING TO THE "CHILDREN OF ASTRAL LOVE," A POPULAR RELIGIOUS MOVEMENT OF THE '70s WIDELY REGARDED AS A CULT. THEY THEN SPENT MONTHS HAVING YOU DEPROGRAMMED.
OBJECTION! IS THERE A QUESTION THERE?
SUSTAINED. GET TO THE POINT, MS. SPENCER.
YOU HAVE A HISTORY OF MENTAL ILLNESS THEN--IS THAT CORRECT?
Y-YES, BUT-- I WAS S-SIXTEEN, AND CONFUSED AND--
WHAT ABOUT LAST YEAR?
WEREN'T YOU PUT UNDER A RESTRAINING ORDER BY YOUR EX-HUSBAND? WEREN'T YOU ARRESTED AFTER VIOLATING SAID ORDER? FIVE TIMES?
WEREN'T YOU INVOLUNTARILY PLACED IN A MENTAL FACILITY FOR 90 DAYS TO DEAL WITH, AND I QUOTE THE COURT DOCUMENTS HERE, "MS. COTTURO'S OBSESSION WITH HER FORMER HUSBAND AND HIS NEW WIFE" AND "HER ISSUES WITH RAGE AND GAINING REVENGE"?
OH, GOOD ONE, KATE...
DEO

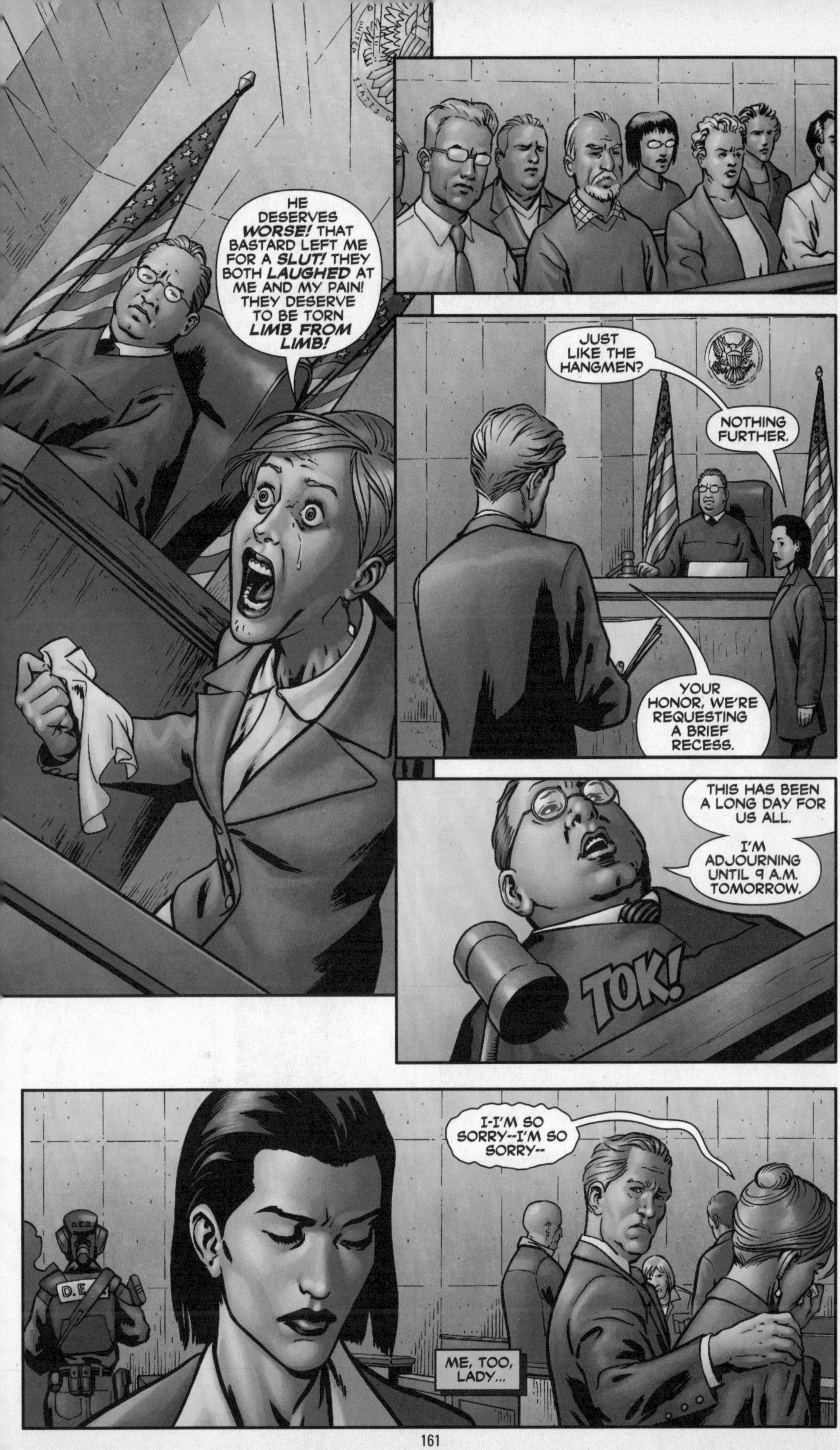

HE DESERVES WORSE! THAT BASTARD LEFT ME FOR A SLUT! THEY BOTH LAUGHED AT ME AND MY PAIN! THEY DESERVE TO BE TORN LIMB FROM LIMB!
JUST LIKE THE HANGMEN?
NOTHING FURTHER.
YOUR HONOR, WE'RE REQUESTING A BRIEF RECESS.
THIS HAS BEEN A LONG DAY FOR US ALL.
I'M ADJOURNING UNTIL 9 A.M. TOMORROW.
TOK!
I-I'M SO SORRY--I'M SO SORRY--
D.E.O.
ME, TOO, LADY...

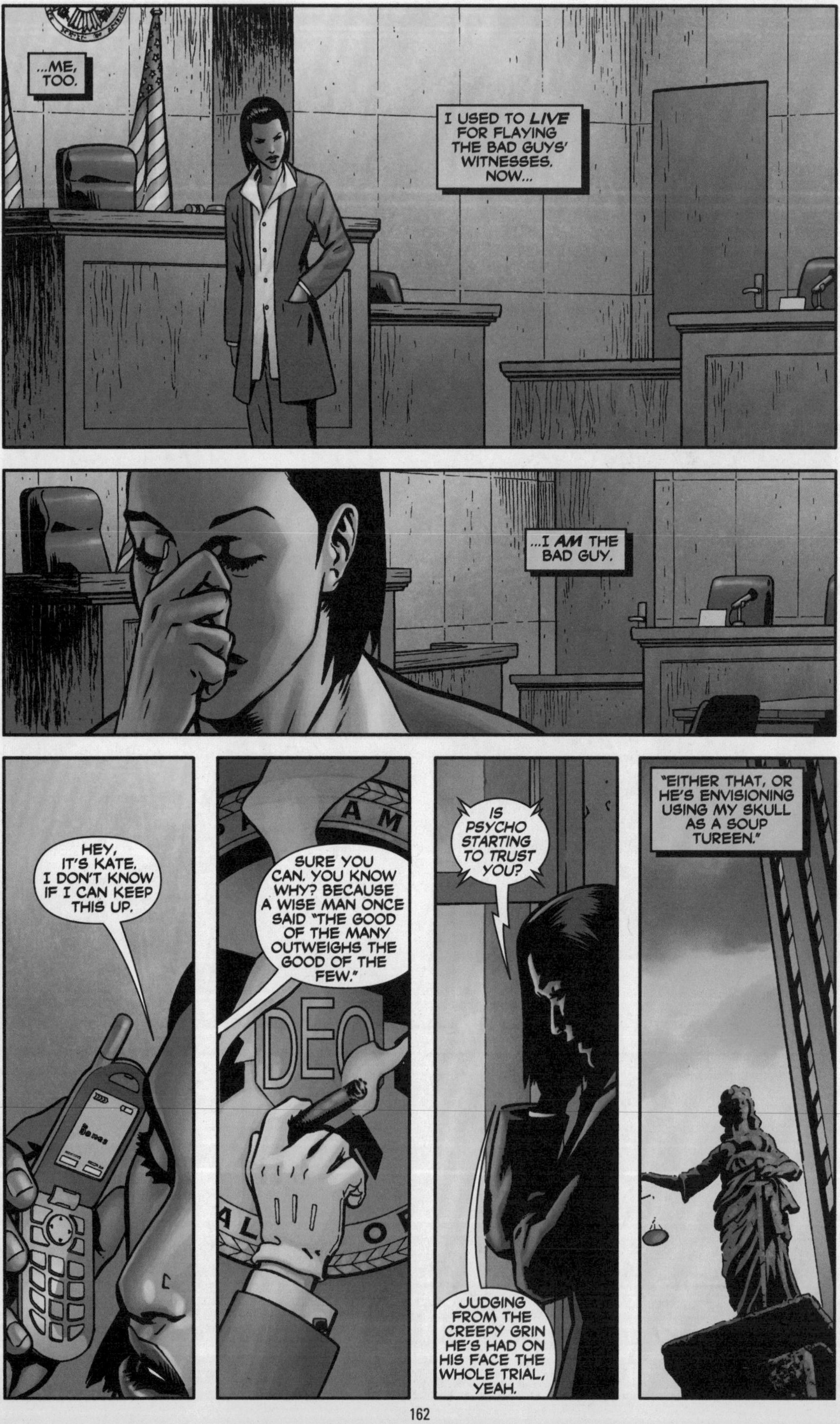
...ME, TOO.
I USED TO LIVE FOR FLAYING THE BAD GUYS' WITNESSES. NOW...
...I AM THE BAD GUY.
HEY, IT'S KATE. I DON'T KNOW IF I CAN KEEP THIS UP.
SURE YOU CAN. YOU KNOW WHY? BECAUSE A WISE MAN ONCE SAID "THE GOOD OF THE MANY OUTWEIGHS THE GOOD OF THE FEW."
IS PSYCHO STARTING TO TRUST YOU?
JUDGING FROM THE CREEPY GRIN HE'S HAD ON HIS FACE THE WHOLE TRIAL, YEAH.
"EITHER THAT, OR HE'S ENVISIONING USING MY SKULL AS A SOUP TUREEN."

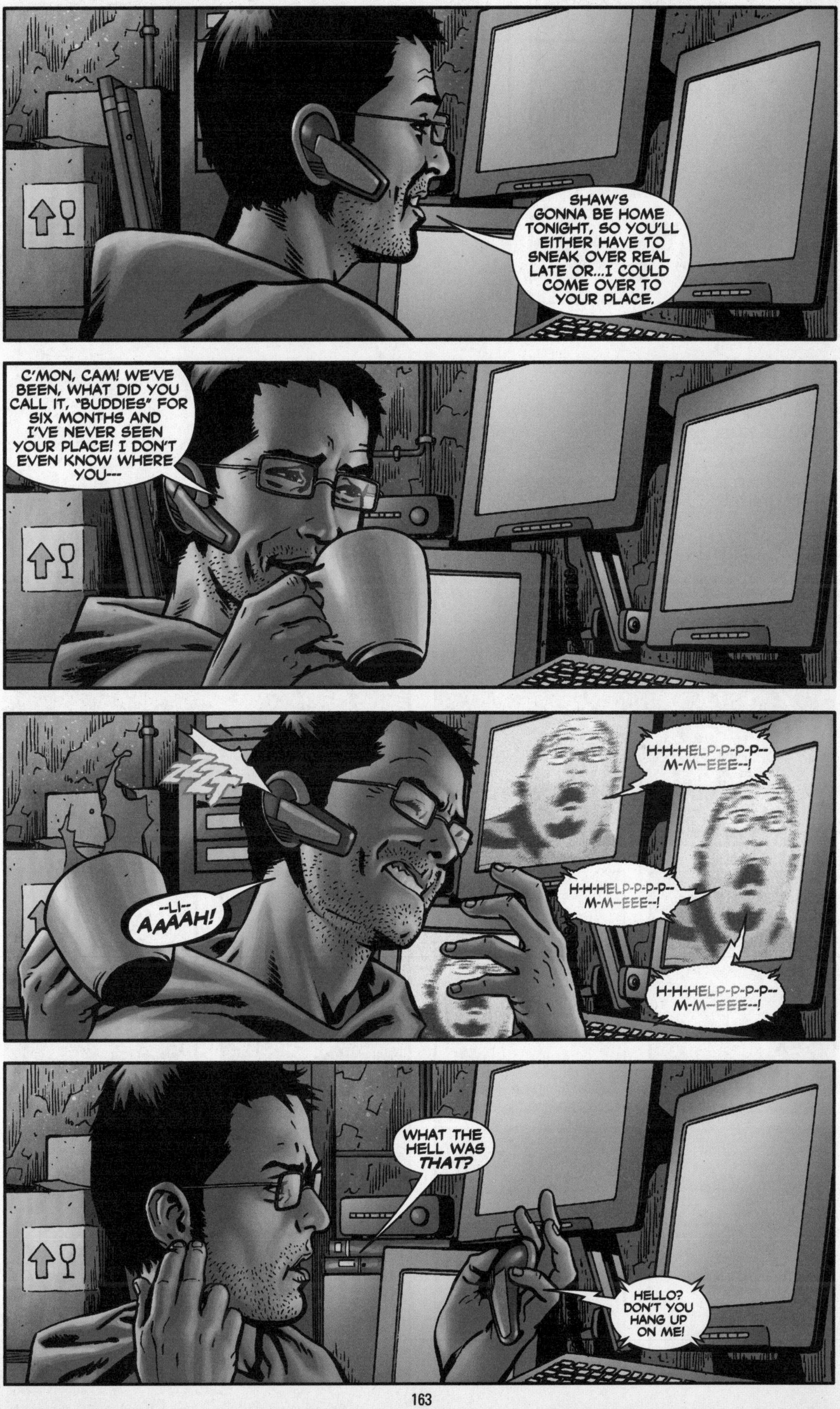
SHAW'S GONNA BE HOME TONIGHT, SO YOU'LL EITHER HAVE TO SNEAK OVER REAL LATE OR...I COULD COME OVER TO YOUR PLACE.
C'MON, CAM! WE'VE BEEN, WHAT DID YOU CALL IT, "BUDDIES" FOR SIX MONTHS AND I'VE NEVER SEEN YOUR PLACE! I DON'T EVEN KNOW WHERE YOU---
ZZZT
--LI-- AAAAH!
H-H-HELP-P-P-P-- M-M--EEE--!
H-H-HELP-P-P-P-- M-M--EEE--!
H-H-HELP-P-P-P-- M-M--EEE--!
WHAT THE HELL WAS THAT?
HELLO? DON'T YOU HANG UP ON ME!

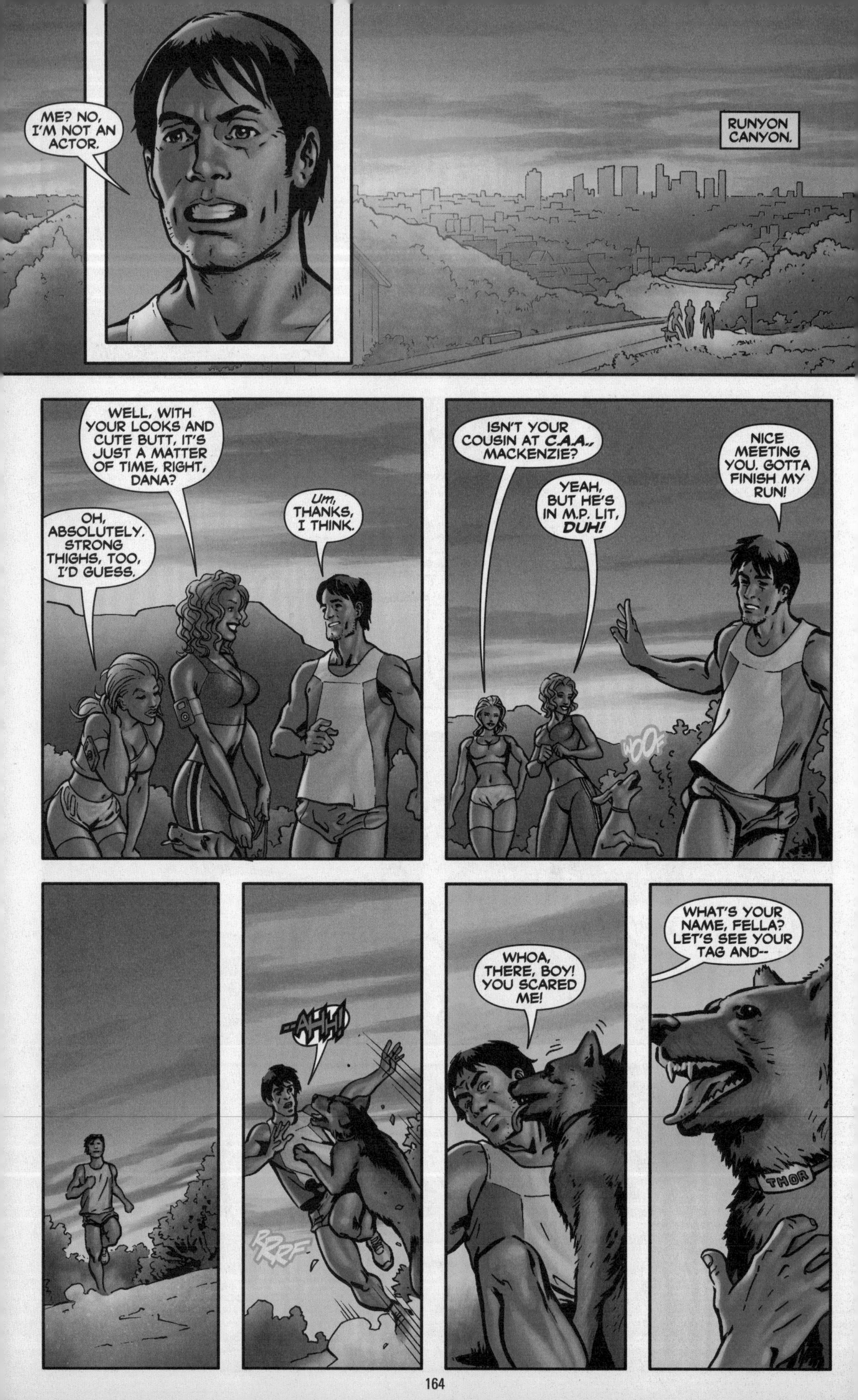
ME? NO, I'M NOT AN ACTOR.
RUNYON CANYON.
WELL, WITH YOUR LOOKS AND CUTE BUTT, IT'S JUST A MATTER OF TIME, RIGHT, DANA?
OH, ABSOLUTELY. STRONG THIGHS, TOO, I'D GUESS.
Um, THANKS, I THINK.
ISN'T YOUR COUSIN AT C.A.A., MACKENZIE?
YEAH, BUT HE'S IN M.P. LIT, DUH!
NICE MEETING YOU. GOTTA FINISH MY RUN!
WOOF
--AHH!
RRRF
WHOA, THERE, BOY! YOU SCARED ME!
WHAT'S YOUR NAME, FELLA? LET'S SEE YOUR TAG AND--
THOR

--"THOR"?

WOOF WOOF

HEY!
THOR!

GET
BACK HERE!
HEY!

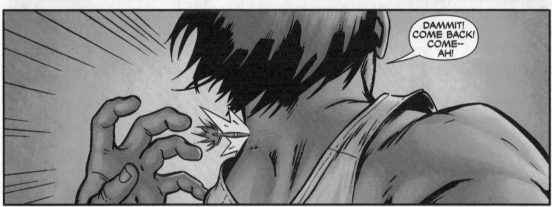

DAMMIT!
COME BACK!
COME--
AH!

W-what's...
goinnning...

...onnnnn...
hereee...?

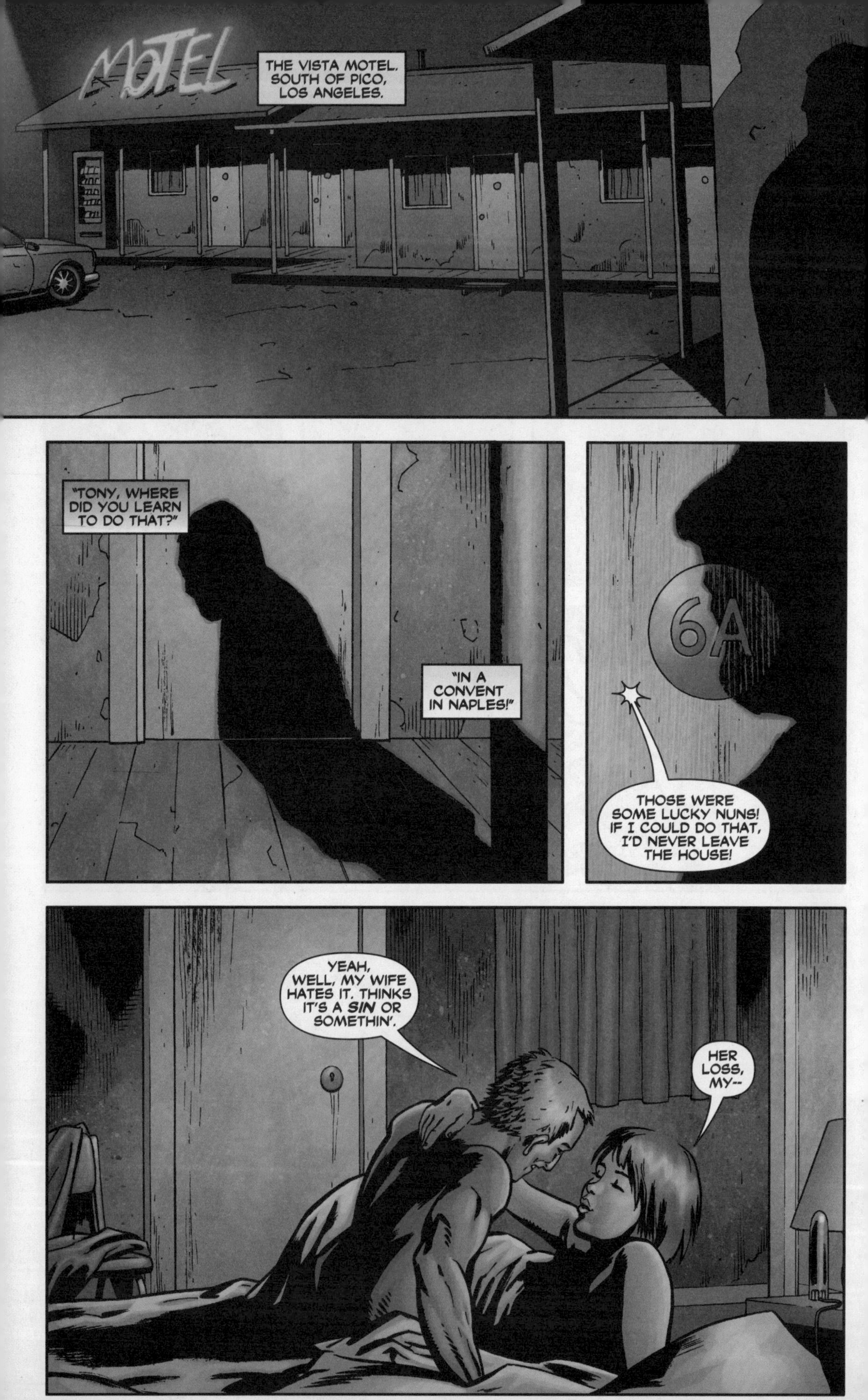
MOTEL
THE VISTA MOTEL. SOUTH OF PICO, LOS ANGELES.
"TONY, WHERE DID YOU LEARN TO DO THAT?"
"IN A CONVENT IN NAPLES!"
6A
THOSE WERE SOME LUCKY NUNS! IF I COULD DO THAT, I'D NEVER LEAVE THE HOUSE!
YEAH, WELL, MY WIFE HATES IT. THINKS IT'S A *SIN* OR SOMETHIN'.
HER LOSS, MY--

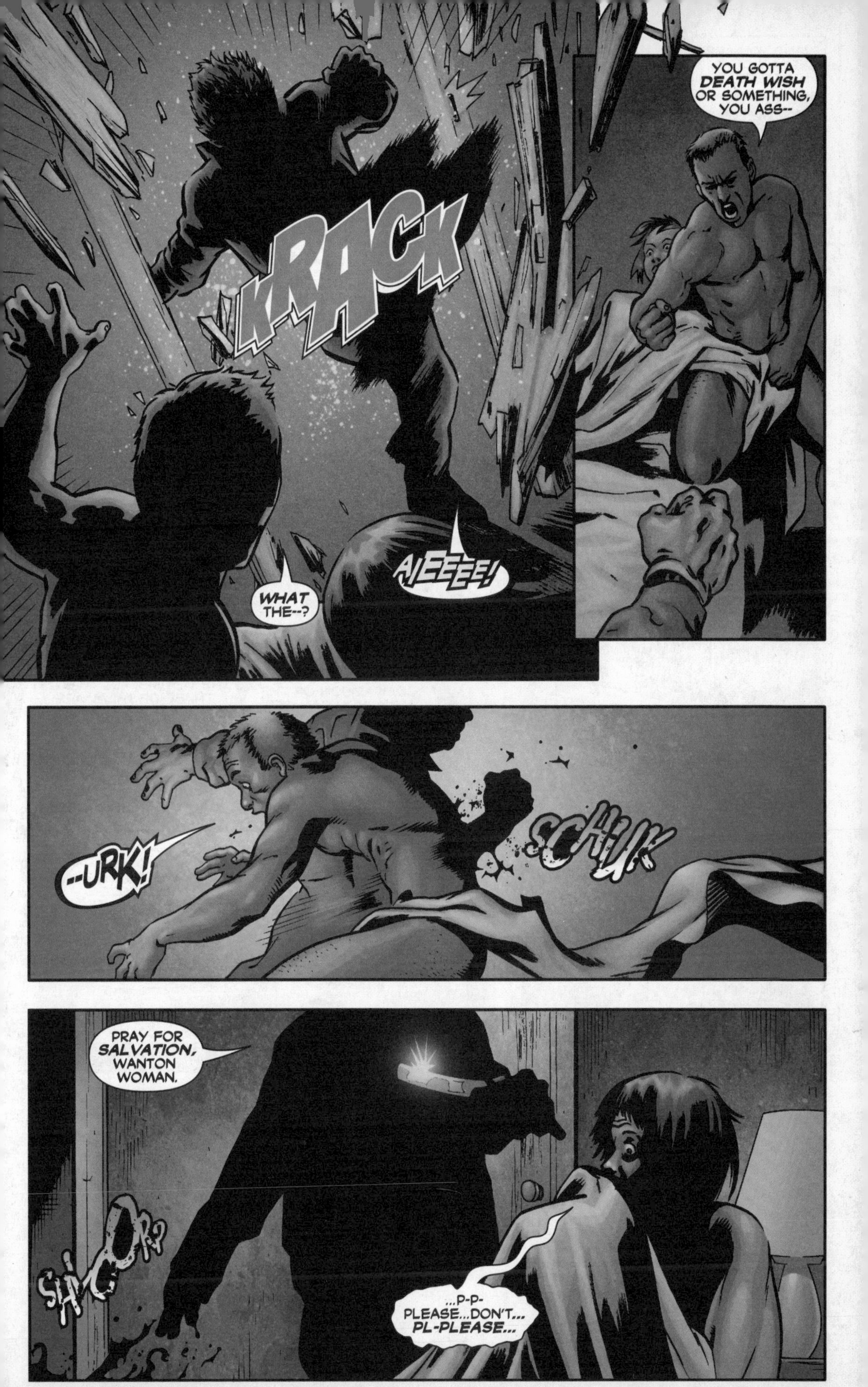
KRACK
WHAT THE--?
AIEEEEE!
YOU GOTTA DEATH WISH OR SOMETHING, YOU ASS--
--URK!
SCHUK
PRAY FOR SALVATION, WANTON WOMAN.
...P-P- PLEASE...DON'T... PL-PLEASE...

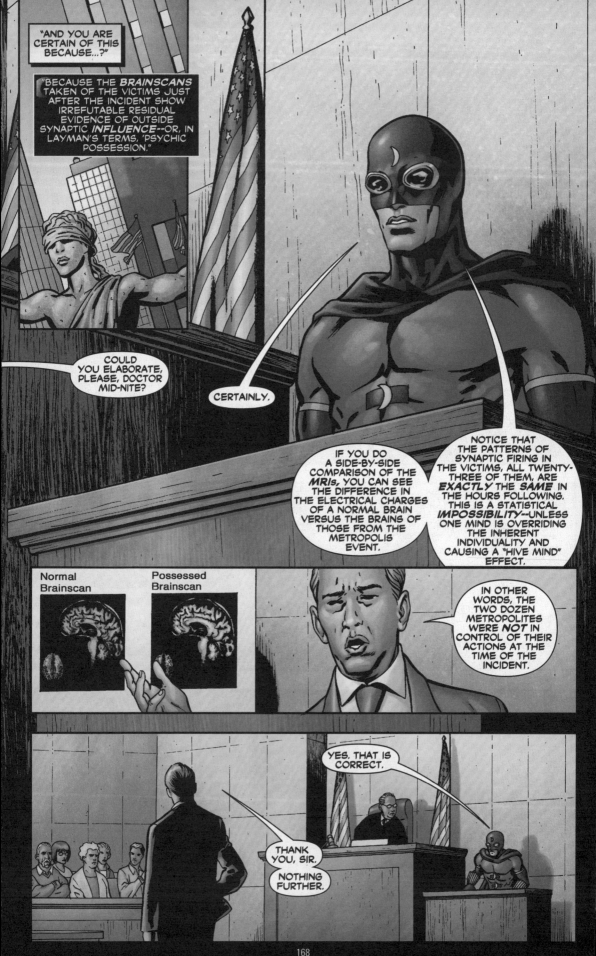

"AND YOU ARE CERTAIN OF THIS BECAUSE...?"

"BECAUSE THE *BRAINSCANS* TAKEN OF THE VICTIMS JUST AFTER THE INCIDENT SHOW IRREFUTABLE RESIDUAL EVIDENCE OF OUTSIDE SYNAPTIC *INFLUENCE*--OR, IN LAYMAN'S TERMS, 'PSYCHIC POSSESSION.'"

COULD YOU ELABORATE, PLEASE, DOCTOR MID-NITE?

CERTAINLY.

IF YOU DO A SIDE-BY-SIDE COMPARISON OF THE *MRIs*, YOU CAN SEE THE DIFFERENCE IN THE ELECTRICAL CHARGES OF A NORMAL BRAIN VERSUS THE BRAINS OF THOSE FROM THE METROPOLIS EVENT.

NOTICE THAT THE PATTERNS OF SYNAPTIC FIRING IN THE VICTIMS, ALL TWENTY-THREE OF THEM, ARE *EXACTLY* THE *SAME* IN THE HOURS FOLLOWING. THIS IS A STATISTICAL *IMPOSSIBILITY*--UNLESS ONE MIND IS OVERRIDING THE INHERENT INDIVIDUALITY AND CAUSING A "HIVE MIND" EFFECT.

Normal Brainscan

Possessed Brainscan

IN OTHER WORDS, THE TWO DOZEN METROPOLITES WERE *NOT* IN CONTROL OF THEIR ACTIONS AT THE TIME OF THE INCIDENT.

YES, THAT IS CORRECT.

THANK YOU, SIR.

NOTHING FURTHER.

DOCTOR MID-NITE, WHEN YOU REFER TO THE "VICTIMS," DO YOU MEAN THE MURDERED *HANGMEN*, OR THE ALLEGEDLY BRAIN-CONTROLLED MURDERERS?

I AM REFERRING TO THOSE WHO WERE PSYCHICALLY *ABUSED* TO COMMIT MURDER.

HM. I SEE.

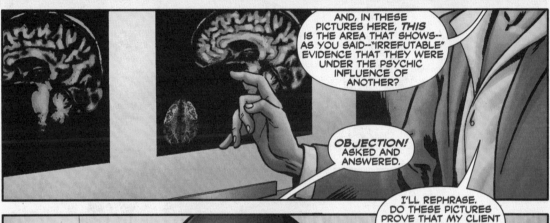

AND, IN THESE PICTURES HERE, *THIS* IS THE AREA THAT SHOWS--AS YOU SAID--"IRREFUTABLE" EVIDENCE THAT THEY WERE UNDER THE PSYCHIC INFLUENCE OF ANOTHER?

OBJECTION! ASKED AND ANSWERED.

I'LL REPHRASE. DO THESE PICTURES PROVE THAT MY CLIENT WAS THE ONE WHO "PUSHED" THESE PEOPLE TO KILL?

THE SCANS SHOW THAT A HIGH-LEVEL TELEPATH WAS MANIPULATING, NO, *OVERPOWERING* THEIR MINDS AND...

A HIGH-LEVEL PSYCHIC? *Hm.* IN MY BRIEF PERUSAL OF META-HUMAN FILES, I'VE FOUND MANY POSSIBLE SUSPECTS *OTHER* THAN MY CLIENT.

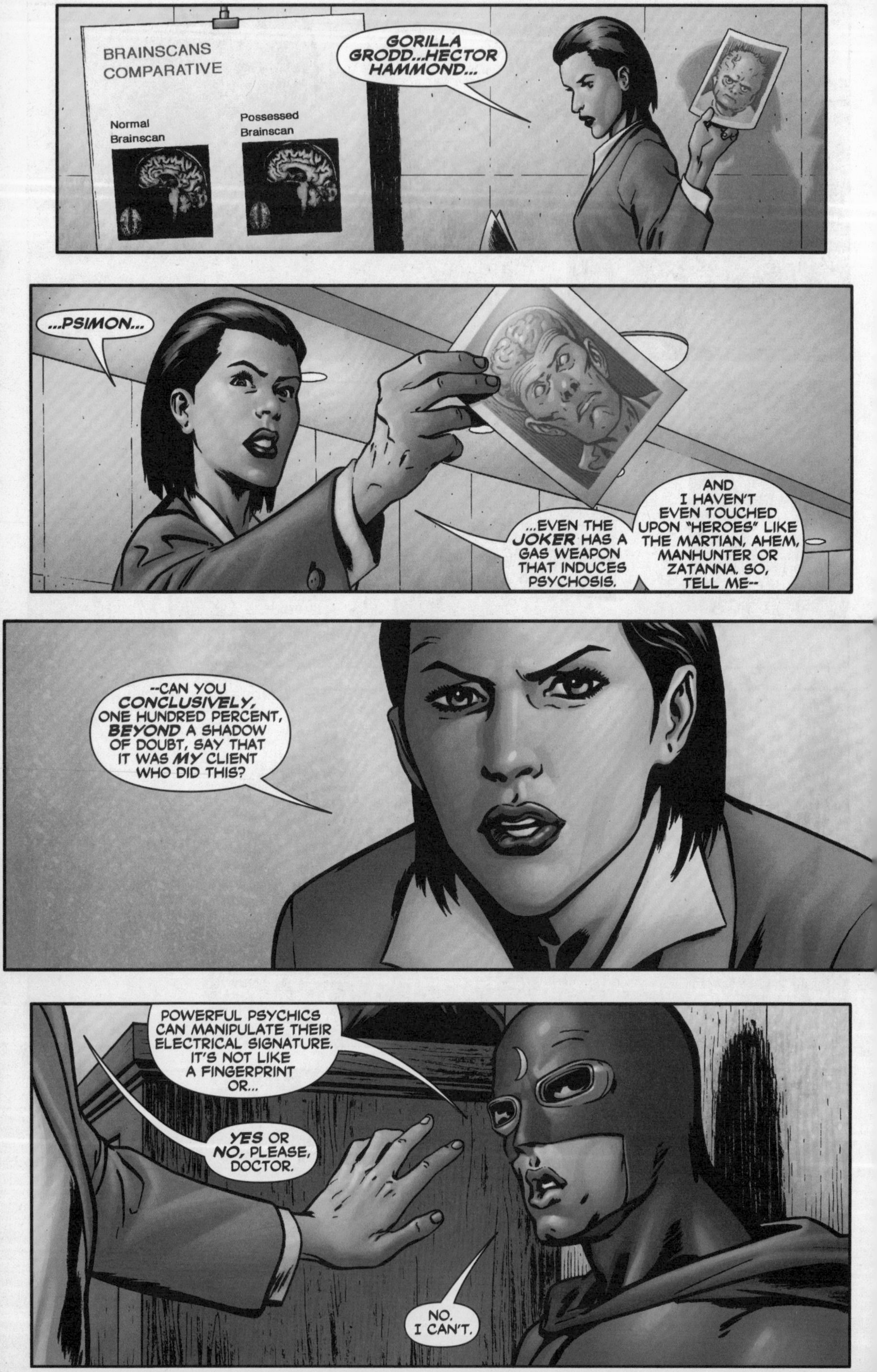
BRAINSCANS COMPARATIVE
Normal Brainscan
Possessed Brainscan
GORILLA GRODD...HECTOR HAMMOND...
...PSIMON...
...EVEN THE JOKER HAS A GAS WEAPON THAT INDUCES PSYCHOSIS.
AND I HAVEN'T EVEN TOUCHED UPON "HEROES" LIKE THE MARTIAN, AHEM, MANHUNTER OR ZATANNA. SO, TELL ME--
--CAN YOU CONCLUSIVELY, ONE HUNDRED PERCENT, BEYOND A SHADOW OF DOUBT, SAY THAT IT WAS MY CLIENT WHO DID THIS?
POWERFUL PSYCHICS CAN MANIPULATE THEIR ELECTRICAL SIGNATURE. IT'S NOT LIKE A FINGERPRINT OR...
YES OR NO, PLEASE, DOCTOR.
NO. I CAN'T.

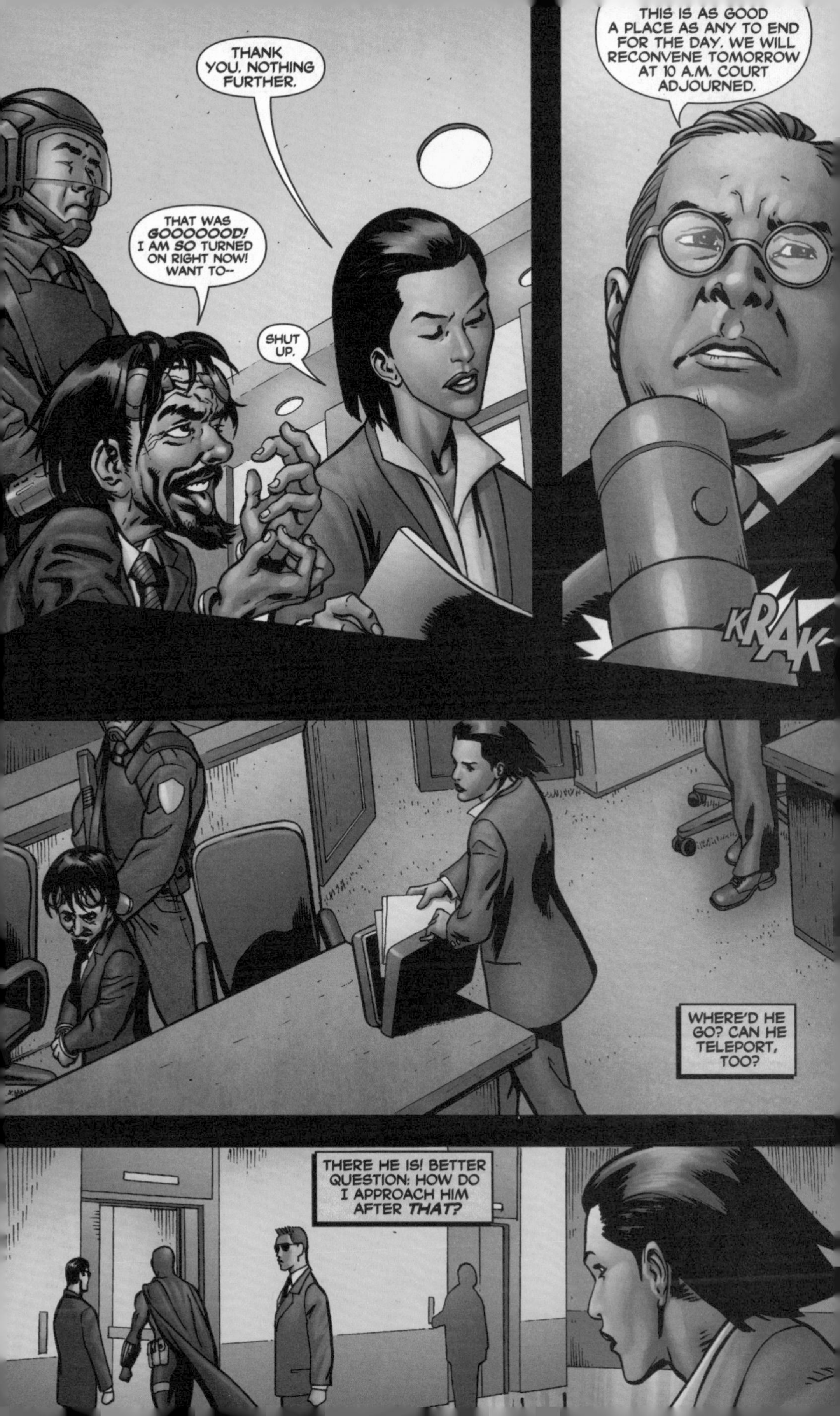
THANK YOU. NOTHING FURTHER.
THAT WAS GOOOOOOD! I AM SO TURNED ON RIGHT NOW! WANT TO--
SHUT UP.
THIS IS AS GOOD A PLACE AS ANY TO END FOR THE DAY. WE WILL RECONVENE TOMORROW AT 10 A.M. COURT ADJOURNED.
KRAK
WHERE'D HE GO? CAN HE TELEPORT, TOO?
THERE HE IS! BETTER QUESTION: HOW DO I APPROACH HIM AFTER THAT?

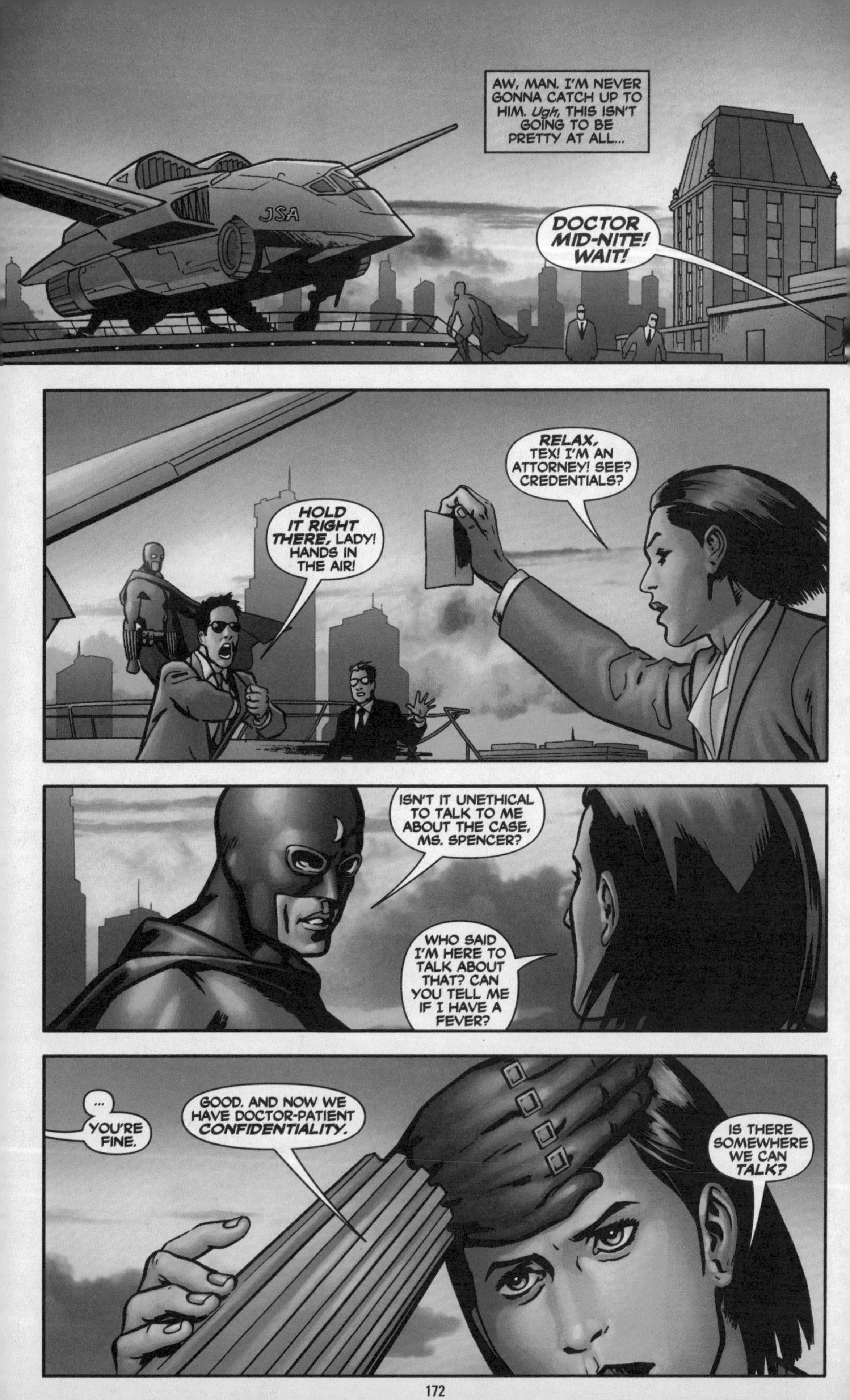

AW, MAN. I'M NEVER GONNA CATCH UP TO HIM. *Ugh*, THIS ISN'T GOING TO BE PRETTY AT ALL...
DOCTOR MID-NITE! WAIT!
RELAX, TEX! I'M AN ATTORNEY! SEE? CREDENTIALS?
HOLD IT RIGHT THERE, LADY! HANDS IN THE AIR!
JSA
ISN'T IT UNETHICAL TO TALK TO ME ABOUT THE CASE, MS. SPENCER?
WHO SAID I'M HERE TO TALK ABOUT THAT? CAN YOU TELL ME IF I HAVE A FEVER?
... YOU'RE FINE.
GOOD. AND NOW WE HAVE DOCTOR-PATIENT CONFIDENTIALITY.
IS THERE SOMEWHERE WE CAN TALK?

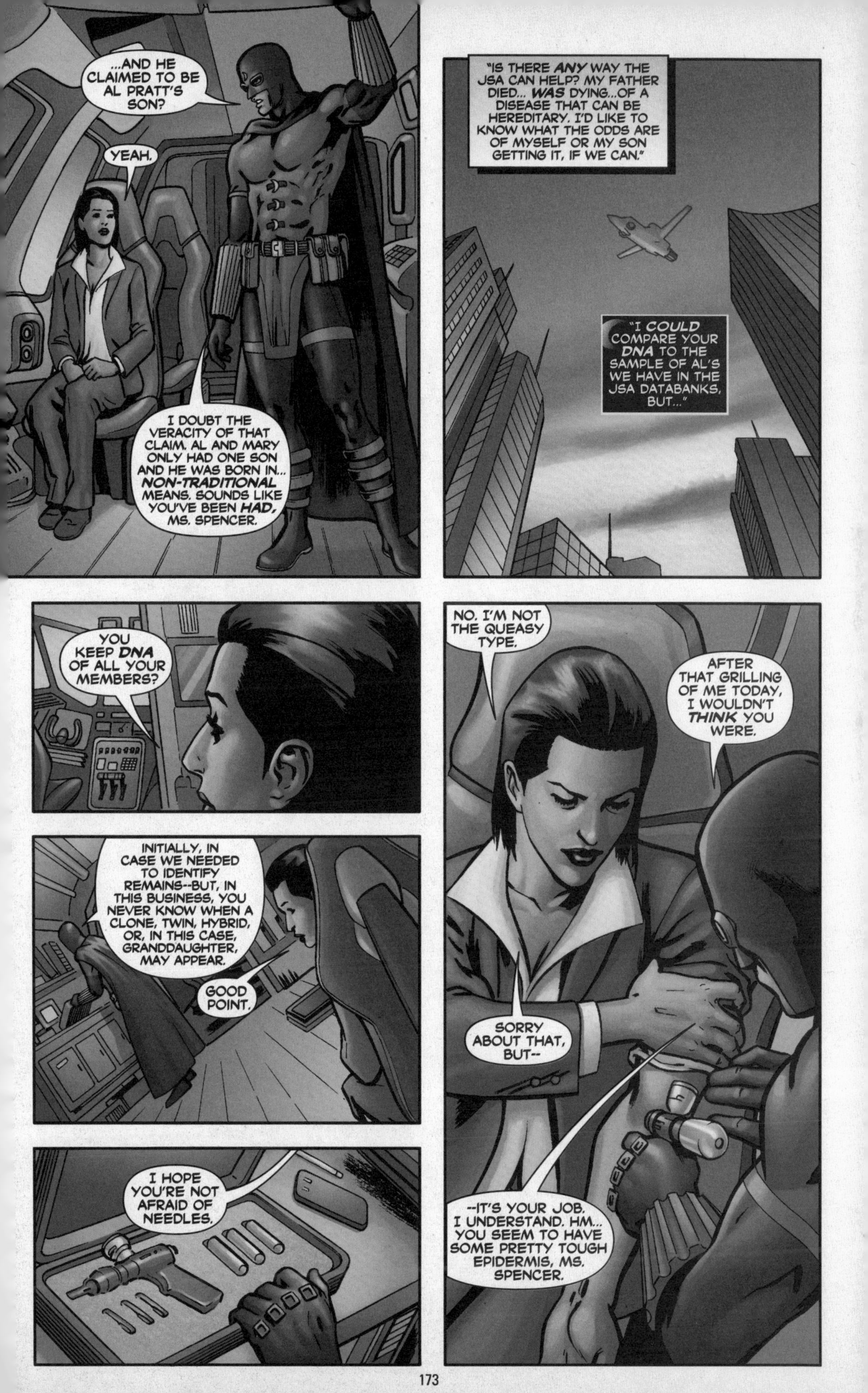

...AND HE CLAIMED TO BE AL PRATT'S SON?
YEAH.
I DOUBT THE VERACITY OF THAT CLAIM. AL AND MARY ONLY HAD ONE SON AND HE WAS BORN IN... NON-TRADITIONAL MEANS. SOUNDS LIKE YOU'VE BEEN HAD, MS. SPENCER.
"IS THERE ANY WAY THE JSA CAN HELP? MY FATHER DIED... WAS DYING...OF A DISEASE THAT CAN BE HEREDITARY. I'D LIKE TO KNOW WHAT THE ODDS ARE OF MYSELF OR MY SON GETTING IT, IF WE CAN."
"I COULD COMPARE YOUR DNA TO THE SAMPLE OF AL'S WE HAVE IN THE JSA DATABANKS, BUT..."
YOU KEEP DNA OF ALL YOUR MEMBERS?
INITIALLY, IN CASE WE NEEDED TO IDENTIFY REMAINS--BUT, IN THIS BUSINESS, YOU NEVER KNOW WHEN A CLONE, TWIN, HYBRID, OR, IN THIS CASE, GRANDDAUGHTER, MAY APPEAR.
GOOD POINT.
I HOPE YOU'RE NOT AFRAID OF NEEDLES.
NO. I'M NOT THE QUEASY TYPE.
AFTER THAT GRILLING OF ME TODAY, I WOULDN'T THINK YOU WERE.
SORRY ABOUT THAT, BUT--
--IT'S YOUR JOB. I UNDERSTAND. HM... YOU SEEM TO HAVE SOME PRETTY TOUGH EPIDERMIS, MS. SPENCER.

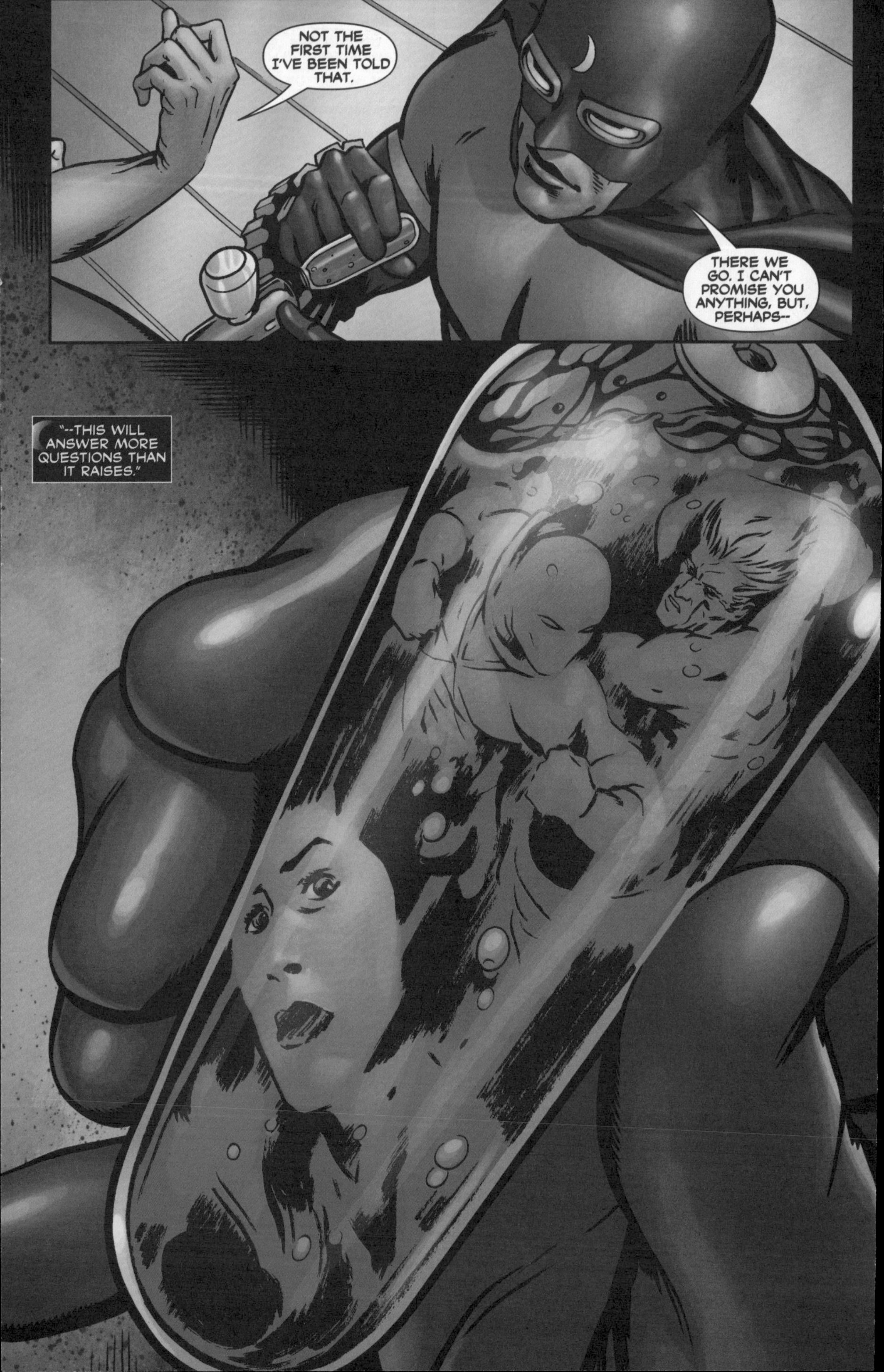
NOT THE FIRST TIME I'VE BEEN TOLD THAT.
THERE WE GO. I CAN'T PROMISE YOU ANYTHING, BUT, PERHAPS--
"--THIS WILL ANSWER MORE QUESTIONS THAN IT RAISES."

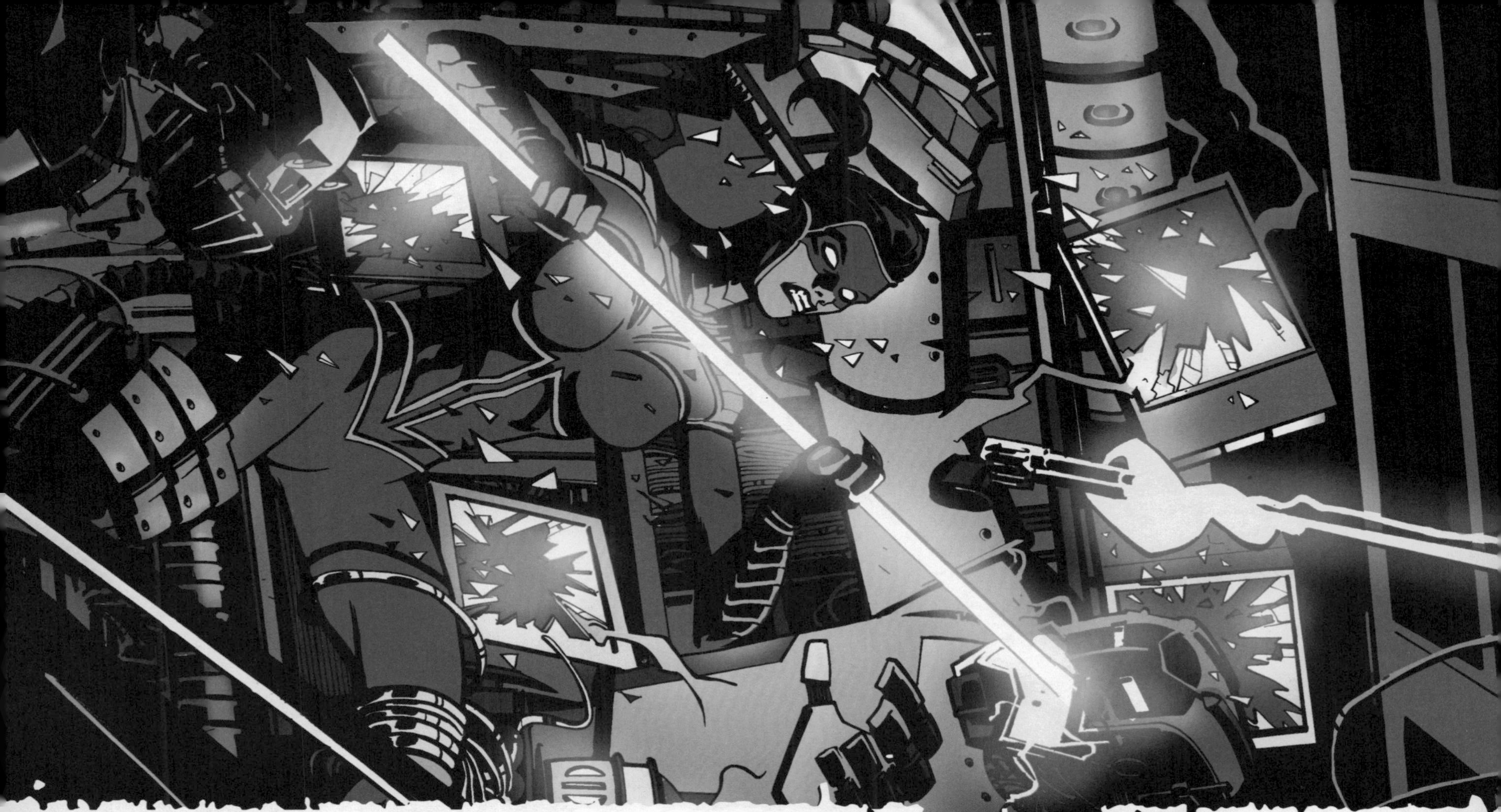

Issue #22 cover by Shawn Martinbrough

Interior art by Javier Pina & Fernando Blanco

IN MY LINE OF WORK, I HAVE COME TO EXPECT THE *UNEXPECTED*.

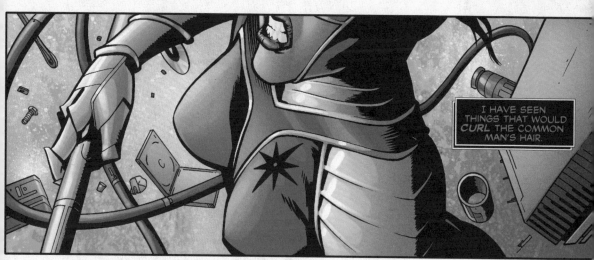

I HAVE SEEN THINGS THAT WOULD *CURL* THE COMMON MAN'S HAIR.

CALL ME OLD-FASHIONED IF YOU MUST, BUT SOME THINGS STILL SURPRISE ME.

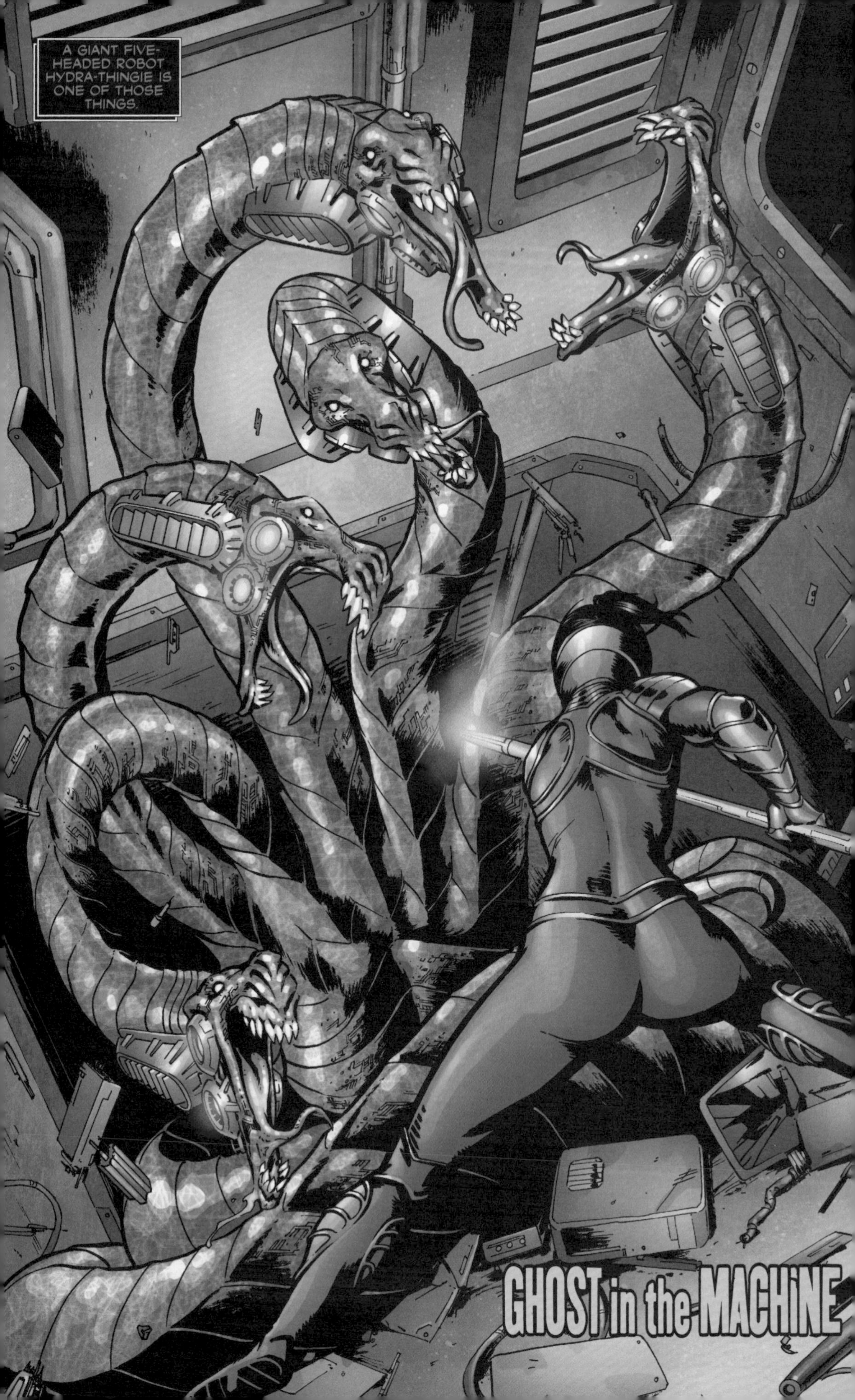
A GIANT FIVE-HEADED ROBOT HYDRA-THINGIE IS ONE OF THOSE THINGS.
GHOST in the MACHINE

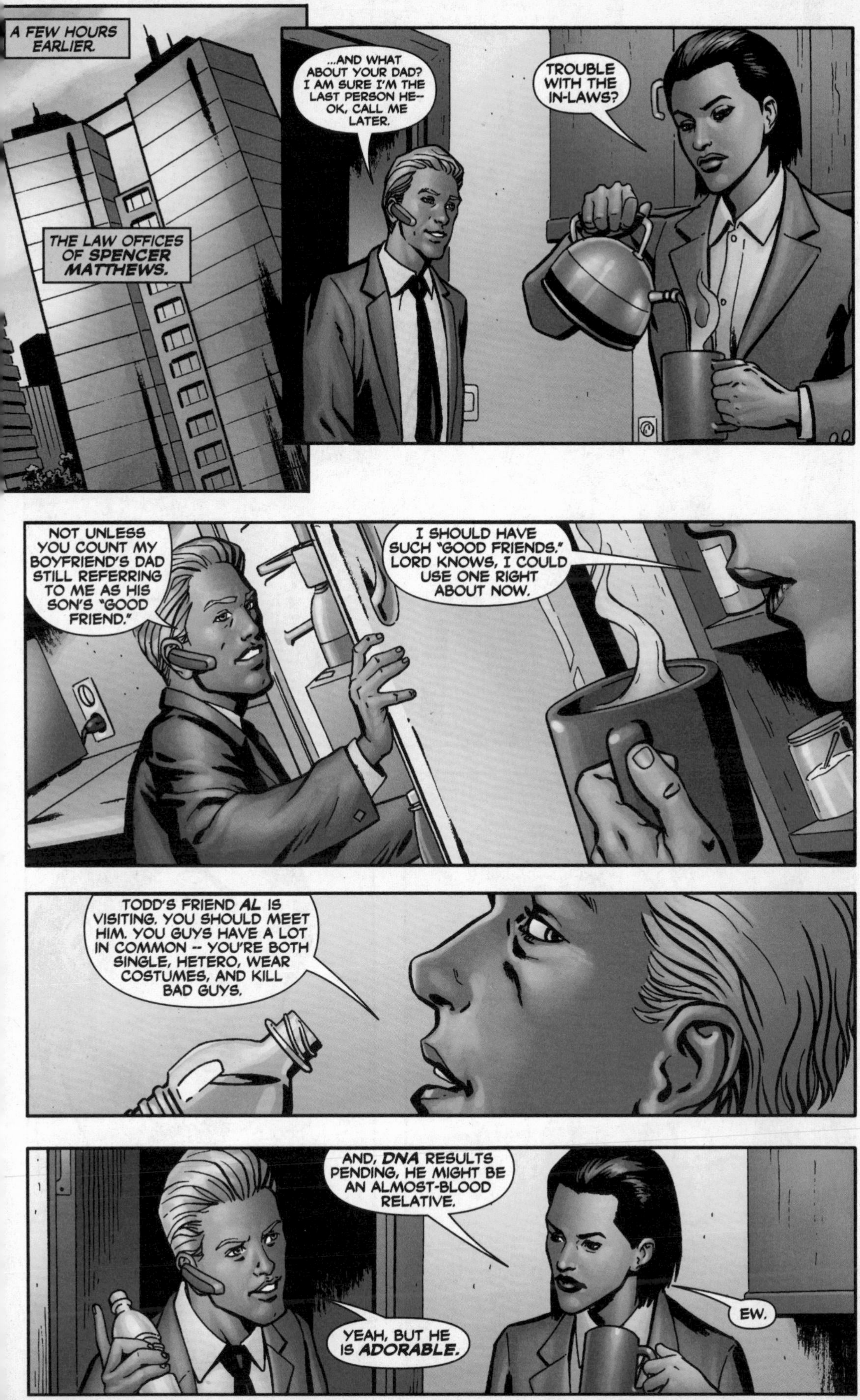
A FEW HOURS EARLIER.
THE LAW OFFICES OF SPENCER MATTHEWS.
...AND WHAT ABOUT YOUR DAD? I AM SURE I'M THE LAST PERSON HE-- OK, CALL ME LATER.
TROUBLE WITH THE IN-LAWS?
NOT UNLESS YOU COUNT MY BOYFRIEND'S DAD STILL REFERRING TO ME AS HIS SON'S "GOOD FRIEND."
I SHOULD HAVE SUCH "GOOD FRIENDS." LORD KNOWS, I COULD USE ONE RIGHT ABOUT NOW.
TODD'S FRIEND AL IS VISITING. YOU SHOULD MEET HIM. YOU GUYS HAVE A LOT IN COMMON -- YOU'RE BOTH SINGLE, HETERO, WEAR COSTUMES, AND KILL BAD GUYS.
AND, DNA RESULTS PENDING, HE MIGHT BE AN ALMOST-BLOOD RELATIVE.
YEAH, BUT HE IS ADORABLE.
EW.

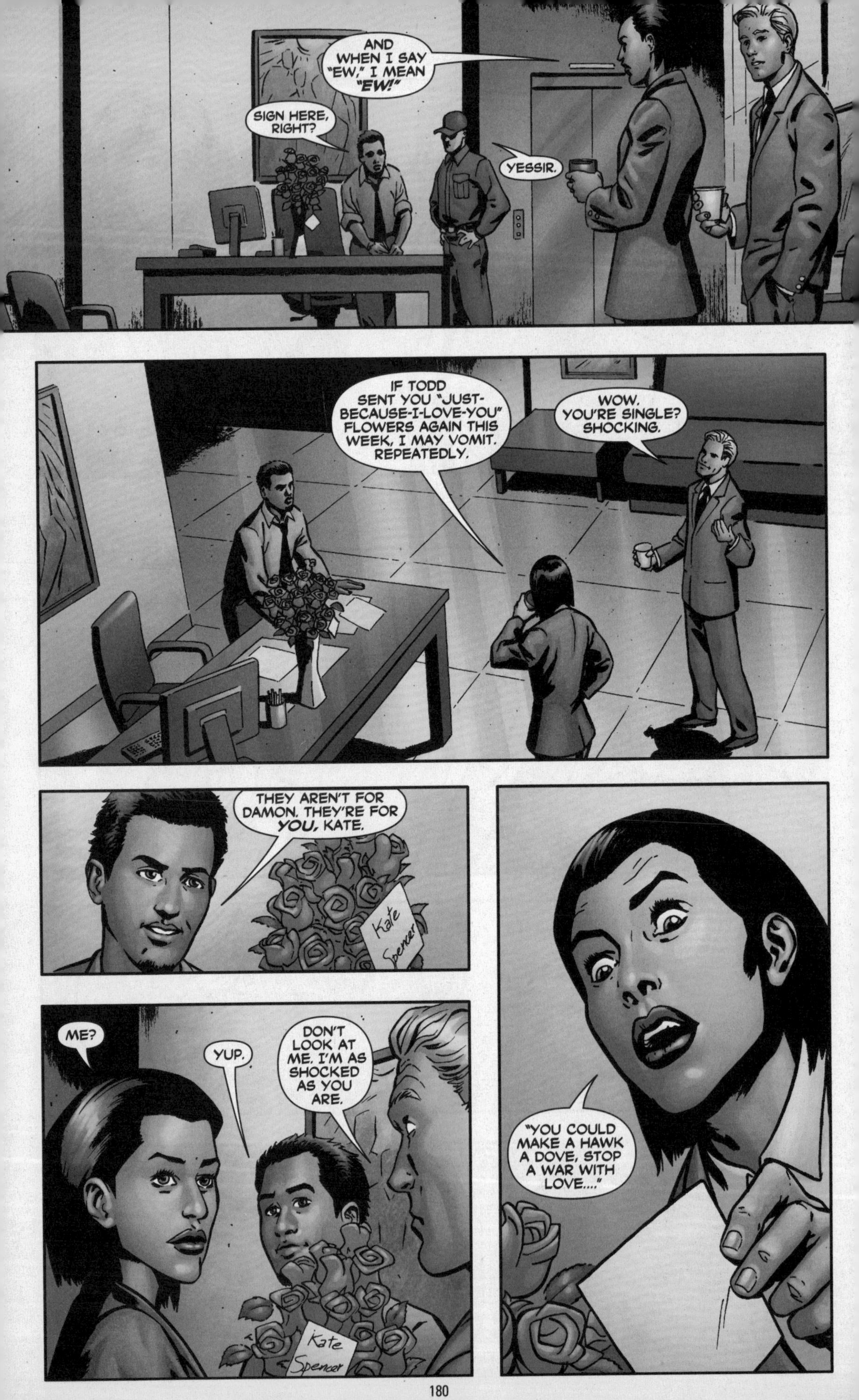
AND WHEN I SAY "EW," I MEAN "EW!"
SIGN HERE, RIGHT?
YESSIR.
IF TODD SENT YOU "JUST-BECAUSE-I-LOVE-YOU" FLOWERS AGAIN THIS WEEK, I MAY VOMIT. REPEATEDLY.
WOW. YOU'RE SINGLE? SHOCKING.
THEY AREN'T FOR DAMON. THEY'RE FOR YOU, KATE.
Kate Spencer
ME?
YUP.
DON'T LOOK AT ME. I'M AS SHOCKED AS YOU ARE.
Kate Spencer
"YOU COULD MAKE A HAWK A DOVE, STOP A WAR WITH LOVE...."

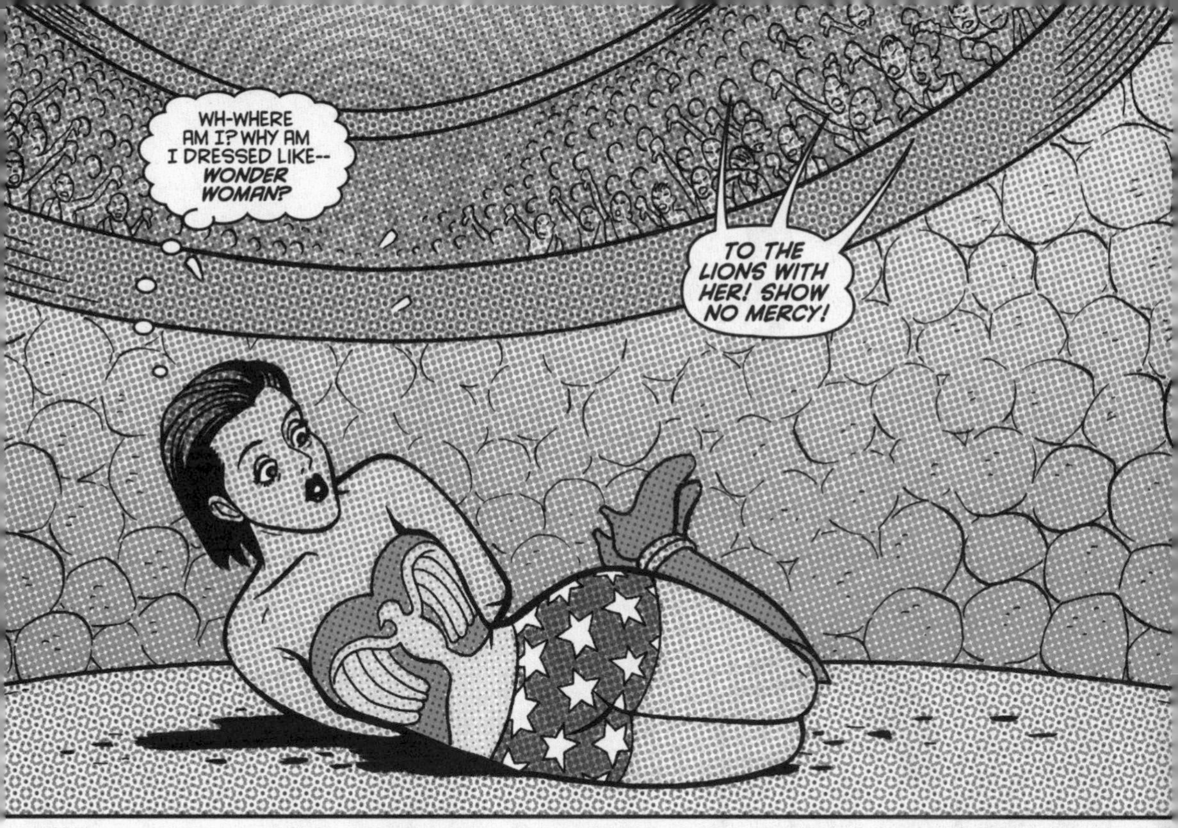
WH-WHERE AM I? WHY AM I DRESSED LIKE-- WONDER WOMAN?
TO THE LIONS WITH HER! SHOW NO MERCY!

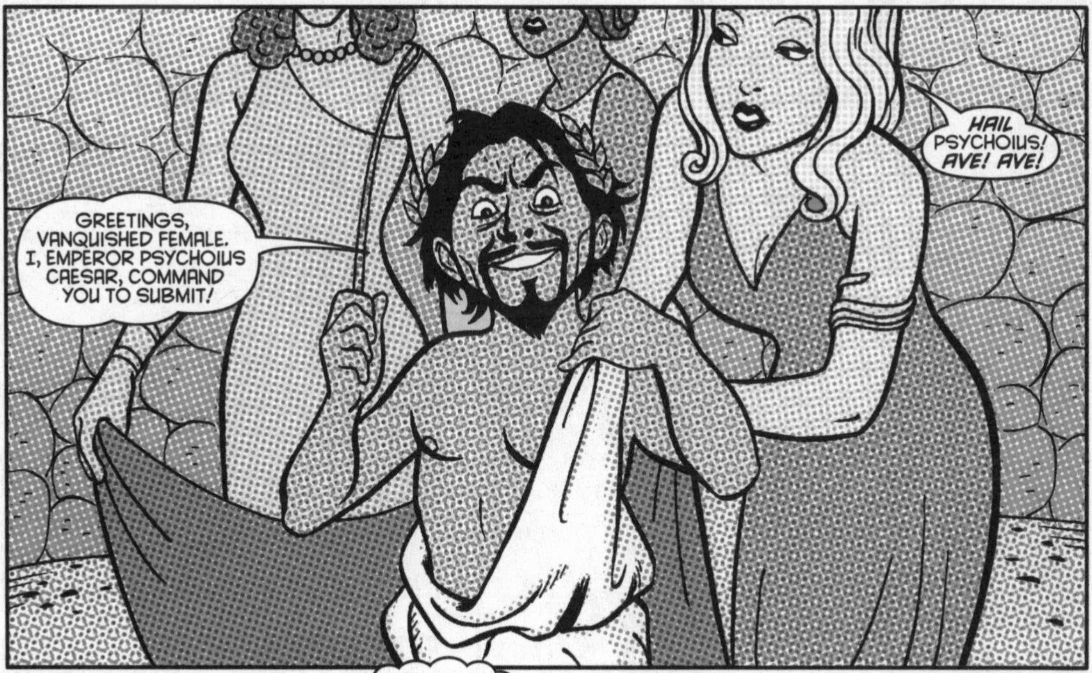
HAIL PSYCHOIUS! AVE! AVE!
GREETINGS, VANQUISHED FEMALE. I, EMPEROR PSYCHOIUS CAESAR, COMMAND YOU TO SUBMIT!

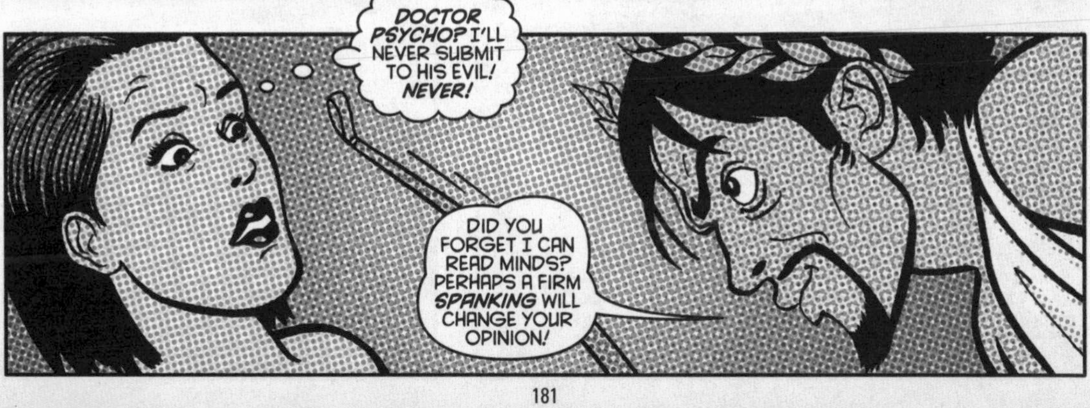
DOCTOR PSYCHO? I'LL NEVER SUBMIT TO HIS EVIL! NEVER!
DID YOU FORGET I CAN READ MINDS? PERHAPS A FIRM SPANKING WILL CHANGE YOUR OPINION!

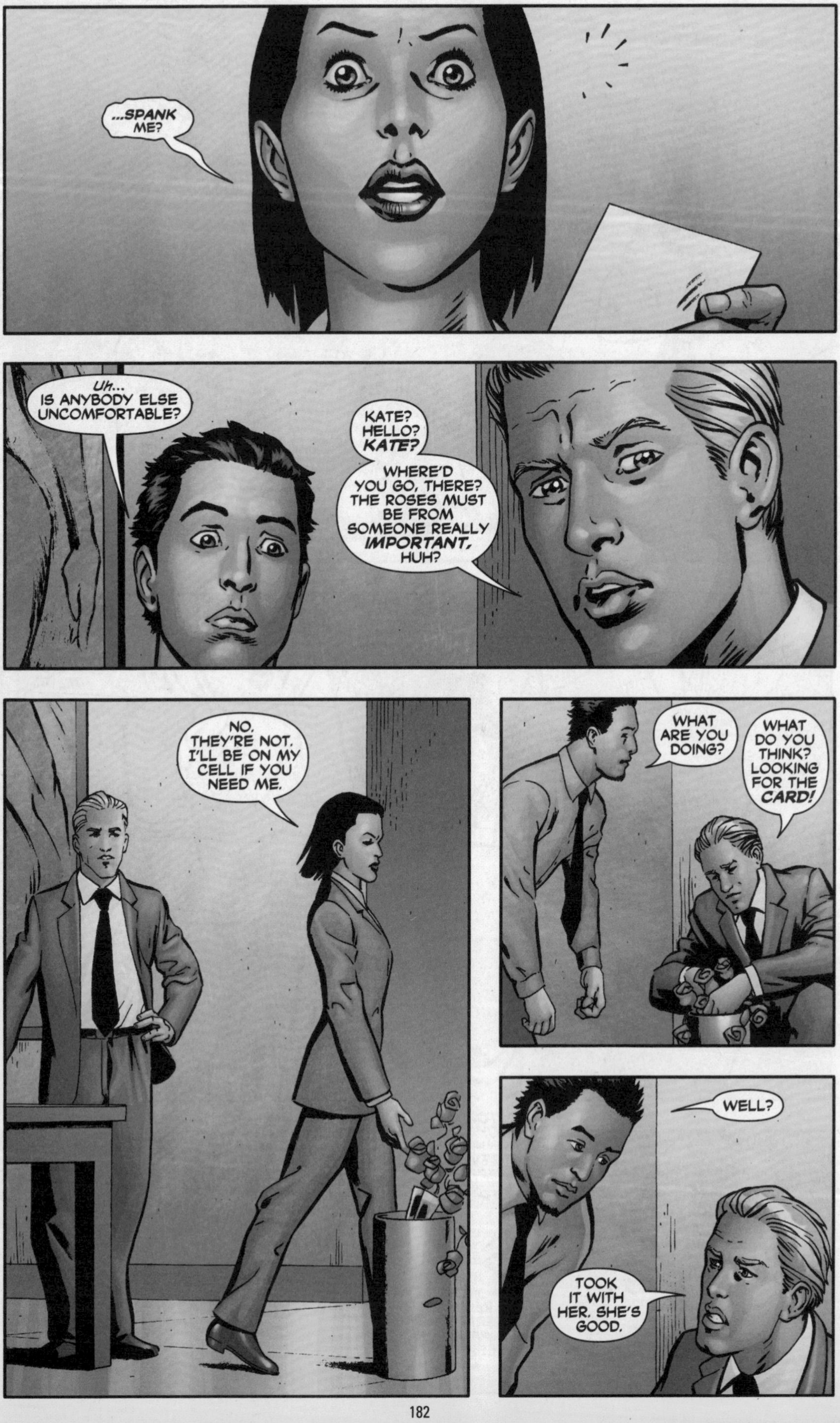
...SPANK ME?
Uh... IS ANYBODY ELSE UNCOMFORTABLE?
KATE? HELLO? KATE?
WHERE'D YOU GO, THERE? THE ROSES MUST BE FROM SOMEONE REALLY IMPORTANT, HUH?
NO. THEY'RE NOT. I'LL BE ON MY CELL IF YOU NEED ME.
WHAT ARE YOU DOING?
WHAT DO YOU THINK? LOOKING FOR THE CARD!
WELL?
TOOK IT WITH HER. SHE'S GOOD.

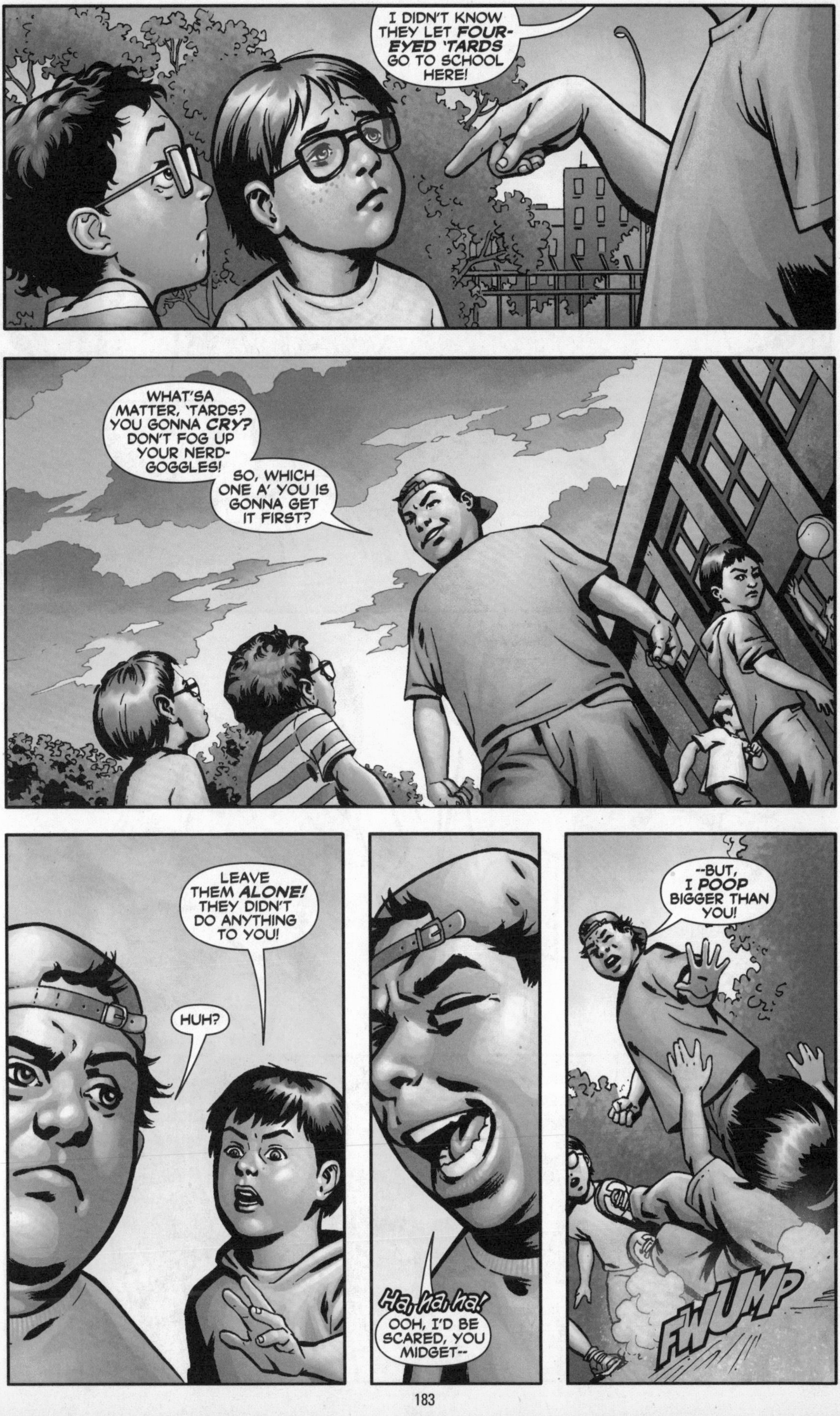
I DIDN'T KNOW THEY LET **FOUR-EYED 'TARDS** GO TO SCHOOL HERE!
WHAT'SA MATTER, 'TARDS? YOU GONNA **CRY?** DON'T FOG UP YOUR NERD-GOGGLES!
SO, WHICH ONE A' YOU IS GONNA GET IT FIRST?
LEAVE THEM **ALONE!** THEY DIDN'T DO ANYTHING TO YOU!
HUH?
Ha, ha, ha! OOH, I'D BE SCARED, YOU MIDGET--
--BUT, I **POOP** BIGGER THAN YOU!
FWUMP

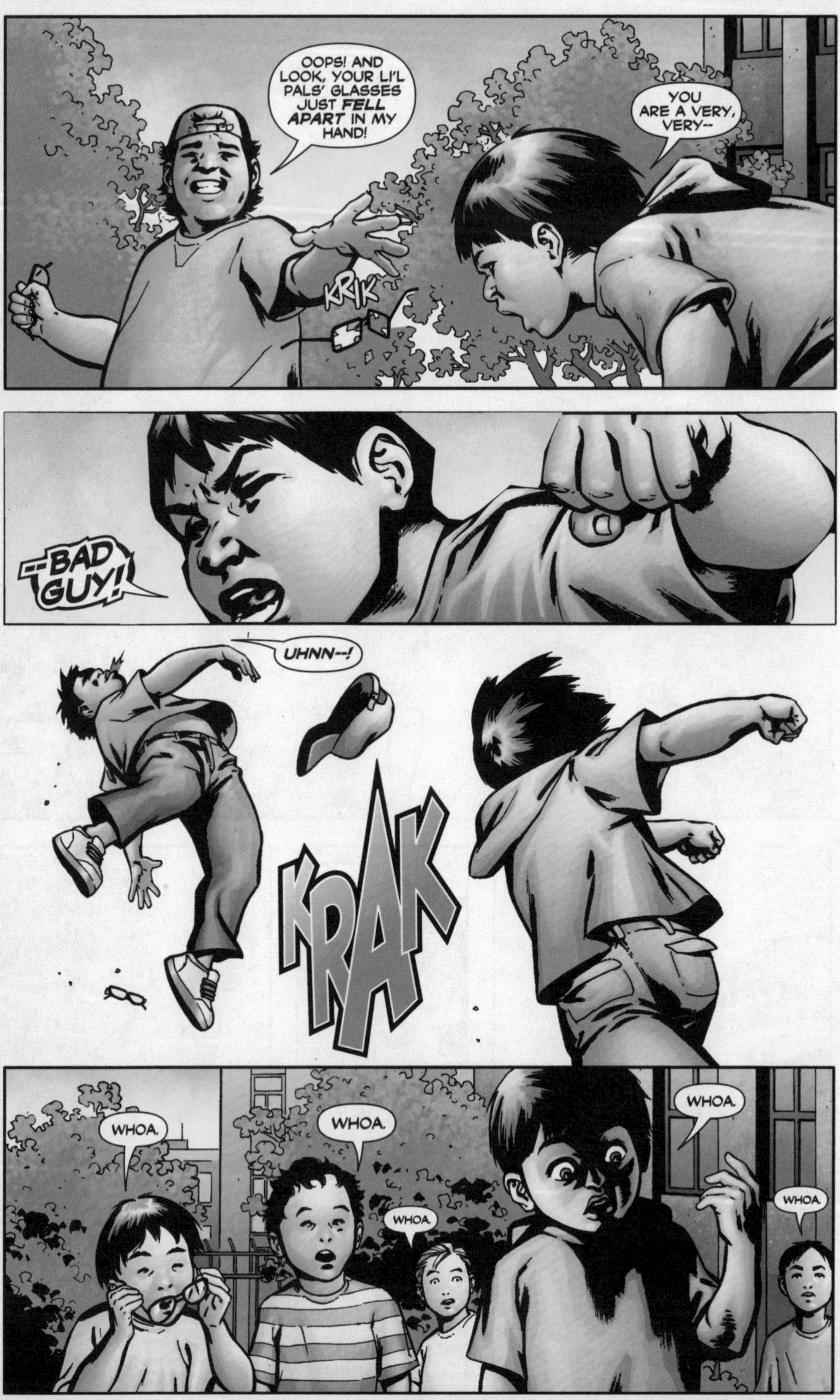
OOPS! AND LOOK, YOUR LI'L PALS' GLASSES JUST FELL APART IN MY HAND!
KRIK
YOU ARE A VERY, VERY--
--BAD GUY!
UHNN--!
KRAK
WHOA.
WHOA.
WHOA.
WHOA.
WHOA.

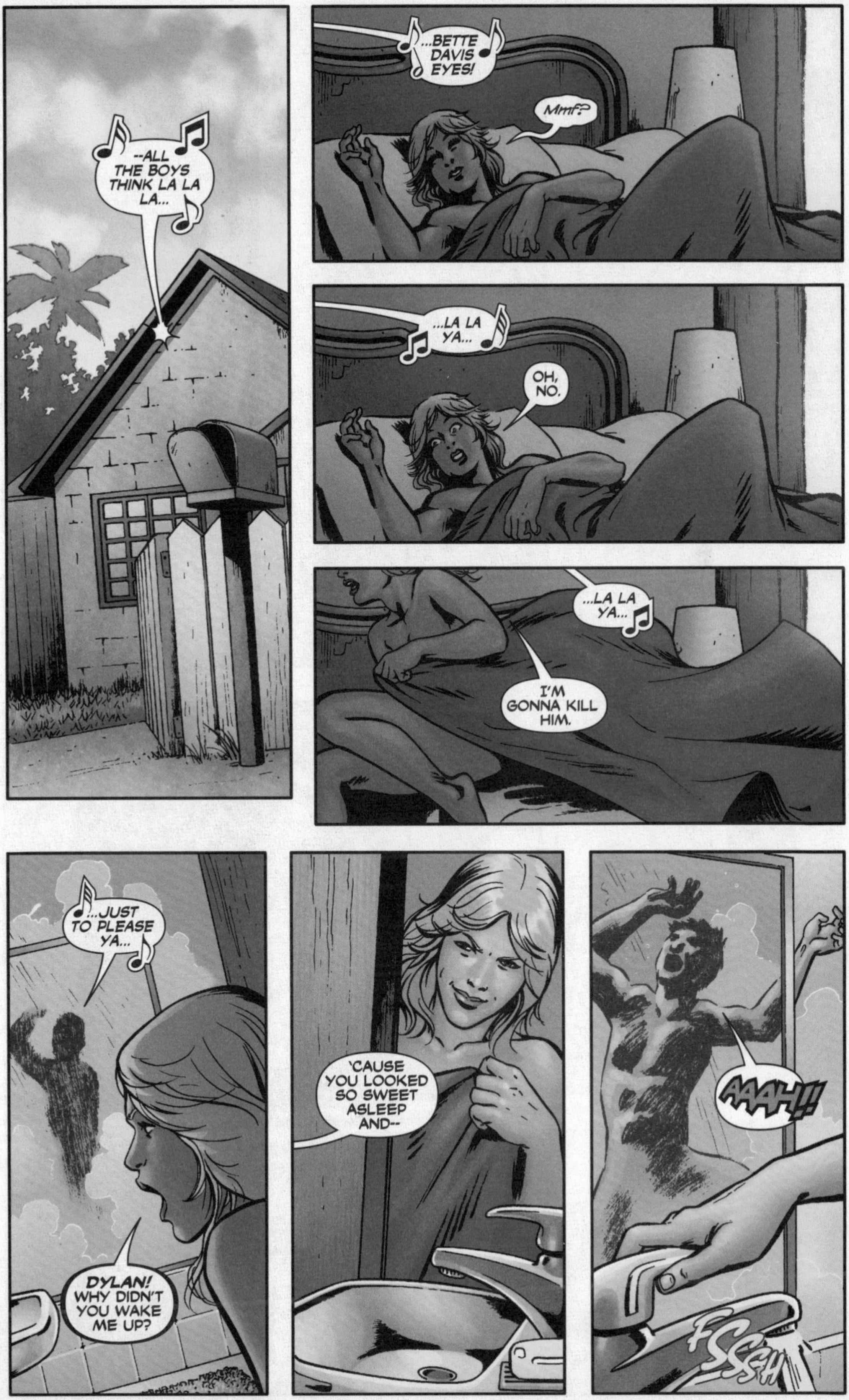
--ALL THE BOYS THINK LA LA LA...
...BETTE DAVIS EYES!
Mmf?
...LA LA YA...
OH, NO.
...LA LA YA...
I'M GONNA KILL HIM.
...JUST TO PLEASE YA...
DYLAN! WHY DIDN'T YOU WAKE ME UP?
'CAUSE YOU LOOKED SO SWEET ASLEEP AND--
AAAH!!
FSSH

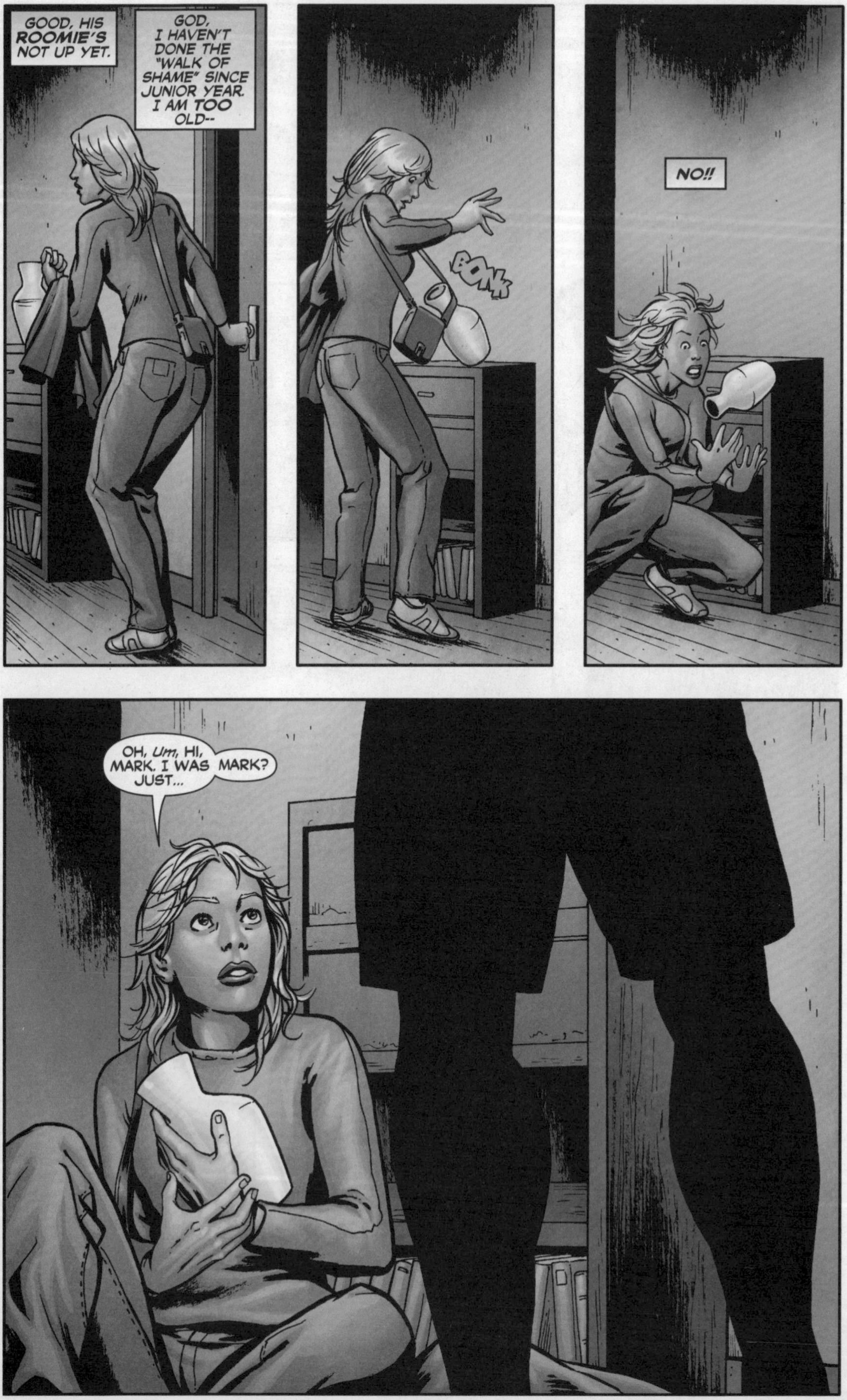
GOOD, HIS ROOMIE'S NOT UP YET.
GOD, I HAVEN'T DONE THE "WALK OF SHAME" SINCE JUNIOR YEAR. I AM TOO OLD--
BONK
NO!!
OH, Um, HI, MARK. I WAS JUST...
MARK?

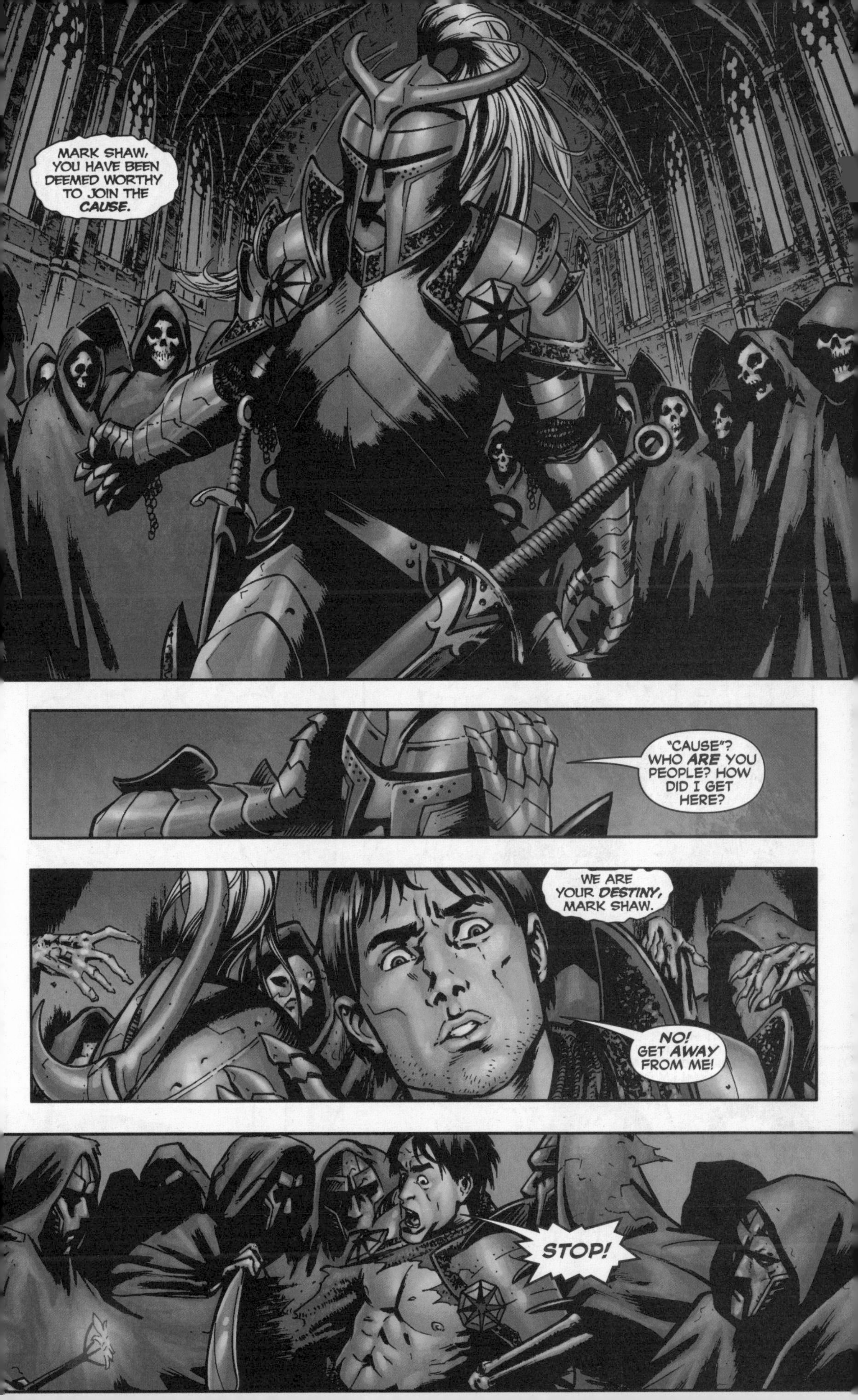
MARK SHAW, YOU HAVE BEEN DEEMED WORTHY TO JOIN THE CAUSE.
"CAUSE"? WHO ARE YOU PEOPLE? HOW DID I GET HERE?
WE ARE YOUR DESTINY, MARK SHAW.
NO! GET AWAY FROM ME!
STOP!

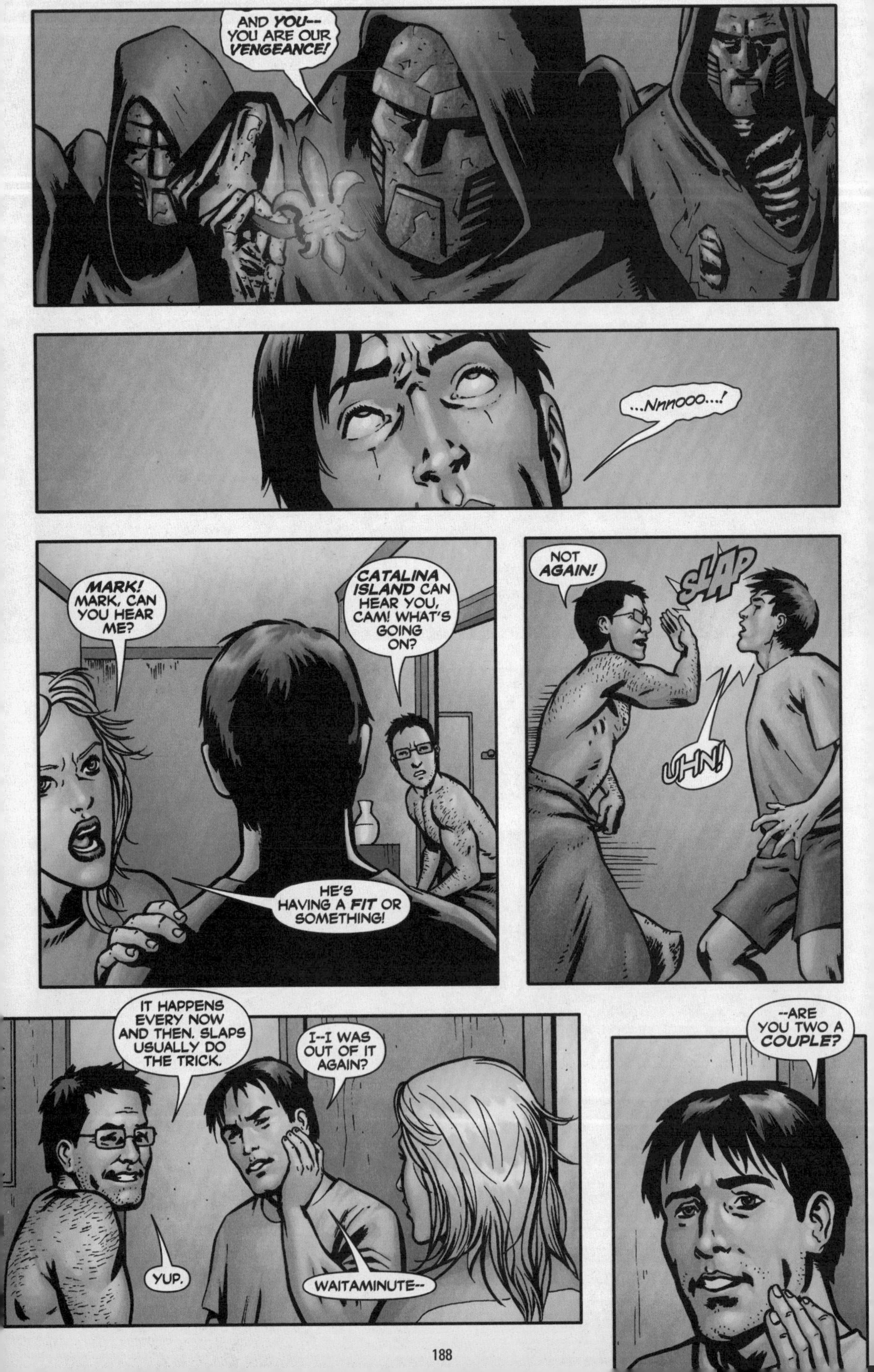

AND YOU--
YOU ARE OUR VENGEANCE!
...Nnnooo...!
MARK! MARK, CAN YOU HEAR ME?
CATALINA ISLAND CAN HEAR YOU, CAM! WHAT'S GOING ON?
HE'S HAVING A FIT OR SOMETHING!
NOT AGAIN!
SLAP
UHN!
IT HAPPENS EVERY NOW AND THEN. SLAPS USUALLY DO THE TRICK.
I--I WAS OUT OF IT AGAIN?
YUP.
WAITAMINUTE--
--ARE YOU TWO A COUPLE?

I SHOULD BE ABLE TO SEPARATE MY EMOTIONS FROM THIS...BUT, IF KATE SPENCER IS AL'S GRANDDAUGHTER, WHO'S GRANDMA?

I CAN'T IMAGINE AL CHEATING ON MARY. BUT THEN AGAIN, MY COLLEAGUES HAVE BEEN SURPRISING ME IN ALL SORTS OF DISAPPOINTING WAYS LATELY.

LISTEN TO ME. I SOUND LIKE A CHILD WHOSE PARENTS ARE GETTING A DIVORCE...

DOC! HEY, DOC, YOU POSSESSED BY THE ULTRA-HUMANITE OR JUST IGNORING ME?

JUST GIVE ME A FEW MINUTES, TED. I'M ALMOST FINISHED HERE.

WHATCHA DOIN'?

YOU KNOW I'M BOUND BY DOCTOR-PATIENT PRIVILEGE.

BLAH, BLAH, BLAH... IF YOU WANNA GRAB A BEER, I'LL BE IN THE GYM.

NOTED.

SEQUENCING COMPARISON COMPLETED.

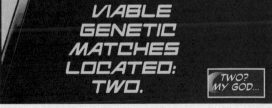

VIABLE GENETIC MATCHES LOCATED: TWO.

TWO? MY GOD...

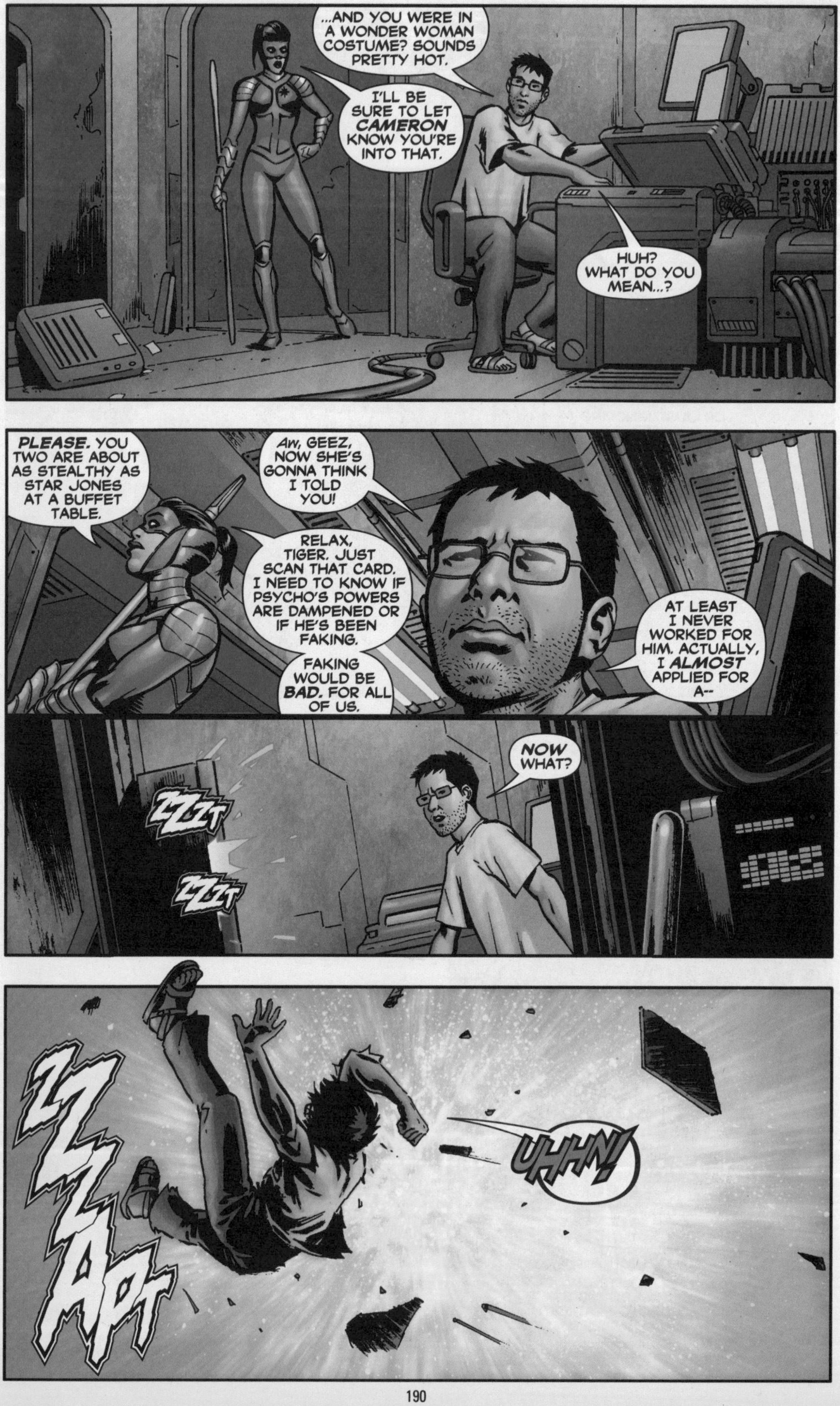
...AND YOU WERE IN A WONDER WOMAN COSTUME? SOUNDS PRETTY HOT.
I'LL BE SURE TO LET CAMERON KNOW YOU'RE INTO THAT.
HUH? WHAT DO YOU MEAN...?
PLEASE. YOU TWO ARE ABOUT AS STEALTHY AS STAR JONES AT A BUFFET TABLE.
AW, GEEZ, NOW SHE'S GONNA THINK I TOLD YOU!
RELAX, TIGER. JUST SCAN THAT CARD. I NEED TO KNOW IF PSYCHO'S POWERS ARE DAMPENED OR IF HE'S BEEN FAKING.
FAKING WOULD BE BAD. FOR ALL OF US.
AT LEAST I NEVER WORKED FOR HIM. ACTUALLY, I ALMOST APPLIED FOR A--
ZZZZT
ZZZZT
NOW WHAT?
ZZZAPT
UHHN!

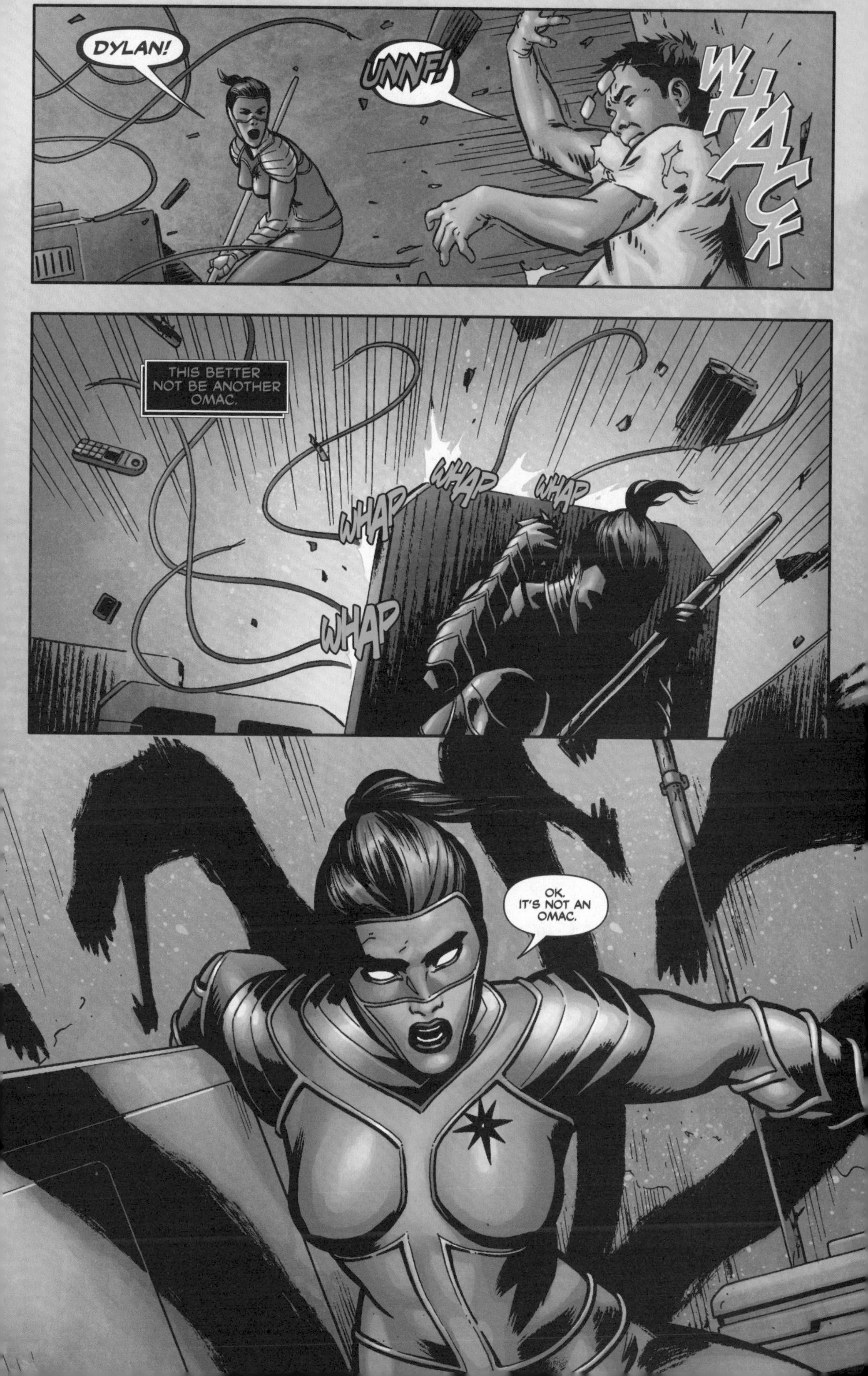
DYLAN!
UNNF!
WHACK
THIS BETTER NOT BE ANOTHER OMAC.
WHAP
WHAP
WHAP
WHAP
OK. IT'S NOT AN OMAC.

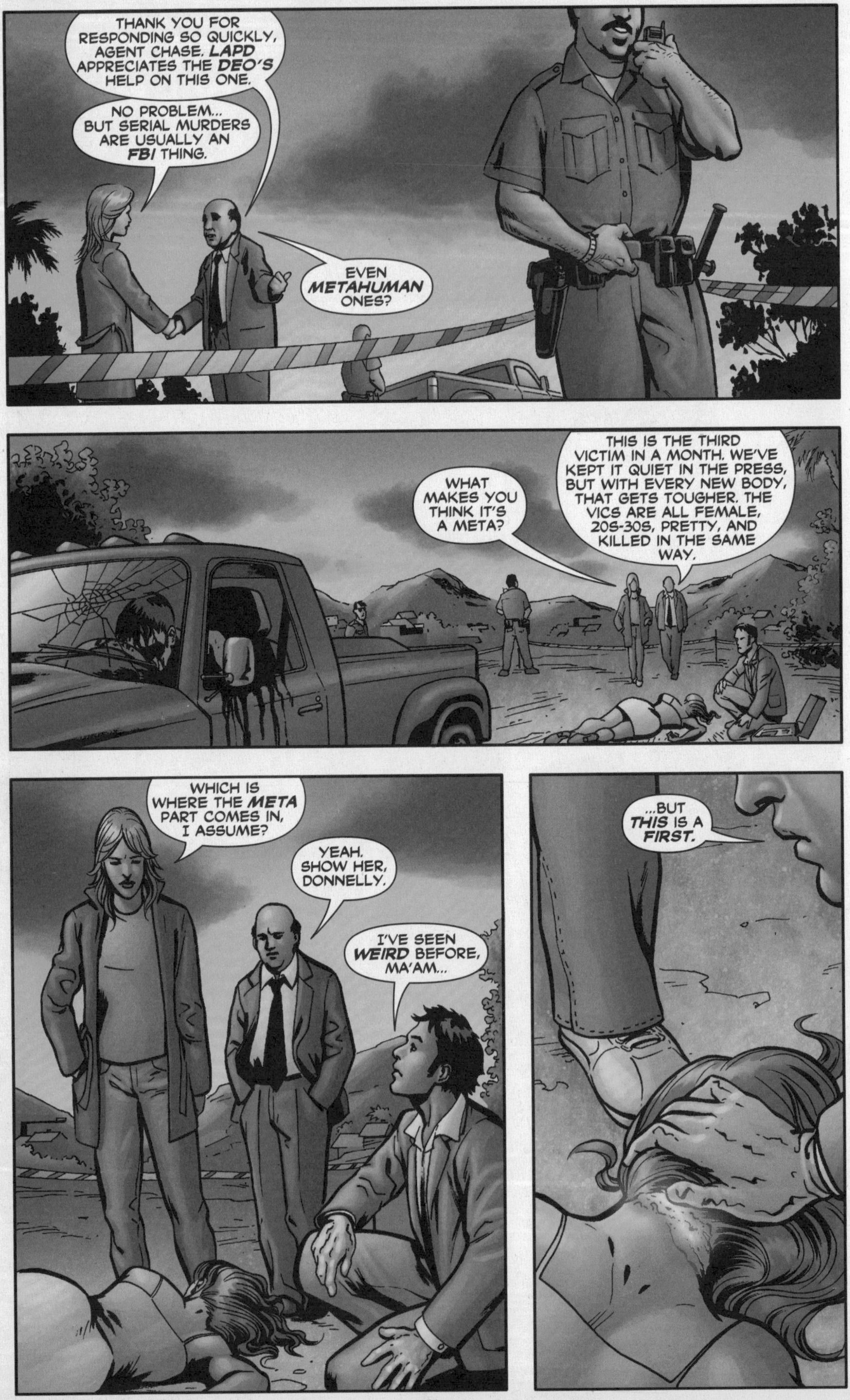
THANK YOU FOR RESPONDING SO QUICKLY, AGENT CHASE. LAPD APPRECIATES THE DEO'S HELP ON THIS ONE.
NO PROBLEM... BUT SERIAL MURDERS ARE USUALLY AN FBI THING.
EVEN METAHUMAN ONES?
WHAT MAKES YOU THINK IT'S A META?
THIS IS THE THIRD VICTIM IN A MONTH. WE'VE KEPT IT QUIET IN THE PRESS, BUT WITH EVERY NEW BODY, THAT GETS TOUGHER. THE VICS ARE ALL FEMALE, 20S-30S, PRETTY, AND KILLED IN THE SAME WAY.
WHICH IS WHERE THE META PART COMES IN, I ASSUME?
YEAH. SHOW HER, DONNELLY.
I'VE SEEN WEIRD BEFORE, MA'AM...
...BUT THIS IS A FIRST.

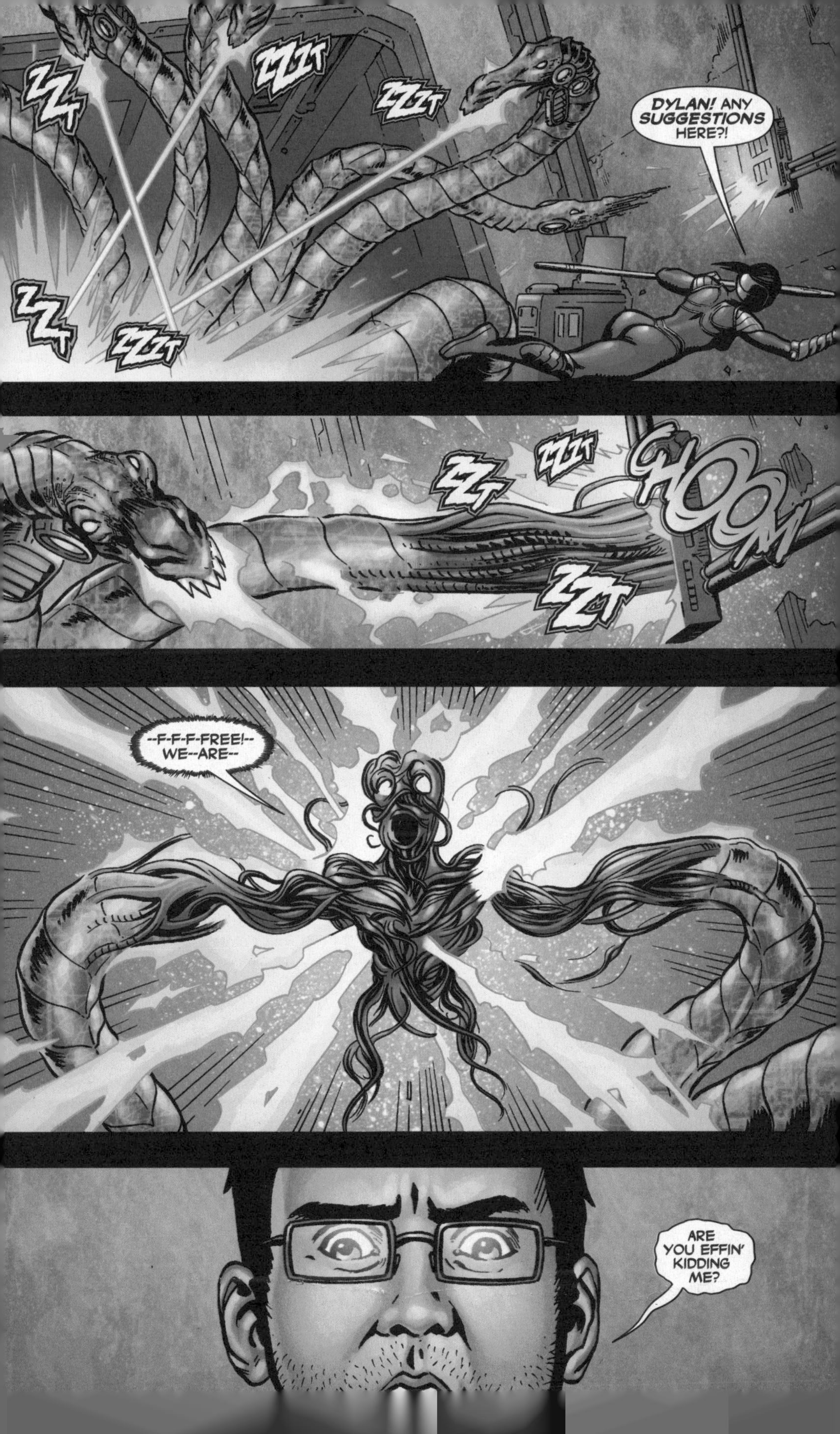
ZZZT
ZZZZT
ZZZZT
DYLAN! ANY SUGGESTIONS HERE?!
ZZZT
ZZZZT
ZZZT
ZZZT
CHOOM
ZZZT
--F-F-F-FREE!-- WE--ARE--
ARE YOU EFFIN' KIDDING ME?

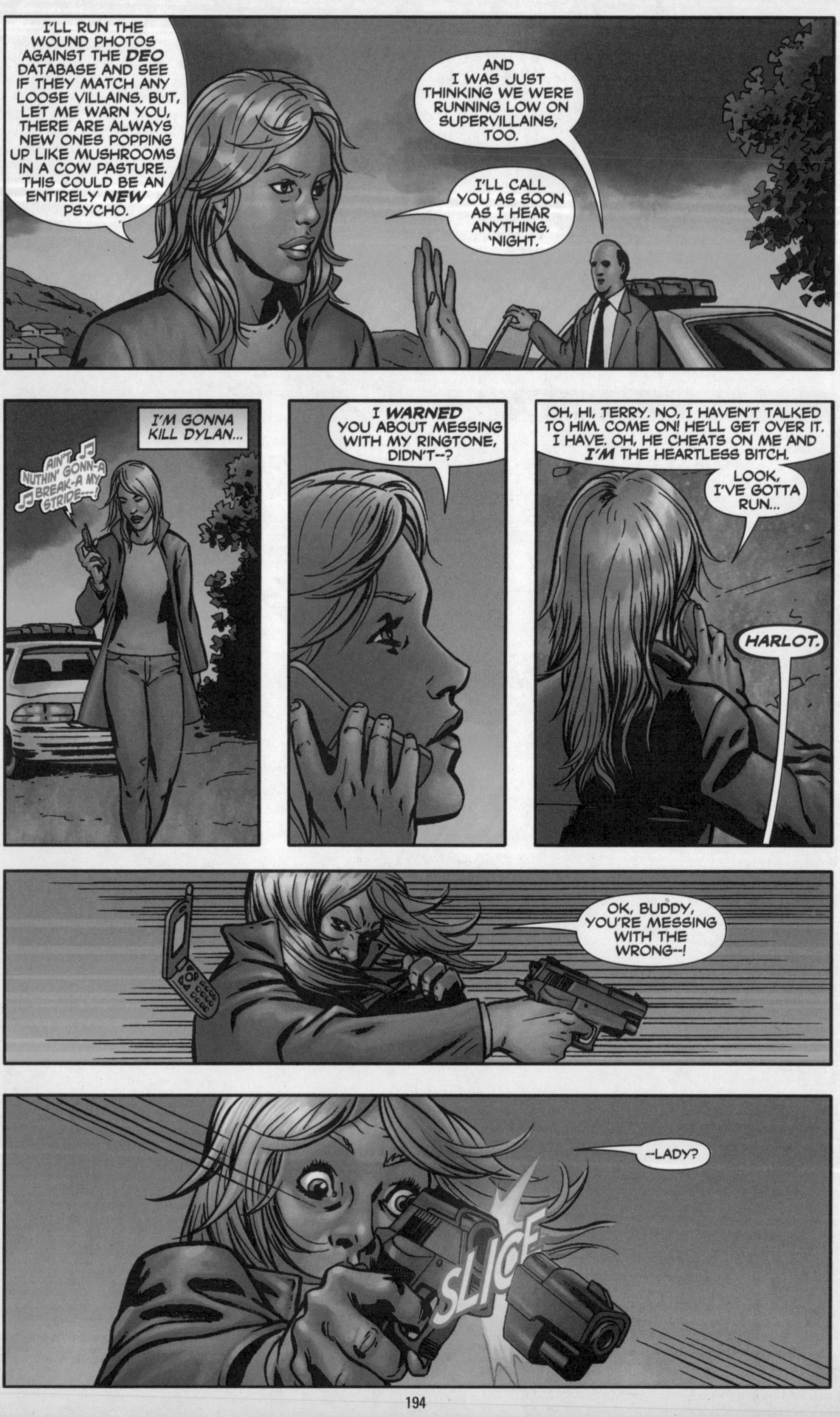
I'LL RUN THE WOUND PHOTOS AGAINST THE DEO DATABASE AND SEE IF THEY MATCH ANY LOOSE VILLAINS. BUT, LET ME WARN YOU, THERE ARE ALWAYS NEW ONES POPPING UP LIKE MUSHROOMS IN A COW PASTURE. THIS COULD BE AN ENTIRELY NEW PSYCHO.
AND I WAS JUST THINKING WE WERE RUNNING LOW ON SUPERVILLAINS, TOO.
I'LL CALL YOU AS SOON AS I HEAR ANYTHING. 'NIGHT.
I'M GONNA KILL DYLAN...
AIN'T NUTHIN' GONN-A BREAK-A MY STRIDE---!
I WARNED YOU ABOUT MESSING WITH MY RINGTONE, DIDN'T--?
OH, HI, TERRY. NO, I HAVEN'T TALKED TO HIM. COME ON! HE'LL GET OVER IT. I HAVE. OH, HE CHEATS ON ME AND I'M THE HEARTLESS BITCH.
LOOK, I'VE GOTTA RUN...
HARLOT.
OK, BUDDY, YOU'RE MESSING WITH THE WRONG--!
--LADY?
SLICE

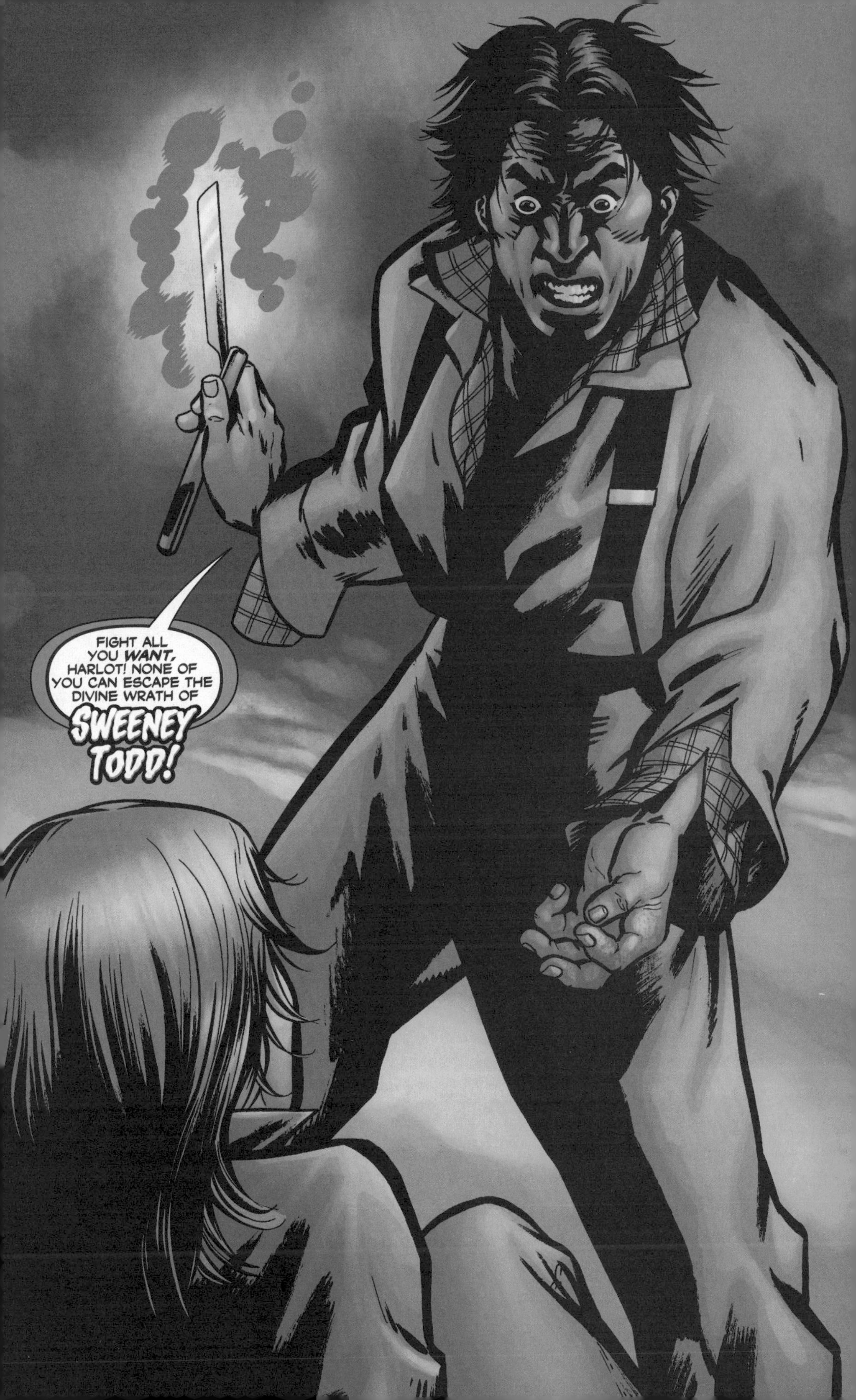
FIGHT ALL YOU WANT, HARLOT! NONE OF YOU CAN ESCAPE THE DIVINE WRATH OF SWEENEY TODD!

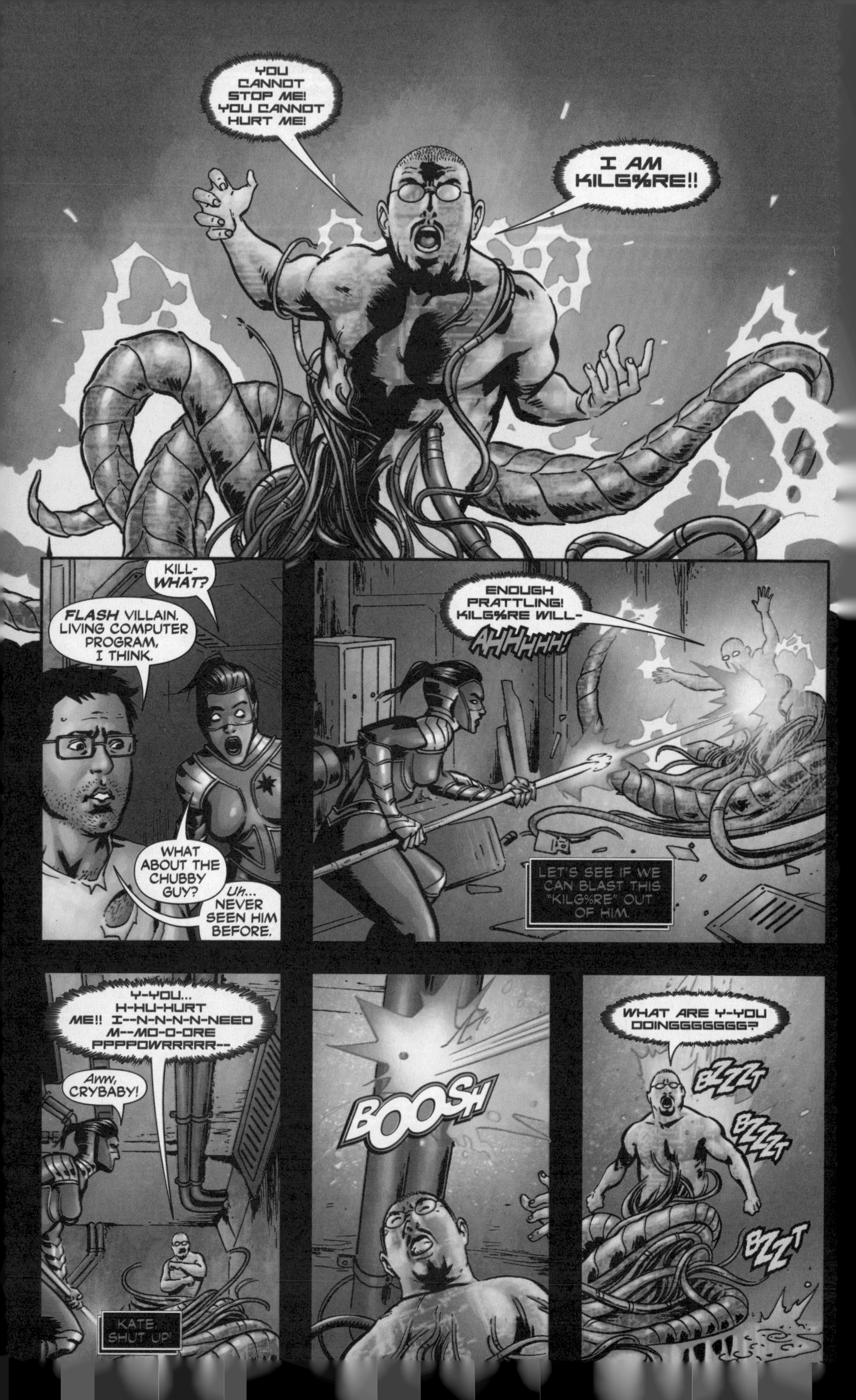
YOU CANNOT STOP ME! YOU CANNOT HURT ME!
I AM KILG%RE!!
KILL-WHAT?
FLASH VILLAIN. LIVING COMPUTER PROGRAM, I THINK.
WHAT ABOUT THE CHUBBY GUY?
Uh... NEVER SEEN HIM BEFORE.
ENOUGH PRATTLING! KILG%RE WILL-
AHHHHH!
LET'S SEE IF WE CAN BLAST THIS "KILG%RE" OUT OF HIM.
Y-YOU... H-HU-HURT ME!! I--N-N-N-N-NEED M--MO-O-ORE PPPPOWRRRRR--
Aww, CRYBABY!
KATE, SHUT UP!
BOOSH
WHAT ARE Y-YOU DOINGGGGGGG?
BZZZT
BZZZZT
BZZT

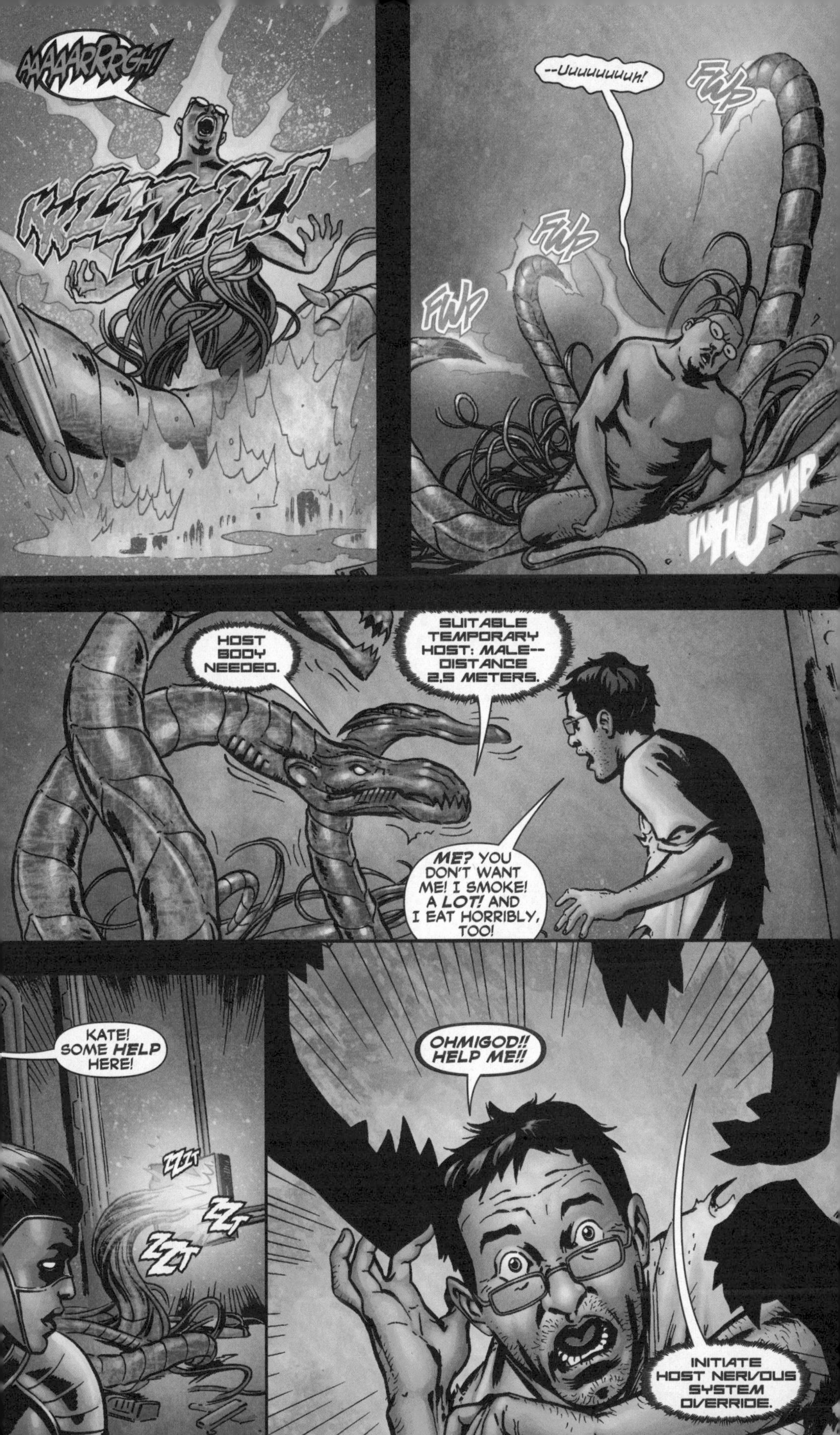
AAAAARRRGH!
KKZZZZZZZT
--Uuuuuuuuh!
FWP
FWP
FWP
WHUMP
HOST BODY NEEDED.
SUITABLE TEMPORARY HOST: MALE-- DISTANCE 2.5 METERS.
ME? YOU DON'T WANT ME! I SMOKE! A LOT! AND I EAT HORRIBLY, TOO!
KATE! SOME HELP HERE!
ZZZT
ZZZT
ZZZT
OHMIGOD!! HELP ME!!
INITIATE HOST NERVOUS SYSTEM OVERRIDE.

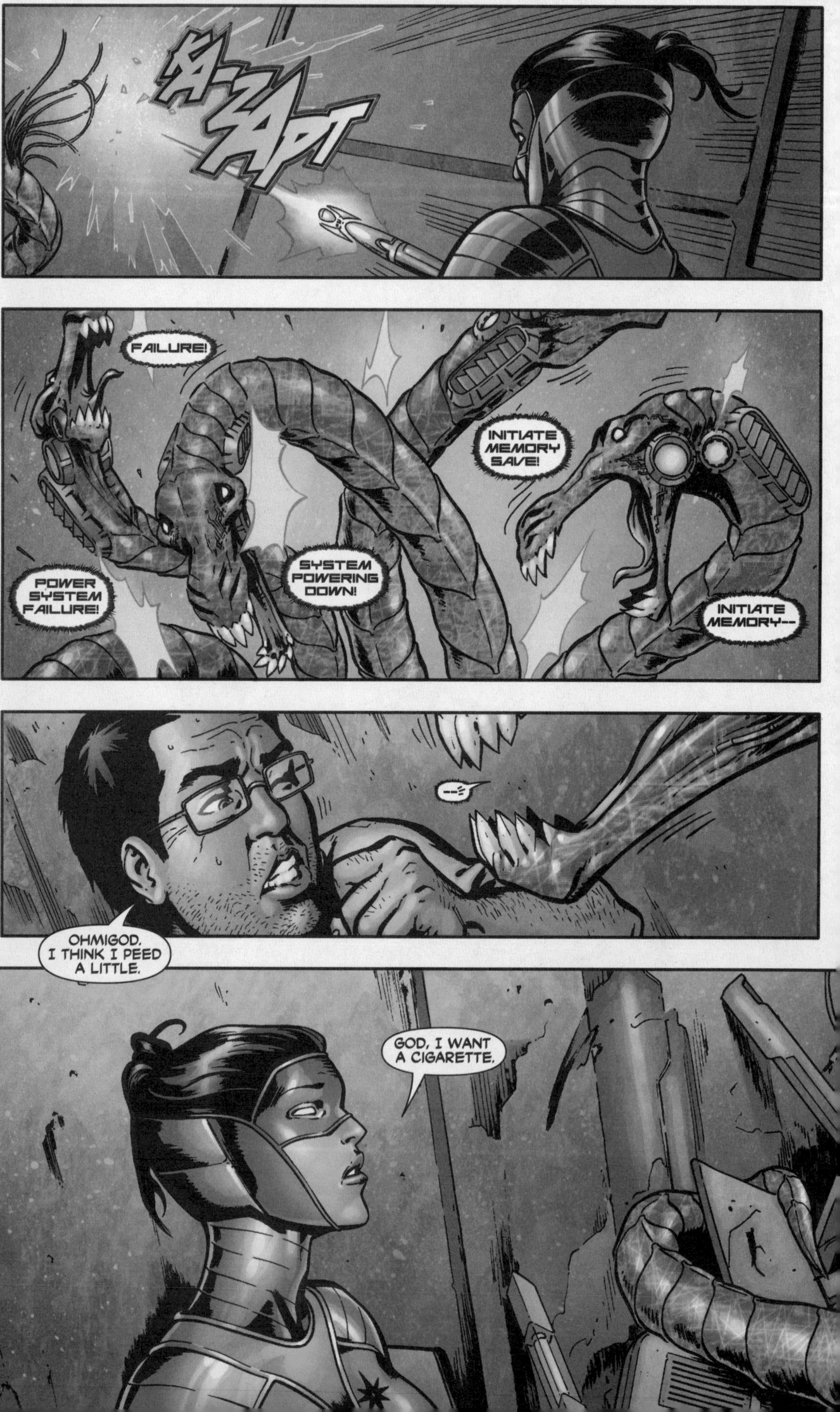
KA-ZAPT
FAILURE!
POWER SYSTEM FAILURE!
SYSTEM POWERING DOWN!
INITIATE MEMORY SAVE!
INITIATE MEMORY--
--!
OHMIGOD. I THINK I PEED A LITTLE.
GOD, I WANT A CIGARETTE.

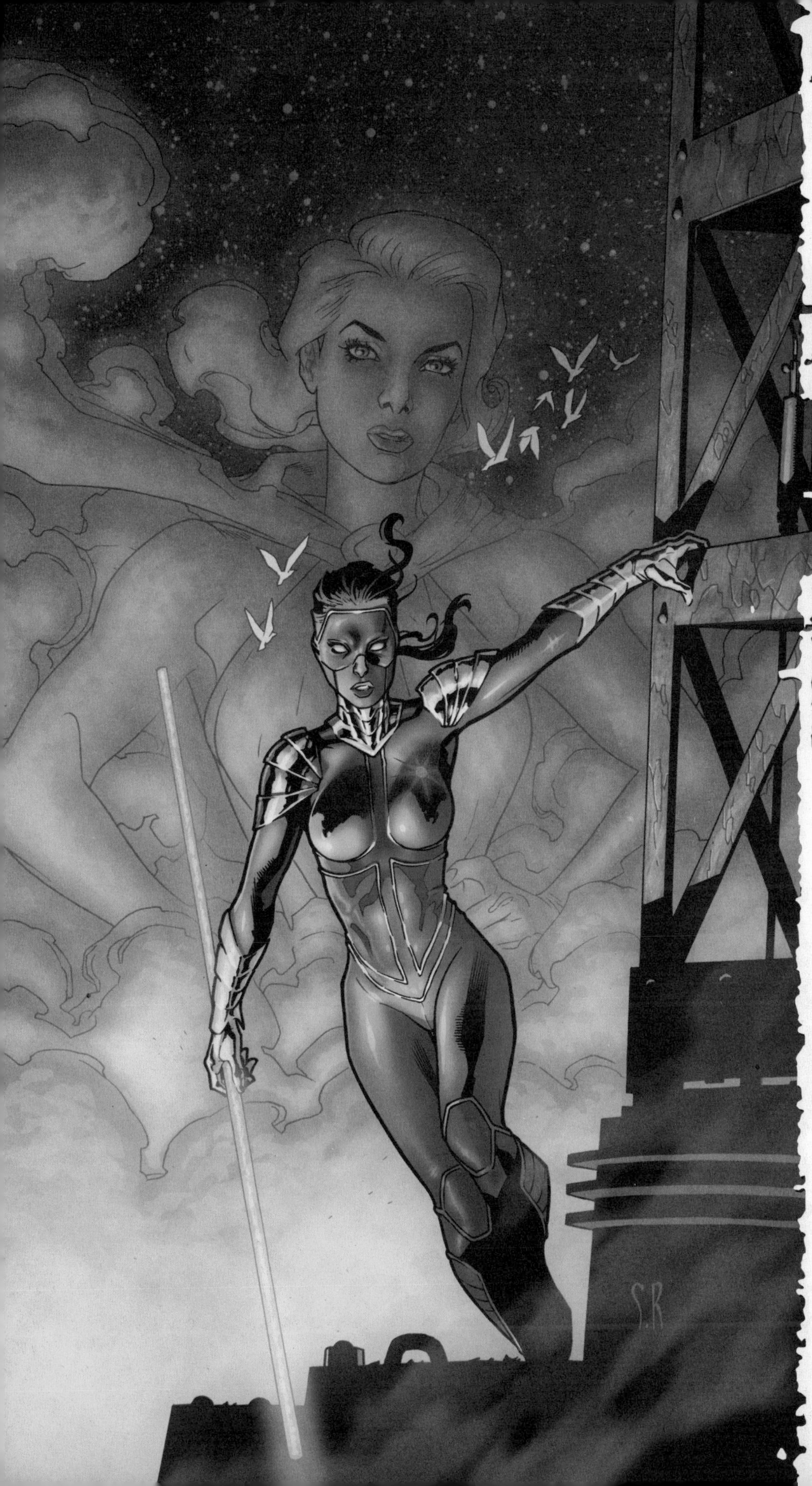

Issue #23 cover by Stephane Roux

Interior art by Javier Pina & Fernando Blanco

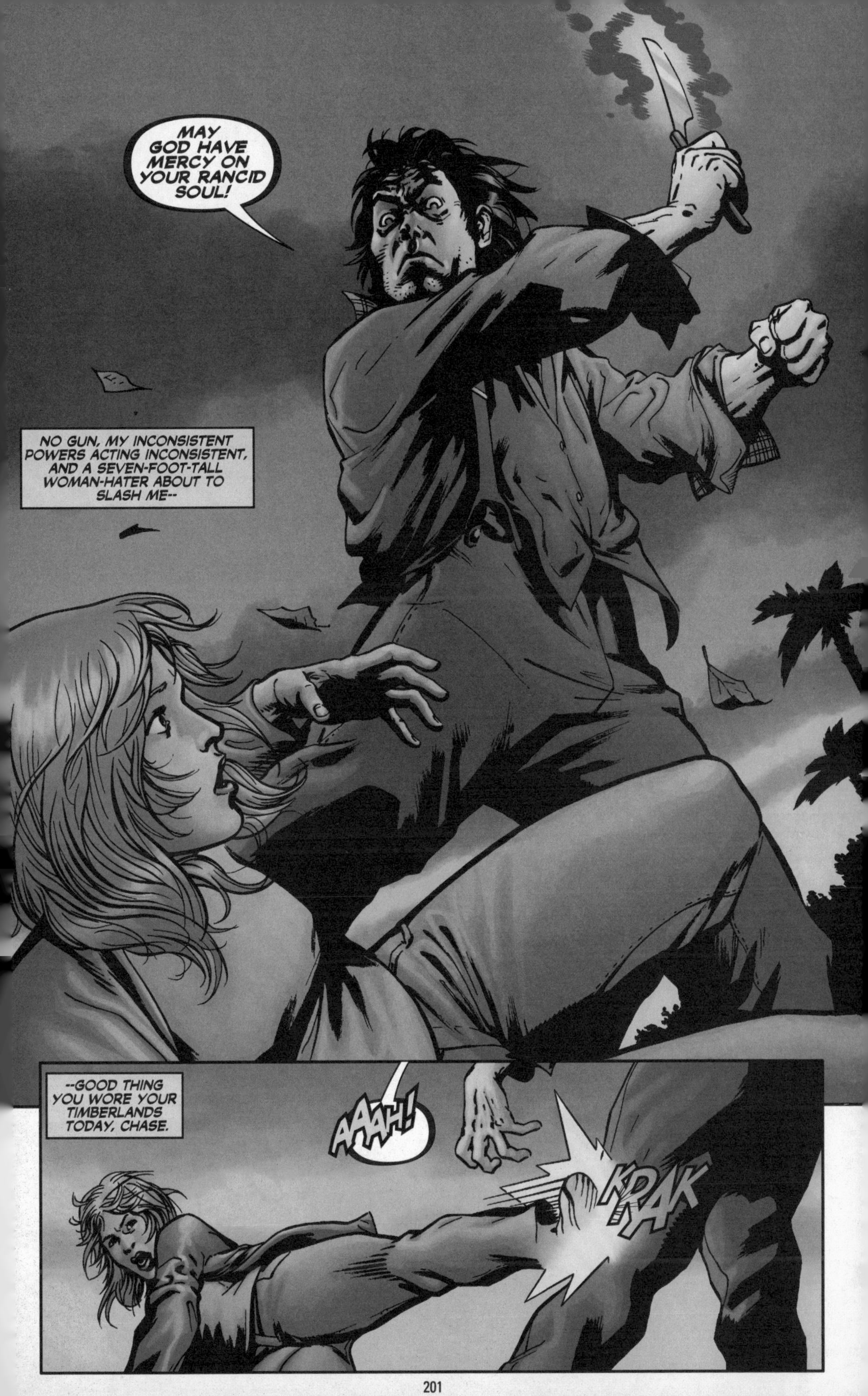
MAY GOD HAVE MERCY ON YOUR RANCID SOUL!
NO GUN, MY INCONSISTENT POWERS ACTING INCONSISTENT, AND A SEVEN-FOOT-TALL WOMAN-HATER ABOUT TO SLASH ME--
--GOOD THING YOU WORE YOUR TIMBERLANDS TODAY, CHASE.
AAAH!
KRAK

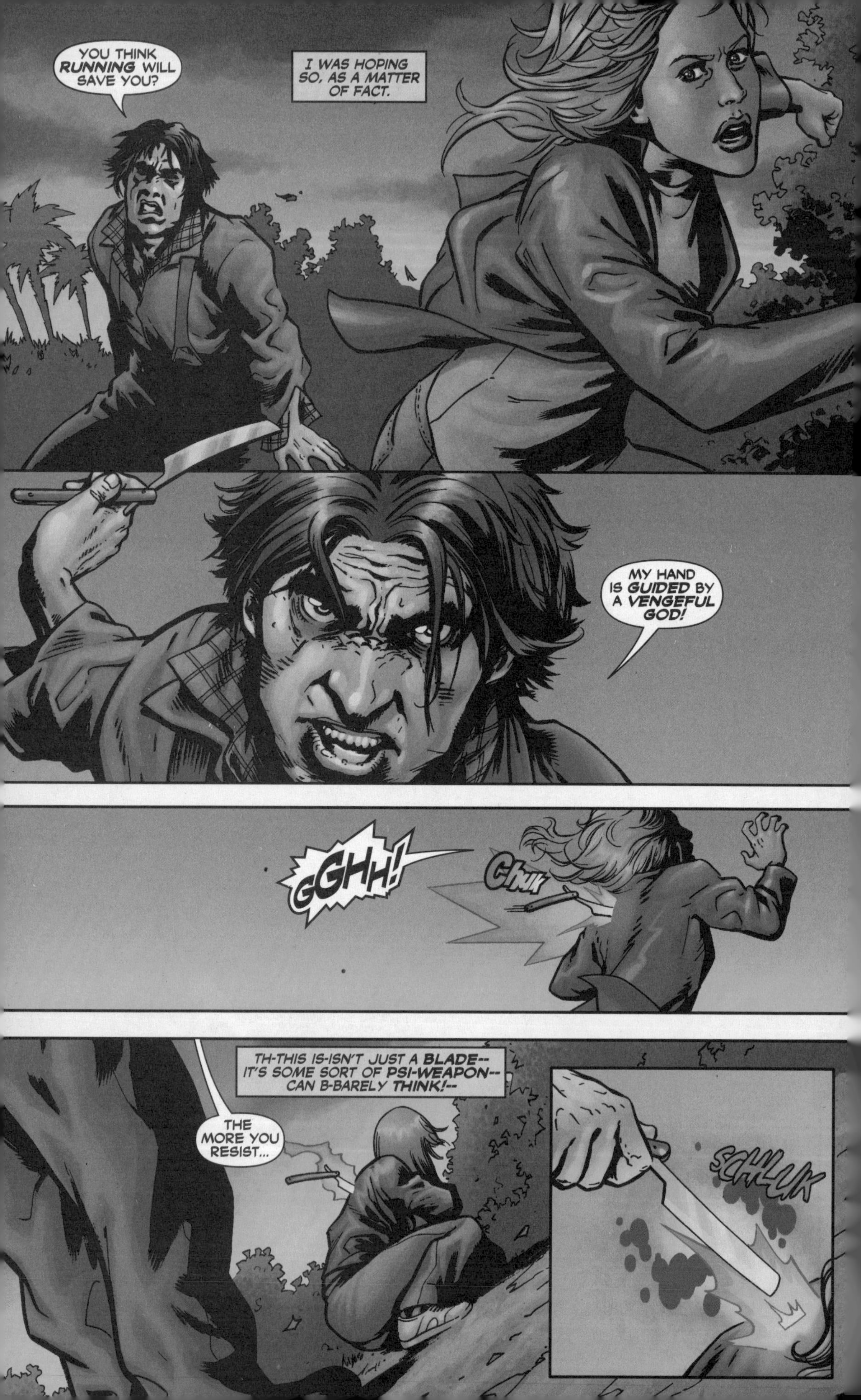
YOU THINK RUNNING WILL SAVE YOU?
I WAS HOPING SO, AS A MATTER OF FACT.
MY HAND IS GUIDED BY A VENGEFUL GOD!
GGHH!
CHUK
TH-THIS IS-ISN'T JUST A BLADE-- IT'S SOME SORT OF PSI-WEAPON-- CAN B-BARELY THINK!--
THE MORE YOU RESIST...
SCHLUK

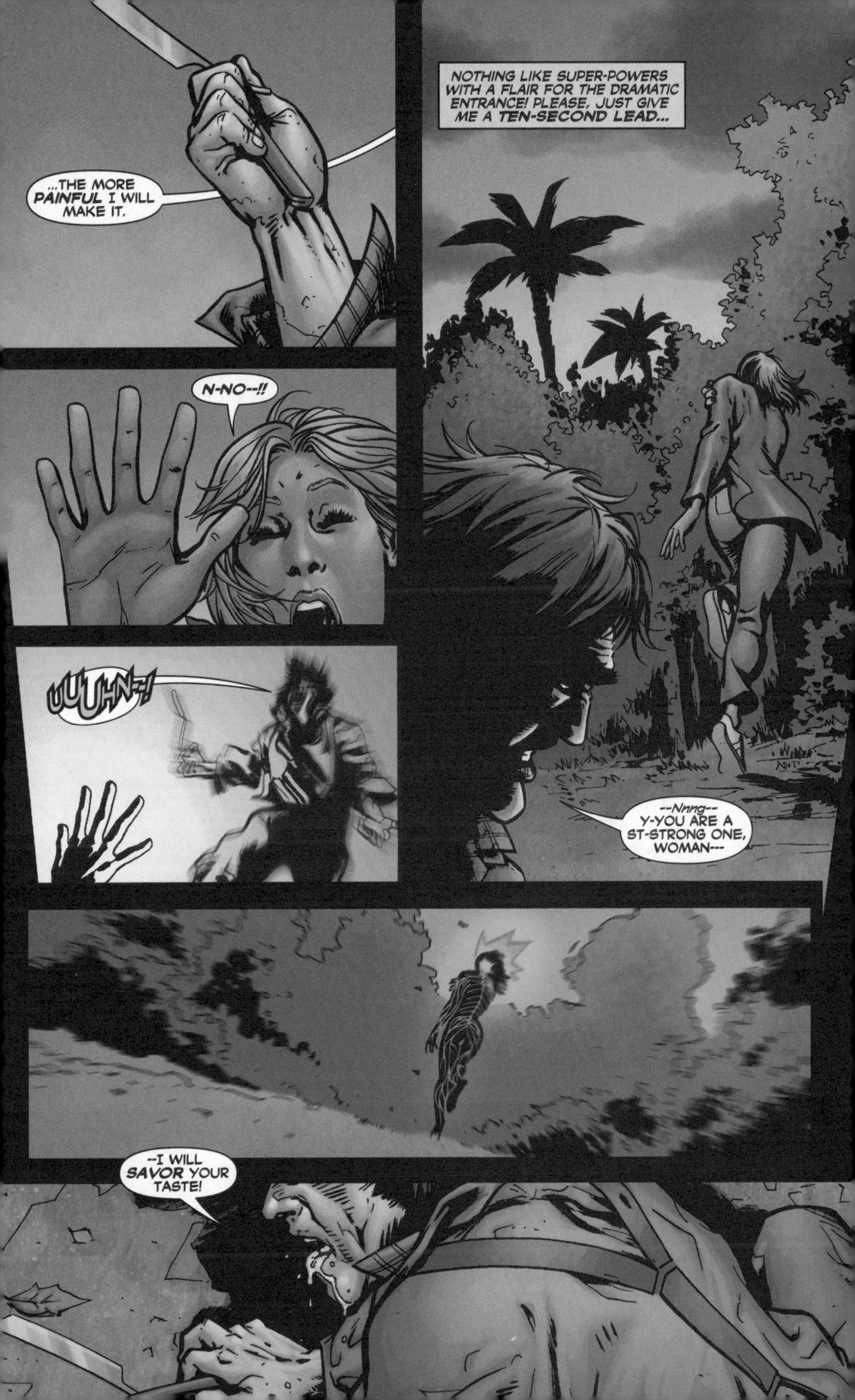
...THE MORE PAINFUL I WILL MAKE IT.
NOTHING LIKE SUPER-POWERS WITH A FLAIR FOR THE DRAMATIC ENTRANCE! PLEASE, JUST GIVE ME A TEN-SECOND LEAD...
N-NO--!!
UUUHN--!
--Nnng-- Y-YOU ARE A ST-STRONG ONE, WOMAN---
--I WILL SAVOR YOUR TASTE!

PHANTOM PAIN

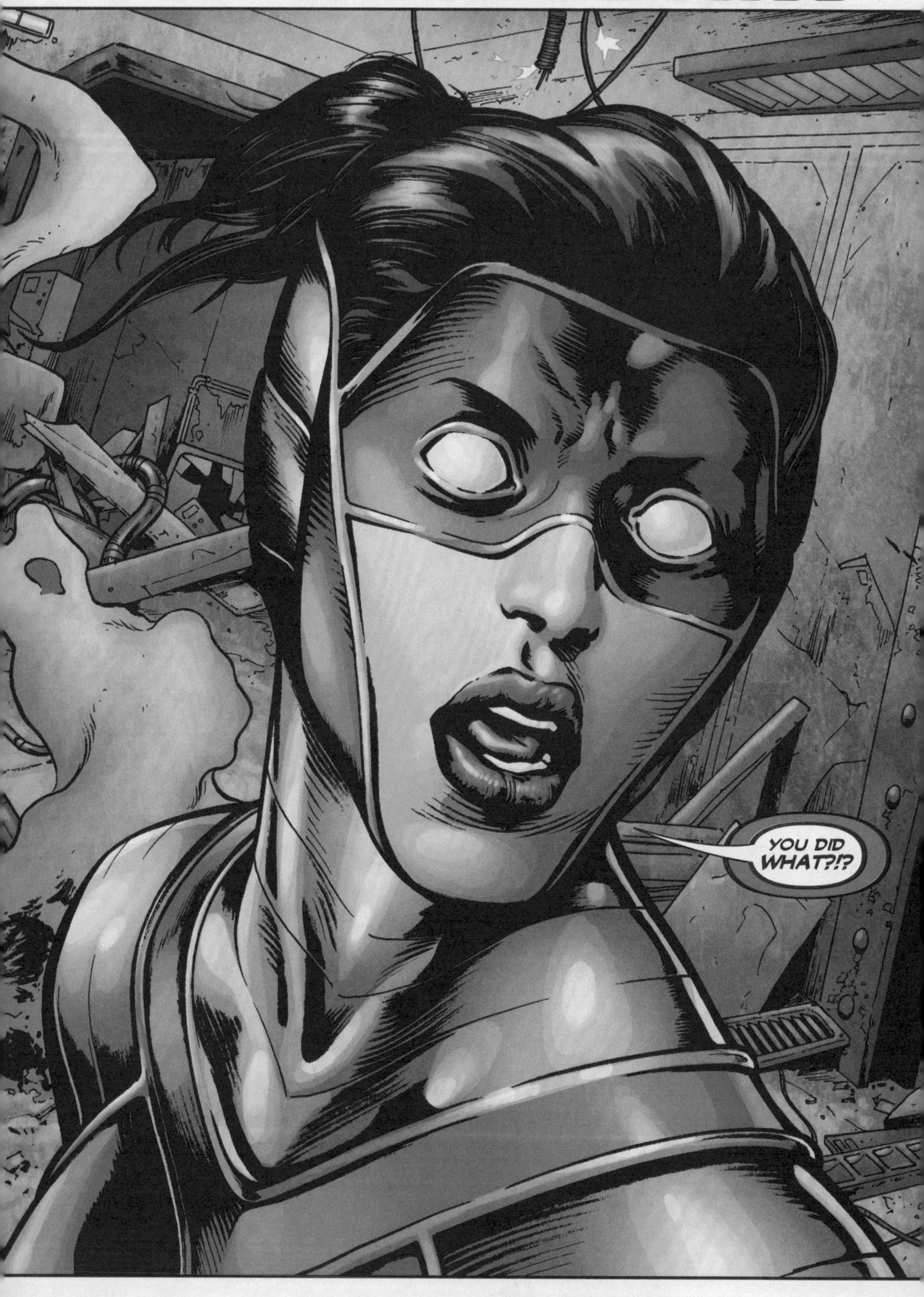
YOU DID WHAT?!?

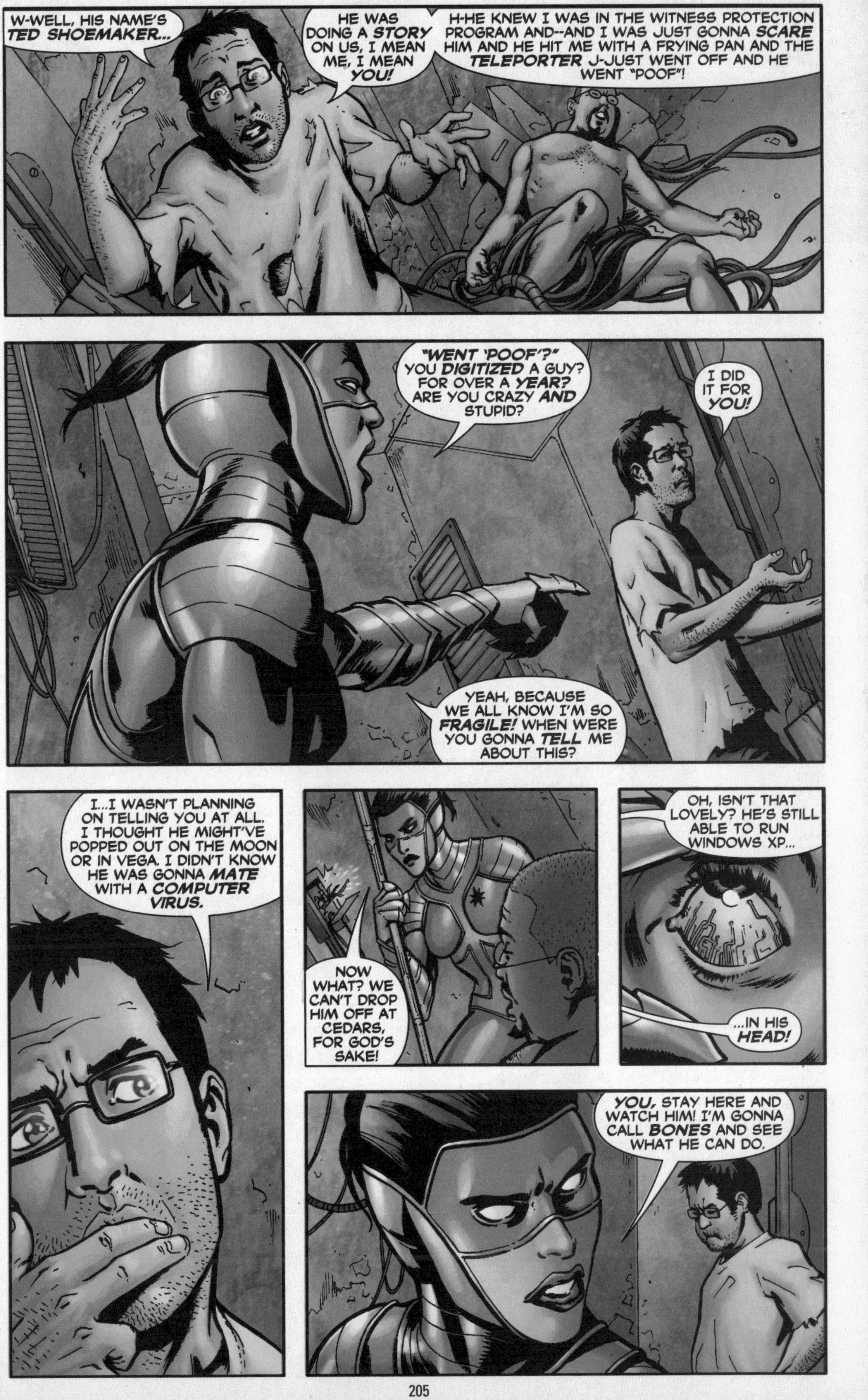
W-WELL, HIS NAME'S TED SHOEMAKER...
HE WAS DOING A STORY ON US, I MEAN ME, I MEAN YOU!
H-HE KNEW I WAS IN THE WITNESS PROTECTION PROGRAM AND--AND I WAS JUST GONNA SCARE HIM AND HE HIT ME WITH A FRYING PAN AND THE TELEPORTER J-JUST WENT OFF AND HE WENT "POOF"!
"WENT 'POOF'?" YOU DIGITIZED A GUY? FOR OVER A YEAR? ARE YOU CRAZY AND STUPID?
I DID IT FOR YOU!
YEAH, BECAUSE WE ALL KNOW I'M SO FRAGILE! WHEN WERE YOU GONNA TELL ME ABOUT THIS?
I...I WASN'T PLANNING ON TELLING YOU AT ALL. I THOUGHT HE MIGHT'VE POPPED OUT ON THE MOON OR IN VEGA. I DIDN'T KNOW HE WAS GONNA MATE WITH A COMPUTER VIRUS.
NOW WHAT? WE CAN'T DROP HIM OFF AT CEDARS, FOR GOD'S SAKE!
OH, ISN'T THAT LOVELY? HE'S STILL ABLE TO RUN WINDOWS XP...
...IN HIS HEAD!
YOU, STAY HERE AND WATCH HIM! I'M GONNA CALL BONES AND SEE WHAT HE CAN DO.

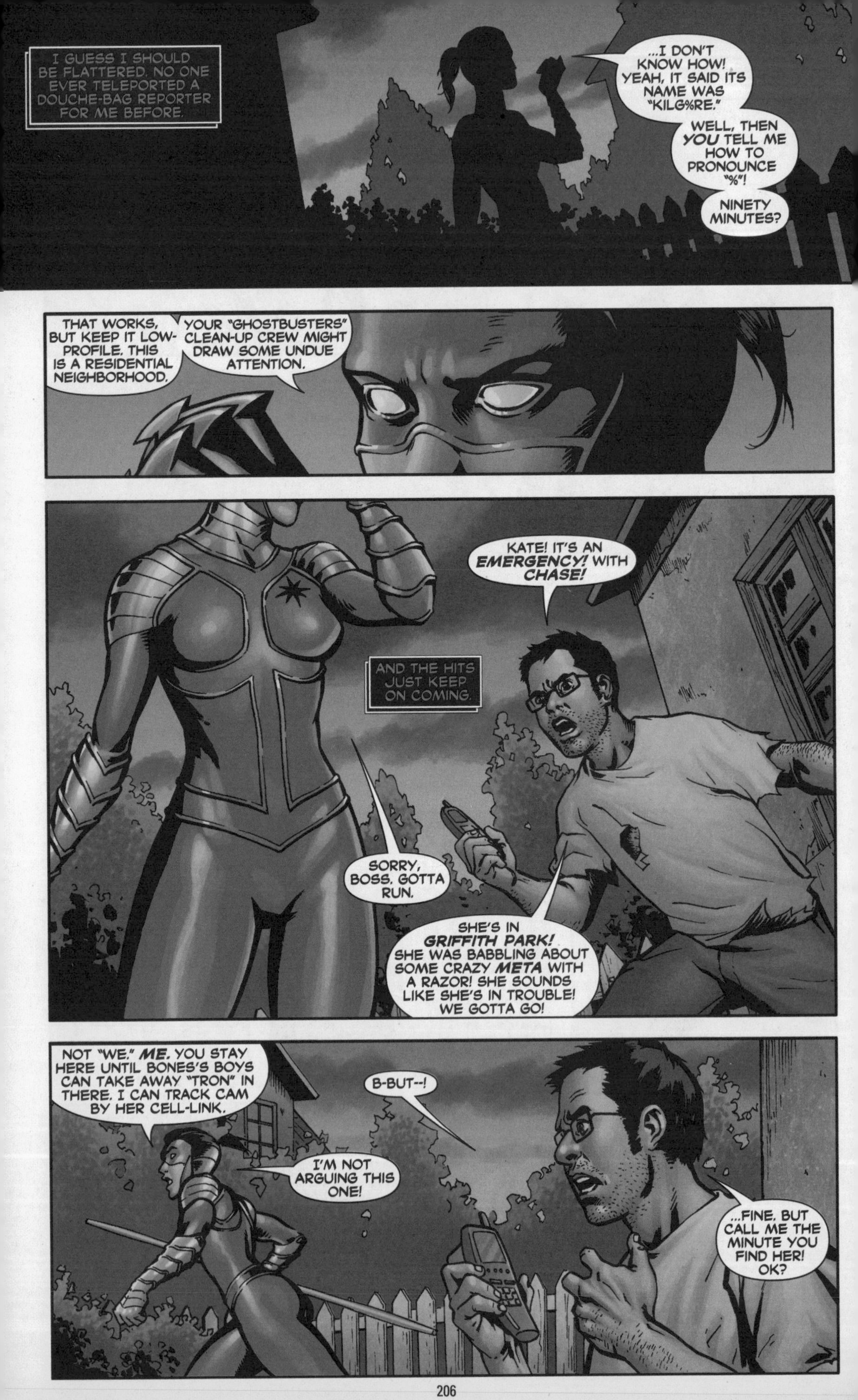

I GUESS I SHOULD BE FLATTERED. NO ONE EVER TELEPORTED A DOUCHE-BAG REPORTER FOR ME BEFORE.
...I DON'T KNOW HOW! YEAH, IT SAID ITS NAME WAS "KILG%RE."
WELL, THEN *YOU* TELL ME HOW TO PRONOUNCE "%"!
NINETY MINUTES?
THAT WORKS, BUT KEEP IT LOW-PROFILE. THIS IS A RESIDENTIAL NEIGHBORHOOD.
YOUR "GHOSTBUSTERS" CLEAN-UP CREW MIGHT DRAW SOME UNDUE ATTENTION.
KATE! IT'S AN ***EMERGENCY!*** WITH ***CHASE!***
AND THE HITS JUST KEEP ON COMING.
SORRY, BOSS. GOTTA RUN.
SHE'S IN ***GRIFFITH PARK!*** SHE WAS BABBLING ABOUT SOME CRAZY ***META*** WITH A RAZOR! SHE SOUNDS LIKE SHE'S IN TROUBLE! WE GOTTA GO!
NOT "WE." ***ME.*** YOU STAY HERE UNTIL BONES'S BOYS CAN TAKE AWAY "TRON" IN THERE. I CAN TRACK CAM BY HER CELL-LINK.
B-BUT--!
I'M NOT ARGUING THIS ONE!
...FINE. BUT CALL ME THE MINUTE YOU FIND HER! OK?

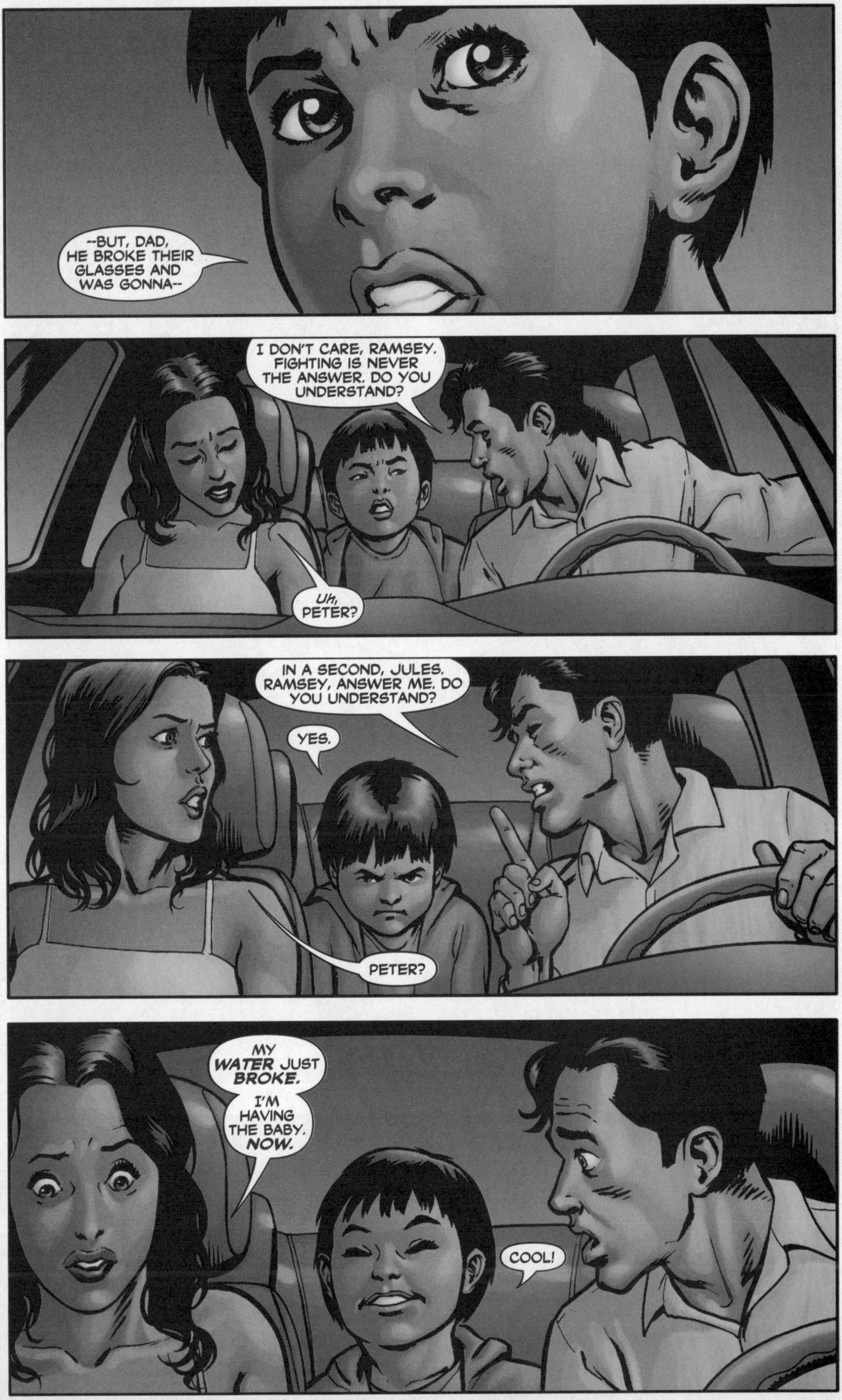
--BUT, DAD, HE BROKE THEIR GLASSES AND WAS GONNA--
I DON'T CARE, RAMSEY. FIGHTING IS NEVER THE ANSWER. DO YOU UNDERSTAND?
Uh, PETER?
IN A SECOND, JULES. RAMSEY, ANSWER ME. DO YOU UNDERSTAND?
YES.
PETER?
MY WATER JUST BROKE.
I'M HAVING THE BABY. NOW.
COOL!

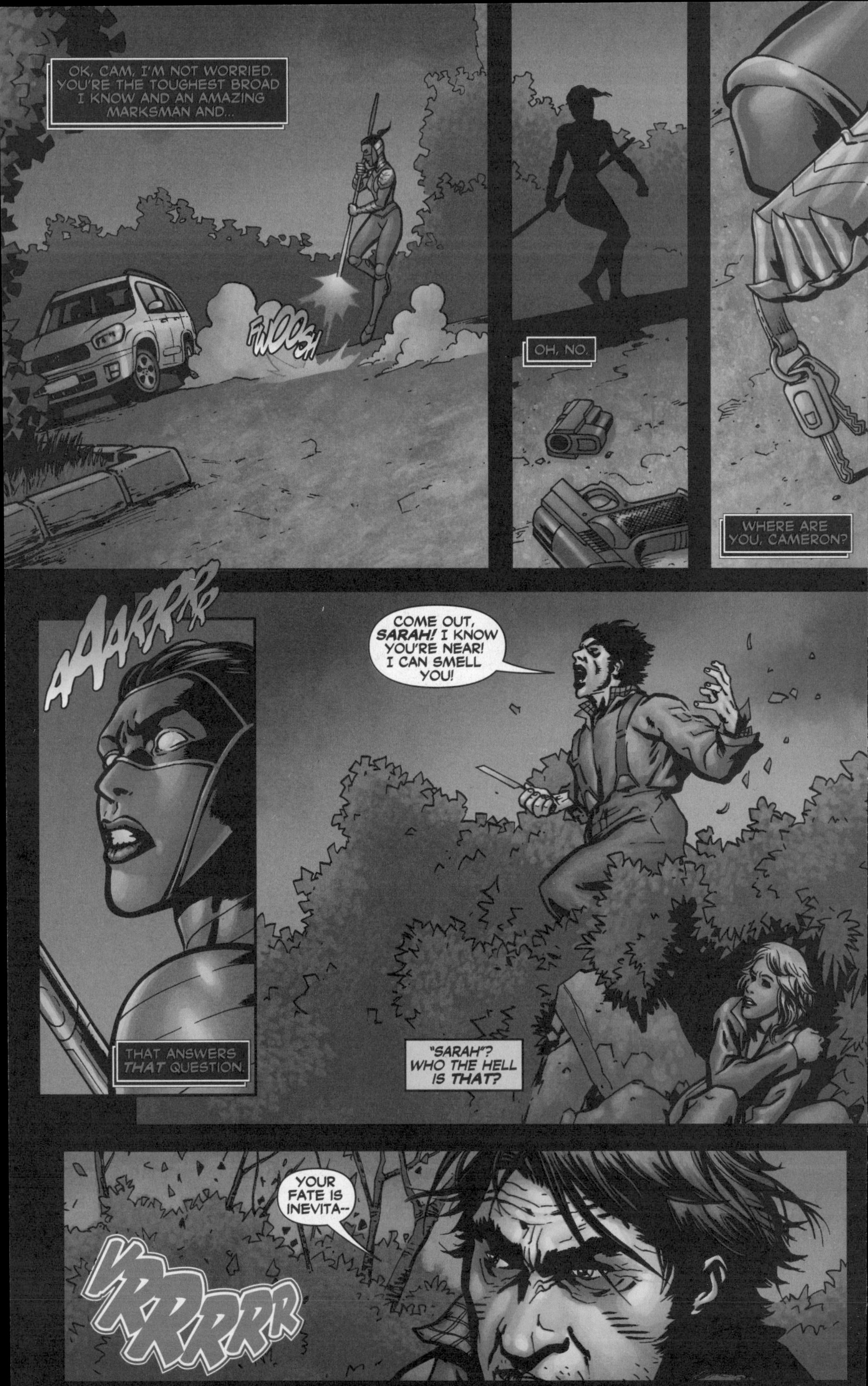
OK, CAM, I'M NOT WORRIED. YOU'RE THE TOUGHEST BROAD I KNOW AND AN AMAZING MARKSMAN AND...
FWOOSH
OH, NO.
WHERE ARE YOU, CAMERON?
AAARRRR
THAT ANSWERS THAT QUESTION.
COME OUT, SARAH! I KNOW YOU'RE NEAR! I CAN SMELL YOU!
"SARAH"? WHO THE HELL IS THAT?
YOUR FATE IS INEVITA--
VRRRRRR

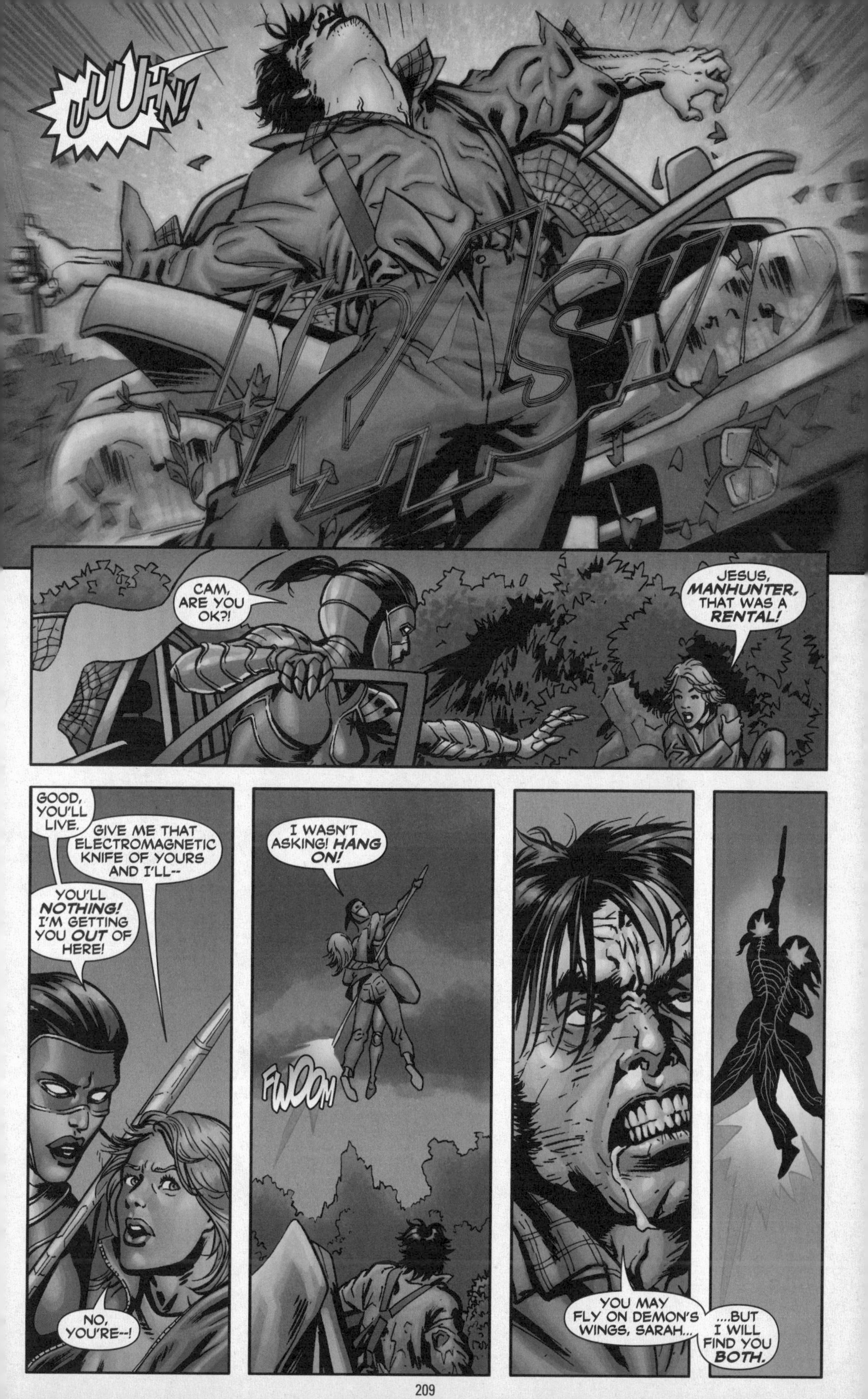
JUUHN!
WHASH
CAM, ARE YOU OK?!
JESUS, MANHUNTER, THAT WAS A RENTAL!
GOOD, YOU'LL LIVE.
GIVE ME THAT ELECTROMAGNETIC KNIFE OF YOURS AND I'LL--
YOU'LL NOTHING! I'M GETTING YOU OUT OF HERE!
NO, YOU'RE--!
I WASN'T ASKING! HANG ON!
FWOOM
YOU MAY FLY ON DEMON'S WINGS, SARAH...
....BUT I WILL FIND YOU BOTH.

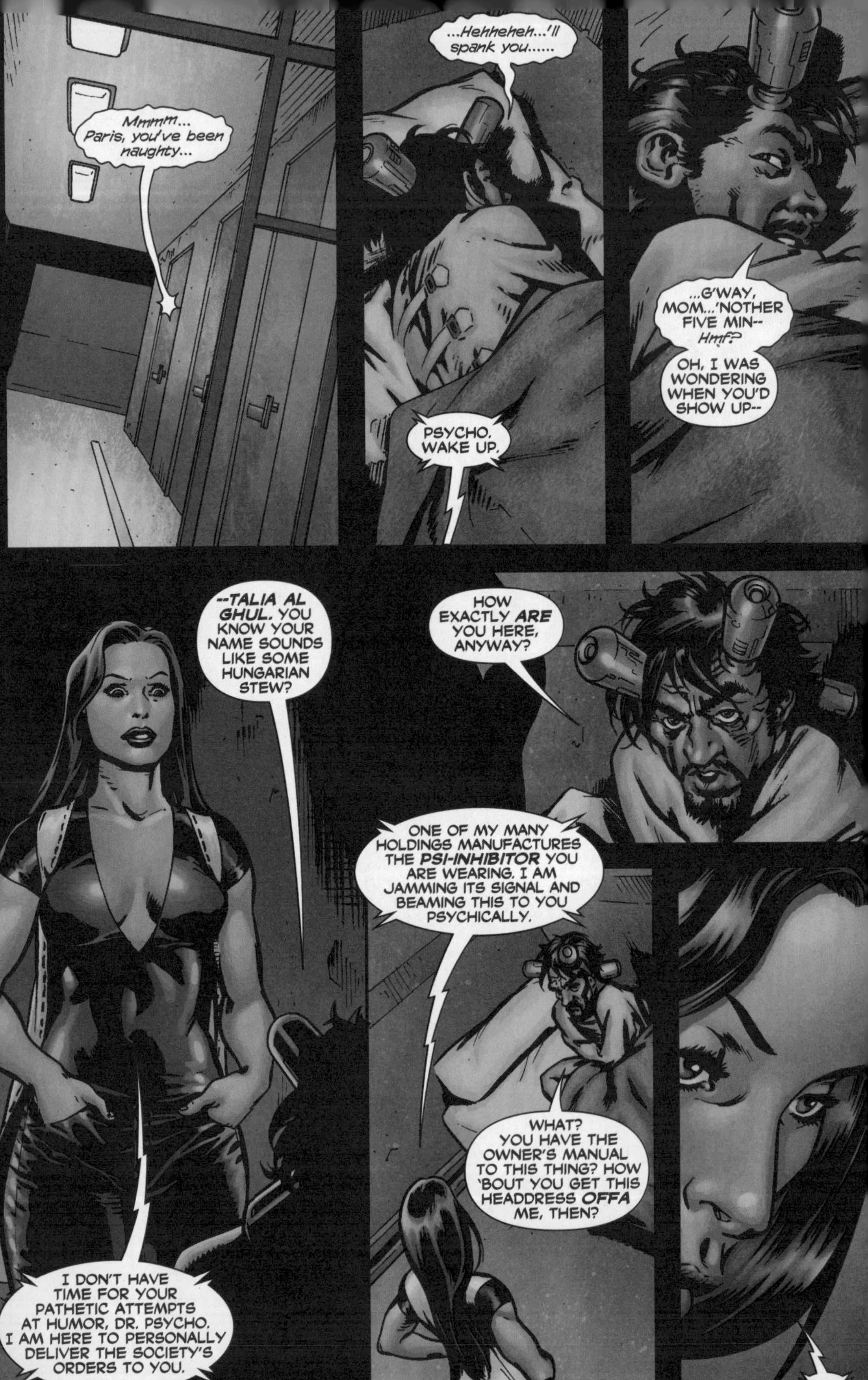
Mmmm... Paris, you've been naughty...
...Hehheheh...'ll spank you......
PSYCHO. WAKE UP.
...G'WAY, MOM...'NOTHER FIVE MIN-- Hmf?
OH, I WAS WONDERING WHEN YOU'D SHOW UP--
--TALIA AL GHUL. YOU KNOW YOUR NAME SOUNDS LIKE SOME HUNGARIAN STEW?
I DON'T HAVE TIME FOR YOUR PATHETIC ATTEMPTS AT HUMOR, DR. PSYCHO. I AM HERE TO PERSONALLY DELIVER THE SOCIETY'S ORDERS TO YOU.
HOW EXACTLY ARE YOU HERE, ANYWAY?
ONE OF MY MANY HOLDINGS MANUFACTURES THE PSI-INHIBITOR YOU ARE WEARING. I AM JAMMING ITS SIGNAL AND BEAMING THIS TO YOU PSYCHICALLY.
WHAT? YOU HAVE THE OWNER'S MANUAL TO THIS THING? HOW 'BOUT YOU GET THIS HEADDRESS OFFA ME, THEN?
NO.

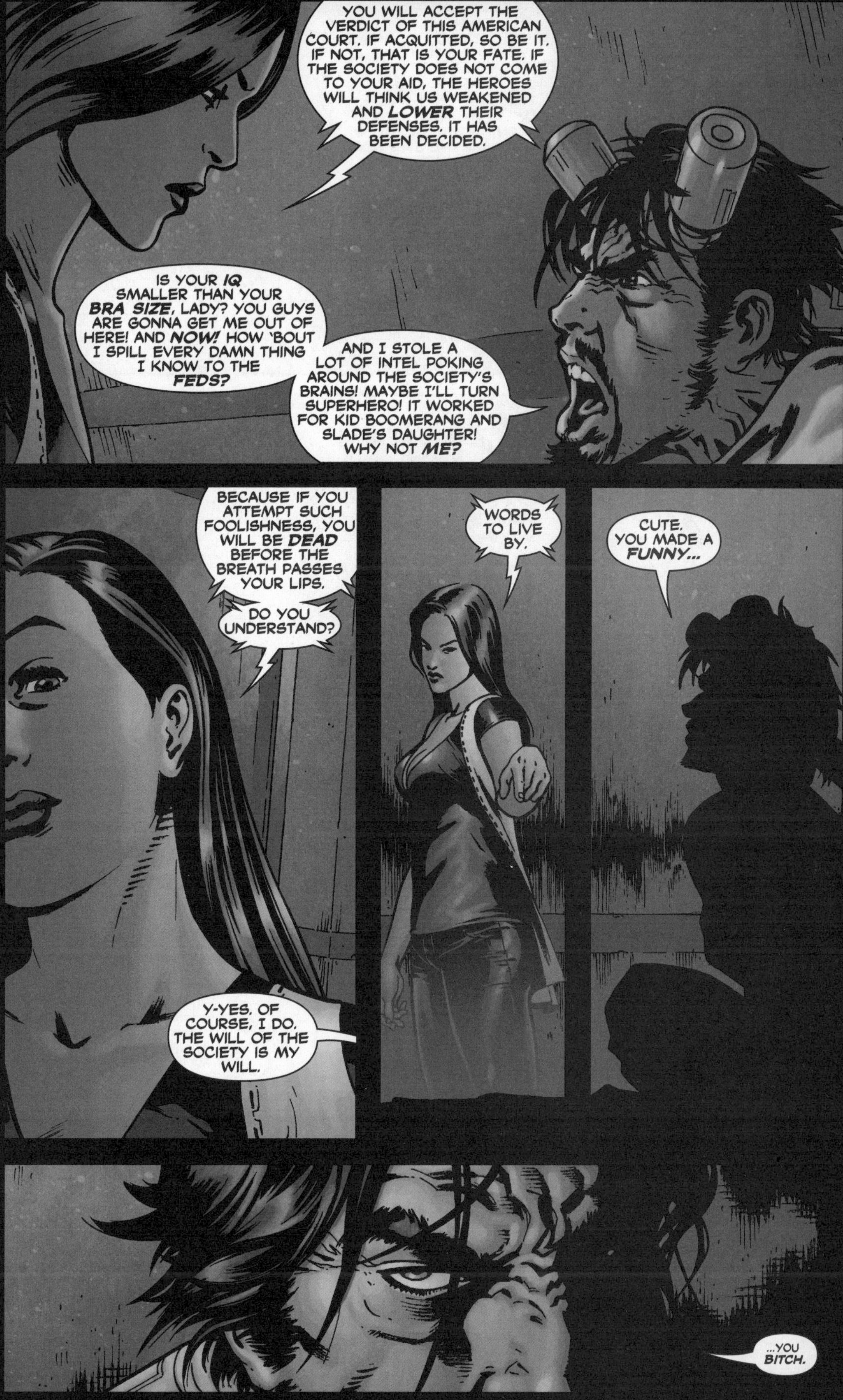
YOU WILL ACCEPT THE VERDICT OF THIS AMERICAN COURT. IF ACQUITTED, SO BE IT. IF NOT, THAT IS YOUR FATE. IF THE SOCIETY DOES NOT COME TO YOUR AID, THE HEROES WILL THINK US WEAKENED AND LOWER THEIR DEFENSES. IT HAS BEEN DECIDED.
IS YOUR IQ SMALLER THAN YOUR BRA SIZE, LADY? YOU GUYS ARE GONNA GET ME OUT OF HERE! AND NOW! HOW 'BOUT I SPILL EVERY DAMN THING I KNOW TO THE FEDS?
AND I STOLE A LOT OF INTEL POKING AROUND THE SOCIETY'S BRAINS! MAYBE I'LL TURN SUPERHERO! IT WORKED FOR KID BOOMERANG AND SLADE'S DAUGHTER! WHY NOT ME?
BECAUSE IF YOU ATTEMPT SUCH FOOLISHNESS, YOU WILL BE DEAD BEFORE THE BREATH PASSES YOUR LIPS.
DO YOU UNDERSTAND?
Y-YES, OF COURSE, I DO. THE WILL OF THE SOCIETY IS MY WILL.
WORDS TO LIVE BY.
CUTE. YOU MADE A FUNNY...
...YOU BITCH.

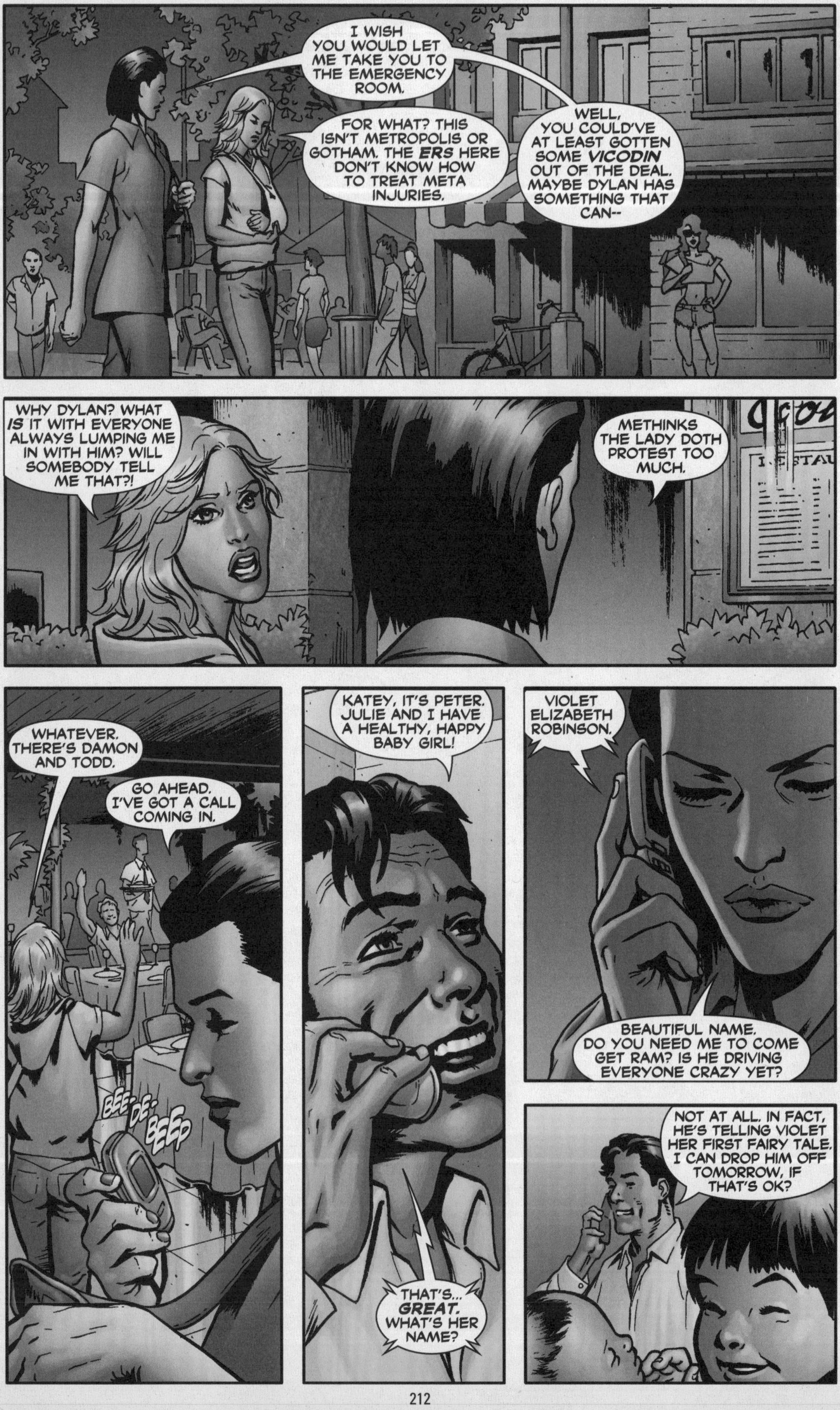
I WISH YOU WOULD LET ME TAKE YOU TO THE EMERGENCY ROOM.
FOR WHAT? THIS ISN'T METROPOLIS OR GOTHAM. THE ERS HERE DON'T KNOW HOW TO TREAT META INJURIES.
WELL, YOU COULD'VE AT LEAST GOTTEN SOME VICODIN OUT OF THE DEAL. MAYBE DYLAN HAS SOMETHING THAT CAN--
WHY DYLAN? WHAT IS IT WITH EVERYONE ALWAYS LUMPING ME IN WITH HIM? WILL SOMEBODY TELL ME THAT?!
METHINKS THE LADY DOTH PROTEST TOO MUCH.
WHATEVER. THERE'S DAMON AND TODD.
GO AHEAD. I'VE GOT A CALL COMING IN.
BEE-DE-BEEP
KATEY, IT'S PETER. JULIE AND I HAVE A HEALTHY, HAPPY BABY GIRL!
THAT'S... GREAT. WHAT'S HER NAME?
VIOLET ELIZABETH ROBINSON.
BEAUTIFUL NAME. DO YOU NEED ME TO COME GET RAM? IS HE DRIVING EVERYONE CRAZY YET?
NOT AT ALL. IN FACT, HE'S TELLING VIOLET HER FIRST FAIRY TALE. I CAN DROP HIM OFF TOMORROW, IF THAT'S OK?

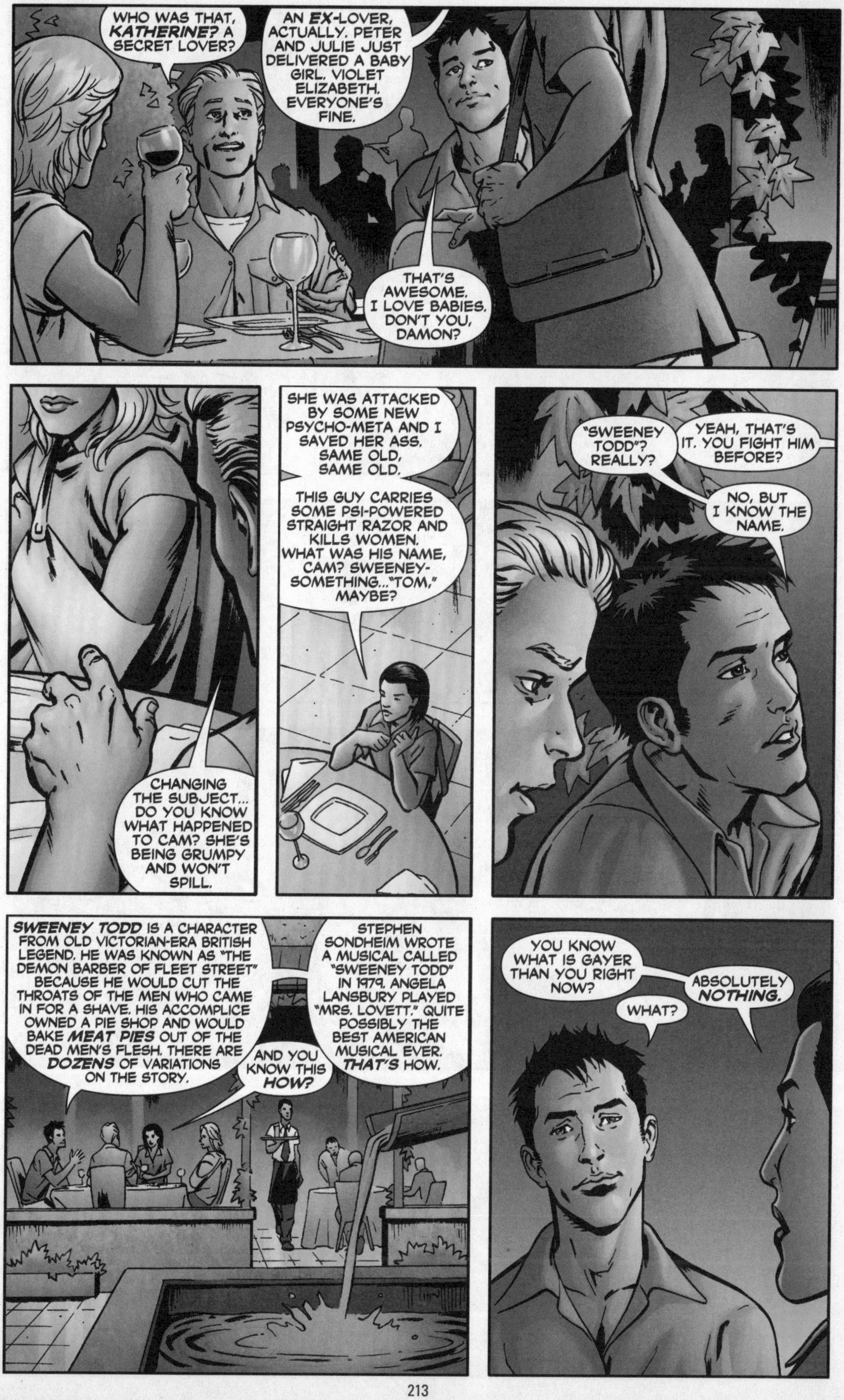
WHO WAS THAT, KATHERINE? A SECRET LOVER?
AN EX-LOVER, ACTUALLY. PETER AND JULIE JUST DELIVERED A BABY GIRL. VIOLET ELIZABETH. EVERYONE'S FINE.
THAT'S AWESOME. I LOVE BABIES. DON'T YOU, DAMON?
CHANGING THE SUBJECT... DO YOU KNOW WHAT HAPPENED TO CAM? SHE'S BEING GRUMPY AND WON'T SPILL.
SHE WAS ATTACKED BY SOME NEW PSYCHO-META AND I SAVED HER ASS. SAME OLD, SAME OLD.
THIS GUY CARRIES SOME PSI-POWERED STRAIGHT RAZOR AND KILLS WOMEN. WHAT WAS HIS NAME, CAM? SWEENEY-SOMETHING..."TOM," MAYBE?
"SWEENEY TODD"? REALLY?
YEAH, THAT'S IT. YOU FIGHT HIM BEFORE?
NO, BUT I KNOW THE NAME.
SWEENEY TODD IS A CHARACTER FROM OLD VICTORIAN-ERA BRITISH LEGEND. HE WAS KNOWN AS "THE DEMON BARBER OF FLEET STREET" BECAUSE HE WOULD CUT THE THROATS OF THE MEN WHO CAME IN FOR A SHAVE. HIS ACCOMPLICE OWNED A PIE SHOP AND WOULD BAKE MEAT PIES OUT OF THE DEAD MEN'S FLESH. THERE ARE DOZENS OF VARIATIONS ON THE STORY.
AND YOU KNOW THIS HOW?
STEPHEN SONDHEIM WROTE A MUSICAL CALLED "SWEENEY TODD" IN 1979. ANGELA LANSBURY PLAYED "MRS. LOVETT." QUITE POSSIBLY THE BEST AMERICAN MUSICAL EVER. THAT'S HOW.
YOU KNOW WHAT IS GAYER THAN YOU RIGHT NOW?
WHAT?
ABSOLUTELY NOTHING.

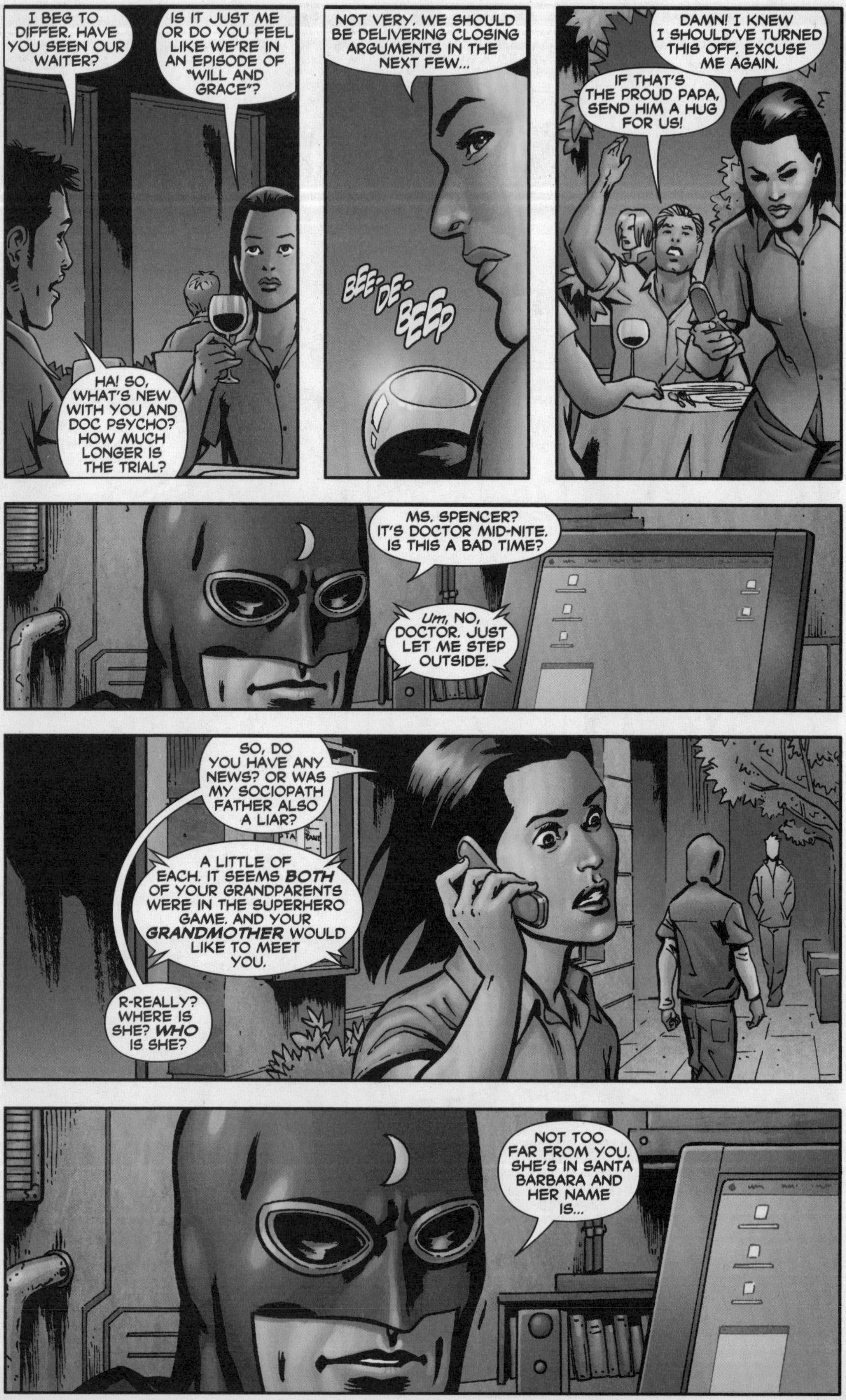
I BEG TO DIFFER. HAVE YOU SEEN OUR WAITER?
IS IT JUST ME OR DO YOU FEEL LIKE WE'RE IN AN EPISODE OF "WILL AND GRACE"?
HA! SO, WHAT'S NEW WITH YOU AND DOC PSYCHO? HOW MUCH LONGER IS THE TRIAL?
NOT VERY. WE SHOULD BE DELIVERING CLOSING ARGUMENTS IN THE NEXT FEW...
BEE-DE-BEEP
DAMN! I KNEW I SHOULD'VE TURNED THIS OFF. EXCUSE ME AGAIN.
IF THAT'S THE PROUD PAPA, SEND HIM A HUG FOR US!
MS. SPENCER? IT'S DOCTOR MID-NITE. IS THIS A BAD TIME?
Um, NO, DOCTOR. JUST LET ME STEP OUTSIDE.
SO, DO YOU HAVE ANY NEWS? OR WAS MY SOCIOPATH FATHER ALSO A LIAR?
A LITTLE OF EACH. IT SEEMS ***BOTH*** OF YOUR GRANDPARENTS WERE IN THE SUPERHERO GAME. AND YOUR ***GRANDMOTHER*** WOULD LIKE TO MEET YOU.
R-REALLY? WHERE IS SHE? ***WHO*** IS SHE?
NOT TOO FAR FROM YOU. SHE'S IN SANTA BARBARA AND HER NAME IS...

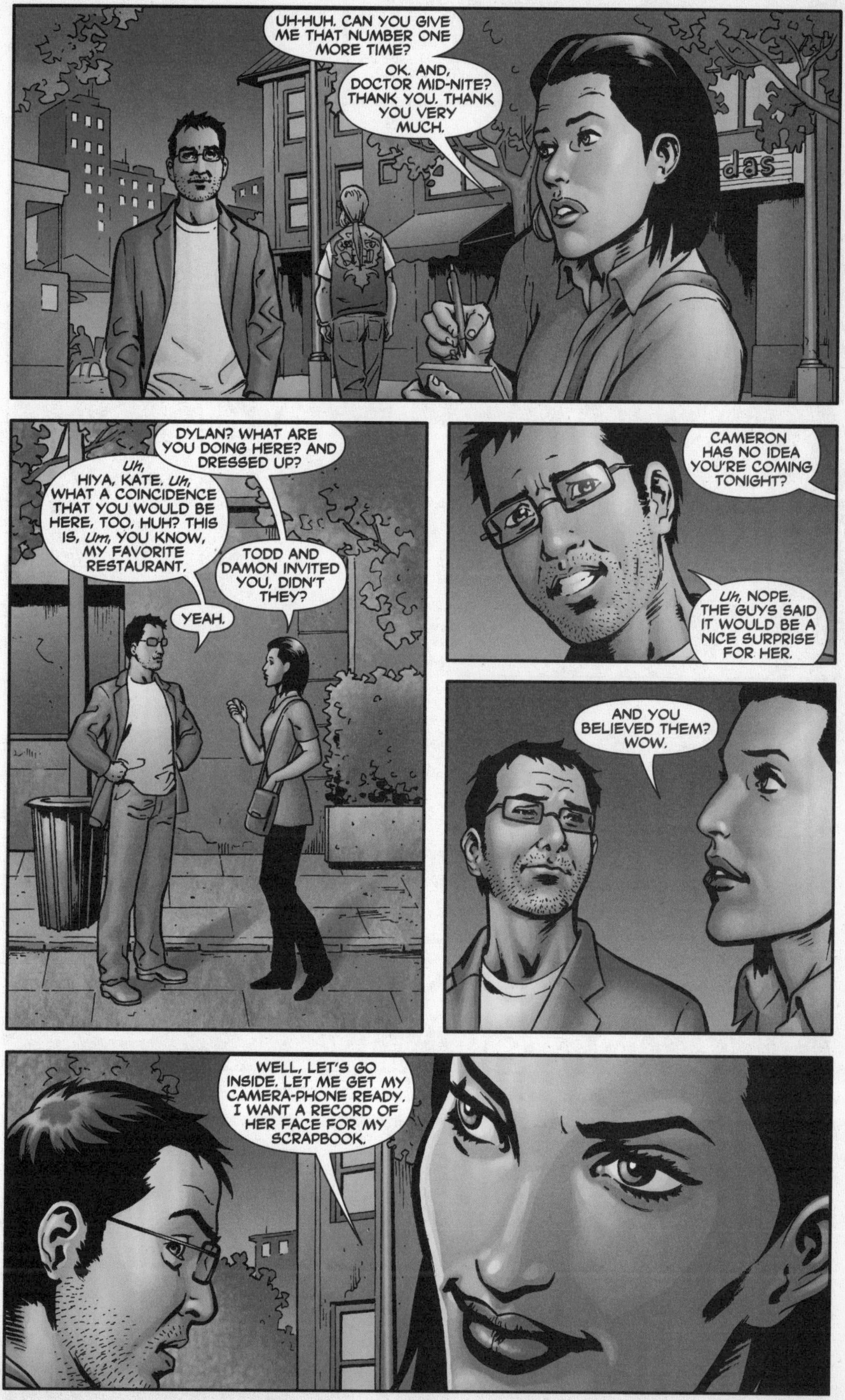
UH-HUH. CAN YOU GIVE ME THAT NUMBER ONE MORE TIME?
OK. AND, DOCTOR MID-NITE? THANK YOU. THANK YOU VERY MUCH.
das
DYLAN? WHAT ARE YOU DOING HERE? AND DRESSED UP?
Uh, HIYA, KATE. *Uh*, WHAT A COINCIDENCE THAT YOU WOULD BE HERE, TOO, HUH? THIS IS, *Um*, YOU KNOW, MY FAVORITE RESTAURANT.
TODD AND DAMON INVITED YOU, DIDN'T THEY?
YEAH.
CAMERON HAS NO IDEA YOU'RE COMING TONIGHT?
Uh, NOPE. THE GUYS SAID IT WOULD BE A NICE SURPRISE FOR HER.
AND YOU BELIEVED THEM? WOW.
WELL, LET'S GO INSIDE. LET ME GET MY CAMERA-PHONE READY. I WANT A RECORD OF HER FACE FOR MY SCRAPBOOK.

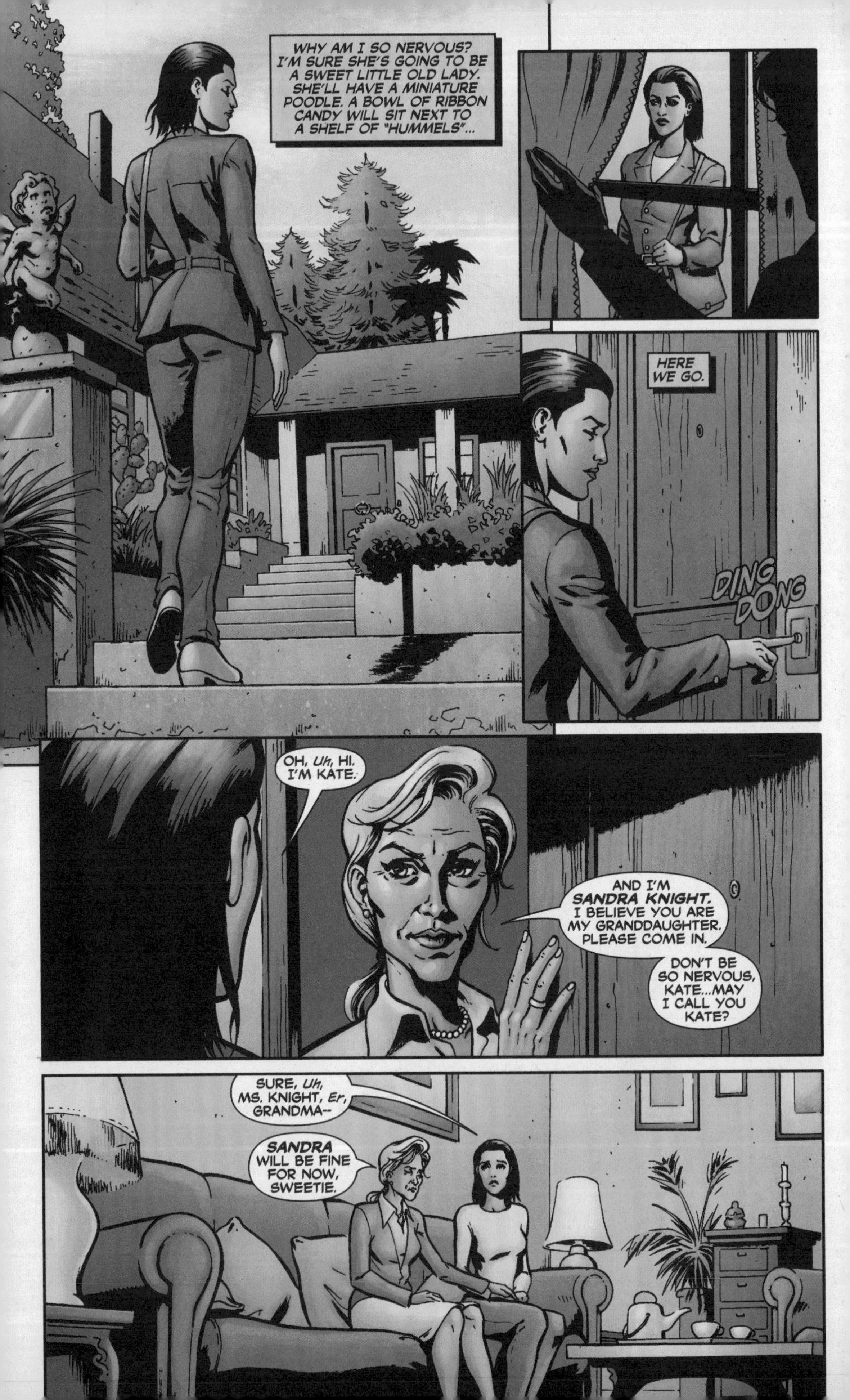
WHY AM I SO NERVOUS? I'M SURE SHE'S GOING TO BE A SWEET LITTLE OLD LADY. SHE'LL HAVE A MINIATURE POODLE. A BOWL OF RIBBON CANDY WILL SIT NEXT TO A SHELF OF "HUMMELS"...
HERE WE GO.
DING DONG
OH, *Uh*, HI. I'M KATE.
AND I'M ***SANDRA KNIGHT.*** I BELIEVE YOU ARE MY GRANDDAUGHTER. PLEASE COME IN.
DON'T BE SO NERVOUS, KATE...MAY I CALL YOU KATE?
SURE, *Uh*, MS. KNIGHT, *Er*, GRANDMA--
SANDRA WILL BE FINE FOR NOW, SWEETIE.

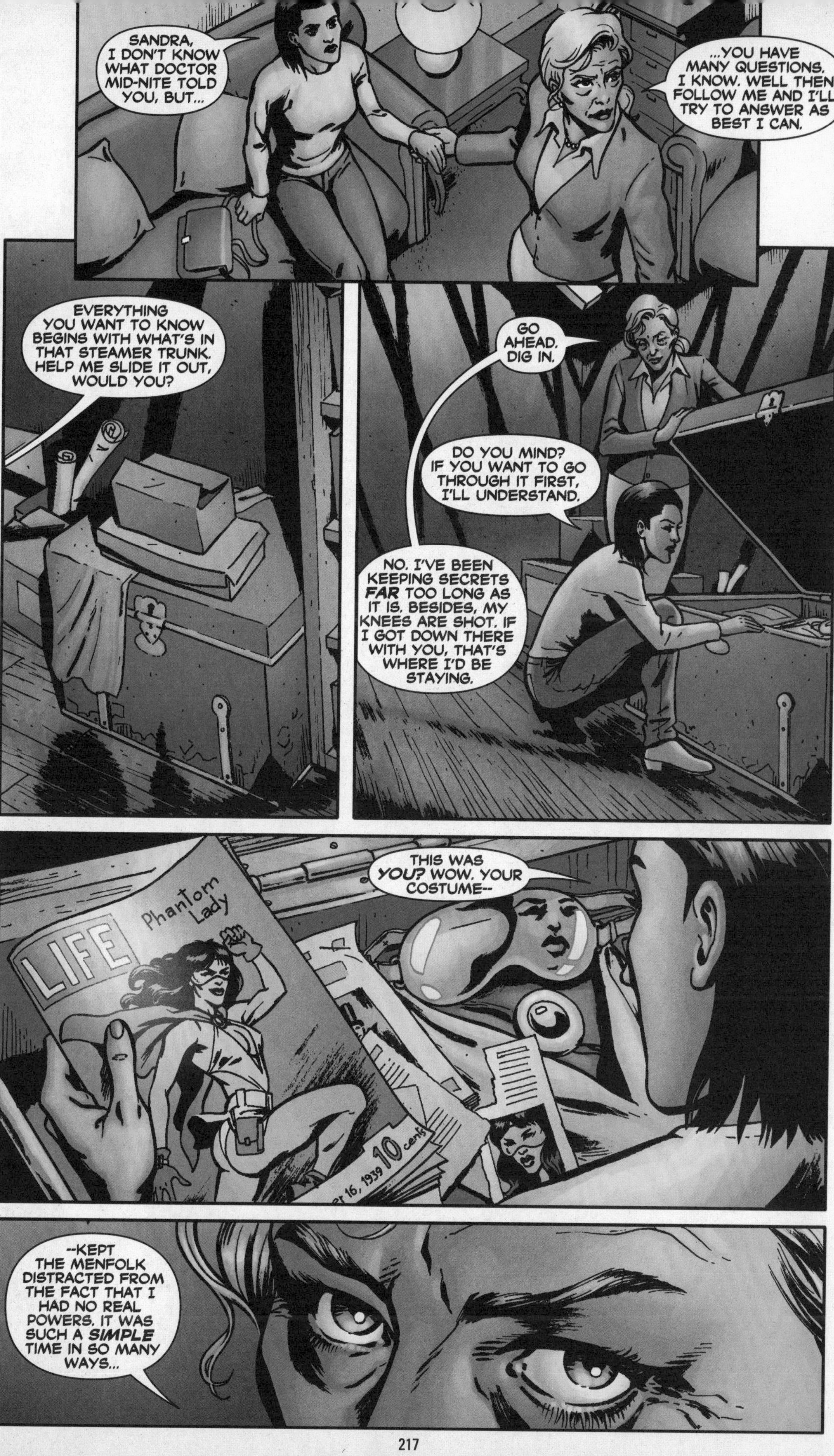
SANDRA, I DON'T KNOW WHAT DOCTOR MID-NITE TOLD YOU, BUT...
...YOU HAVE MANY QUESTIONS. I KNOW. WELL THEN, FOLLOW ME AND I'LL TRY TO ANSWER AS BEST I CAN.
EVERYTHING YOU WANT TO KNOW BEGINS WITH WHAT'S IN THAT STEAMER TRUNK. HELP ME SLIDE IT OUT, WOULD YOU?
GO AHEAD. DIG IN.
DO YOU MIND? IF YOU WANT TO GO THROUGH IT FIRST, I'LL UNDERSTAND.
NO. I'VE BEEN KEEPING SECRETS FAR TOO LONG AS IT IS. BESIDES, MY KNEES ARE SHOT. IF I GOT DOWN THERE WITH YOU, THAT'S WHERE I'D BE STAYING.
THIS WAS YOU? WOW. YOUR COSTUME--
LIFE
Phantom Lady
10 cents
--KEPT THE MENFOLK DISTRACTED FROM THE FACT THAT I HAD NO REAL POWERS. IT WAS SUCH A SIMPLE TIME IN SO MANY WAYS...

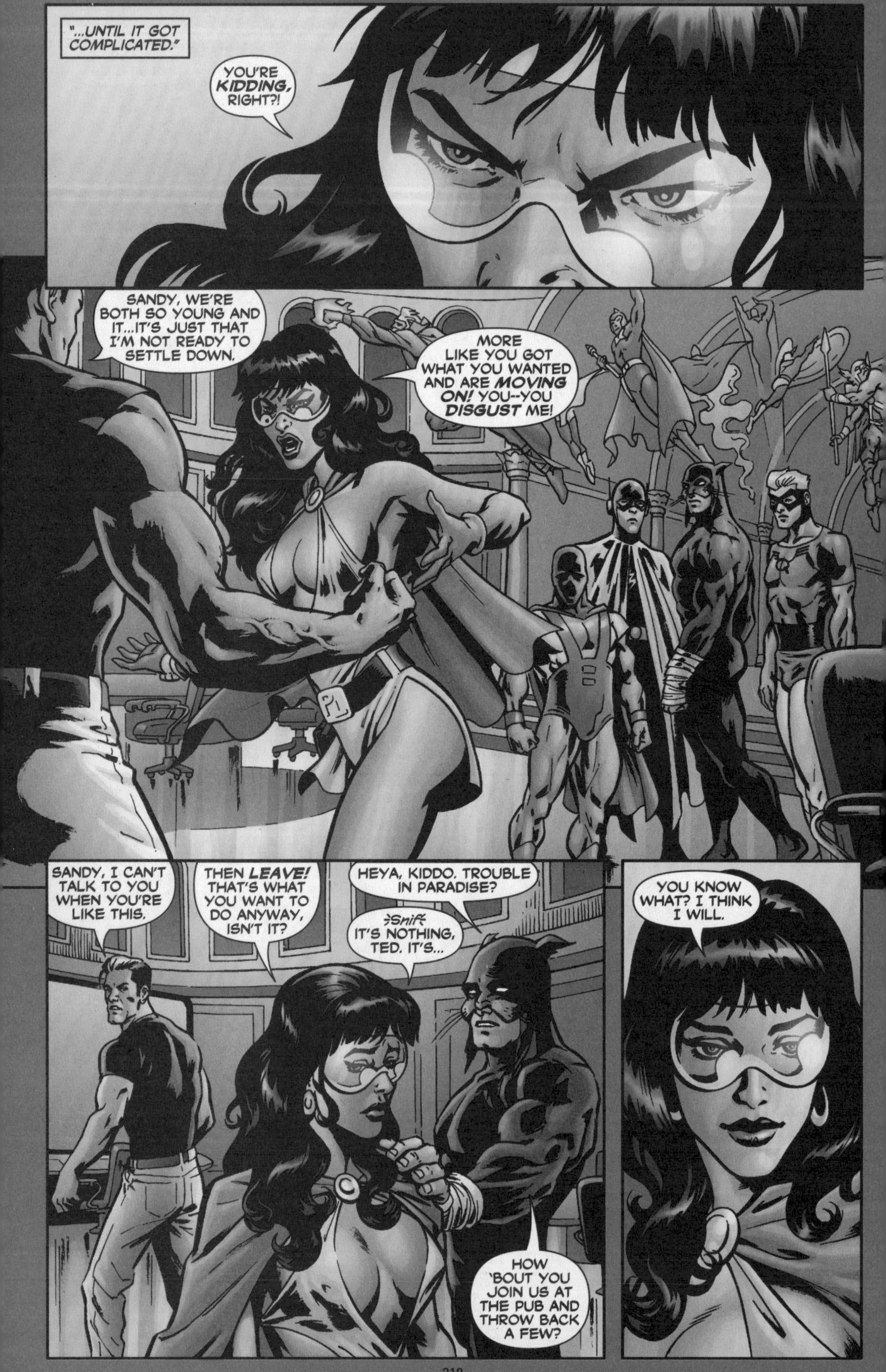
"...UNTIL IT GOT COMPLICATED."
YOU'RE KIDDING, RIGHT?!
SANDY, WE'RE BOTH SO YOUNG AND IT...IT'S JUST THAT I'M NOT READY TO SETTLE DOWN.
MORE LIKE YOU GOT WHAT YOU WANTED AND ARE MOVING ON! YOU--YOU DISGUST ME!
SANDY, I CAN'T TALK TO YOU WHEN YOU'RE LIKE THIS.
THEN LEAVE! THAT'S WHAT YOU WANT TO DO ANYWAY, ISN'T IT?
HEYA, KIDDO. TROUBLE IN PARADISE?
SNIF
IT'S NOTHING, TED. IT'S...
HOW 'BOUT YOU JOIN US AT THE PUB AND THROW BACK A FEW?
YOU KNOW WHAT? I THINK I WILL.

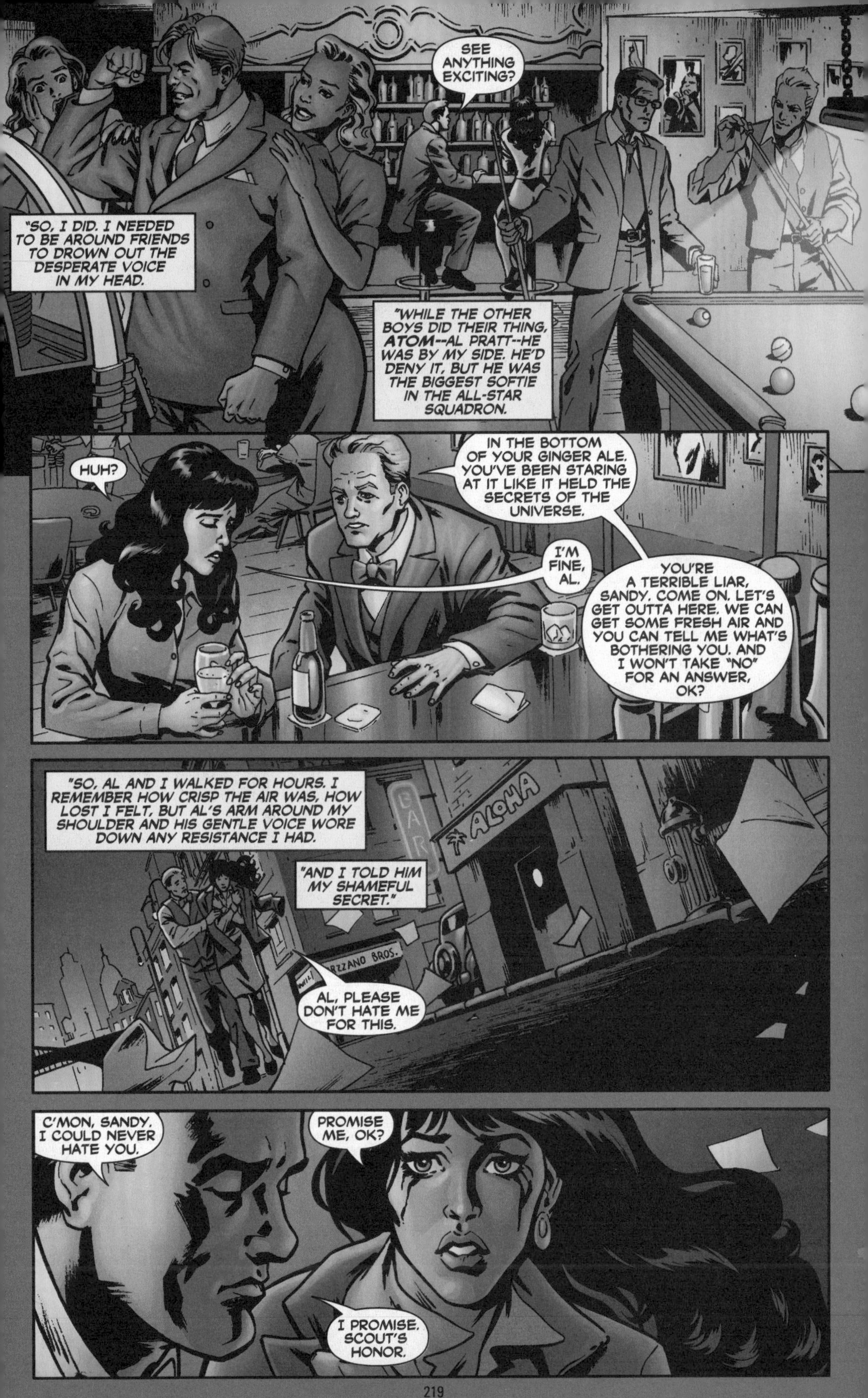
SEE ANYTHING EXCITING?
"SO, I DID. I NEEDED TO BE AROUND FRIENDS TO DROWN OUT THE DESPERATE VOICE IN MY HEAD.
"WHILE THE OTHER BOYS DID THEIR THING, ATOM--AL PRATT--HE WAS BY MY SIDE. HE'D DENY IT, BUT HE WAS THE BIGGEST SOFTIE IN THE ALL-STAR SQUADRON.
HUH?
IN THE BOTTOM OF YOUR GINGER ALE. YOU'VE BEEN STARING AT IT LIKE IT HELD THE SECRETS OF THE UNIVERSE.
I'M FINE, AL.
YOU'RE A TERRIBLE LIAR, SANDY. COME ON. LET'S GET OUTTA HERE. WE CAN GET SOME FRESH AIR AND YOU CAN TELL ME WHAT'S BOTHERING YOU. AND I WON'T TAKE "NO" FOR AN ANSWER, OK?
"SO, AL AND I WALKED FOR HOURS. I REMEMBER HOW CRISP THE AIR WAS, HOW LOST I FELT, BUT AL'S ARM AROUND MY SHOULDER AND HIS GENTLE VOICE WORE DOWN ANY RESISTANCE I HAD.
BAR
ALOHA
"AND I TOLD HIM MY SHAMEFUL SECRET."
RZZANO BROS.
AL, PLEASE DON'T HATE ME FOR THIS.
C'MON, SANDY. I COULD NEVER HATE YOU.
PROMISE ME, OK?
I PROMISE. SCOUT'S HONOR.

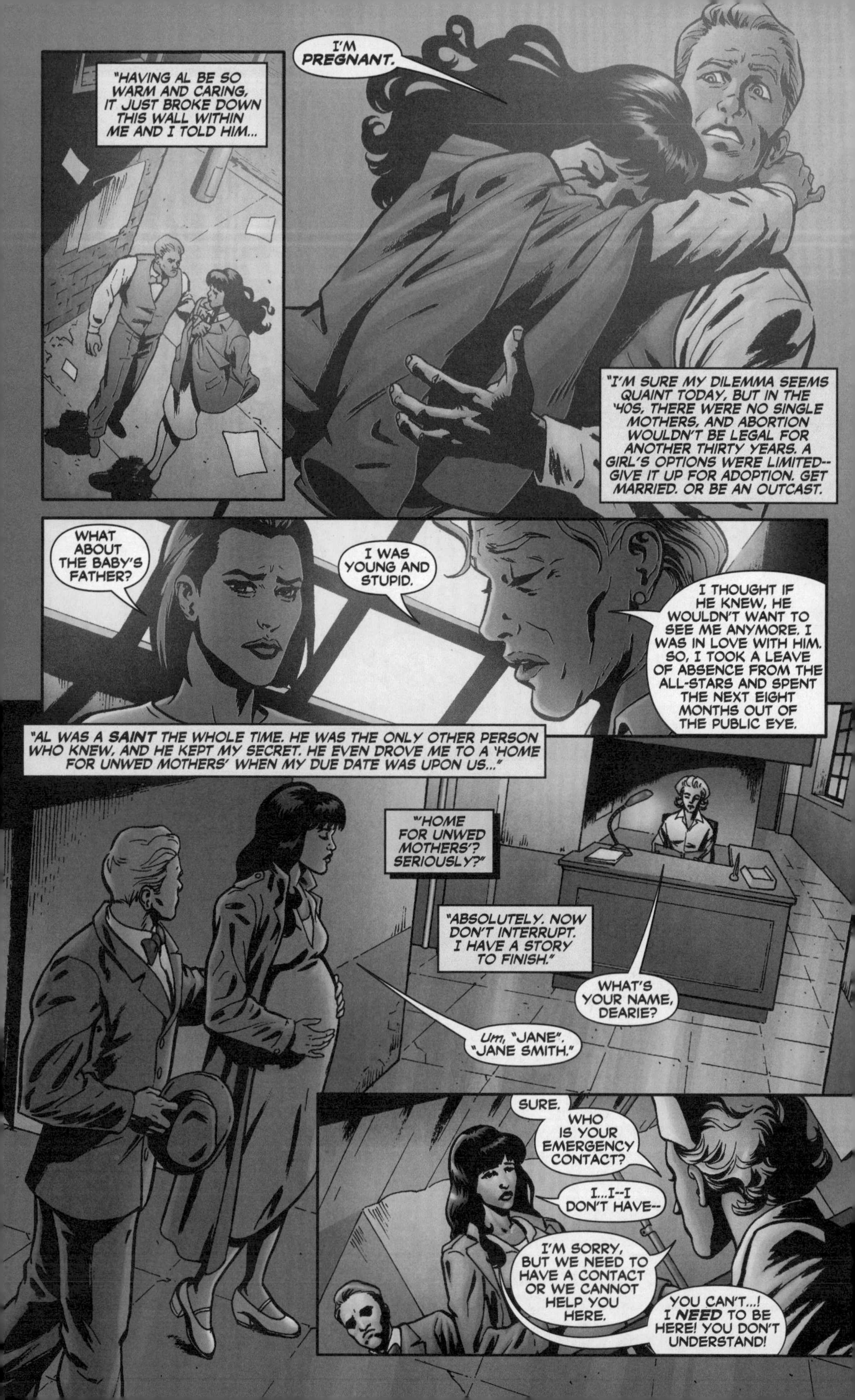
"HAVING AL BE SO WARM AND CARING, IT JUST BROKE DOWN THIS WALL WITHIN ME AND I TOLD HIM...
I'M PREGNANT.
"I'M SURE MY DILEMMA SEEMS QUAINT TODAY, BUT IN THE '40S, THERE WERE NO SINGLE MOTHERS, AND ABORTION WOULDN'T BE LEGAL FOR ANOTHER THIRTY YEARS. A GIRL'S OPTIONS WERE LIMITED-- GIVE IT UP FOR ADOPTION. GET MARRIED. OR BE AN OUTCAST.
WHAT ABOUT THE BABY'S FATHER?
I WAS YOUNG AND STUPID.
I THOUGHT IF HE KNEW, HE WOULDN'T WANT TO SEE ME ANYMORE. I WAS IN LOVE WITH HIM. SO, I TOOK A LEAVE OF ABSENCE FROM THE ALL-STARS AND SPENT THE NEXT EIGHT MONTHS OUT OF THE PUBLIC EYE.
"AL WAS A SAINT THE WHOLE TIME. HE WAS THE ONLY OTHER PERSON WHO KNEW, AND HE KEPT MY SECRET. HE EVEN DROVE ME TO A 'HOME FOR UNWED MOTHERS' WHEN MY DUE DATE WAS UPON US..."
"'HOME FOR UNWED MOTHERS'? SERIOUSLY?"
"ABSOLUTELY. NOW DON'T INTERRUPT. I HAVE A STORY TO FINISH."
WHAT'S YOUR NAME, DEARIE?
Um, "JANE". "JANE SMITH."
SURE. WHO IS YOUR EMERGENCY CONTACT?
I...I--I DON'T HAVE--
I'M SORRY, BUT WE NEED TO HAVE A CONTACT OR WE CANNOT HELP YOU HERE.
YOU CAN'T...! I NEED TO BE HERE! YOU DON'T UNDERSTAND!

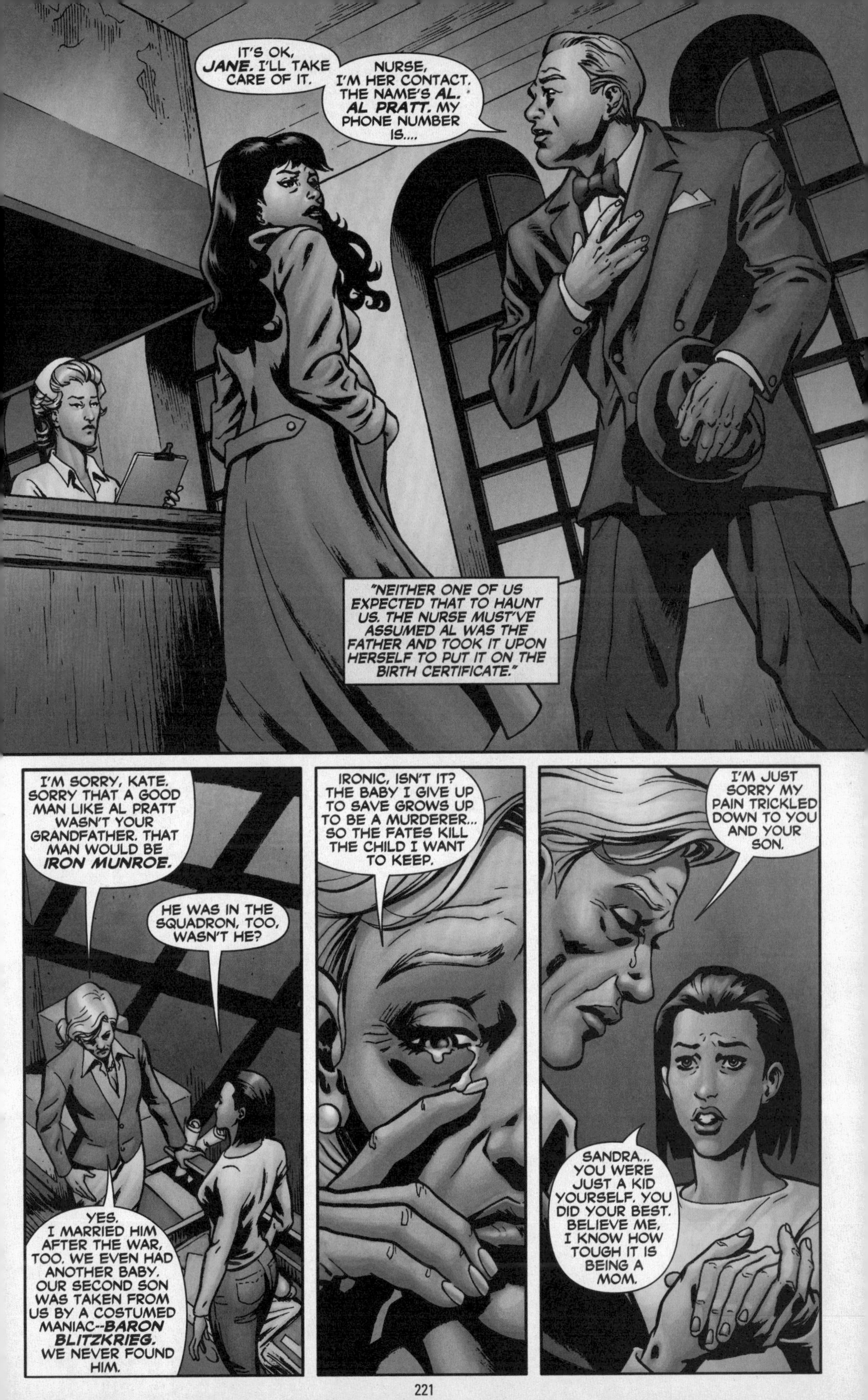
IT'S OK, JANE. I'LL TAKE CARE OF IT.
NURSE, I'M HER CONTACT. THE NAME'S AL. AL PRATT. MY PHONE NUMBER IS....
"NEITHER ONE OF US EXPECTED THAT TO HAUNT US. THE NURSE MUST'VE ASSUMED AL WAS THE FATHER AND TOOK IT UPON HERSELF TO PUT IT ON THE BIRTH CERTIFICATE."
I'M SORRY, KATE. SORRY THAT A GOOD MAN LIKE AL PRATT WASN'T YOUR GRANDFATHER. THAT MAN WOULD BE IRON MUNROE.
HE WAS IN THE SQUADRON, TOO, WASN'T HE?
YES. I MARRIED HIM AFTER THE WAR, TOO. WE EVEN HAD ANOTHER BABY. OUR SECOND SON WAS TAKEN FROM US BY A COSTUMED MANIAC--BARON BLITZKRIEG. WE NEVER FOUND HIM.
IRONIC, ISN'T IT? THE BABY I GIVE UP TO SAVE GROWS UP TO BE A MURDERER... SO THE FATES KILL THE CHILD I WANT TO KEEP.
I'M JUST SORRY MY PAIN TRICKLED DOWN TO YOU AND YOUR SON.
SANDRA... YOU WERE JUST A KID YOURSELF. YOU DID YOUR BEST. BELIEVE ME, I KNOW HOW TOUGH IT IS BEING A MOM.

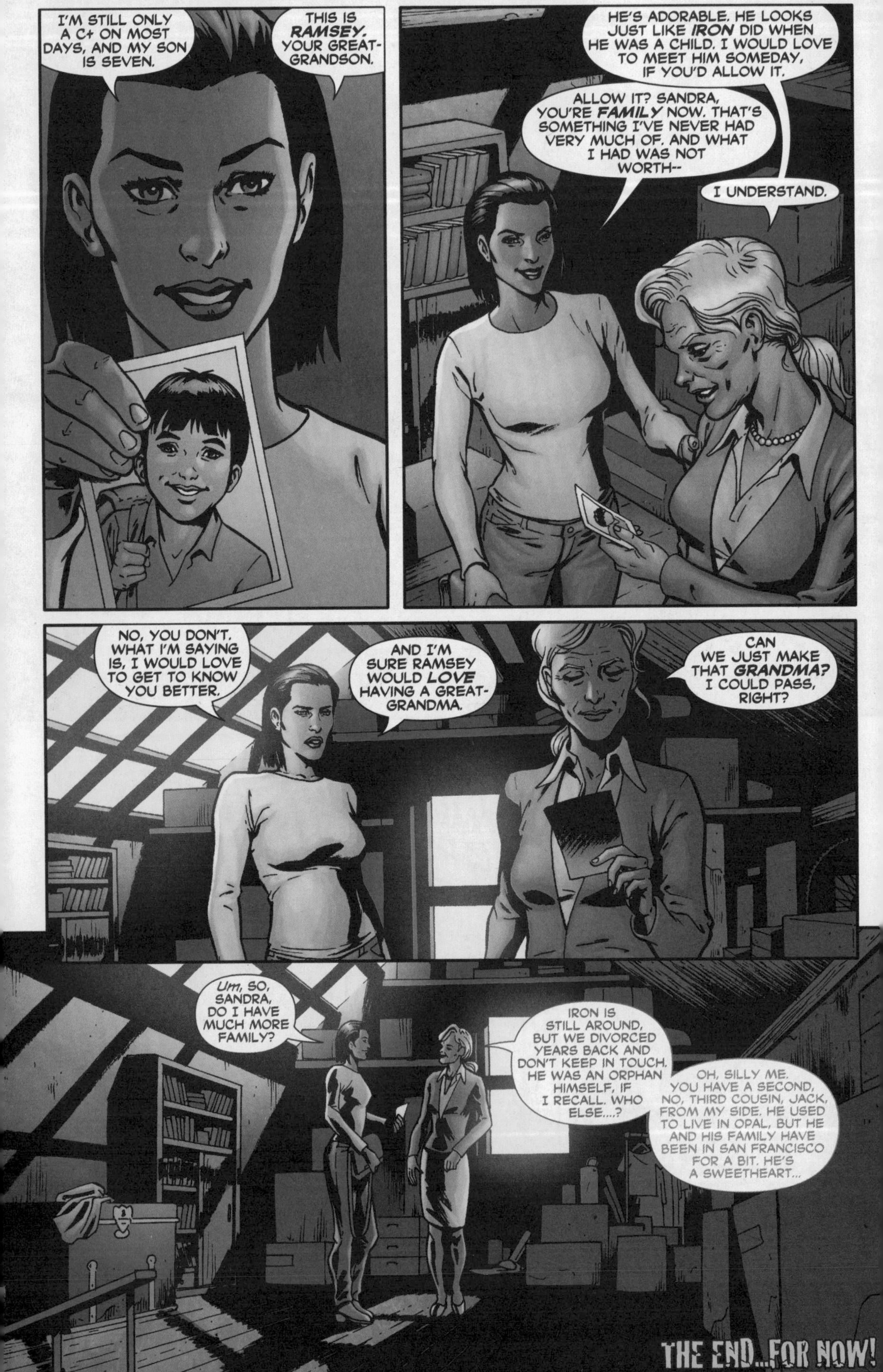

I'M STILL ONLY A C+ ON MOST DAYS, AND MY SON IS SEVEN.
THIS IS RAMSEY. YOUR GREAT-GRANDSON.
HE'S ADORABLE. HE LOOKS JUST LIKE IRON DID WHEN HE WAS A CHILD. I WOULD LOVE TO MEET HIM SOMEDAY, IF YOU'D ALLOW IT.
ALLOW IT? SANDRA, YOU'RE FAMILY NOW. THAT'S SOMETHING I'VE NEVER HAD VERY MUCH OF. AND WHAT I HAD WAS NOT WORTH--
I UNDERSTAND.
NO, YOU DON'T. WHAT I'M SAYING IS, I WOULD LOVE TO GET TO KNOW YOU BETTER.
AND I'M SURE RAMSEY WOULD LOVE HAVING A GREAT-GRANDMA.
CAN WE JUST MAKE THAT GRANDMA? I COULD PASS, RIGHT?
Um, SO, SANDRA, DO I HAVE MUCH MORE FAMILY?
IRON IS STILL AROUND, BUT WE DIVORCED YEARS BACK AND DON'T KEEP IN TOUCH. HE WAS AN ORPHAN HIMSELF, IF I RECALL. WHO ELSE...?
OH, SILLY ME. YOU HAVE A SECOND, NO, THIRD COUSIN, JACK, FROM MY SIDE. HE USED TO LIVE IN OPAL, BUT HE AND HIS FAMILY HAVE BEEN IN SAN FRANCISCO FOR A BIT. HE'S A SWEETHEART...
THE END...FOR NOW!